# Praise for *He*

"Benor, Krasner, and Avni have written 〰〰〰 〰〰〰〰〰ng work that promises to reshape Jewish educators' basic approaches to the whys and hows of language learning."

—Shaul Kelner, author of *Tours That Bind:*
*Diaspora, Pilgrimage, and Israeli Birthright Tourism*

"What a fascinating teach-in about a subject so often discussed in passing but rarely seen up close—the use (or not) of Hebrew in Jewish schools and camps and why (or whether) it matters to modern American Jewish identity. Finally, a book about that elusive creature 'Hebrew School Hebrew'!"

—John H. McWhorter, author of *The Creole Debate*

"A lively, evocative, and wide-ranging account of American Jewry's complex and often-maligned relationship with Hebrew, this important book is as much about community as it is about language. In finding creativity where others have found fault, *Hebrew Infusion* challenges us to rethink our assumptions about the cultural grammar of the modern Jewish experience."

—Jenna Weissman Joselit, author of *Set in Stone:*
*America's Embrace of the Ten Commandments*

"An extremely important contribution towards the study of a major aspect of the American Jewish Diaspora community and to sociolinguistics."

—Bernard Spolsky, author of *The Languages of the Jews:*
*A Sociolinguistic History*

"This engaging book delves into the use of Hebrew in the Jewish summer culture camps of the United States. While there is a call by some leaders to do Hebrew immersion to create proficient speakers, camps find immersion difficult to accomplish. Paralleling Native American language/culture camps and other language revitalization programs, infusion of heritage language allows Hebrew speakers to feel personally attached to their own beloved language by using what they know in daily conversations, even as the rest of the conversation is English. While there are differences between the situations of endangered indigenous languages vs. Hebrew for the Jewish Diaspora, the many similarities establish this volume as a recommended read for everyone involved in endangered and minoritized language survival."

—Leanne Hinton, author of *Bringing Our Languages Home:*
*Language Revitalization for Families*

"The first serious work on Hebrew in Jewish summer camps is as important a work of history as it is an ethnographic study of a range of contemporary camps. This book will become an essential work not only for those interested in Jewish American cultures, but other diaspora communities in the United States, who face remarkably similar issues. An outstanding contribution to all of those interested in language, culture, and identity."

—Riv-Ellen Prell, author of *Fighting to Become Americans: Jews, Gender, and the Anxiety of Assimilation*

"Summer camps are rarely studied as significant social and linguistic experiences. This book is a first, as it shows how the infusion of Hebrew into English in Jewish summer camps emblematically establishes local solidarity and diasporic identity. The book offers an enlightening, new perspective on American Jewry in relation to Hebrew and Yiddish at the same time that it stands as a sociolinguistic landmark."

—Walt Wolfram, author of *The Development of African American Language: From Infancy to Adulthood*

"Funny things happen on the way to heritage language revival. Creolized languages develop to serve even more useful functions for identity and community for migrants. This book offers a fascinating study into the emergence of 'camp Hebraized English' in American Jewish summer camps. It provides another rich example of how translingual practices serve the needs of diaspora communities."

—Suresh Canagarajah, author of *Translingual Practice: Global Englishes and Cosmopolitan Relations*

"In this lively and engaging account of the rise of Hebrew content at Jewish-American summer camps, the authors illuminate the cultural work of language across generations."

—Leslie Paris, author of *Children's Nature: The Rise of American Summer Camp*

"Hebrew Infusion is the remarkable result of a seven-year collaboration to explore and illuminate Hebrew language use, teaching, and learning in American Jewish camps. Bringing together historical, sociolinguistic, and applied linguistic perspectives, the authors examine the organization and meanings of Hebrew infusion practices and how they have varied over time and across settings. The authors effectively apply multiple theoretical frameworks to tell the story of how Hebrew has been deployed in camp contexts to construct local, national, and transnational understandings of Jewishness. For any scholar interested in the relationship between language and community, this book is essential reading."

—Leslie C. Moore, Associate Professor of Teaching & Learning and Linguistics at The Ohio State University

# Hebrew Infusion

# Hebrew Infusion

*Language and Community at
American Jewish Summer Camps*

SARAH BUNIN BENOR
JONATHAN KRASNER
SHARON AVNI

RUTGERS UNIVERSITY PRESS
NEW BRUNSWICK, CAMDEN, AND NEWARK,
NEW JERSEY, AND LONDON

Library of Congress Cataloging-in-Publication Data

Names: Benor, Sarah Bunin, 1975—author. | Krasner, Jonathan B., 1966—author. |
   Avni, Sharon, 1970—author.
Title: Hebrew infusion: language and community at American Jewish summer camps /
   Sarah Bunin Benor, Jonathan Krasner, and Sharon Avni.
Description: New Brunswick, New Jersey; London: Rutgers University Press, [2020] |
   Includes bibliographical references and index.
Identifiers: LCCN 2019037924 | ISBN 9780813588735 (paperback) | ISBN 9780813588742
   (hardback) | ISBN 9780813588759 (epub) | ISBN 9780813588766 (pdf) |
   ISBN 9781978804593 (mobi)
Subjects: LCSH: Jewish camps—United States—History—20th century. | Hebrew
   language—Study and teaching—United States—History—20th century. | Languages in
   contact—United States. | Non-formal education—United States—History—20th century.
Classification: LCC BM135 .B46 2019 | DDC 796.54/22—dc23
LC record available at https://lccn.loc.gov/2019037924

A British Cataloging-in-Publication record for this book is available from the British Library.

♾ The paper used in this publication meets the requirements of the American National Stan
dard for Information Sciences—Permanence of Paper for Printed Library Materials, ANSI
Z39.48-1992.

www.rutgersuniversitypress.org

Manufactured in the United States of America

*Dedicated to our happy campers,*
*Aliza, Dalia, and Ariella*
*Ariel and Gideon*
*Mia and Gali*

# Contents

Introduction   1

### PART I
### Past

1   Hebrew Infusion in American Jewish
    Summer Camps, 1900–1990   19

2   Camp Massad in the Poconos and the Rise and
    Fall of Hebrew Immersion Camping   50

3   Camp Ramah: A Transition from
    Immersion to Infusion   82

### PART II
### Present

4   A Flexible Signifier: Diversity in Hebrew
    Infusion and Ideology   113

5   The Building Blocks of Infusion   142

6   "Sign" Language: Visual Displays of
    Hebrew and Jewish Space   172

7   Bringing Israel to Camp: Israeli Emissaries
    and Hebrew   198

8   Conflicting Ideologies of Hebrew Use   215

    Epilogue   248

    Acknowledgments   253
    Notes   257
    References   275
    Index   295

# Hebrew Infusion

# Introduction

"We love Jewish summer camp, don't we?" This was the opening of a comedy routine by Benji Lovitt, an American Jew who attended a Young Judaea (Zionist) summer camp and eventually immigrated to Israel.[1] Lovitt, performing in 2013 for Diaspora Jews spending the year in Israel, continued, "We learn so much. We learn about Jewish culture, Jewish community, Jewish peoplehood. You know what we didn't learn? The Jewish language of Hebrew. We thought we learned Hebrew. We learned nouns. You see, nobody ever left camp actually able to construct a sentence." As the vaguely uncomfortable giggles became louder, he continued. "Well I guess if you ever find yourself in a situation where you have to say 'singing, dancing, camper, counselor, dining room,'" Lovitt paused for effect, "you might be okay. If you think you learned Hebrew at Jewish summer camp, try telling them that at El Al security." Lowering his voice an octave and putting on a heavy Israeli accent, he stepped into the role of Israeli airport security officer: "So, do you know Hebrew?" "Why sure, I went to Jewish summer camp," he responded, mimicking an oblivious American. "*Az ma ata oseh po* [So what are you doing here]?" he asked in his security officer voice. "Umm," Lovitt hesitated, shrugging his shoulders as the American, and muttered, "*Sheket b'vakasha* [quiet, please]? *Shabbat Shalom* [peaceful Sabbath]." The audience exploded. "*Chadar ochel* [dining room], mofo!"[2]

The audience's collective nodding and laughter affirm how widespread the phenomenon of using seemingly random Hebrew words in English sentences is at American Jewish camps. Lovitt's critique is technically accurate. At most American Jewish summer camps, Hebrew use is limited primarily to select nouns within English sentences and does not help campers become proficient in Israeli Hebrew. This is a variety of English that we call "camp Hebraized English" (CHE), a register of Jewish American English that includes Hebrew words: both Jewish life words (words used in other Jewish communal settings such as *Shabbat Shalom*) and camp words (words used primarily at camp like *chadar ochel*). By

1

definition, CHE is a variety of English, not Hebrew. CHE is one aspect of a broader phenomenon we call "Hebrew infusion," the process in which camp staff members incorporate elements of Hebrew into the primarily English-speaking environment through songs, signs, games, and words. As we demonstrate in this book, camp leaders intend these infusion practices to strengthen campers' affective or ideological relationships with Hebrew, and they are less concerned with developing fluency in Hebrew.

Lovitt's routine—as well as the audience's response—affirms how widespread CHE is, as well as the contempt in which it is held in American Jewish camping discourse and education more broadly. There is a large and vocal force that perceives this noun-centric use of Hebrew as troubling, inferior, and "not really Hebrew." Its critics argue that CHE is a bastardization of the Hebrew language, making its very use a lost opportunity to teach Hebrew, a language that the majority of American Jewish youth do not know. Many American Jewish educators and public intellectuals think that developing Hebrew skills among American Jews is crucial to the goals of instilling and strengthening a sense of Jewish belonging, thereby ensuring a vital American Jewish community and a strong connection between American and Israeli Jews.[3] However, most contemporary Jewish overnight camps do not strive to teach Hebrew fluency. Although a few camps in the mid-twentieth century focused on proficiency and had strict language policies dictating the use of Hebrew in all activities, camps since then have widely turned to an alternate model of language attachment: Hebrew infusion.

Using historical and sociolinguistic methods, this book explores how camp leaders came to accept and rely on Hebrew infusion and how they approach it, experience it, and critique it today. We explain the social, economic, and cultural conditions that created this wholly American diasporic register and why ideology about language supersedes language fluency. We probe why some Jewish leaders perceive CHE as alarming and unacceptable. At the same time, we expose the important function and creativity of CHE and demonstrate how it is a distinctive cultural phenomenon for American Jews in its own right. These two contradictory positions—that CHE is an inferior form of Hebrew and that it is an important component of American Jewish life—lead us to discourses of language authenticity, revealing distinct understandings of what American Jews should know, feel, and do and how they should relate to Israel. Thus the story we tell here of Hebrew at American Jewish camps offers a new perspective on the changing dynamics of American Jewry over the past century and its highly creative response to the challenge of fashioning a diasporic identity.

## INFUSION

Consisting of a wide range of spoken and written activities in which Hebrew is integrated to various degrees into a primarily English environment, Hebrew infusion takes place in songs, blessings, signage, games, and routinized sentences (announcements and other utterances with established wording that are regularly used as part of the camp routine). The primary goal of this infusion, as articulated by camp officials, is for campers to strengthen their feelings of connection with being Jewish through the use of Hebrew; therefore infusion works as a socializing process that reaffirms Hebrew as an emblematic language of Jews and Judaism. In contrast to immersion, where the goal is full language competency, Hebrew infusion in the camp context focuses on young Jews developing an ideology about Hebrew and its importance in Jewish culture, without necessarily being able to use it for full communicative purposes.

Just as an infused drink can have only a hint of berry or a strong flavor, the infusion metaphor emphasizes that Hebrew can be integrated to varying degrees. We refer to camps with a "strong dose" of Hebrew infusion as "Hebrew-rich," recognizing that this categorization is one end of a continuum. At Hebrew-rich camps, such as the Conservative movement's Ramah network, the Young Judaea network, and the Reform movement's Olin-Sang-Ruby Union Institute (OSRUI), participants can perceive the flavor of Hebrew in most activities. Camps on the other end of the continuum infuse Hebrew in more limited ways, such as during Shabbat prayers and Israeli dancing. Across the continuum, Hebrew infusion can be seen as a top-down and intentional language policy that highlights symbolic and affective dimensions of language over communicative ones. In other words, infusion privileges the development of a relationship to Hebrew over its full acquisition or mastery. Infusion operates in the ideological realm, and its measure of success is different from that of traditional language-learning programs.

Camp leaders often speak of "connection" when they discuss summer camp experiences, crediting camp with "connecting" campers to the camp community, to Israel, and to Jews around the world. This discourse of connection extends to Hebrew infusion. Infusing Hebrew to forge communal and transnational connections presupposes that these connections only require a nominal and symbolic acquaintance with Hebrew, and it assumes that English is insufficient to meet this purpose, despite the fact that the vast majority of Israeli Jews and Jews throughout the world speak English. In other words, one of the central rationales for infusing Hebrew is to create and promote an "imagined community" of Jews around the world who value Hebrew and use elements of it, even if many of them cannot use it for day-to-day communication.[4] One Jew will never meet all other Jews, but is expected to feel connected to them not only via shared historical narratives and religious observance but also through shared ideologies about the importance of Hebrew and the capacity to engage in Hebrew prayers and use modern Hebrew words. Thus, the notion of Hebrew as a connecting language is symbolic or aspirational.

We base our notion of Hebrew infusion on other models of emblematic language use that conceptualize speakers having an affective relationship with a language they are not fully proficient in or whose use is limited in scope but is still central to the identity of the group. This phenomenon is not limited to Jews using Hebrew at American summer camps. Cultural studies scholar Jeffrey Shandler's notion of postvernacularity concerns the privileging of the symbolic register of Yiddish over its primary value for communication among American Jews.[5] In postvernacular Yiddish use, the goal is not proficiency but rather the commitment to Yiddish and what it represents. Interestingly, Shandler shows that the postvernacular mode can also occur among speakers fluent in the language in question when there is a deliberate choice to use that language rather than another because it has value beyond the semantic content of what is being expressed. Hebrew infusion draws on postvernacularity but differs in two significant ways. First, postvernacularity implies the phase following the historical vernacular use of the language, a situation that does not apply to Hebrew at camp because Hebrew was never the vernacular of American Jews. Second, infusion is an intentional pedagogical practice initiated by educators (even if it eventually becomes reflexive), whereas postvernacularity can occur organically.

Linguistic anthropologist Netta Avineri's "metalinguistic community," which grows out of postvernacularity theory, also informs Hebrew infusion. Focusing on secular Americans learning Yiddish, Avineri defines a metalinguistic community as a group of people "engaged primarily in discourse *about* language and cultural symbols tied to language."[6] In metalinguistic communities, participants are socialized to have certain knowledge and ideologies about the language, and connection is more of a priority than linguistic competence. Avineri analyzes how teachers, performers, and others use the language in pedagogical ways, especially in songs, greetings, closings, and evaluations. These features are also found in Hebrew use at Jewish summer camps, and we see infusion practices as one means by which metalinguistic communities are formed. However, contemporary camps are not metalinguistic communities; the primary purpose of a camp is to provide a Jewishly rich summer experience, not to engage in discourses about language. Yet, like in metalinguistic communities, Hebrew infusion acts as a site of socialization for Jewish youth because camp leaders perceive it as a means of instilling campers with particular Jewish values, beliefs, and behaviors.

Postvernacularity and metalinguistic community are central to our conceptualization of Hebrew infusion because they capture how communities grapple with language maintenance and "loss," even when the language is not (and has never been) a vernacular of the community. Our analysis is also informed by other theoretical treatments of immigrant and indigenous groups' emblematic and hybrid uses of language, as well as analysis of how they modify their relationship to a language in the face of cultural, political, and social dynamics.[7] Many groups respond to such dynamics by incorporating elements of a language into an environment conducted primarily in another language, a phenomenon we refer to as "ethnolinguistic infusion," which highlights the ideological link between the language and the group.[8] For example, in Sri Lankan immigrant communities in the United States, Canada, and the United Kingdom, English-speaking children are taught to recite chants and speeches in Tamil, despite their limited comprehension.[9] In California, most Elem Pomo Indians speak English and are not proficient in Elem Pomo, but leaders use the endangered ancestral language for ceremonies and openings and closings that frame meals or presentations.[10] These situations differ from Hebrew use among American Jews, because Hebrew is not currently threatened with endangerment, is many centuries removed as an ancestral language, and is currently seen as a sacred textual language and a language of a far-away center of communal life. However, there are also important similarities. Although the immigrant and indigenous groups, as well as American Jews, speak English as their primary or only language, leaders of all these groups infuse loanwords and routinized passages from their group languages—Tamil, Elem Pomo, and Hebrew—in communal events. Within each group, there is diversity in how much of the language individuals speak and how they relate to the language. Even so, leaders of each group wish to promote their language within their community and foster group connection, despite the prevalence of a dominant language.

## Jewish Summer Camping

Summer camp is a quintessentially American institution with roots that can be traced as far back as the mid- to late 1800s. By the early twentieth century, Jews were attending residential summer camps (used interchangeably here with sleepaway and overnight camps) in disproportionate numbers, due in part to the relative popularity of summer camps in the urban northeastern and midwestern centers where they tended to live. Jews also gravitated to camp as an agent of American acculturation. For upwardly mobile Jews, sending one's children to camp, like other bourgeois summer leisure practices, was a status symbol. For working-class and poor families, philanthropically supported vacation camps (or fresh air camps) provided an opportunity for kids to escape the heat and unsanitary city streets. When Jews established their own camps, they were indistinguishable from the Christian camps in their general aesthetic and menu of activities. What marked some of these camps as Jewish, in addition to their ownership and clientele, was the incorporation of some type of Sabbath observance (typically a brief prayer service) and kosher or kosher-style food. But these features were by no means ubiquitous.[11] It was only after World War I that a significant number of Jewish camps of various ideological stripes began incorporating a robust program of Jewish religious and cultural practices, including the use of Hebrew and Yiddish. Many new camps were founded in the mid-twentieth century, some oriented toward Hebrew immersion but many more toward various types and degrees of Hebrew infusion.

Jewish overnight camping is now experiencing another historical surge, with enrollments rising and new camps emerging to join long-established ones. Since the publication of the 1990 National Jewish Population Survey and the consolidation of a loosely organized "Jewish continuity" movement in the United States, Jewish summer camping has been identified as "a unique educational setting poised to deliver powerful Jewish formative experiences to children, teens, and young adults."[12] The Foundation for Jewish Camp (FJC), founded in 1998 to expand and professionalize the nonprofit Jewish camping industry, makes this bold statement: "The key to the Jewish future is Jewish camp. We know from research—and nearly two decades' experience—that this is where young people find Jewish role models and create enduring Jewish friendships. It's where they forge a vital, lifelong connection to their essential Jewishness."[13] Families looking for a Jewishly oriented summer environment have never had as many options as they have today. In 2018, the American Camping Association, the largest professional camping organization in North America, accredited approximately 2,400 camps employing more than 320,000 staff people and serving over 7.2 million children.[14] Jewish camps operate as a discrete submarket. In 2017, FJC was working with 160 residential camps, which employed about 21,400 counselors and served more than 82,000 unique campers (as well as many day camps, which we do not analyze in this book).[15] Many Jewish Community Centers (JCCs) and a few synagogues maintain residential summer camps. There are camps for every major religious denomination, various Zionist movements, subgroups like Russian Jews and Jews of Color, and several special interests, including sports, arts, science, organic farming, and entrepreneurship.

Camp is about the psychosocial experience, but it is also an industry, and decision making is necessarily refracted through the prism of the market. Camp leaders make choices about food, facilities, and activities with an eye toward filling beds. Hebrew is also a part of this calculus. One theme that weaves its way throughout this book is how camps conceptualize and navigate the notion of a threshold of language exposure and pedagogy. In other words, camps grapple with how much Hebrew is too much and may be counterproductive to their sustainability and growth as they seek to recruit campers, many of whom have little knowledge of or interest in Hebrew either because of their less-than-positive experiences in religious schools or lack of exposure to Hebrew speakers. We refer to this as a Hebrew "tipping point": a determination of the correct dosage of Hebrew that fits the clientele a camp serves. For some camps, including those in the Ramah network, which serves about 8 percent of campers attending nonprofit Jewish camps,[16] Hebrew speaking is constitutive of their brand identity and central to their ideological mission. Not surprisingly, such camps are particularly fertile terrains for our analysis and receive disproportionate attention here. But even where Hebrew is more peripheral, Jewish camps are continually negotiating how much Hebrew is too much or too little.

Schools, synagogues, JCCs, and philanthropic organizations also infuse Hebrew in their activities and rituals to some degree. Yet camps have the potential to infuse more Hebrew because of the many distinctive locations, activities, and roles that need to be named, as well as the many opportunities for rituals, from wake-up to bedtime. The very features that distinguish camp from other social and educational environments make studying their Hebrew use a particularly worthy project. Generally speaking, overnight camps enculturate children into particular attitudes and behaviors, whether they be religious, ethnic, socioeconomic, or political. They represent a "total institution,"[17] removed from the routines and pressures of everyday life, in which participants' activities are highly regulated. Cheers, songs, rituals, and other traditions abound as part of a distinctive camp culture and as conveyors of particular values and worldviews. Jewish camping is no different: American Jewish communities have long turned to summer camps to socialize their youth to know, feel, and behave as American Jews.[18] This socialization happens not only through prayers and educational programming but also through everyday activities. Virtually everything at camp has the potential to be infused with Jewishness. But the very ingredients that make camp a powerful socializing environment can also limit its impact—campers' ability to transfer what they learn at camp to other contexts.[19] Bounded in time, space, and age range, overnight camp creates cultural moments that often cannot extend to the camper's year-round life. This limitation raises questions about the long-term impact of camp language practices, particularly the ways in which CHE is an isolated cultural product that may never be fully embraced at Jewish schools or synagogues.

## Language as a Lens into Jewish Life

Jewish camping has garnered considerable attention over the years, but *Hebrew Infusion* shines a unique analytic light on language within the camping experience.[20] Similar books could be written analyzing other cultural practices at Jewish camps—the use of music, color war, prayer, the Sabbath—each of which offers insight into American Jewish ideologies and orientations.[21] We chose to focus on language because of its ubiquity and scope. Language "happens" every time somebody speaks—when a loudspeaker announcement calls someone to the office, a volleyball specialist divides up teams, or a camper requests a Band-Aid. For some camps, each of these moments involves decisions about whether and how to use Hebrew words. Should the announcement be prefaced by "*Hakshivu!*" (Attention/listen [plural])? Should the volleyball teams be given Hebrew names? Should the counselor tell the camper to get her Band-Aid at the infirmary, the *mirpaa*, or the *marp*? Language materializes every time someone creates or notices writing on a songsheet, a sign, or a mural. Should such written materials be in English or Hebrew? Should they have block letters, cursive, vowel markings, transliteration, or translation? Other questions focus on what type of Hebrew to use. The ancient Hebrew of the scriptures? The classical Hebrew of the prayer book? The Hebrew religious terminology of the American Ashkenazi synagogue? The modern Hebrew spoken by young people in Israel today? Collectively, these questions reflect the complexity of Hebrew infusion.

Language has several attributes that make it a strong resource for building community beyond simple communication. It is social: it allows us to bond with some people and exclude others. It is manipulable: we can use it in creative ways to form new sounds, words, sentences, and visual representations. It is semiotic: we can intend and interpret language to symbolize something else—stances, social groups, historical ties. It is combinable: we can blend elements of two or more languages to emphasize multiple and hybrid identities. It is ideological: linguistic decisions can reflect and constitute various stances and worldviews. It is multimodal: it can be spoken and written, perceived aurally and visually. Finally, it can also be metalinguistic: conversations about language are opportunities to discuss belonging and identity.

Our primary focus is on English and Hebrew, but language use at the camps in our study is not restricted to those languages. Sephardic Adventure Camp infuses Ladino (Judeo-Spanish), including in songs, color war banners, and the Ladino word of the day.[22] At Gesher and other camps with many children of Russian Jewish immigrants, staff and campers communicate in Russian and English. Many camps use elements of Yiddish, which is not surprising given its history as an ancestral language for many North American Jews.[23] Orthodox camps, such as the Lubavitch Camp Emunah, use many Yiddish words and grammatical influences, and the historically Yiddishist Camp Kinder Ring infuses Yiddish through songs and activities. Non-Orthodox, non-Yiddishist camps use several Yiddish words that have become part of the American Jewish lexicon: religious terms like *daven* (pray) and *treyf* (nonkosher), as well as secular words like *shmooze* (chat) and *mensch* (good person).

The relative paucity of Yiddish in American camping outside of Hasidic communities is not surprising. Hebrew and Yiddish hold different sociolinguistic roles for Jews. With the revernacularization of Hebrew as part of the Zionist project came the denigration of Yiddish as a weak diasporic language, in contrast to Hebrew as the language of Jewish power and ingathering.[24] Yiddish is now associated with older generations, not with the youth of summer camp, and it potentially excludes Jews whose ancestors did not come from Eastern Europe. In addition, many Yiddish words within English no longer constitute an insider code because of their spread to non-Jewish circles. Finally, Yiddish is increasingly associated with its vernacular use among growing Hasidic populations, who are marginal in the discourse of many American Jewish camps. In contrast, Hebrew is now seen as the unifying symbolic language of Jews around the world. Yiddish and Hebrew loanwords might be used at camp because they are part of Jewish English spoken in many Jewish communal settings (Jewish life words). But when camp leaders incorporate additional Hebrew loanwords—especially those referring to camp locations, roles, and activities—they transform English into a camp code, a youth code, and an insider Jewish and/or Zionist code.

Historically, the flourishing of modern Hebrew in the new state of Israel led to several overlapping changes in ideologies and practices regarding Hebrew in the United States. First, the revernacularization of Hebrew affected the calculus of Diaspora Hebrew revivalists in the mid-twentieth century, relieving them of the onus of speaking Hebrew as a means of ensuring Jewish survival. We see evidence of this in the rise and decline of Massad Poconos (1941–1981) and other Hebrew-speaking camps. Second, American Jewish communities incorporated more modern Hebrew words and pronunciations into their Jewish English. Third, American Jewish educational institutions began focusing not only on textual Hebrew but also on modern Hebrew. The increasing number of Israelis working at camps in the United States, as well as in schools, synagogues, and other American Jewish communal institutions, as well as the thousands of Americans who visit and study in Israel, has led to a reshuffling of language priorities and ideologies.

Although we can speak about Hebrew use at camp, at times it is necessary to distinguish between textual Hebrew and modern Hebrew.[25] We use "textual Hebrew" as an umbrella term to refer to Hebrew in the Bible and in rabbinic literature from ancient to premodern times, including the Mishnah, *midrashim*, and liturgy. Some rabbinic literature is written in (Judeo-) Aramaic, most notably the Gemara/Talmud, the *Kaddish* prayer, and parts of the Passover seder. Historically, textual Hebrew and Aramaic have been referred to under the umbrella term *lashon kodesh* (language of holiness).[26] Thus our use of the term "textual Hebrew" sometimes includes Aramaic, especially regarding prayers. Modern Hebrew, in contrast, refers to revernacularized Hebrew used in Israel. Many words and constructions used in modern Hebrew are also found in biblical and rabbinic literature; after all, despite the many influences of Yiddish and other languages on modern Hebrew, the revived language was, quite intentionally, based on textual Hebrew.[27] In line with communal discourse, we sometimes distinguish between textual and modern Hebrew, and we sometimes use Hebrew as an umbrella term referring to both. Although some scholars capitalize the term "Modern Hebrew," we opted for "modern" to underscore the fluid and dynamic nature of contemporary varieties of Hebrew.

## RESEARCH METHODS

During the summers of 2012–2015, we conducted observations at thirty-six camps, representing diversity in religiosity, movement, size, and geography.[28]

Many were in New York, Pennsylvania, and Southern California, but we also visited camps in Washington State, Northern California, Colorado, Manitoba, Wisconsin, Mississippi, North Carolina, New Hampshire, and Maine. Camp types included pluralistic, B'nai B'rith, JCC, private, Reform, Conservative, Hebrew-speaking, modern Orthodox, Zionist, progressive Zionist, Israeli American, Russian American, Sephardic, eco-Jewish, Jews of color, Orthodox girls, and Chabad girls. We arranged our visits so we could experience parts of the full camp schedule at various camps: staff week, first day, last day, weekday, Shabbat, awards ceremonies, outside performers, visitors day, talent show, *Tisha B'Av*, and *maccabiah*. Our stays ranged from three hours at Camp Sternberg to sixteen days over three summers at Ramah California, with an average of two days per camp. Overall, we spent about 78 days visiting camps (21 at Ramah camps, 14 at Zionist movement camps, 13 at Union for Reform Judaism (URJ) camps, and 30 at others).

At each camp, we tried to observe the following events, as applicable: meals, prayers, educational programs, social programs, song sessions, dance sessions, sports, art, and cooking. We observed large groups, small staff meetings, and informal interactions. We photographed signs, posters, artistic placards, and camp "swag" in various venues, from dining halls to bunks, from waterfronts to prayer spaces, from horse sheds to radio broadcasting rooms. The three of us visited only one camp together; nonetheless, we use "we" throughout the book. We also conducted observations at three gatherings in the spring of 2015: a Jewish Agency for Israel training session in Israel for Israeli emissaries/*shlichim* (with the help of a research assistant), a convening of the Goodman Camping Initiative and Bringing Israel to Camp Workshop, and the Foundation for Jewish Camp's biennial Leaders Assembly.

We were aware that our presence and stated research interest influenced people's language use at some camps, and we tried various techniques to mitigate the effects of the observer's paradox.[29] In a few cases, camp participants "performed" Hebrew for our benefit, such as the camper who said, "*Shalom* [hello]. Do I get a point for that?," or the administrator who introduced a Hebrew word skit in the middle of the session, inspired by our research interest. Nevertheless, we are confident that the practices described in this book are characteristic of Jewish summer camps even when researchers are not present.

In addition to brief conversations with hundreds of staff members during our camp visits, we had longer interviews with about 150 staff members at contemporary camps and support organizations, such as national offices of camp networks, the Foundation for Jewish Camp, the iCenter (which supports Israel education in North America), the Jewish Agency for Israel, and funders that support camps and camp initiatives. We also conducted interviews or focus groups with about seventy campers ages 8 to 16, with parental consent, from three camps—OSRUI, Ramah California, and Tel Yehudah—and with a few campers and parents at additional camps. Campers were selected to represent diversity in educational background and prior Hebrew exposure. Some interviews were in person; others were conducted via phone or video. Most were recorded and transcribed.

In fall 2015, we sent a survey invitation to camp directors from all Jewish-identified camps we could find in North America. Of the 161 camps we invited, 103 responded to the survey (64% response rate). In some networks—Habonim Dror, Hashomer Hatzair, and Ramah—all the camps were represented, and in others the response rate was lower, especially from the JCC Association, Association of Independent Jewish Camps (AIJC), and camps with no network. Our sample included camps of all sizes, from 100 to more than 1,000 campers.[30]

We conducted historical research at several archives—American Jewish Archives, American Jewish Historical Society, Hadassah Archives, Jewish Theological Seminary, and Western Reserve Historical Society—and examined published historical, biographical, and journalistic accounts. We interviewed dozens of people who founded, worked at, and/or attended various Jewish summer camps (in addition to the interviews with contemporary camp constituents described above), and we analyzed historical interviews conducted by others.

All of this research led to thousands of pages of notes and transcripts, as well as thousands of images, documents, and artifacts. With the help of research assistants, we coded and analyzed the transcripts and field notes (136 codes with 16,132 applications). Given that our research and writing extended over seven years, it is possible that some of the observations in the contemporary sections are outdated. Some camps have changed locations, logos, Hebrew practices, and even names; for example, Camp JRF became Havaya, and Moshava Malibu moved to the mountains and became Moshava Alevy.

## Unpacking Our Personal "Duffel Bags"

The three of us came to this project with "baggage" that included diverse disciplinary orientations and experiences with Jewish summer camp. Sarah, a sociolinguist, studies language and ethnicity and language contact, especially American Jews' mixing of English, Hebrew, and Yiddish. She attended day camps at the JCC of Greater Washington, some of which had Hebrew names, like Atid (future, a computer camp) and Maccabiah (a sports camp), others of which had English names, like S.T.A.Y. (Summer Theater of the Arts for Youth). Although she never attended a Jewish sleepaway camp, her husband often shares Hebrew phrases and songs he learned at Camp Solomon Schechter. Their daughters attend Ramah California, Ramah in the Rockies, and Habonim Dror Camp Gilboa,[31] and they joke that mom uses them for research. This is partly true: with permission, she gathered data from camp communications and on visitors' days. But she also used her research to find the perfect camp for each child. At times, she wore two hats simultaneously: mom scouring posted photos to find her children and researcher scanning for interesting uses of Hebrew; mom listening intently to her happy campers' stories about new activities and friendships and researcher remembering their Hebrew activity names to write down later.

Jonathan, a historian, studies the history of Jewish education and American Jewish culture. He attended several Jewish camps as a child and worked as a counselor and division head at Camp Raleigh, a modern Orthodox camp in Livingston Manor, New York, and as a member of the educational staff at Ramah in Nyack, New York. His eldest child spent five happy summers at Eden Village Camp, a pluralistic, Jewish environmental camp in Putnam Valley, New York. But his formative camp experience was his time as a camper at Massad Bet, in the Poconos, where for three summers he both imbibed the Hebrew-speaking environment as a "theater kid," performing in all-Hebrew productions, and largely ignored it in his cabin, where his counselors mesmerized him with a folk rock soundtrack that included Led Zeppelin and Crosby, Stills, & Nash. Many of his camp memories during his third summer were overshadowed six months later by his beloved counselor's death in an antisemitic attack while chaperoning a group of kids to a New York Rangers game. Although Massad probably taught Jonathan more Hebrew than he learned in twelve years of Jewish day school, his experience there also demonstrated that campers (and counselors) internalize myriad, sometimes conflicting messages even in intentional and immersive educational environments.

As a camper and a staff member at Camp Young Judaea Sprout Lake, Camp Judaea, and Tel Yehudah (for a total of eight years), Sharon spent much of her childhood and teenage years using CHE. Her Hebrew skills were put to the test when she moved to Israel in the early 1990s and adapted to Israeli life as an *olah chadasha* (new immigrant). With her own Hebrew learning experiences as her guide, she developed her interest in Hebrew in the American context into an academic pursuit that has, in various twists and turns, weaved its way through her professional work for the past twenty years. Her participation in this book drew on her disciplinary training in language pedagogy, applied linguistics, and linguistic anthropology. With both her children currently attending Young Judaea camps, CHE remains a household vernacular that continues to challenge her to better understand what Hebrew means to American Jews.

## DECISIONS

### Names and Pseudonyms

Unlike some other research on Jewish camping,[32] we often name camps to portray the diversity of camps and so that others might contact them for more information about particular activities. In line with historians' conventions, we use real names for historical figures, including those still living, in the historical sections of the book. In line with sociolinguists' conventions, we use pseudonyms or descriptors for staff members, campers, and others in the contemporary sections. Common descriptors, such as "leader" and "administrator," encompass director, associate director, Judaic director, education director, and other leadership positions.

### Sample of Camps

We concentrated much of our research on Hebrew-rich camp networks, especially Massad Poconos, Ramah, URJ, and Young Judaea. We recognize that the Hebrew practices and histories of these camps are not representative of all Jewish overnight camps. In addition, our research focuses only on residential camps and does not include day camps. Future studies might include more in-depth research at camps with fewer Hebrew practices, including JCC camps, and at day camps, focusing on how campers in those settings understand the uses and meanings of Hebrew. Although we focused our research on the United States, nine Canadian camps participated in our survey, and we observed and interviewed participants at Massad in Manitoba, Canada. Therefore, when we write "America," we are sometimes also referring to Canada.

### Transcription/Transliteration

We chose not to follow an academic system of Hebrew transcription, transliteration, or romanization, such as those from the Library of Congress or the International Phonetic Alphabet. These systems can yield unwieldy combinations and involve unfamiliar characters and diacritics. We believe an American standard is emerging for the spellings of many Hebrew words, such as *maccabiah*, *mitzvah*, *challah*, *aliyah*, *Shabbat*, *havdalah*, and *tikkun olam*. When such spellings are common, we use them in this book. For words that have not yet developed a standardized form, we made decisions for the sake of consistency. We use <ch> for [x] (both ח - *chet* and כ - *chaf*) and <tz> for [ts] (צ - tsadi), as in *chug* and *tzrif*, rather than *hug* and *tsrif*. We avoid <h> at the end of a word and double consonants, as in *kehila kedosha*, not *kehillah kedoshah*. And we use <'> to indicate a morphological boundary, as in *v'ahavta* and *l'chaim*, but not between vowels, as in *mirpaa* and *moadon*, rather than *mirpa'a* and *mo'adon*—except where we feel it is necessary to avoid confusion, as in *marpe'a*. However, when we use quotes and examples from written sources, we maintain the original transliterations. Therefore readers will notice some inconsistency, which is in line with the diversity we encountered.

### ORGANIZATION OF THE BOOK

*Hebrew Infusion* is divided into two parts: historical and contemporary. The historical section explores how Hebrew infusion came to be the dominant paradigm of Hebrew use in Jewish camping. Its three chapters introduce the underlying rationales that camp leaders and Jewish educators developed and relied on in mobilizing Hebrew, and they set up the thematics of Hebrew that are taken up in the contemporary section.

Chapter 1 traces the historical arc of how Jewish culture camps—camps promoting Jewish cultural activities—adopted Hebrew infusion practices. Using the Reform movement as a case study, this chapter examines how camp leadership transformed Hebrew words and songs into a tool for identity development, even in camps that initially rejected Hebrew. This infusion of camp Hebrew words created a distinctive register, CHE, which functioned as a powerful agent for the cultivation of identification and belonging. In all its forms, Hebrew infusion became a marker of distinction, a vehicle for cultural expression, a connector to tradition, and a force for social cohesion.

Chapter 2 focuses on the rise and fall of Massad Poconos (1941–1981) as a case study of a camping movement that was fully committed to Hebrew immersion. Massad was born out of the ideology of the *Histadrut Hanoar Haivri* (the Hebrew Youth Cultural Federation), an organization dedicated to building a culturally generative, Hebrew-speaking Jewish community in North America. Massad thrived until the 1970s, when the need for an autonomous Hebraic cultural Zionism in America disappeared as the state of Israel matured.

The demise of Massad stands in direct contrast to the trajectory of the Ramah camp network, the subject of chapter 3. This chapter's singular focus on Ramah attests to the outsized role this network and its staff had in developing and fostering a Hebrew culture at American Jewish summer camps by ritualizing Hebrew speaking in public, popularizing a specialized vocabulary of camp Hebrew, and using Hebrew in the performing arts. The case of Ramah also underscores how and why Hebrew infusion, including CHE, ultimately responded better to the historical and cultural context, not to mention the enculturation goals, of American Jewish educational camping than Hebrew immersion.

The first part of the book, then, sets the stage for understanding how Hebrew infusion took root as the dominant paradigm in American Jewish camping. It shows how Hebrew was deployed to address a range of perceived challenges, threats, and opportunities in the American Jewish community. In telling the history of Hebrew at American Jewish summer camps, we can identify the various permutations of these efforts and contextualize how contemporary camps have come to embrace Hebrew infusion, including CHE, in the service of meeting their articulated or implicit educational and ideological goals.

Part II jumps forward in time and offers a contemporary analysis of Hebrew infusion practices. Chapter 4 begins with "day in the life" portraits of Hebrew infusion practices at three ideologically distinct contemporary camps, demonstrating how infusion practices are flexible enough to accommodate diverse educational goals and ways of "doing Jewish." The analysis shows that infusion practices share similarities, including privileging fragmentary and routinized engagement over Hebrew proficiency and balancing Hebrew exposure and pedagogy with concerns about remaining commercially vital. Drawing on interviews and the results of a survey of camp directors, chapter 4 also examines the rationales camp leaders and participants give for using Hebrew infusion. Some of these rationales emphasize textual Hebrew, some modern Hebrew, some a combination. Together they form a constellation of ideologically related meanings, all of which constitute understandings of what it means to be Jewish in America.

Chapter 5 provides an in-depth look at language infusion practices. It grounds Hebrew-English hybridity in theories of "translanguaging," a term describing how speakers mix resources from multiple languages without concern for their boundaries.[33] Although campers may perceive these activities as fun and games, leaders intend them to serve serious purposes: creating a distinctly American Jewish camp community and culture while fostering campers' positive connections to Hebrew and Jewishness. Camp staff also accomplish these goals through frequent metalinguistic conversations (talk about language), including translation and pedagogical questions about Hebrew. Through these activities and interactions, camps socialize campers not only to use language appropriate for the camp setting but also to be part of a metalinguistic community of Jews who value Hebrew.

Whereas chapter 5 focuses on spoken infusion practices, chapter 6 shifts attention to visual displays of Hebrew at camp on signs, banners, song sheets, and other material objects, as well as online. Hebrew in camps' "linguistic landscape"[34] serves largely symbolic functions. Hebrew signage, in conjunction with English writing and other visual cues, helps constitute camp as an American Jewish space, in contrast to other American (and Israeli) spaces. However, Hebrew signs also reflect and engender local hierarchies of Hebrew expertise and articulate ideologies about Jewish expertise and knowledge.

Chapter 7 examines the connections that camps seek to establish between Hebrew and Israel, largely through the use of *shlichim* (Israeli emissaries) who are often tasked with "bringing Israel to camp." One of the mechanisms in reaching this goal is the use of Israeli Hebrew. This chapter takes a critical look at the intersection of Hebrew authenticity, Jewish nationalism, and CHE by examining the complicated project of building affective ties between the American and Israeli Jewish communities through emissaries' language. Negotiations regarding which type of Hebrew is legitimate and how to square Hebrew nationalism with local camp sociolinguistic norms raise unresolved questions about what it means to be an authentic speaker of Hebrew in the American camp context and how American Jews evaluate their culture in relation to their vision of Israel.

Chapter 8 expands on these themes by exploring conflicting stances surrounding Hebrew infusion. In other words, this chapter focuses on language ideologies—people's conscious and unconscious beliefs about language, including the hierarchical values of different ways of speaking and the ways that language can align and distinguish individuals and groups.[35] Questions about how much Hebrew to use and whether to translate are both ideological and practical, as camps deal with their existential need to fill beds. Some leaders denigrate CHE, especially innovative forms like *chadar* (a clipping of *chadar ochel*), reflecting what we call "sociolinguistic projection," seeing their language through the eyes of others, in this case, Israelis. Exploring these discourses brings us full circle from the leaders of the vanguard Hebrew camps in the mid-1900s who looked to language to ensure diasporic Jewish survival and to embody a commitment to the Jewish state.

The epilogue analyzes renewed calls for Hebrew proficiency and underscores that Hebrew still serves mostly symbolic roles for American Jews and continues to be a touchstone for debates about community building.

In sum, this book applies multiple research methods and theoretical frameworks to bring issues of Jewish education and sociolinguistics into sharper focus. By analyzing Hebrew ideologies and practices at Jewish overnight camps, we offer new ways of thinking about American Jewish communities and the relationship between language and group identity.

## BOOK WEBSITE

Our book website, http://www.brandeis.edu/mandel/projects/hebrewatcamp .html, includes a glossary, an index of camps and camp networks, additional reports, blog posts, and photos.

PART I

# Past

# CHAPTER 1

# Hebrew Infusion in American Jewish Summer Camps, 1900–1990

Over the past century, administrators and educators have advanced a variety of rationales for Hebrew in Jewish summer camps. For example, in the early 1960s, the education director at the pluralistic Cejwin Camps, in Port Jervis, New York, viewed the cultivation of "a Hebraic atmosphere" as one element in a wider religious and cultural program designed to expose campers to "Jewish group living." In 1970, an educator at the Goldman Union Camp Institute (GUCI), a Reform-affiliated camp in Zionsville, Indiana, connected the camp's incorporation of "Hebrew, history and worship" into its program to an overarching goal of "Jewish identity" development. And in 1993, the educational director at Young Judaea's Tel Yehudah camp called for a renewed emphasis on Hebrew to promote connections between Israeli and Diaspora Jews and bolster the movement's commitment to Zionism.[1]

Interestingly, the lack of unanimity in articulated goals did not translate into radically different approaches to Hebrew on the ground. A few camps experimented with immersive Hebrew environments, and some structured formal opportunities for Hebrew speaking and teaching. But most maintained that such efforts were impractical, counterproductive, or even antithetical to the purposes of camp. "These kids are coming to camp to have fun," cautioned the Union Camp Institute educator. "If we do too much we . . . enact the law of diminishing returns."[2] When it came to Hebrew, a more fruitful educational approach, most camp officials agreed, was informal and indirect—through Hebrew songs, skits, games, and posters, and the reflexive use of Hebrew terms in everyday camp language. In other words, a wide swath of Jewish culture camps, ranging from the nondenominational JCC camps to the private camps to the religious and Zionist movement camps, coalesced around the strategy of Hebrew infusion. To be sure, ideological and practical considerations at various camps, as well as historical contingencies, affected the dosage of Hebrew infusion and contributed to change over time. And although each camp developed independently, they were not closed systems: the circulation of staff and campers among camps ensured a measure of similarity, but not uniformity, in the manifestation of Hebrew infusion practices and CHE varieties.

## THE ORIGINS OF HEBREW IN AMERICAN JEWISH SUMMER CAMPS

Few Jews attended summer camps before 1900 because of pervasive social anti-semitism and the explicitly Christian character of many early camps.[3] By the beginning of the twentieth century, however, Jews became avid supporters of their own summer camps, sending their children to them in disproportionate numbers—and Hebrew has been heard in some form at these camps since the first Jewish ones were founded. During this initial era of Jewish camping, most camps were either privately owned—solidly middle- or upper-class establishments—or institutional "fresh air" camps for working-class and indigent children, run by settlement houses, local chapters of voluntary organizations, community centers, and citywide philanthropic federations.[4]

At both the private and institutional camps, Hebrew was probably first heard in the context of prayer. Some privately owned camps, such as Schroon Lake Camp (1906), Kamp Kohut (1907), Camp Kawanga (1915), and Camp Che-Na-Wah (1923), held Sabbath services, even as others like Camp Kennebec (1907) were Jewish owned and mostly Jewish patroned, but included little or no Jewish content. In addition, the Yiddish vernacular that immigrant campers sometimes spoke in the institutional camps such as Surprise Lake Camp (1902), Tamarack Camps (1902), and Camp Wise (1907) also included Hebrew words. Although more robust Jewish cultural programs were gradually introduced after World War I into select institutional camps, including the ones just mentioned, initially these camps were primarily concerned with promoting Americanization. Only gradually did camp leaders conclude that healthy acculturation was facilitated rather than stymied by ethnic and religious awareness and pride.[5]

When Jewish camping became a vehicle for reconstructing American Jewish life, educators and activists quickly recognized the power of language as a social organizing and meaning-making force. Hebrew assumed a much larger role in the cultural Zionist camps that emerged after World War I, whose development was fueled by optimism about the prospects of the Zionist project in Palestine. A parallel Yiddish-language camping movement was also initiated during this period, and some of those camps, particularly the ones affiliated with the Sholem Aleichem Folk Institute and the Farband (the Labor Zionist fraternal order), arguably shared analogous socialization goals with the cultural Zionist camps, even if they were ideologically distinctive.[6] The groundwork for the cultural Zionist camps was laid in the decade and a half before World War I, when several Jewish educators in New York, Boston, Baltimore, and a few other cities began experimenting with teaching Hebrew as a living language in Talmud Torahs—Jewish communal supplementary schools. In 1910, Hebraist educator Samson Benderly became the first director of the Bureau of Jewish Education, the inaugural central agency for Jewish education in New York City. Benderly and three of his protégés were ultimately responsible for creating three of the earliest "Jewish culture camps"; that is, camps where the promotion of Jewish cultural activities was mission driven.

Cejwin Camps (est. 1919) incorporated Hebrew more frequently and in different ways than any Jewish camp had before.[7] Benderly disciple Albert P. Schoolman, who directed Cejwin and was a co-owner of Camp Modin (est. 1923), recognized that the cloistered and immersive environment was an ideal educational setting because it combined three features that did not apply in a conventional supplementary school program: plenty of time, community living, and freedom from curricular constraints. Under Schoolman's guidance, Cejwin, which was initially founded as a fresh air camp for the Talmud Torah children at Manhattan's Central Jewish Institute, was reenvisioned as an educational camp, in which Hebrew and Judaica classes accompanied a conventional camp program.[8] The camp thereby became an extension of the supplementary school, and modern Hebrew became an object of study using *Ivrit b'Ivrit*, the immersive "natural method" of Hebrew instruction.[9] Hebrew was also reinforced at other times during the day—in activities like music and arts and crafts; in daily services, where campers used an abridged Hebrew and English prayer book; and at mealtimes, when they chanted an abbreviated *Birkat Hamazon* (Grace after Meals). At a minimum, Schoolman expected every first-time camper to be able to read Hebrew and participate in the camp's prayer services by the end of the summer.[10] This model of the study camp was adopted in the 1940s and '50s by second-generation Jewish cultural camps like Camp Yavneh (est. 1944), a project of Boston's Hebrew Teachers College; Camp Sharon (est. 1946), which was operated by the Chicago College of Jewish Studies; and Camp Ramah (est. 1947), which was overseen by the Jewish Theological Seminary's Teachers Institute.

Schoolman was forced to abandon Cejwin's formal Hebrew study program as financially unsustainable during the Depression. But before this setback he recognized that the Indian lore and iconography that permeated many American camps could be replaced by Hebrew and Jewish culture. At Cejwin, not only did camp induct youngsters into an environment punctuated with Jewish ritual and prayer but it also drew on Jewish history, literature, symbols, and motifs to create a richly textured camp culture.[11] From its unit and division names to the musical numbers that enlivened its pageants, and from the blessings in its dining hall to the brightly colored murals that adorned its building walls, Hebrew was an integral part of Cejwin's manufactured landscape. Hebrew was a link between past and present, imbuing the camp project with meaning. As the language of the Bible, it connected the camp community with glorious and heroic days of yore, while as the language of the Zionist colonists in Palestine, it represented Jewish rebirth and renewal. Decades later, Cejwin's Jewish culture camp model with its emphasis on informal Jewish education was adopted by many Reform camps, as well as by some federation and JCC camps.[12]

Modin, a private camp that Schoolman and his wife Bertha opened with two other couples, Isaac and Libbie Berkson and Alexander and Julia Dushkin, in Canaan, Maine, catered to a wealthier clientele and did not include required formal classes, but adopted a similar cultural Zionist program.[13] Modin encouraged Hebrew learning by instituting what was likely the first *Shulchan Ivrit* (table where participants speak Hebrew) in the dining hall, for campers and counselors, at an American camp. Significantly, however, Cejwin and Modin were not conceived as Hebrew-speaking camps, and language proficiency was not identified as a goal. Hebrew worked in tandem with other symbols to posit and reinforce a bond between the camp community and the new Hebrew society in Palestine. The intensity of Hebrew and Jewish culture at Modin has waxed and waned over the years in response to changes in ownership and market forces. Yet Modin's general model became a blueprint for other privately owned Jewish camps that offered a cultural and religious program, such as Blue Star (est. 1948) in North Carolina.

## Hebrew in Zionist Youth Movement Camps

The first camps to systematically infuse modern Hebrew into the warp and weft of day-to-day camp life were sponsored by the Zionist youth movements. Most were designed to extend youth group activities into the summer months. Explicitly committed to promoting migration to Palestine and the diffusion of Zionist culture in the Diaspora, the camps used Hebrew to reinforce movement identification and contribute to the construction of a distinctive movement culture. Indeed, much of their nomenclature was specific to the particular youth movement. Thus Habonim referred to its first camps as *kvutzot* (groups), whereas Hashomer Hatzair and the religious Zionists referred to them as *moshavot* (semi-collective villages in Palestine).

North American Zionist movement camping began in 1928 when a group of Hashomer Hatzair youths, mostly in their late teens and early twenties, pitched a few surplus army tents on some rented farmland in Highland Mills, New York. The leaders of the two-week *moshava*, Abraham Zeiger and Yudke Ya'ari, were fluent Hebrew speakers who succeeded in creating a "Palestinian atmosphere."[14] According to one account, "Hebrew was predominant in speech as well as in song, in daily use in the kitchen as well as at the discussions around the campfire." Dov Vardi recalled a mixture of Hebrew and Yiddish. He remembered the *shomrim* (Hashomer Hatzair youth movement members) sitting at picnic tables, impatiently waiting for their food and singing "*Od lo achalnu* [We haven't yet eaten]" and the Yiddish ditty "*Montik bulbes . . . Dinstik bulbes . . .* [Potatoes Monday . . . potatoes Tuesday . . .]." Relating another camp memory, he conjured an image of Zeiger leading a procession of *shomrim* dressed in their "Sabbath whites" on Friday evening and speaking to them "in exquisite Hebrew about our strong ties to the past, with former generations" and to the present pioneers in Palestine's young agricultural villages.[15]

Hashomer Hatzair's success inspired other Zionist youth groups, including Habonim, Gordonia, Mizrachi (Bnei Akiva), Betar, and Young Judaea, to set up their own camps in the 1930s and early 1940s. Although the language of the Zionist movement camps and most of the youth group chapters was English, it was liberally infused with Hebrew vocabulary. "The revival of Hebrew in Palestine has demonstrated the key position that the national tongue holds in our new life," declared Habonim's 1935 prospectus. "A *chalutz* [pioneer] organization requires of its members the study and utilization of the language."[16] Much of the Hebrew nomenclature at the camps was carried over from the year-long youth groups, thereby connecting members to their particular chapter and to the larger youth movement. At Habonim camps, for example, terms like *menahel* (group leader) and *chaver* (comrade) were adopted from its youth groups. Some of this terminology changed in 1960, including the substitution of *madrich* (counselor/guide) for *menahel* and *machanot* (camps) for *kvutzot*, when World Habonim, the umbrella agency for Habonim organizations in English-speaking countries, merged with *Ichud Hanoar Hachalutzi*, the Labor Zionist youth organization in French- and Spanish-speaking countries, to form *Ichud Habonim*.

Supplemental everyday vocabulary was appropriated from the kibbutzim, many of which were organized by youth movements. The use of kibbutz Hebrew promoted the camps' association with the collectivist agricultural settlements in Palestine. Because many Zionist movement camps were designed to simulate kibbutz life, appropriation of its prevailing terminology was almost intuitive. For example, the camp dining hall became known as the *chadar ochel*, the infirmary was dubbed the *mirpaa*, and the communal fund the *kupa*. In addition, Zionist movement camps used Jewish life words, such as *oneg Shabbat*, the Sabbath festive gathering. When necessary, scouting, kibbutz, and Jewish life words were supplemented with a utilitarian camp vocabulary mined from 1930s-era modern Hebrew; for example, *hitamlut* (exercise) and *schiya* (swimming). It was while serving as a counselor at a Gordonia camp in the mid-1930s that Camp Massad founder Shlomo Shulsinger first encountered this vocabulary, and some of these words found their way into that Hebrew immersion camp's widely disseminated Hebrew-English dictionary. From Massad, they spread to both immersion and infusion camps, including Yavneh and Ramah, where the *Massad Dictionary* was issued to campers and counselors in the late 1940s and early 1950s.[17]

Even in the better-documented Zionist youth movement camps, it is difficult to know just how much Hebrew was infused in their early years. Very little in the way of ephemera, let alone audio recordings, has survived from these years, so one is compelled to extrapolate from participants' published and unpublished accounts of camp life. The extent to which Hebrew loanwords and sentences were used seemed to vary from camp to camp. Hebrew words were apparently used most frequently when employing movement nomenclature and for specific camp activities. It is telling that when Shalom Altman published his *Judaean Songster* in 1934, the table of contents and index appeared in transliteration, and the songs themselves appeared both in Hebrew characters and in transliteration. Apparently, not all Young Judaeans were capable Hebrew readers.[18]

Although the youth movements hoped that campers would eventually immigrate to Palestine, they did not generally prioritize the cultivation of Hebrew proficiency at their camps. Movements like Hashomer Hatzair, Habonim, Mizrachi, and Betar, all European imports, were oriented toward *chalutziut* (pioneering) and *hachshara* (preparation for immigration to Palestine and kibbutz life). Hebrew study was a significant component of *hachshara* programs. But because the major youth movements, except for Young Judaea, were Palestine-centric and did not see a long-term future for Jewish Diaspora communities, they found no reason to promote an indigenous Hebrew culture in North America. Nevertheless, Hebrew still played a critical role in these camps, because it oriented movement members toward Palestine and effectively differentiated otherwise mundane camp activities from virtually identical goings-on at other camps.

Not all Zionists were *sholelei hagolah*, Diaspora negationists (a term used by many Zionist thinkers). Indeed, there were cultural Zionists in the United States (and elsewhere) who viewed the revival of Hebrew as a living language in both Palestine and the Diaspora as integral to a larger transnational Jewish revival project. Many also believed that the Jewish future in North America would only be safeguarded if the bonds of community were reinforced through the production of an indigenous American Jewish culture. Using Hebrew as the language of cultural expression was viewed as a strategy that would allow Jews to retain their distinctiveness in the United States and withstand the overwhelming pressure to assimilate. By encouraging creative Jewish expression in diasporic communities, as well as in Palestine, cultural Zionists used Hebrew as a vehicle to promote a transnational Jewish identity. This political commitment required far more than the incorporation of Hebrew words; cultural creativity demanded linguistic proficiency. This view animated young Hebraists in the late 1930s and '40s who were members of *Histadrut Hanoar Haivri*, the Hebrew Youth Cultural Federation, including Shlomo Shulsinger, who nurtured a Hebrew-speaking haven in the Poconos at Camp Massad, as well as Moshe Davis and Sylvia Ettenberg, the architects of the Conservative movement's Ramah camps.[19] It similarly found support at the Hebrew teacher colleges, two of which founded their own Hebrew study camps in the 1940s: Camp Yavneh in New Hampshire and Camp Sharon in Michigan.

## Hebrew in Postwar Camps

Hebrew infusion in American Jewish summer camps became more common-place between 1940 and 1970, when Jewish camping was enjoying a boom.[20] Its growth can be measured both qualitatively and quantitatively. To borrow best-selling author and rabbi Chaim Potok's felicitous phrase, a sojourn to camp was appreciated as "a worthy use of summer."[21] In the wake of the Holocaust, the weight of history and the imperative of Jewish survival were on these young Jews' shoulders. Thus, many mid-century Jewish camp directors and educators strove to surround campers with compellingly animated expressions of Jewish culture, including various Hebrew practices at select camps.

Because these postwar Jewish culture camps were designed to prepare youth for a fully integrated American Jewish lifestyle, rather than a segregated exis-tence in a Jewish bubble (whether in North America or Israel), their approach to Hebrew was often instrumental.[22] Leaders felt that the cultivation of propri-etary feelings for Hebrew language and culture would contribute to the fashion-ing of a dynamic and durable diasporic identity. When Hebrew was taught for fluency, it was usually because camp educators were focused on molding a Jew-ish elite, rather than normativizing Hebrew proficiency among American Jews.[23] In those cases, educators also spurred camper and staff engagement with classi-cal Jewish texts as sources of inspiration, wisdom, and ethical behavior.

The annihilation of roughly two-thirds of European Jewry, with its eviscera-tion of cultural and religious life, broadened and elevated American Jewish cul-tural distinctiveness into a mission of survival.[24] Among the ways in which American Jews resolved to meet this challenge was through formal and infor-mal education. American society in general became more child-centered,[25] an orientation attributable to the countrywide baby boom and the accompanying ethos that child-rearing was "the key not only to responsible citizenship and a secure future but to a personally fulfilling life."[26] Although these tendencies were also on view in Jewish communities, there was an added dimension to Ameri-can Jews' expectant posture toward the young that was associated with post-Holocaust trauma and the anxiety many felt about American Jewry assuming the mantle of leadership in Jewish culture and world affairs.

In a powerful address before the Conservative Movement's Rabbinical Assem-bly, Mordecai Kaplan painted the emergent generation as a "saving remnant" that would redeem the Jewish people. Kaplan's calculated use of a term that was hitherto applied to Holocaust survivors was enthusiastically appropriated by other leading Conservative figures.[27] But as anthropologist Riv-Ellen Prell doc-uments, Jewish leaders were skeptical about parents' capacity to be cultivators of Jewish identification within their children and thereby turn this "saving rem-nant" into "redeemers." As such, the onus was on rabbis and educators to save Jewish youth from the "apathy and ignorance" that prevailed in most of their homes by socializing them within compelling Jewish environments. Even more than youth groups and schools, residential summer camps became favored sites for cultivating a sense of Jewish belonging, because they removed children and youth from their homes and immersed them in highly controlled environments substantially shut off from the outside world. Camps, Prell wrote, were "conceptualized by their founders and leaders as incubators of a more authentic Judaism."[28]

Many of the Jewish camps that emerged in the mid- to late 1940s and early 1950s were shaped by this dynamic. Chaim Potok's description of his first year as a division head at Ramah Poconos in 1951 captures the anticipation and sense of mission that camp leaders at institutions like Ramah felt as they groomed their charges: "We lived, it seemed to me, in a permanent state of exhilaration born of a sense of high purpose and accomplishment. We were educating the next generation of Jews in a living Judaism."[29] The founders of institutions like Ramah, Brandeis Camp Institute, Young Judaea's Tel Yehudah, and the Reform movement's Union Institute were attracted to camp as an educational environment for the same reasons, and they shared a similar pedagogical outlook, at least in its broadest strokes. They also agreed that camps were countercultural institutions designed to provide an alternative to and thereby subvert the status quo. Where the camps differed from one another was in how they defined the "ideal Jewish life" and how they fashioned their "total Jewish environment." These differences in ideology and praxis played a significant role in dictating the use of Hebrew in each camp.

Some camps, like Ramah, which initially focused on training a Conservative elite, viewed Jewish textual literacy as a *sine qua non* of Jewish leadership. Others, like Brandeis Camp Institute, aspired to stir the hearts of Jewish youth through a steady diet of cultural activities, religious ceremonies, and study. Like the interwar Zionist camps, these newer camps used Hebrew to construct an environment that felt authentically Jewish and symbolically set apart from the dominant American culture, even as they partook in quintessential American summer pastimes like playing sports and staging popular musical theater productions. Although many camp professionals were interested in fostering a connection between campers and the newly established state of Israel, their emphasis was squarely on American Jewish life.

Consider Young Judaea's leadership camp, Tel Yehudah, founded in 1947 to address a perceived "dearth of adequate and trained leadership within Young Judaea," as well as a discernible lack of "spirited interest" from older youth group members. It is not surprising that this Zionist camp approached Hebrew through the prism of national revival. Yet Young Judaea was also the most Americanized of the Zionist youth movements, and it struggled with how to support *chalutziut* (pioneering) while affirming the long-term viability of American Jewish life. Writing about Young Judaea's approach to *chalutziut*, historian Arthur Goren noted an ongoing tug-of-war between those who wished to fashion the movement into a conduit for immigration to Palestine and those who insisted on maintaining its appeal as a Jewish consciousness-building program for a wide swath of American Jewish youth.[30]

Under Young Judaea executive director Norman Schanin, who directed Tel Yehudah from 1947–1952 and was a student of Mordecai Kaplan, the movement and its camps were receptive to Zionist culture as the embodiment of Jewish rebirth and cultural effervescence—but not as a negation of the Diaspora. Schanin's elevation of transnational Jewish peoplehood over narrow Israeli nationalism tacitly weakened the rationale in the Diaspora for a Hebrew-centered educational program. Modern Hebrew fluency was hardly a prerequisite for participation in American Jewish life, even if the ability to read or understand some Hebrew (textual and modern) was a marker of Jewish belonging.[31] The Americanization of *chalutziut* gave Zionist camp directors the license to balance fostering Hebrew literacy against other priorities. Challenges like the availability of Hebrew-speaking staff, the educational background of the campers, and the prevailing American culture of monolingualism were more easily regarded as fixed factors than surmountable obstacles. But the imperatives of Jewish unity and attachment to Israel motivated directors to encourage camper identification with Hebrew as a Jewish language and, more specifically, to foster a sense of linguistic ownership through the use of infusion.

At Herzl Camp, a private Zionist camp about ninety minutes from Minneapolis in Webster, Wisconsin, camp director Zvi Dershowitz gradually introduced Hebrew nouns into the day-to-day language of the camp during the late 1950s. For example, counselors in training were called *ozrim* (helpers), the infirmary became known as the *marpe'a*, and English announcements on the public address system would begin with the phrase, "*Hakshivu! Hakshivu!*" (Attention! Attention!). From the outset, many of these words were clipped. Thus, the dining room was universally known as the *chadar*, rather than the *chadar ochel*. According to Dershowitz, his goal was to "stimulate [campers'] Jewish and Zionist identities. . . . I tried to create an atmosphere where Hebrew was common around camp." Campers and staff reportedly adapted easily to the innovation in formal settings but were more resistant to using the terminology in private conversations. In addition, a Hebrew immersion initiative called Ivriah was introduced in 1960 by Dershowitz and program director Moshe Dworkin, but it only lasted a few seasons.[32]

Dershowitz became a proficient Hebrew speaker while spending a year at the Jewish Agency-sponsored *Machon L'Madrichei Chutz La'Aretz* (Institute for Youth Leaders from Abroad), but he probably picked up most of the camp Hebrew loanwords that he introduced to Herzl Camp from his years in Zionist youth groups. Dershowitz grew up in Young Judaea and Masada, the Young Men's Zionist Organization of America, and before leading Herzl Camp he served as director of Camp Young Judaea in Winnipeg, Canada.[33]

## Camp Hebraized English and the Ethnic Revival

By the 1960s, Jewishness was becoming more visible in American popular culture, and Jewish public figures were becoming more comfortable in their Jewish skins.[34] Historian Kirsten Fermaglich detected a new "spirit of cultural transgression" in the early 1960s and viewed the era as "a bridge that transformed the quietism of the early McCarthy years into the angry radicalism that dominated the headlines in 1968."[35] Of course, Jews were not the only group to become more ethnically assertive in the early 1960s. The election of America's first (and to date only) Catholic president, in 1960, came to symbolize the ascendancy of an Americanness that was elastic enough to encompass the so-called white ethnics.[36]

This trend toward unguarded and confident Jewish self-expression accelerated in the late 1960s and '70s, catalyzed not only by the catharsis that many American Jews experienced during and after the June 1967 Six Day War but also by America's more general ethnic revival. By then, as scholar Matthew Frye Jacobson put it, "normative whiteness" was recast "from what might be called Plymouth Rock whiteness to Ellis Island whiteness."[37] This fundamental change in the way many Americans viewed their nation's origin narrative effectively gave Jews permission to find inspiration and meaning in performances of Jewish ethnicity, including identification with Israel and the use of Hebrew. At the same time, unprecedented acceptance in American society prompted widespread anxiety about Jewish continuity from a variety of Jewish insiders.[38] Fostering Jewish ethnic and religious identification became a preoccupation of Jewish educators, community leaders, and young Jewish activists.

In this atmosphere of experimentation, some Jewish young people, including but by no means limited to those connected with the countercultural *havurah* (fellowship) movement, found that using Hebrew-infused English reinforced a sense of Jewish connection and belonging. *Response* magazine editor William Novak viewed counselors' use of (what we call) CHE at Ramah as an attempt to "Judaize" summer camp, and a 1970 Reform camp manual linked Hebrew usage to Jewish self-awareness because it promoted an affective rather than a merely cognitive connection to Jewishness: "To be a Jew, one must do more than think himself a Jew: he must feel himself to be Jewish. One important aspect of feeling Jewish is a full knowledge of Hebrew."[39] Significantly, such convictions were increasingly articulated by staff at Jewish culture camps that were traditionally American-centered. Thus, the late 1960s and '70s marked a gradual (and incomplete) convergence of the Hebrew practices of a wide swath of Jewish educational and culture camps of varying ideological stripes. Although significant differences remained in philosophy and praxis, a consensus developed around the efficacy of Hebrew and Israel as building blocks of Jewish identity—together with the realization that Hebrew proficiency was often an unworkable educational objective. Even though creating an entirely Hebrew-speaking camp environment was deemed an overly ambitious and largely unattainable project, the champions of Hebrew infusion engaged in a comparably transformational educational endeavor. In this radical project of American Jewish reconstruction, Hebrew infusion was thought to confer a veneer of authenticity and promote linkages to biblical heroes and classical Jewish texts, as well as a young and vibrant state of Israel and its Hebrew culture.

Accordingly, concerns about Jewish adjustment to America began giving way to fears about Jewish survival. It was also in the 1960s and '70s that American Jewish educators and communal leaders appropriated the concept of "identity" to describe and measure indices of Jewish group belonging and individual attachment to Jewish heritage. The very term "identity," which was popularized in the 1950s by developmental psychologist Erik Erikson, was appropriated by Jewish public intellectuals, educators, and sociologists to discuss manifestations of Jewish group belonging and express nascent anxieties about Jewish continuity. By the late 1960s, it was also being used to describe an individualized sense of connection to one's heritage.[40] In line with the wider turn to ethnicity in America, Jewish countercultural publications like *The Jewish Catalog* (1973) urged American Jewish youth to explore Judaism and thereby make meaning of their lives. The hothouse environment of summer camp presented an ideal site for investigation and experimentation. The emphasis on identity did not fundamentally change the programmatic spine of highly ideological Jewish educational and culture camps, but it did encourage some mainstream and pluralistic camps, particularly those affiliated with JCCs and federations, to intensify their Jewish character.

Even when the programmatic and linguistic changes were modest, they were discernible to counselors and campers, who reported that exposure to Hebrew made them feel more Jewishly connected. Performing one's Jewish identity through using Hebrew loanwords was analogous to wearing a Star of David pendant or eating matzah on Passover. But how much Hebrew and what kind of Hebrew varied from camp to camp, as did the extent to which using Hebrew conferred cultural capital.[41]

A sign of the changing times was the serious-minded response by communal professionals to the publication of a 1963 American Association for Jewish Education report that criticized JCC- and federation-sponsored camps for their poorly conceived objectives and anemic Jewish content. In response, the National Jewish Welfare Board (JWB), which served as the umbrella organization for JCCs, encouraged its approximately 100 affiliated camps to "actively engage" campers in Jewish activities and concerns and not to limit Jewish programming to religious services and rituals. Some camp directors like Asher Melzer at Surprise Lake Camp in Cold Spring, New York, and Michael Zaks, at Camp Tamarack in Ortonville, Michigan, took the appraisal to heart and spent the next two decades enhancing the Jewish content in their camps. For example, they replaced

Indian names and iconography around camp with Hebrew appellations and themes.[42]

The JWB also supported the Summer Shlichim (Emissaries) Program, inaugurated in 1965–1966, which brought Israeli emissaries to camp as counselors and specialists. The emissaries program, which was initially confined to only a few camps, spread quickly in the aftermath of the 1967 Six Day War. The presence of Israelis inspired and enabled the infusion of more Hebrew into the camp program through the inclusion of Israeli music and folk dancing, as well as camp Hebrew loanwords. Introducing Israeli culture, including Hebrew, into nondenominational camps was often viewed as a less controversial approach to increasing Jewish content in the 1960s and '70s than heightening religious observance. Hebrew and Israeli cultural programming could be made playful and thus encounter minimal resistance from campers or their parents.[43] Israel's ascent to a regional superpower on the geopolitical stage may have contributed to the more central role that it played in American Jewish educational settings. Where the image of Israel besieged was a potent motivational device for the promotion of *chalutziut* in Zionist camps, the power and romance of post-1967 Israel played to a wider audience, becoming a vehicle for enhancing Diaspora Jewry's self-esteem.[44] According to former staffers, campers and even counselors venerated emissaries who served in the 1967 war and sometimes made them into sex symbols. Hebrew, as the language of these Israelis, was likewise alluring. Thus, enhanced identification with Israel led to an increased interest in Israeli culture, including modern Hebrew.[45]

## Hebrew in Reform Movement Camps: A Case Study

To appreciate how and why Hebrew infusion practices became habitual in Jewish culture camps in the 1960s and '70s, it is useful to consider the case of the Reform movement's camping network, the Union of American Hebrew Congregations' (UAHC) Camp Institutes for Living Judaism. (The UAHC changed its name to the Union for Reform Judaism in 2003.) Reform camps offer an ideal case study because of their ideological orientation and the richness of the archival record. The most liberal and universalistic of American Judaism's major streams, Reform promoted American integration and catered to an acculturated clientele. Save for their incorporation of Jewish worship and study and their interest in leadership cultivation, Reform camps were hardly distinguishable from contemporaneous YMHA or private nondenominational Jewish camps. Additionally, with the exception of Camp Saratoga (later known as the Swig Camp Institute) in Northern California, Israel and modern Hebrew were generally peripheral to Reform camps' mission and programming in the 1950s, as they were in most private, JCC, and federation-sponsored camps. Hebrew and Israel-related programming began figuring more prominently by the 1960s, and by the 1970s and '80s most Reform camps had adopted a register of CHE as their lingua franca. The normalization of ethnic identity politics in the late 1960s and 1970s meant that even highly acculturated Reform youth saw no conflict between their Americanness and their growing romance with Israel and its language. Institutions that historically did not view promoting Hebrew proficiency as part of their mission often embraced Hebrew with two purposes in mind: suffusing the camps with a more Jewish atmosphere and fostering identification with Israel. Although there is no intrinsic link between using modern Hebrew and feeling a connection to Israel, camp officials reinforced the association through Zionist-themed Hebrew songs, Israeli folk dancing, and the presence of Israeli staff. The scant qualitative data available on Reform campers in the 1960s and '70s, which are almost exclusively retrospective, suggest that staff were at least partially successful in forging such bonds.[46]

The parameters of "Living Judaism" developed and expressed at the oldest Reform movement camp—the Union Institute in Oconomowoc, Wisconsin (known today as the Olin-Sang-Ruby Union Institute or simply by the acronym OSRUI)—made no mention of Hebrew. It is also noteworthy that an early set of camp guidelines stipulated, among other things, that only the American flag (and not the Israeli one) would be raised and lowered and that the discussion of both Zionism and communism at camp was *verboten*.[47] Given the Reform movement's historical opposition to political Zionism (which was repudiated in 1937 but still found support in some quarters), its concern with American integration, and its minimalist approach to liturgical Hebrew in prayer, these omissions and stipulations may seem unexceptional.[48] But many of the founders and rabbinical faculty at the Union Institute were sympathetic to the Zionist cause— some, including Rabbis Herman Schaalman, Ernst Lorge, and Karl Weiner, were German Jewish refugees who had grown up in the Blau-Weiß and Habonim youth movements—and Israel and Zionist culture occasionally found their way into the camp's early programming. Some camp insiders speculate that the state of American political discourse contributed to the reticence around Zionism and the lack of spoken Hebrew. The Union Institute was founded in 1952 at the height of the Cold War and the second Red Scare, which swept up a disproportionate number of Jews and placed many others on the defensive about their political loyalties. Rabbi Ernst Lorge's son, Michael, who has written about the founding of the Union Institute, characterized the Oconomowoc camp's guidelines as a subterfuge, designed to allay the concerns of the Chicago laity. Either way, Israel was peripheral during the early years of the Union Institute. Perhaps for this reason, the camp gave little or no attention to modern Hebrew.[49]

The Jewish energy at the Union Institute in the early and mid-1950s was channeled into creative worship and clergy-facilitated study sessions focusing on ethics, theology, history, and current events. The Hebrew language did not figure prominently in either of these realms. In the case of worship, Hebrew was used only for a few central prayers like the ceremonial call for worship (*Bare-chu*) and the central creed (*Shma*).[50] The liturgy with which most campers were familiar from their home congregations came out of the Reform movement's mostly English *Union Prayer Book*. When campers were encouraged to write their own services, the liturgy was inevitably primarily in English. Likewise, when rabbis conducted study sessions and discussions, typically around a unifying theme, the classical sources they shared were offered in English translation. When Hebrew was heard at camp, it was often textual and ceremonial, with speakers routinely using the Ashkenazi pronunciation that was normative in most Reform synagogues. A 1959 Union Institute Hebrew vocabulary list included Jewish life words like "*Oneg Shabbos*," "*Havdoloh*," "*Hamotzee*," "*Mazal Tov*," and "*Mezuzah*." Hebrew did not appear on the printed camp schedule, nor were Hebrew signs visible on the camp grounds. The one exception was in the realm of music, where simple Hebrew songs were taught and sung alongside English standards.[51]

If Hebrew initially played a modest role in the Reform camping program, by the mid-1950s there were indications of impending change. The most noteworthy harbinger was the establishment of a twelve-day Hebrew-intensive, Zionist program called Solel at Camp Saratoga, which became affiliated with the UAHC in 1952. Developed by Los Angeles Bureau of Jewish Education officials Samuel Kaminker and Irwin Soref, and Hebrew teacher Sarah Kaelter, Solel (Trailblazer) included "daily Hebrew classes and a multitude of activities that were interwoven with Hebrew." The idea for the program likely originated with Kaminker, who began experimenting with Zionist-centered camp programming a few years earlier while directing Camp Avodah near Chicago. It met with little resistance because Jewish Angelinos were generally supportive of the newly established state of Israel.[52] Solel blazed a path for the introduction of modern Hebrew and intensive Israel-related programming at other Reform camps.

The winds of change could be felt in Wisconsin by 1960. When Rabbi Victor Weissberg visited the Oconomowoc camp during the summer of 1957, he was struck both by the absence of Hebrew in the camp's program and the campers' professed interest in learning the language. In a report to the director, Weissberg recommended that "the camp should plan to teach Hebrew in some form or another."[53] The senior rabbi at Temple Beth El in Northbrook, Illinois, Weissberg represented a new generation of rabbis who were ordained after World War II. A child of Eastern European immigrants and an alumnus of Young Judaea, Weissberg was also a World War II navy veteran who felt no conflict between his Zionism and his allegiance to America. By the late 1950s and early 1960s, Jews like Weissberg were increasingly comfortable with expressions of ethnic identity.

When the Union Institute introduced Hebrew instruction, it created little dissonance, even for its highly acculturated clientele. An initial attempt was made to teach campers how to read vocalized Hebrew on an optional basis in 1959. Hebrew Union College rabbinical student and future professor Stephen Passamaneck reported mixed success using the idiosyncratic *Rocket to Mars* (1953) primers, a phonetic approach to Hebrew reading that employed Hebrew letters to spell English words. The choice of *Rocket to Mars* indicates that the emphasis of the program was on synagogue skills, especially decoding liturgical Hebrew. One correspondent in the camp newspaper reported, "At the end of the six books, after landing back on Earth, the campers found to their amazement that the most exciting part of their experience on the rocket was that they could now read Hebrew and recognize some of the *Union Prayer Book* prayers." Another camper explained that Passamaneck also devoted class time to translating Hebrew prayers into English.[54]

The *Rocket to Mars* curriculum was soon dropped in favor of more conventional pedagogies, and the Hebrew program at the Union Institute expanded, so that by 1962, Hebrew instruction was elevated to a mandatory activity on the daily schedule. Classes were tracked by language ability, with camper placement accomplished at the beginning of each camp session through a short reading and comprehension exam. The Hebrew classes were only part of a more pervasive transformation. By the early 1960s, the Union Institute's campers were increasingly exposed to modern Hebrew words and phrases as the camp embraced Hebrew infusion. This changeover, engineered by program director Oscar Miller and education director Howard Bogot, accelerated on the arrival of camp director Irv Kaplan in 1963. This shift is well documented, thanks to the preservation at the American Jewish Archives of schedules, song sheets, camper newspapers, class materials, and other camp realia. For example, by 1962, daily activities that were listed in English on schedules from the 1950s were itemized in both transliterated Hebrew and English in an attempt to acclimate both campers and staff to the use of selected Hebrew terms. Thus, "*avodat ha'kodesh*" replaced the "Call to Worship," and "special interest activities" became known as "*chugim*." By 1966, the daily schedule was almost entirely in transliterated Hebrew, with words already familiar to campers, like "*Aruchat Haboker*" (breakfast) and "*M'nuchah*" (rest), rendered without translation and with more recently introduced words and phrases, like "*Hanafat Hadegel*" (flag raising), appearing with parenthetical translations.[55]

Contemporaneous camper-written newspaper articles and camper-composed ditties illustrate that the use of Hebrew on official camp documents was more than symbolic. Consider, for example, the lyrics for a 1962 Song Fest, where each cabin presented a theme song using a popular melody. Cabin 6's reworking of the show tune "Hernando's Hideaway," from *The Pajama Game*, included these lyrics:

This cabin doesn't look like home
You'll never win the *Nakayon* [a competitive cabin-cleaning activity]
Clean up this place without a moan
Clean up! Without a moan or groan—*Oy vey!*

Similarly, Cabin 4 reimagined Neil Sedaka's "Breaking up Is Hard to Do":

We love the *Medura, ra, ra, ra, ra* [campfire]
We even love *Sicha, cha, cha, cha, cha* [faculty-facilitated discussions]
We also love *Chugim, gim, gim, gim, gim, gim* [electives]
And Canteen . . . shuvi doo doo.[56]

Although the songs' cleverness is debatable, the lyrics illustrate that Hebrew loanwords were ensconced in daily conversation.

The Union Institute's dialect of CHE emerged from a deliberate process. During the 1962 season, under the supervision of Miller, rabbinical student Donald Splansky prepared a twenty-six-item Hebrew word list that was later mailed to soon-to-be campers in June 1963. The accompanying explanatory letter identified the words as those "commonly used by the Program Director and staff," and it directed campers to familiarize themselves with them before arriving at camp. In contrast to a shorter list of Hebrew terms created in 1959, which included Jewish life words like *Shabbos*, none were explicitly religious or liturgical in nature. Rather, the list was customized for a camp environment and included words like *madrich/madricha* (counselor) and *tzrif* (cabin). Significantly, each word was typed in Hebrew block letters with vowel markings, transliterated, and translated into English. "That's when the word *Bayit* replaced the term 'Big House,'" Splansky recalled, referring to the camp's main building.[57]

Director Irv Kaplan's previous experience directing the Chicago Board of Jewish Education-sponsored camps, Avodah and Sharon, convinced him of the power of Hebrew to promote Jewish identification. Both he and Miller grew up in the Conservative movement, which used more Hebrew than Reform in its liturgy and educational programming. Kaplan's Hebrew was rusty, but he was an ardent Zionist, Splansky remembered, and "under his directorship Zionism was the hidden agenda in his vision of the camp." That summer, educator Fradle Pomp Freidenreich introduced an activity-based Hebrew program that emphasized aural skills and simple conversation, as well as reading, through the use of manipulatives, games, and songs. Freidenreich's gimmicks reportedly included a striptease (down to her bathing suit), which she performed to teach the Hebrew names for various articles of clothing. Additionally, Kaplan directed Splansky to place signs in the dining room featuring meal-related vocabulary with corresponding pictures. The following summer, the Union Institute inaugurated the Hebrew-intensive Pioneer Program for high school students, which became known as Chalutzim.[58] All of these additions indicated a transformation in the language ideologies of Union Institute leaders and participants.

## HEBREW IMMERSION PROGRAMS IN INFUSION CAMPS

Chalutzim was one of a modest number of specialized Hebrew-speaking camp programs that were launched in the 1960s and '70s; other such programs included the Ulpan program at Tel Yehudah and Herzl Camp's MABA program. Unlike the Hebrew immersion camps like Massad and Yavneh that were inaugurated in the 1940s, these programs were nested in larger Jewish camps. At some camps, such as the Union Institute in Oconomowoc, the programs were optional, whereas in others, like Tel Yehudah, they were built into the camper sequence. Because the participants typically had only rudimentary Hebrew skills, the programs were overtly didactic. In this respect, they bore some resemblance to the programs at Camp Yavneh and the Ramah camps in their early years. Although routinized and nonroutinized Hebrew speaking was encouraged during formal activities and in public spaces, there was little pretense at making Hebrew the language of camper conversations in the tents or cabins.

Tel Yehudah's Ulpan program was initiated in 1961 as part of Young Judaea's more forthright turn in its approach to *chalutziut*. In 1955, Young Judaea leaders inaugurated a work-study gap year program in Israel, known today as "Year Course," which combined five months of Hebrew and Jewish study in Jerusalem with four months of volunteer work on a kibbutz or moshav. The Ulpan, which stressed Hebrew language and culture, was developed a few years later as a preparation course. "We used our imagination, and we made a program where Hebrew was essentially part of the very living of camp," recalled longtime *merakez* (unit head) Mel Reisfield. Movement leaders were transparent in their hope that some Year Course participants would choose to remain in Israel or return after university.[59]

MABA, an acronym for *Machanaut B'avirah Ivrit* (Camping in a Hebrew Environment), was a three-week session at Herzl Camp that combined an immersive modern Hebrew program in the mornings with regular camp activities in the afternoons. Developed in 1970 as a joint project of the camp and the Hebrew-intensive Minneapolis Talmud Torah, it served students from among the Talmud Torah's ranks.[60] Campers learned everyday Hebrew vocabulary and grammar by memorizing and acting out conversational dialogues, many of which focused on camp life and activities. Hebrew signage was erected around camp to reinforce these lessons. MABA campers also participated in Hebrew electives, which centered around activities like publishing a Hebrew camp newspaper and staging a musical with Hebrew songs and select Hebrew phrases. They also sat together and practiced their Hebrew in the dining room.[61]

Of all these Hebrew-speaking camp programs launched during the 1960s and '70s, Chalutzim was the most enduring and served as the poster child for Hebrew-language intensive programming in the Reform camping context.[62] Two other Reform camp programs—Solel, at the Swig Camp Institute, in Saratoga, California, and Torah Corps, at Kutz Camp, in Warwick, New York—were also Hebrew centered, although not immersive. The Chicago-area Reform rabbis who stood behind the Chalutzim program were eager to see the Union Institute engage more substantively with Israel and the Hebrew language and also supported attempts to infuse Hebrew into the main camp. After two years of planning, the Pioneer Program was inaugurated in 1964 as a six-week session for eighteen to twenty high school students who had "at least a reading ability in Hebrew" and a recommendation letter from their congregational rabbi.[63]

The extent to which the program was driven by American Jews' growing romance with Israel is evident in its Hebrew name, Chalutzim (pioneers). Participating campers were pioneers in intensive Hebrew study at Oconomowoc, just as the six-week length of the session was also unprecedented at the Union Institute, where two-week sessions were the norm. But the word *chalutzim* also evoked the first waves of Zionist immigration to Palestine, particularly the Jews who engaged in agricultural labor. Consider, also, this letter to campers from the Pioneer Program's first unit director, Donald Splansky, who had become a rabbi by that time: "We will be pioneering in many ways, both in the work at the camp farm and the cabin life away from the main camp area. We will be pioneering in studying Hebrew intensively and in learning to speak Hebrew in everything we do. Finally, the whole program will be a pioneer project, the first time at Union Institute and the first time in all the Reform camps."[64]

Evidently, Splansky did not view the pioneering aspect of the session as limited to its intensive emphasis on Hebrew study and acquisition. The teens would simulate the experience of early Zionist *chalutzim*: they would live in separate cabins from their peers and would work in the fields and in the barnyard.[65] Still, Hebrew was always a central component of Chalutzim. Splansky instructed the inaugural cohort to "brush up" on their Hebrew before the start of camp. Likewise, the information guide for parents explained that campers would be "learning Hebrew by using it as their everyday language." A general information sheet for prospective campers included a basic camp vocabulary list and the assurance that it will "prove to be handy in the beginning when you arrive at 'little Israel.'" Soon-to-be campers were also told to learn their Hebrew names before arrival and to "give some thought to a Hebrew name for the Pioneer camp mascot," which they would choose from among the farm animals.[66]

Splansky and his team, including counselors Rachel Zohar Dulin and Sam "Shmulik" Alpert, struggled during the first summer to place the program on solid footing.[67] For example, campers resisted the dictum that prayers be conducted entirely in Hebrew, insisting on maintaining a mostly English service on the grounds that it would be more meaningful.[68] Of course, their objection to reciting the liturgy in Hebrew was completely consistent with the Reform movement's contemporaneous prayer practice and values, indicating the countercultural nature of the Pioneer Program. By the end of the season, the staff was able to agree on a range of policy changes for the following summer, many of which were designed to bolster Hebrew speaking, including the complete isolation of the Pioneer Program from other units, except on the Sabbath. The camp built a separate meeting house and playing fields for the program. According to Dulin, segregation was a key ingredient to the program's subsequent success. So too was staff buy-in. It was only when the counselors began speaking solely in Hebrew that camper outcomes measurably improved. At first, the counselors protested that the counselor–camper bond was dependent on heart-to-heart conversations. Consequently, the camp leadership team acceded to a compromise that allowed English to be spoken in the cabins after lights out. Dulin, a Soloman Schechter teacher who later became a professor of Hebrew, recalled that great attention was dedicated to staff training. "You have to prepare the staff to know what they are trying to do, and don't talk to me about *sababa* and *shmababa*. That's not the purpose of this," she said, brushing off the idea that kids could be turned on simply by teaching them a little Israeli slang. "The focus was Israel and Israeli culture."[69]

The Hebrew program attained a measure of stability as the staff became better acclimated. Much of it was driven by the force of Dulin's personality. She became a master at using song as a teaching device. She also standardized Chalutzim's formal Hebrew education program, developing graded, thematic curricular materials. Prospective campers were required to pass an entrance examination— they could take it multiple times until they received a passing grade—which was also used for placement purposes. In addition, Dulin was well known for using what she termed *kuntzim* or stunts to heighten campers' interests. One example from the 1967 camp season, which was still recalled decades later by multiple former staff members, was born out of Dulin's desire to teach the campers about Eliezer Ben-Yehuda, the editor and lexicographer whose single-minded devotion to Hebrew was the driving force behind its modern revival. Dulin managed to co-opt one of the least compliant Hebrew speakers, a boy whose Hebrew name was Gershon, to use only Hebrew for an entire day. "Let them be shocked by the fact that you, the biggest problem here, are really turned on to the idea," she recalled telling the camper. The plan worked marvelously. Whenever one of his comrades began speaking with him in English, Gershon would respond: "*Mah ata omer*? *Rak ivrit*! [What are you saying? Only Hebrew!]." At the end of the day, Gershon was publicly decorated with a Ben-Yehuda Award. Splansky recalled that for the next few days the faculty would exhort the campers during announcements in the dining room: "*Gershon medaber ivrit. Kol ehad yachol l'daber ivrit* [Gershon speaks Hebrew. Everyone can speak Hebrew]."[70]

Another influential early staff member was Rabbi Hillel Gamoran, an alumnus of the Hebrew-speaking Massad camps, who arrived in 1966. According to Dulin, the example of Gamoran speaking modern Hebrew and not simply using it as a language of prayer or study made a big impression on the campers. By the late 1960s, the program staff became more insistent on maintaining an immersive environment. They also adopted another stratagem out of the Massad playbook: the use of a reward system for Hebrew speaking. But unlike Massad, where the coveted prize was a patch that could be affixed on a camper's scouting uniform, the coin of the realm at Chalutzim was M&Ms.[71]

At the end of the 1966 season, the editors of the Pioneer unit's newspaper, the *Halutzon*, declared, "We are Chalutzim, not Pioneers." Even so, the newspaper itself was written almost entirely in English. A year later, however, at least some of the campers were sufficiently advanced that the newspaper could publish articles written exclusively in Hebrew.[72] Part of Chalutzim's allure was its success in imbuing campers with an *esprit de corps* and creating a sense of anticipation about the program among the younger campers. Being a Chalutzim camper or alumnus conferred status and prestige. Arguably, Chalutzim's success, like that of Massad, hinged on the force of larger-than-life, single-minded personalities who made Hebrew speaking their holy mission. Dulin, who played this role in the 1960s, was followed by two other dynamic and forceful female leaders, Tamar "Timi" Mayer, and Etty Dolgin, both of whom, like Dulin, were native Israelis. Former campers recalled that Mayer ran Chalutzim like an army unit, and her toughness and high standards were effective motivational tools.[73] Chalutzim endures today because its leaders made Hebrew speaking their sacred mission and because its placement in the older division created a sense of anticipation about the program among the younger campers; being a Chalutzim camper or alumnus was a form of cultural capital.

### HEBREW, YIDDISH, AND JEWISH CULTURAL PROGRAMMING AT REFORM CAMPS

Although the Hebrew dosage—even outside of Chalutzim, Solel, and Torah Corps—was strongest at Oconomowoc, Saratoga, and Kutz, Hebrew infusion was not confined to those camps. Even though the UAHC camps were programmatically decentralized, leaving camp directors and their staff with flexibility, virtually all were using some modern Hebrew by the 1960s. For example, the Goldman Union Camp Institute in Zionsville, Indiana (GUCI), was on the more minimalist end of the spectrum, but by the mid-1960s modern Hebrew terms like *boker tov* (good morning) were being used there alongside Jewish life words like *havdalah* (the ceremony marking the end of the Sabbath).[74] A new spirit was ushered in with the arrival of Herzl Honor as Zionsville's director in 1968. The Reform movement's interest in hiring someone with Honor's background telegraphed its shifting stance in relation to Israel. Honor was active in Habonim in his youth and joined a *garin*, a nucleus of prospective immigrants who train and learn together in preparation for kibbutz life. Honor and his young family lived on Kibbutz Bet Hashita in the early 1950s, but they eventually returned to the United States where he worked in various cities as a religious school principal and camp leader.[75] Honor spent four summers at Zionsville, after two years as program director at the Reform movement's Union Camp Institute in Cleveland, Georgia (later renamed Camp Coleman). He quickly set about intensifying the use of CHE, introducing terms like *chadar ochel* (dining hall), *tiyul* (hike), *menucha* (rest), and *machanayim* (a variant of dodgeball). Hebrew singing and

Israeli folk dancing became more prominent. He also initiated a daily camp work and beautification hour that he called *avoda*, a word that carries the dual connotation of work and service.

The transition to Hebrew infusion at UAHC camps was facilitated by several factors, including demographic and cultural shifts within the Reform movement in the postwar years. The influx of Eastern European Jews into Reform temples, which reached a tipping point during the interwar years[76] and accelerated in the postwar period, was accompanied by growing interest in Jewish rituals, greater identification with the state of Israel, and increased use of Hebrew in prayer. In 1961, NFTY (National Federation of Temple Youth) initiated its semester-long high school Israel exchange program. Two years later, Hebrew Union College–Jewish Institute of Religion (the Reform seminary) established a branch in Jerusalem, and 1964 witnessed the publication by the Union of American Hebrew Congregations of the first textbook on Israel (*Israel Today* by Harry Essrig and Abraham Segal) for use in Reform religious schools.

During the 1960s, Hebrew and Yiddish were developing different connotations for American Jews. Hebrew indexed Jews' relationship to liturgy, ritual, Zionist culture, and Israel. Yiddish, the vernacular of many campers' grandparents and even some parents, was familiar and homey, and increasingly a focus of nostalgia. But it also indexed foreignness, the old country, the immigrant neighborhood, and working-class status. American Jews linked Yiddish to locales like the *shtetl* and the Lower East Side that they turned into sites of memory through processes of reclamation, embellishment, fetishization, and commodification. But most American Jews had no actual desire to turn back the clock or revive Yiddish culture,[77] and they maintained Yiddish only in postvernacular ways, including as loanwords in Jewish English.[78] In this way, Jews were able to invoke their ethnicity through the selective deployment of distinctive language without paying a social penalty. However, Yiddish was no longer completely an insider code: select Yiddish and Yinglish words like "shmo" and "maven" were being appropriated as part of American English more broadly.[79] When *The Joys of Yiddish* author Leo Rosten claimed, "We are witnessing a revolution in linguistic values," he was referring to the English language rather than Yiddish.[80] The increasing use in mainstream America of Yiddish words, formerly an in-group Jewish language, complicated the maintenance of communal boundaries. In contrast, Hebrew loanwords remained the equivalent of a secret handshake that authenticated one's membership in an exclusive club. They maintained this currency even in the 2010s, as comic Jon Stewart demonstrated on a 2017 episode of *Jimmy Kimmel Live*, when he elicited peels of laughter from a Kimmel-worshiping bar mitzvah boy and a quizzical look from the non-Jewish host by yelling "*Sheket b'vakasha!* [Quiet, please!]," a common Hebrew refrain at many Jewish camps.[81] In contrast, Kimmel himself used the Yiddish word *mensch*, demonstrating its spread beyond Jewish circles and its limited availability as an insider code.

Honor's cultural programming at the Union Camp Institute in Zionsville sheds light on how CHE was functionally different from the Yiddish-influenced Jewish English spoken by children and grandchildren of Eastern European immigrants. It also helps clarify why staff at postwar Jewish culture camps typically found Hebrew to be more felicitous than Yiddish for their educational and identity-building purposes. Honor's most creative and arguably impactful innovation was cultural programming that foregrounded Israel and Jewish peoplehood. In the years before his arrival, special programming had often revolved around the Jewish holiday cycle, and festivals like Passover and Sukkot were celebrated (out of season) in camp. This had several benefits: it was a creative way of compensating for the lack of summertime Jewish holidays; it addressed the discontinuity between camp and year-round life by teaching the campers rituals, songs, and traditions that they could bring home; and for some campers who hailed from small Jewish communities where they might not partake in communal holiday celebrations with peers, it served as a substitute for, rather than an enhancement of, a home-based experience.

Nevertheless, Honor and his program director, Ike Eisenstein, phased out these religiously centered activities for more ethnically focused programming. Initially, Yiddish, as well as Hebrew, figured prominently. In 1969, for example, the theme was "The Shtetl: From the Old World to the New." Campers were introduced to a new Yiddish word each day, culled from *The Joys of Yiddish*, Rosten's newly published witty lexicon of "Yiddish-in-English."[82] Honor told the camp newspaper, which the editors that summer dubbed *The Shtetl Schmatah* (Yiddish for "small town rag"), that he hoped the program would "give a bit of Yiddishkeit to those who are several generations removed from Eastern Europe."[83] However, Hebrew soon took center stage at the camp, both in terms of content knowledge and creating an ambiance. The following summer, Zionsville's program revolved around the theme "An American in Israel." The camp was turned into an Israeli absorption center as the staff conducted a three-week simulation of the Israeli immigrant experience. Study sessions, electives, sports competitions, and cultural festivals were all Israel themed or recast with an Israeli veneer. A staff-produced camp newspaper, which was published three times per week, provided campers with news about Israel (in English, adapted from Jewish Telegraphic Agency articles), stories, and information spotlights on Israeli destinations and issues. *Chugim* were organized around Israeli culture, such as cooking and dance.

The use of Hebrew nouns for camp buildings and activities increased exponentially. A Hebrew "word of the day," often plucked from daily Israeli life, such as *kol tuv* (best wishes), *b'seder* (okay), and *tachana merkazit* (central bus station), was taught each morning in the *chadar ochel*. Cabins were named for Israeli cities, such as Lod and Rehovot. Simulating the experience of new *olim* (immigrants), campers were assigned to daily *ulpan* classes based on their prior Hebrew knowledge; they were taught Israeli games like *chamor chadash* (lit. new donkey) that might be played by a typical Israeli Scouts troop; and they participated in a *zimriya*, an Israeli song festival, and a *tzaada*, a hybrid color war and hiking program named after the annual three-day march from Israel's Mediterranean coast to the Judean hills, commemorating the siege of Jerusalem in 1948–1949.[84] Staff members viewed these programs as fundamentally constructivist "identity-building" exercises, not merely as "games."[85] The staff's dedication to producing such creative and multifaceted simulations—and campers' reciprocal receptivity to performances of alternate archetypes of Jewishness—exemplified the late 1960s quest among many Jewish young people for authenticity, belonging, and a connection to heritage. Jewish language was integral to these simulations and lent them an air of realism. But identity affirmation was not premised on an expectation that campers would actually immigrate to Israel or become fluent Hebrew or Yiddish speakers. It is not surprising, then, that the Hebrew that Zionsville campers learned during the 1970 season had more staying power than Yiddishisms in the subsequent life of the camp or that context-specific Hebrew words like *tachana merkazit*, which could not easily be appropriated into daily camp life, fell away, while others, like *sheket b'vakasha*, which had immediate currency, survived beyond that season.

In the 1970s and '80s, Hebrew infusion practices accelerated at Zionsville. Hebrew signage dotted the camp landscape, and activities, divisions, and roles were increasingly given Hebrew names. Staff performed an entertaining, pedagogical program about Hebrew called *"Al Hamirpeset"* (On the Porch), inspired by Sesame Street, and Hebrew classes became mandatory for all units. The teachers were given a five-page Hebrew-English vocabulary list with more than 200 modern Hebrew words, including sections on the cabin, dining room, infirmary, activities, canteen, calendar, sports, clothing, body parts, colors, weather, and time. According to the teacher's guide, among the first recommended ulpan activities was a tour of the camp using Hebrew.[86] Although Zionsville eventually dropped the Hebrew classes, the other infusion practices—signage, entertaining/pedagogical skits, and CHE—have become entrenched in camp tradition at the Union Camp Institute/GUCI and other Reform-affiliated camps.

### Hebrew Infusion through Song

Another important aspect of Hebrew infusion at Reform camps was music. Of course, music is a feature of most camps; as folklorist I. Sheldon Posen observed, songs and singing provide "continuity" and "a means of identification" for the camp community. He characterized a camp's songbook as the "greatest single body of folklore shared by the camp folk group."[87] Communal singing was a popular urban pastime in the late nineteenth century when it was imported into camps and became a quintessential summer camp tradition. In important respects, communal singing was perfectly fitted for summer camp: it was participatory and "offered children self-made entertainment within the isolated camp environment." The enjoyment and delight it stimulated could be guided by adults and used to further a camp's ideological and spiritual goals.[88]

By the 1930s, singing became more structured as camps began to employ official song leaders tasked with maximizing group involvement. Folk songs predominated in most camp repertoires, although religious songs could be heard in YMCA and church camps, and labor songs and other overly political songs were favorites at socialist and communist camps. "Spirit songs," such as unit theme songs and camp cheers, and "ritual songs," including religious hymns and prayers, as well as "Taps" and ritualized dining room cheers, were also part of a camp's songbook. Alongside this official repertoire, which Posen referred to as the camp "liturgy," existed an unofficial "lay tradition" of camp songs, ranging from popular music to camp music parodies to bawdy songs. These were sung by campers in unofficial settings and on their own initiative.[89]

Jewish culture camps valued singing for similar reasons as did non-Jewish camps, and their musical landscapes were comparable in that they included both liturgical and lay traditions. The Jewish camp songbook typically included selections from a variety of musical genres in at least three languages—English, Yiddish, and Hebrew (and occasionally Ladino)—although individual repertoires reflected each camp's political and cultural orientation and philosophical approach. By the 1960s and '70s, Hebrew songs had become more prominent and numerous in many camp songsters, reflecting their increased importance in the camp culture, while the number of Yiddish songs dwindled. (Yiddishist camps were an exception to this trend, although they were declining in number.) Thus, singing became a central Hebrew infusion practice at various Jewish culture camps. For many campers, music offered their most sustained and powerful exposure to Hebrew.[90]

Singing was a relatively low-bar way to introduce Hebrew to camps. The repetitive nature of camp singing encouraged Hebrew memorization and a greater comfort with the Hebrew language, but it was seldom intended to promote Hebrew proficiency. The champions of Hebrew song articulated affective goals, including religious and spiritual uplift, connection to Israel and the Jewish collective, and love of Hebrew language and culture. Singing in a Jewish language, whether Hebrew, Yiddish, or Ladino, marked camp as a Jewish space and the camp community as a Jewish community. In some cases, Hebrew set pieces were ritualized, like prayers over candles, wine, and challah bread on the Sabbath or the Grace after Meals. Occasionally, there was carryover between various camp settings, such that a prayer set to a contemporary melody might be used in both a religious service and a dining room singsong or sing-along. New campers were often expected to pick up a camp's liturgy, including its Hebrew songs, through repetition. But when new Hebrew songs were introduced, they were typically translated by song leaders. Indeed, songs were often chosen for their social or religious messages.[91] Thus, Arik Einstein's idealistic 1971 song, "*Ani v'Ata*" ("Me and You"), with its refrain, "You and I will change the world," became a popular anthem at many Jewish camps in the aftermath of the dispiriting 1973 Yom Kippur War and amidst the United States' crisis of confidence in the 1970s; similarly, Moshe Ben-Ari's 1996 song "*Salaam/Od Yavo Shalom Aleinu*" ("Peace Will Yet Be upon Us") became a standard in liberal Jewish camps as dovish American Jews struggled to salvage hope following the outbreak of the Al-Aqsa Intifada and the failure of the peace negotiations in 2000–2001.

The influence of Hebrew singing was arguably most profound in camps that incorporated only a modest amount of Hebrew in other aspects of camp life but where Jewish living was taken seriously and Jewish experimentation was encouraged. In those environments, Hebrew music became a vehicle for expressing ownership over Jewish (and camp) tradition. Ethnomusicologist Mark Kligman observed that Reform camps were far more active "seedbed[s] for new music" in the mid- to late twentieth century than the Conservative Ramah camps. Ramah tended to be more deferential to expertise and more tied to the canon of songs in its printed songbooks. Kligman speculated that the all-Hebrew repertoire at Ramah discouraged songwriting, because most would-be composers lacked the requisite Hebrew vocabulary and grammatical skills. At Reform camps, novices felt comparatively less pressure to defer to experts and more easily overcame their inhibitions around singing, leading, and composing.[92]

Select Palestinian Zionist folk songs, *Shirei Eretz Yisrael* (Songs of the Land of Israel), could be found in Zionist camp songbooks in the 1930s and '40s, but a breakthrough of sorts occurred when the Weavers released a cover of Issachar Miron and Yehiel Haggiz's song, "*Tzena, Tzena*," in 1950, with both the original Hebrew and new English lyrics. The song skyrocketed to No. 2 on the u.s. Billboard charts. Ari Kelman writes about how "*Tzena, Tzena*" "fed American Jews' sense of what Israel was—a land brimming with tanned and muscular kibbutznik-soldiers singing, dancing the hora, and making the desert bloom." Yet, as Kelman perceptively adds, "Despite the song's pedigree, it took [Weavers' member Pete] Seeger's *hechsher* [stamp of approval] to make Israel audible to American Jews." In the wake of the popularity of "*Tzena, Tzena*," Hebrew songs from Israel were increasingly incorporated into the musical repertoires of Jewish culture camps.[93]

Under the influence of music directors like Cantor William Sharlin, who worked at Camp Saratoga, singing was one of the few nondevotional activities in which Reform campers in the 1950s were exposed to Hebrew. From the outset, song leaders led the campers in sing-alongs after every meal. Their repertoires included simple Israeli pioneer songs, Hebrew children's music, and liturgical selections (typically sung using the Ashkenazic pronunciation), as well as some Yiddish folk melodies. Even so, they were often overshadowed by American folk music, brotherhood songs, and spirituals. According to Rabbi Hillel Gamoran, who spent many years on the Union Institute's faculty, the rule of thumb in those early years was that the campers would not be able to handle more than a line or two of Hebrew.[94] A 1956 Union Institute songster included short Hebrew folk tunes like "*Zum Gali, Gali*" and "*Hee-Nay Mah Tov*," alongside "On Top of Old Smoky" and "Shenandoah." A few others were loose English translations of popular Zionist folk songs like "*Finjan*." In all, fully half of the songs were partially or entirely in Hebrew.

Hebrew folk music emanating from Israel fit easily into the liturgical repertoire that was dominated by folk songs and Negro spirituals. Cantor Sharlin recalled carefully balancing the number of folk and protest songs with an equal number of Hebrew and Yiddish songs. In other Reform camps, the ratio between English and Hebrew songs was closer to three to one. When Sharlin introduced and taught new Hebrew songs, the lyrics were transliterated and handprinted on butcher paper, which was hung around the dining room.[95] The spirit that he created in rollicking dining room sing-alongs is legendary. According to one eyewitness, "Sharlin wanted us to sing well, he wanted us to have a good time, he wanted it to be a vehicle for Jewish expression—at that time, not very much Hebrew, but just enough to let us know that we were Jewish."[96] The statement suggests that even in Reform camp circles, at least in the minds of some, using Hebrew words and singing Hebrew songs were markers of Jewishness. JCC camps, as well as select private Jewish camps like Blue Star, also participated in this trend.

The prevalence of Hebrew music in the liturgy and soundtrack of Reform camps increased in the mid- to late 1960s and '70s. Reform camps began incorporating more Israeli songs into the camp repertoire as staff sought to foster campers' emotional bonds to Israel. The transition to a more Israel-centered musical repertoire occurred as a byproduct of the euphoria unleashed by Israel's victory in the June 1967 Six Day War and the arrival of the first Israeli emissaries to camps as part of the Summer Shlichim Program (see chapter 7). Merri Lovinger Arian, a former camper at Eisner Camp, in Great Barrington, Massachusetts, who became a song leader and choral arranger in multiple Reform camps in the 1970s and later a faculty member at the Debbie Friedman School of Sacred Music at Hebrew Union College, recalled the Israelization process. During the summer of 1967, her first at Eisner, most of the energy in the song sessions was generated by the American folk music of singers like Pete Seeger, Bob Dylan, Ed McCurdy, Phil Ochs, Simon and Garfunkel, and Peter, Paul, and Mary. The folk genre was popular across the board in the Reform camping network, as well as at other left-leaning camps. Joan Baez was even brought in to perform at Camp Swig. "The ethics and morals that we learned were reflected in the lyrics of [the folk singers'] songs," Arian explained. The following summer, however, the repertoire noticeably shifted toward Israeli Hebrew songs. "By singing

Israeli folk songs, music provided a portal to identifying with Israelis," she explained. "It didn't matter that we hardly understood the words—we were making a connection with our homeland. We felt the heartbeat of Israelis through their music."[97]

Israeli songs also facilitated the introduction of Sephardic-influenced Hebrew pronunciation to Reform camps. Hebrew-speaking camps like Massad, Ramah, and Yavneh had adopted a Sephardic-influenced pronunciation of Hebrew from the outset. For the Hebraists who staffed these camps in the early years, speaking Hebrew in the manner of the Zionists in Palestine represented an ideological commitment to a transnational Hebrew culture. Even the Jewish Theological Seminary leaders' initial ambivalence about political Zionism at the Ramah camps did not translate into fealty to Ashkenazic-influenced Hebrew pronunciation. In camps where Hebrew was more peripheral, Hebrew pronunciation tended to mirror that of the predominantly Ashkenazi synagogues from which the campers and staff hailed. In the mid- to late 1950s, Reform camps adopted a bifurcated approach to Hebrew, using a Sephardic-influenced pronunciation when singing Zionist songs but retaining the Ashkenazic pronunciation in prayer and when using Jewish life words like *Shabbos*. According to campers and staff at the Union Institute in Oconomowoc, this hybrid approach was organic and did not reflect a conscious attempt to legislate from the top. Song sheets from that era reflect this bifurcation, with modern Hebrew songs transliterated using the Sephardic-influenced pronunciation and transliterated prayers reflecting the Ashkenazic pronunciation. A transition to completely Sephardic-influenced pronunciation at the Union Institute in Oconomowoc occurred in the early to mid-1960s, and somewhat later at camps like Eisner. Ethnomusicologist Judah Cohen explained that campers and younger staff viewed the adoption of the newer pronunciation as "a source of empowerment," in part because it "provided a connection to a hegemonic Jewish culture that until then they had only known in spirit."[98]

The inauguration of Israel's Chassidic Song Festival in 1969 provided another source and genre of Hebrew music that the song leaders eagerly welcomed. In one important respect, neo-Hasidic songs were often easier to teach than Israeli folk music, because their lyrics were typically shorter and were often adapted from liturgical or biblical sources. The two breakout hits from the initial festival were Nurit Hirsh's "*Oseh Shalom*" and Shlomo Carlebach's "*V'Haer Einenu*." According to composer and songleader Jeffrey Klepper, these songs often arrived in North America via the Israeli emissaries and "spread through a network of Hebrew teachers and young rabbis, helped along by high school students returning from their Israeli exchange programs. For those of us strumming our guitars at Jewish camps in 1970 (I was 16) and learning it for the first time, it hit like a bolt of summer lightning." "*Oseh Shalom*" was followed in 1971 by Hirsh's almost equally popular "*Bashana Habaa*," which she wrote with Ehud Manor.

Recordings of both songs, sung by Klepper and his singing partner Daniel Free-lander, were included in the first *NFTY Sings* album, released in 1972.[99] By this time, the camp liturgy had grown to include more ritual songs; for example, Hebrew chanting of the first paragraph of the Grace after Meals became norma-tive at most camps using Cantor Moshe Nathanson's popular melody. Campers and counselors alike often referred to the prayer simply as "the *Birkat*," using a clipped form of the Hebrew term *Birkat Hamazon*.[100]

Arian's reference to American folk music gestured toward another musical trend at Reform camps in the 1960s: the replacement of the professional cantors and musicians who traditionally led camp music programs with homegrown, amateur, guitar-playing song leaders.[101] Song leading became a coveted role at camp, a source of cultural capital. At Camp Hess Kramer, for example, song lead-ers were given the honor of leading the entire camp in the Sabbath eve pro-cession to the open-air chapel. In the 1970s, Kutz Camp Institute director Allan Smith offered need-based scholarships to many an aspiring song leader on the theory that his investment would pay dividends in camp spirit. In the late 1960s, Kutz began hosting a song-leading seminar as part of its annual National Lead-ership Institute under the direction of Jim Schulman. Aspiring song leaders were compelled not only to hone their singing and guitar-playing skills but they were also motivated to practice proper Hebrew pronunciation—and their pedagogi-cal role obliged them to learn the meaning of the Hebrew words they taught.[102] The phenomenon of song leading also underscored how Hebrew was policed at camp. Song leaders without a strong command of Hebrew occasionally taught incorrect Hebrew lyrics, leading to the intervention of rabbis or other Hebrew-literate staff.

If Hebrew became a staple of Reform camps' soundtrack and liturgy, so did CHE. Counselors and campers incorporated CHE into spirit songs, as exem-plified by the Song Fest lyrics discussed earlier, and it could even be heard in the lay songs that were sung without adult supervision. Indeed, it was a mea-sure of the success of Hebrew infusion that at least some Reform campers reflex-ively and effortlessly performed these linguistic practices outside of top-down contexts.

By the 1970s, some camp musicians were not only song leading but also com-posing their own original Hebrew music. Inspired stylistically by political folk music, and drawn to Hebrew by Israel's cathartic victory in 1967 and the neo-Hasidic musical wave ushered in by Carlebach (itself informed by American folk), song leaders/composers created a unique American Hebrew sound. Pio-neering this endeavor was Michael Isaacson, who composed an entire youth ser-vice in the late 1960s, "*Avodat Amamit*: A Folk Service," which he and musician Doug Mishkin performed on one side of the first *NFTY Sings* album in 1972.[103] But the quintessential composer/song leader was Debbie Friedman, who made her song-leading debut at Kutz in 1969 and established herself as a gifted song-

Figure 1.1. Debbie Friedman, the "Joan Baez of Jewish song," c. 1972. In the 1970s and '80s, Friedman and her protégés infused Reform camps with Hebrew through music. (Credit: American Jewish Archives)

writer and rising star with her 1972 album *Sing unto God* (see figure 1.1).[104] Friedman attended a six-month program in Israel in 1969–1970 that combined kibbutz life and Hebrew study with heritage tourism. While in Israel she became an ardent Zionist and a proficient Hebrew speaker, which later gave her the confidence to compose Hebrew songs. The following summer she mentored a new crop of budding song leaders, including Klepper and Mishkin.[105]

It was precisely Friedman's ability to compose in the musical idiom of the day that endeared her to her early enthusiasts. Friedman burst onto the Jewish music scene with a folk melody set to the *Union Prayer Book*'s translation of the *V'Ahavta* prayer ("Thou Shalt Love the Lord Thy God") that she composed to overcome her peers' estrangement from the traditional prayer liturgy.[106] The next step, in Friedman's view, was to address the estrangement between liberal Jews and the Hebrew language. The shift to Hebrew was consciously engineered by Friedman and her protégés, including Klepper and Freelander, and can be traced through their albums in the 1970s and early 1980s. "Between the camping system and the emerging Reform musical tradition, we were able to normalize the use of Hebrew in the Reform movement," Freelander asserted. According to one estimate, by the mid-1970s more than 80 percent of the NFTY and Reform camp music repertoire was in Hebrew.[107] The movement's shift from the eighty-year-old Union Prayer Book to the more Hebrew-intensive and eclectic *Gates of Prayer: Shaarei Tefila* in 1975 accelerated the trend toward Hebrew singing, as did attempts to popularize and standardize an ever-expanding Reform musical canon, most notably through the production and release of the *Songs NFTY Sings* albums between 1972 and 1989, as well as the establishment in 1992 of the annual *Hava Nashira* song leaders and composers workshop (notably, named in Hebrew, in contrast to *Songs NFTY Sings*).[108]

Yet the musicians' success in bringing Hebrew music into Reform camps and congregations did not presage a national Reform initiative to prioritize the study of Hebrew. Thus, Friedman and a younger generation of songwriters were presented with a dilemma. Should they sacrifice the desideratum of Hebrew in order to facilitate a deeper connection between the singer and the song? By the mid- to the late 1980s, their lyrics begin taking a turn toward English, with Hebrew loanwords and Hebrew-English code switching. Among the most widely adopted of Friedman's liturgical songs, "*Mi Shebeirach*," with lyrics co-written with Drorah Setel, exemplifies this trend. Consider the second verse:

> *Mi shebeirach imoteinu* [The one who blessed our foremothers]
> *Mekor habracha l'avoteinu* [The source of blessing for our forefathers]
> Bless those in need of healing with *refua shleima* [complete healing],
> The renewal of body, the renewal of spirit,
> And let us say, *Amen*.

According to Freelander, the decision to compose bilingually emerged from the reality that performers found themselves devoting a significant portion of their camp and youth group concerts to translation. "Putting both languages in the same song saved time. In fact, you get much deeper emotional meanings to people than [with] Hebrew. For me that was an affirmation of our comfort level in America, not feeling second class because we used some English."[109] It is not coincidental that Friedman transitioned to bilingual composition around the same time she began composing more personal and emotional prayers. Friedman's example continues to be emulated by American Jewish composers who frequent the camp circuit, not only in Union for Reform Judaism camps but also in Jewish camps of many types.

———

As we have seen, most Jewish camps, including the Reform-affiliated institutions that we explored in depth here, had little interest in the campers attaining proficiency but still brought Hebrew to their participants in the form of dozens of camp Hebrew loanwords and phrases, as well as Hebrew songs, prayers, and signs. Familiarity with elements of Hebrew was viewed as integral to a healthy Diaspora Jewish identity, connecting campers with their heritage, the state of Israel, and the camp community. The infusion of camp Hebrew words at Jewish summer camps created a distinctive register, CHE, which functioned as a powerful agent for the cultivation of identification and belonging. Hebrew infusion, like the Sabbath and to a lesser extent the dietary laws, became a marker of distinction, a vehicle for cultural expression, a connector to tradition, and a force for social cohesion.

For some American Jewish educators, however, any outcome short of Hebrew proficiency was deemed insufficient. In particular, cultural Zionists in the 1930s and '40s, who believed that a national Jewish revival was contingent on the flowering of a productive modern Hebrew culture in the Diaspora, were dedicated to cultivating a Hebrew-speaking elite in North America. Moreover, in their view, conditions at residential summer camps were ideal for creating an immersive environment, which would be favorable for language acquisition. Efforts to simulate such conditions in the conventional school classroom had not yielded the desired outcomes. The most significant experiment in immersive Hebrew camping was Massad in the Poconos, a network of Hebrew-speaking camps that operated between 1941–1981, the subject of the next chapter.

CHAPTER 2

# Camp Massad in the Poconos and the Rise and Fall of Hebrew Immersion Camping

Richard "Rafi" Starshefsky vividly recalls the moment when it hit him that he was going to spend the summer in an immersive Hebrew environment. Despite his enthusiasm for Jewish learning and observance, Starshefsky—who transferred from public school to a Jewish day school in the fourth grade—had struggled to pick up the Hebrew language. A few years later, when one of his teachers suggested that he spend the summer of 1963 at Massad Bet[1] as a form of Hebrew boot camp, Starshefsky was amenable but utterly unprepared. What he saw when he arrived at the bus stop, in front of the camp's Manhattan offices, nearly convinced him to retreat to his parents' car and make a quick getaway. A man in his twenties who seemed to be in charge was barking Hebrew orders at campers and counselors alike. "I remember, until today," Starshefsky remarked in a 1994 interview, "he absolutely refused to say anything to me in English. Refused. I walked up to him, I spoke to him in English, he answered me in Hebrew, and I couldn't understand him. Then he started to speak a little bit slower and I was able to understand at least what he wanted me to do, because between the Hebrew and the hand motions, I was able to figure it all out."[2]

Starshefsky's parents, who spoke little or no Hebrew, "were absolutely stunned." So when their son began to panic and share his second thoughts about going to camp, they were inclined to give in to his wishes. Once he calmed down, however, Starshefsky began watching the boys who were boarding the bus with their baseball gloves and other sports equipment. "The other kids looked like they were going to have a good time," so Starshefsky decided to take a chance and join them. Much to his relief, the boys on the bus were conversing with one another in English. But the bus monitor Bernie Horowitz was relentless, making announcements only in Hebrew.

Once they arrived at the camp in Dingmans Ferry, Pennsylvania, Starshef-sky's bunkmates also switched to Hebrew for most of their conversations. Starshefsky's friends were his lifeline in the first days and weeks of Massad, play-ing the parts of translator and cultural interpreter. But in time, Starshefsky caught on and ended up enjoying his summer enough that he returned for the following twelve seasons.

The Massad Poconos Camps, which operated from 1941 to 1981, exemplify the effort to offer Hebrew-language instruction through immersion at an American summer camp. Massad was not the first camp to do so, but as a project of the *Histadrut Hanoar Haivri* (the Hebrew Youth Cultural Federation), which stood at the vanguard of American Hebraism, its approach was arguably the best the-orized. Massad was also the most influential of these camps. Many of its alumni went on to work at other camps and assume positions of authority in the Jewish world, and the camp's functional Hebrew-English dictionary was disseminated widely. Thus, many of Massad's innovative approaches to teaching Hebrew and its idiosyncratic camp Hebrew vocabulary influenced later immersion and infu-sion camps. Moreover, Massad exemplified how Hebrew camping was both a response to and an artifact of a cultural Zionist vision of Jewish national revival. The camp's history was intertwined with that of the *Tarbut Ivrit* (Hebrew culture) movement in America. Massad's founding represented the signal achievement of a second generation of American Hebraists, and its fate would be ultimately bound up with the decline of Hebraism in America.

Massad's founders and supporters believed that Hebrew embodied the character and values of the Jewish people and expressed their spiritual core. In the words of medievalist and Hebraist Shalom Spiegel, whose book *Hebrew Reborn* (1930) traced the development of modern Hebrew, "Within language lies concealed magic forces of nature and of blood, lees of instinct and culture, a heritage of emotions, habits of thought, traditions of taste, inheritances of will—the imperative of the past."[3] Massad's shapers viewed Hebrew as integral to cementing kinship bonds among Jewish communities in disparate lands, offering them a means of communication and a common culture. In sum, they viewed a thriving Hebrew culture as essential to Jewish survival. Zionist edu-cator Rabbi Samuel Blumenfield encapsulated this view in a widely circulated apologia:

> The problem of Jewish survival in America is . . . intimately linked up with the question [of] whether American Jewry will have a Jewish language of its own and what language could serve today as a Jewish language. . . . To Jewry at large, Hebrew can serve as a potent factor in Jewish survival, for it links the Jew to his past, binds him to his present, and enables him to share in the pres-ervation of Jewish life in the future.[4]

Massad's founders were fanatically dedicated to Hebrew immersion and elevated it above all other educational, social, and even religious objectives. Their inability to adapt their model to an increasingly wealthy, denominationally fractured, and thoroughly Americanized Jewish community ultimately led to Massad's demise. Linguist and Zionist educator Shimon Frost put the matter succinctly: "The Massad camps were really islands of Hebrew in an ocean of linguistic assimilation."[5] If most American Jews did not defend monolingualism in principle, neither did they elevate modern Hebrew fluency to a desideratum. Most historically Hebraist camps that managed to survive eventually transitioned to an infusion approach. At the same time, Massad demonstrates how Hebrew could be used effectively to promote a broad-based Jewish identity that transcends denomination and political ideology.

### Dreamers and Builders of a Hebrew World

Any discussion of Massad's origins must begin with the motivations and ideology of its sponsoring organization, the Histadrut Hanoar Haivri, and of the camp's prime mover, Shlomo Shulsinger (see figure 2.1). Massad was distinct both from earlier Jewish culture camps like Cejwin, which were vehicles for socializing the children of immigrants and fashioning an Americanized Judaism, and postwar movement camps like Ramah, that were designed to shape a "redeemer generation" in the wake of the Holocaust.[6] But Massad was no less interested in molding campers into a vanguard that would transform Jewish society in response to a perceived existential Jewish challenge. Shlomo Shulsinger and his supporters were committed to the proposition that the twin scourges of assimilation and antisemitism could be combated only through a Jewish cultural transnationalist rebirth centered on the revival of Hebrew as a modern pan-Jewish language. More specifically, the camp was an especially fecund outgrowth of the Tarbut Ivrit movement, the Hebrew culture movement in North America dedicated to making Hebrew the cultural language of the Jewish elite. As Hebrew literature scholar Alan Mintz explained, the propagators of Tarbut Ivrit, Shulsinger among them, "identified the essence of Judaism with its linguistic and literary manifestations."[7] Shulsinger described Massad's mission in countercultural terms: "By giving the child a living and creative Hebrew environment during his summer vacation, the camp attempts to provide that spiritual supplement which does not find its place in the Hebrew school, thus obviating the artificial duality from the life of the Hebrew child and substituting in its place completeness and harmony."[8]

Shulsinger benefited from being in the right place at the right time. A native of Jerusalem, he arrived in the United States in 1929 at the age of 16. His identity as a Zionist educator was shaped in Baltimore, where he came under the influ-

Figure 2.1. Shlomo Shulsinger, director of Camp Massad Poconos (middle), with camper and staff member. (Courtesy of Estates of Noam and Nehama Shudofsky and Massad Camps, Inc.)

ence of Baltimore Hebrew College president Dr. Louis Kaplan.[9] While working part-time as a Hebrew teacher in Baltimore's United Talmud Torah, Shulsinger became involved in Gordonia, a secular, vaguely socialist Zionist youth movement dedicated to enacting the principles of ideologist Aaron David Gordon—principally, the revival of Hebrew and redemption through agricultural labor in *Eretz Yisrael*.[10] His first encounter with American Zionist camping came as a staff member at Gordonia's Camp Moshava, near Annapolis, Maryland.[11] Although Gordonia used Moshava as a site for *hachshara* (preparation for emigration to Palestine and kibbutz life), Shulsinger's experience convinced him of camping's broader educational potential. A few years later, while teaching at Yeshivah of Flatbush, a modern Orthodox day school in Brooklyn, New York, Shulsinger became active in the Histadrut Hanoar Haivri. As the Hebrew camp project came to fruition, Shulsinger benefited from the support and counsel of this coterie of committed Hebraists who adopted the camp project as their own.[12]

Massad was not simply the brainchild of a single zealot, but the crowning achievement of the Histadrut Hanoar Haivri. Emerging out of a 1936 student conference in New York, the federation's prime mover was Moshe Davis, then a student leader at the Jewish Theological Seminary's (JTS) Teachers Institute. Davis initially envisioned Hanoar Haivri as a social and Hebrew cultural group that would bring together the students at the three New York Hebrew teacher-training institutions. The response was enthusiastic, and the interschool association began to gel through a weekly Saturday evening Hebrew book club. As news of the group spread and attracted interest, chapters were established in Hebrew teacher colleges outside New York. Over the next two years, the federation flowered into a wider Jewish youth movement, although it never attracted more than a few thousand adherents. American Hebraists always represented an elite and arguably rarified subculture.[13]

Davis fell under the sway of the JTS Teachers Institute's dean, Rabbi Mordecai Kaplan, and his conception of Judaism as a civilization. The pressing topic that was debated by Hanoar Haivri in those years was whether it was possible to build a culturally generative, indigenous Jewish community in North America. In other words, could American Jews live simultaneously in two worlds, contributing as full members to American society while building a rich and vibrant American Judaism? In expanding the parameters of Jewish life beyond the religious realm, Kaplan provided Davis and his coterie with a template for creative and organic Diaspora Jewish living. In Davis's view, Hanoar Haivri extended Kaplan's vision even further. "It wasn't only a matter of living in two civilizations," he recalled. "I was very much concerned with developing maximal Hebrew experiences."[14] Davis and his colleagues often used the term "experience" to connote an encounter that furthers self-actualization and leads to fulfillment, a process that Zionist writers like A. D. Gordon explored, but also in a way that was reminiscent of what psychologist Abraham Maslow later termed "peak experiences."[15]

In the Hanoar Haivri platform, Davis excoriated American Jewry for its "vicarious Zionism" and complained that existing youth movements were singularly focused on political Zionism and the upbuilding of Palestine, rather than also prioritizing the revival of Hebrew culture in North America.[16] One can similarly detect in the platform a Kaplanian transnational approach to Zionism.[17] The essence of Zionism, Davis asserted, was not territorialism but "the inner reconstruction of Jewish life." The Jewish cultural revival in Palestine should be "a source of inspiration" and a spur to a similar process of "organic creation" in North America rather than "an object of imitation."[18]

In planting this flag in the ground, Hanoar Haivri was not only seeking to distinguish itself from the older Zionist youth movements, like Hashomer Hatzair, Habonim, Betar, and Hashomer HaDati; it was also challenging an older generation of Hebraists, those who were affiliated with the *Histadrut Ivrit*, which was founded in 1916 to promote modern Hebrew language and culture in North America. In the eyes of Histadrut Ivrit's stalwarts, *tarbut* essentially meant literary culture, as exemplified by the Histadrut Ivrit's weekly newspaper, *Hadoar*.[19] For Davis and his comrades, tarbut was a more democratic idea that encompassed the visual and performing arts. The American Jewish masses would not be won over with dense ideological tracts and feuilletons in a language that few read or understood. "The question," Davis insisted, "was could we get people to enjoy life, Jewish life, through Hebrew? And it was clear that in an American environment you needed more than language." To this end, the youth federation created a variety of forums for Hebraic artistic expression, particularly in drama, dance, and music.[20]

As their interest in a holistic definition of tarbut and the creation of an indigenous, non-imitative Hebrew culture in America suggested, the Hanoar Haivri contingent also differed from the first generation in its orientation toward the Diaspora. Whereas the Histadrut Ivrit's immigrant ideologists decried American Jewish life as materialistic, boorish, and ethically compromised, the mostly American-born members of Hanoar Haivri were at home in their surroundings. Moreover, the rise of fascism and the specter of war in Europe reinforced in them an appreciation for American democracy and freedom.[21]

In the short run, the emergence of the Jewish state as a political reality threw into sharp relief the fledgling nature of Hanoar Haivri's enterprise. In the long run, the nurturing of an indigenous Hebrew culture under the aegis of an autonomous Jewish political entity called into question a central rationale for American Jewish Hebraism. The paradigm of Jewish survival through a transnational Hebraic renaissance was effectively replaced by the dynamics of Israeli-Diaspora Jewish relations and cultural diffusion. The considerable import of these implications for American Hebrew camping is discussed later in the chapter.

Relying on a minimal budget and a generous dollop of idealism, Hanoar Haivri's initiatives during its first decade were typically the pet projects of a single member or a small group of members. These included *Niv*, its monthly magazine; *Pargod*, its theater group; *Kinor Sinfonietta*, its orchestra; and *Rikud Ami*, its dance troupe. The camp project found its champion in Shulsinger. But its scale and cost dwarfed Hanoar Haivri's other cultural activities, which initially gave members pause. *Niv*, for example, was initially supported through a $10-per-issue subsidy from renowned Hebrew publisher Avraham Yosef Stybel. A camp would not be able to survive on such charity.[22]

Shulsinger initially won over his colleagues at a 1940 Hanoar Haivri convention where he laid out his vision and rationale for the camp. If the movement were serious about creating an indigenous Hebrew culture, there could be no better setting than the overnight camp, a cloistered, total environment where campers and staff alike could eat, play, pray, and socialize in Hebrew without distraction or inhibition. Massad's novelty was that it accomplished its countercultural goals by grafting Hebrew onto an established American pastime like

summer camp. Shulsinger's argument for Massad was encapsulated in a *Niv* editorial: "We must seek the means to help us build a Hebrew world comprising
Hebrew and American culture, in which the child will be able to live a full life
of creativity and joy."[23] The second generation looked askance at their elders'
largely stillborn efforts to raise a generation of Hebrew-speaking youth through
the supplementary schools. The implementation of *Ivrit b'Ivrit* in hundreds of
Jewish schools was arguably one of the most consequential accomplishments of
the Histadrut Ivrit. But by the 1930s and 1940s, it appeared that the experiment
had paid few dividends. The remedy, in Hanoar Haivri's view, was the creation
of an entirely Hebrew-speaking environment nested in an informal educational
setting. A Hebrew summer camp, they believed, could serve as "a kind of hothouse, a hermetic lab in which Hebrew could flourish naturally and without
restraint." The Hebrew-speaking camp was not designed to replace the rigorous
Hebrew-centered school curriculum, but rather to complement and complete its
Hebraic mission.[24]

### Immersive Hebrew and Yiddish Antecedents

The prospect of a Hebrew-speaking camp was not entirely novel when Shulsinger
first raised it at the Hanoar Haivri convention in 1940. Camp Achvah, which was
established by New York Bureau of Jewish Education director Samson Benderly
in 1927, briefly operated as a Hebrew immersive environment.[25] Achvah began
as a component of a leadership training initiative known as the Kvutzah, a
cohort-based, work-study fellowship program for aspiring Jewish educators.
Achvah, which opened in Arverne, New York, in 1927, and moved to Godeffroy,
New York, in 1929, was a summer retreat, where Kvutzah members lived com-
munally, studying in the mornings and engaging in recreational activities in the
afternoons and evenings. Kvutzah members themselves chose the name "Achvah," the Hebrew word for brotherhood. Non-Kvutzah members were also
admitted to Achvah as campers in those early years, but the camp was primarily a vehicle for professional development for educators. The camp's official language was Hebrew, and Kvutzah members were expected to conduct themselves
entirely in Hebrew during both formal and informal interactions. In fact, Kvutzah members organized a *Vaad Maginei Ha'safah* (Language Patrol Council),
which heard cases brought by fellow members against perennial backsliders.
Members recalled that the Hebrew atmosphere enriched and heightened virtually every aspect of religious and cultural life at camp.[26]

The term "Kvutzah" (group or collective) was intentionally reminiscent of the
early Zionist collective agricultural settlements in Palestine. Another important
way in which the Kvutzah members telegraphed their connection to Palestine
was their decision to imitate the Sephardic-influenced Hebrew pronunciation
favored by the Zionist Jews in Palestine.[27] Operating a Hebrew-speaking camp
required the invention of a Hebrew camp vocabulary for distinctively Ameri-

can foods, customs, sports, and leisure activities. If a camp dictionary was ever compiled, it is, unfortunately, lost to history.[28] Since a few of the Kvutzah members worked decades later at other Hebrew-speaking camps, it is tempting to draw a connecting line between Achvah's original Hebrew vocabulary and that of the second generation of Hebrew camps.[29] Unfortunately, this is only conjecture, and many of the terms that have survived in the historical record appear to be unique to Achvah.[30]

If Achvah had any antecedents in American Jewish education, they were arguably the earliest Yiddishist camps founded after World War I, many of which were also immersive. But there were significant differences between Achvah and most Yiddishist camps. The latter were part of larger efforts to promote Yiddish language and Yiddish cultural literacy for the children of immigrants—who, even if they heard Yiddish at home, had a very different relationship with the language than did their immigrant parents. Even as the Yiddishist camps embodied progressive, secular ideas, they situated them in continuity with an old world vernacular culture that was still thriving in Europe. Hebraists, by contrast, were disrupting that continuity by promoting a new vision of Jewish vernacularity and a different cultural model that sought to transform, if not repudiate, the Diaspora.[31] In addition, Yiddishist camps were more conventional, programmatically and financially, than Achvah in that they were focused primarily on children ages 7–15. Many Yiddishist camps also housed adjacent, Yiddish-speaking adult summer colonies, which was not the case at Achvah.

### Building the Foundation

The Kvutzah and Achvah's Hebrew immersive environment were abandoned in the midst of the Depression as financially unsustainable, and the camp was converted into a Jewish culture camp along the lines of Cejwin. But the idea did not die. In the late 1930s, Davis and his close collaborator in Hanoar Haivri, Sylvia Cutler Ettenberg, daydreamed while sitting under the trees at Cejwin Camps about sponsoring a Hebrew immersion camp. The pair would eventually cofound Camp Ramah in 1947, but from 1940 to 1944, they offered invaluable support to Shulsinger as he struggled to get Massad on a solid footing. They arranged a consultation with Schoolman, Cejwin's longtime camp director who was considered one of the best in the Jewish camping business. Though Schoolman would later go on to advise Shulsinger, in that early meeting he tried to disabuse his visitors of their seeming naiveté about what it takes to run a camp with a barrage of questions about drowning, ptomaine poisoning, and frantic phone calls from parents. Davis finally blurted out, "Mr. Schoolman, I don't know the answers to these questions, and the others you plan to pose. But one thing I do know: If I stay another five minutes, there will never be a Hebrew camp in this country."[32]

Davis and Shulsinger had more luck winning the backing of Alexander Dushkin, head of New York's central Jewish education agency, the Jewish Education Committee, who offered to financially assist them if Shulsinger agreed to lay the groundwork with a day camp, a cheaper and less risky testing ground than an overnight camp. Despite his belief that a day camp offered limited educational possibilities, Shulsinger agreed.[33] In the summer of 1941, Shulsinger and four counselors opened a Hebrew-speaking day camp with twenty-two campers in Far Rockaway, Queens.[34] Despite struggling with enrollment, Shulsinger depicted the summer as a programmatic success in his report to Hanoar Haivri's 1941 convention, where he secured approval to forge ahead with the overnight camp.[35] The first summer also facilitated a budding romance between Shulsinger and one of his counselors, Hanoar Haivri secretary Rivka Wolman. Indeed, it was while they were "leafing through some Zionist literature after a long day's work" that they happened on Chaim Nachman Bialik's 1894 paean to the First Aliyah, "*Techezakna* [Strengthen]," also known as "*Birkat Am* [The People's Blessing]." Their eyes were drawn to the first line of the fourth stanza:

> If you have not built the rafters—but only the foundation (*massad*),
> be content, my brothers, your toil is not in vain!

Shulsinger recalled that he and Wolman were immediately captivated by the word *massad*, and "decided to call the camp Massad as a symbol of the fact that Hebrew camping would be the foundation for Hebrew education—and through it, for Jewish life."[36] As Shimon Frost explained, "The name Massad itself testifies to the vision of the Hebrew renaissance in its widest meaning; it connotes only a beginning, the foundation, the underpinnings. Upon these must be erected an edifice of cultural-national renewal, of a return to Jewish sources and a deepening of the nation's historic roots. Within this ideological framework, the Hebrew language was seen as a principal instrument in the struggle against assimilation and estrangement, and as the bond with a glorious shared past."[37] "*Techezakna*," which was set to a Russian marching song, later became Massad's unofficial anthem.[38] Massad also served as a foundation for Shulsinger's and Wolman's relationship. The couple was married in 1942, and Rivka eventually became a full partner in the Hebrew camping project.

During its second summer in operation—its first as an overnight camp— Shulsinger operated Massad on the grounds of Camp Machanaim, an English-speaking Orthodox camp in Monticello, New York, until sufficient money was raised to rent and eventually buy his own site in Tannersville, Pennsylvania. Massad moved to Tannersville in 1943 and remained on the property until the camp folded in 1981. Bialik's line from "*Techezakna*" that inspired the camp's name was affixed at the front of the camp's auditorium (see figure 2.2).[39]

Figure 2.2. The name "Massad" was inspired by Bialik's poem, "Techezakna." The first line of the fourth stanza adorned the top of the stage in Massad Aleph. (Courtesy of Estates of Noam and Nehama Shudofsky and Massad Camps, Inc.)

### INVENTING CAMP HEBREW

As Massad's reputation spread, its popularity soon outpaced the number of its beds, resulting in a long waiting list. Over Shulsinger's objections, in 1948–1949, a second camp, Massad Bet, was purchased and opened in Dingmans Ferry. A compulsive micromanager, Shulsinger would have preferred to adopt the Cejwin model and expand in a single facility. In hindsight, Shulsinger and his wife argued that a single enlarged camp would have been more cost effective, allowing Massad to adapt more easily to variable market demands. But the existence of separate Massad camps in Tannersville and Dingmans Ferry and, later, Effort, Pennsylvania, allowed each to develop its own character, despite Shulsinger's weekly visits.

As at Jewish culture camps like Cejwin, and Zionist movement camps like Habonim, the divisions at Massad were referred to by Hebrew names; given that the camp emblem was a date palm, Shulsinger chose to designate Massad's divisions using the Hebrew words for various parts of a tree (*shoresh, geza, anaf, tzameret*). The camp roads were named for famous Jewish figures past and present. Thus, at Massad Aleph, the road that led to the synagogue was named Shveel

HaRav Kook, for Mandate Palestine's first Ashkenazi chief rabbi, whereas the path to the infirmary was aptly named Rechov Rambam, for the renowned medieval philosopher and physician Maimonides.[40]

What set Massad apart from those other camps was its immersive Hebrew environment. It is not an oversight that a detailed planning memorandum for the camp, drafted in 1940, contains only two sentences about the facility. The focus of the memorandum was squarely on Hebrew, and the experiment was framed in terms of the Zionist project of "cultural rebirth and national reawakening." And although Hanoar Haivri lined up Schoolman as a consultant, camp operations were of little interest beyond their instrumental necessity. The passion was reserved for the oversized section on the camp's mission and rationale:

> In order that Hebrew shall become a living language it is necessary that it be lived, not only for five or six hours a week in the school, nor even for twenty hours a week in a Yeshibah. To live a language means to use it twenty-four hours a day, seven days a week for as many weeks as possible. In Palestine this means for fifty-two weeks a year, for American Jews and their children it means about nine or ten weeks a year, that is to say during the summer vacation when the children are free from school.[41]

Although Massad's success can be attributed in part to the marriage of ideological fervor and dogged determinism, as personified by Shulsinger, it also benefited from impeccable timing. Massad burst on the scene in the midst of World War II, when support for Zionism was running high, grew into maturity while basking in the glow of the new state of Israel, and reached the apex of its popularity in the immediate aftermath of the 1967 Six Day War. Equally important, the founding of Massad coincided with the development of the first modern Orthodox day schools, including the Yeshiva of Crown Heights (1923), Yeshivah of Flatbush (1928), the Ramaz School (1937), the Hebrew Institute of Long Island (1937), and the Yeshiva of Central Queens (1940). In 1948, Yeshivah of Flatbush and Ramaz alone supplied 56 percent of the 239 campers. Since both schools were strongly Zionist and committed to immersive Hebrew pedagogy in their Jewish studies classes, these campers came in with a stronger Hebrew background than campers attending Talmud Torahs or public and supplementary schools.[42]

Shulsinger curated the environment by interviewing prospective campers to be certain that their Hebrew was up to snuff. Massad's founders were transparent in their conviction that the camp was unsuitable for the children of the masses: "The Hebrew camp is designed for that minority of children who are able to master the language with sufficient facility to use it and thereby to gain the advantages of a Hebrew camp set-up. It is this minority whom we wish to train as the future leaders in every walk of Jewish and Zionist life."[43] It is hardly accidental that the camps declined at the same moment when day schools were abandoning immersion as a Hebrew teaching pedagogy. According to longtime

Massad cultural director and Ramaz School administrator Rabbi Mayer Moskowitz, by the mid-1970s it was becoming increasingly difficult to find a sufficient
number of Hebrew-fluent counselors.[44]

In the camps' early years, compliance with the Hebrew-speaking policy was
reputedly almost universal, leading some visitors to marvel at the achievement:
adult visitors to Massad were often awed by the sight of American-born children
speaking a fluent and almost *maskilic* (European Jewish Enlightenment-style),
if American-accented, Hebrew.[45] (Internal documents suggest that the reality
was more complicated; as early as 1945, the rapid growth of the camp was being
blamed for some falloff in the extent and level of Hebrew usage.[46]) Journalist Harold Ribalow assured his readers that the children "are not forced to speak Hebrew.
They want to speak Hebrew; they think in Hebrew, they live with Hebrew and
they accept it as they do food and water."[47] But author Hillel Halkin, who was a
camper at Massad Bet in the late 1940s, while confirming Ribalow's observation
that Hebrew speaking was the norm, offered a more sardonic perspective:

> Massad was a unique place, a combination of an American summer camp, a
> kibbutz and a Soviet gulag. The gulag part had to do with the fact that speak-
> ing Hebrew all day long was not only mandatory, even if you knew only a few
> words of it, but also something you were punished for not doing, and the coun-
> selors actually went around like police spies, keeping their ears open for for-
> bidden English words. If you fulfilled your daily quota of Hebrew, you were
> awarded with an *Ayin*, which was the first letter of the word *Ivrit* ("Hebrew"),
> and every evening at flag lowering—we flew both the Stars and Stripes and
> the Star of David, although the latter, I believe, flew higher—each counselor
> had to announce how many *Ayin*s his bunk had been awarded. Bunks that did
> poorly could be docked from activities, or given kitchen duty, and at the end
> of the summer the lucky Stakhanovites were presented with an *Ayin*
> sweatshirt.[48]

Halkin's quest for *Ayin*-emblazoned apparel that summer—elsewhere he
recalled that the prize was a t-shirt rather than a sweatshirt—was almost stopped
cold during one baseball game when his counselor, Sam Sonnenschein, who was
serving as umpire, called Halkin out on a low pitch. When Halkin reacted by
barking a vulgar expletive at Sonnenschein, in English, his counselor not only
threw him out of the game but also threatened to take away his *Ayin*:

> I could make peace with being tossed out of the game; in the Majors, players
> were thrown out for far lighter infractions. But losing the "*Ayin*" was a whole
> other ballgame. Not only had I scored twice that day, but my Hebrew was bet-
> ter than that of all of the other team members combined, and I made a point
> of speaking more Hebrew than anybody else.
>     "All right, then. How do you say it in Hebrew?" I challenged him.
>     "Say what?"

Figure 2.3. *Mifkad* lineup at Camp Massad, c. 1945. (Courtesy of Estates of Noam and Nehama Shudofsky and Massad Camps, Inc.)

"Say what I said just now. Go find it in the [Massad Dictionary]."
Sammy Sonnenschein scratched his head. . . .
"So am I getting my '*Ayin*' back?" I asked.
"You little son of a bitch!" said Sammy Sonnenschein—in English.
But that night, around the flagpole, I got my letter, and my season of success was extended by another day. The t-shirt was almost mine.[49]

Psychologist and genocide scholar Israel Charny, who began attending Massad in 1942 when the camp was located in Monticello, recalled *mifkad*, the twice-daily military-style lineup at the flagpole that became like "loyalty oath ceremonies" (see figure 2.3). In the early years, they were sometimes run by Shulsinger himself, and, later, by the head counselors or division heads: "Each day we stood like soldiers and we were told whether we were living trees or wilting trees on the basis of whether we had been heard speaking Hebrew or *chas v'chalilah* [Heaven forbid] another language." Charny characterized the ritual as "pretty creepy and totalitarian," but it did not sour him on the camp or on the Hebrew language.[50]

The enforcement regime depended on the counselors, and in the early years many took their jobs seriously. More than fifty years later, Rabbi Jack Bloom, who also attended Massad in the 1940s, was still able to parrot his counselor's daily reports to Shulsinger at the flagpole: "*Kevutzat Dekel, hayom arba'ah mishmonah kiblu ayin* [Today, four out of eight [campers] in the Palm Tree Group received *ayin*s]." Campers generally spoke a mixture of English and Hebrew in their cabins, but they quickly learned that their counselors had no compunction about dispensing penalties for lapsing into English on the ball field or in the dining hall.[51]

If counselors were zealous in policing the Hebrew immersion environment, they were likely taking their cue from Shulsinger, whose almost single-minded obsession with rooting out any backsliding into English made him an object of both fear and gentle ridicule. Shulsinger always seemed to be lurking behind a tree or bush waiting to catch an unsuspecting camper in an act of linguistic infidelity. Veteran campers and staff honed their antennas and instantly switched into Hebrew if they sensed his presence. Ileane "Chaya" Altman Colodner, who first attended Massad in 1947, recalled that Shulsinger would even patrol the cabins at night to make sure that the children were not speaking English to their bunkmates in bed. "Shlomo was what we call in Hebrew a *meshugaon* [a crazy genius]," Bloom recalled. "I say that with great respect because he achieved something phenomenal. But he was a monomaniac, and the whole thing was Hebrew." Others pointed out that Shulsinger's obsessive behavior around Hebrew speaking reflected a wider tendency toward micromanagement and perfectionism.[52] In time, language policing became a recognized and accepted feature of Massad and even the subject of humor among insiders.

Yiddish poet and editor Mordechai Strigler, who visited Massad in 1963 and shared his observations (in Hebrew) in *Hadoar*, characterized Shulsinger and the other young educators he met there as "stubborn." He meant it as a compliment. Strigler approvingly pointed out that although Israelis could be found at Massad in ample numbers, the backbone of the camp consisted of American staff, which he believed was indicative of its viability. And it bothered him not at all that they spoke an American-accented, highly customized Hebrew.[53] In fact, the dearth of Hebrew words for everyday camp activities compelled Shulsinger and staff member Hillel Rudavsky to create a camp dictionary, known informally as the *Milon Massad* (Massad Dictionary), edited by Hebraist Daniel Persky; it was distributed to campers before camp started or at their first *mifkad* (lineup and roll call). The earliest edition was mimeographed; later editions were published in hardcover.[54] The dictionary was designed to teach functional Hebrew and included sections devoted to daily life and camp activities. So vital was the need it filled that the dictionary accompanied staff when they moved on to other Hebrew-speaking camps, like Boston Hebrew College's Camp Yavneh in Northwood, New Hampshire. During its earliest years, the Massad Dictionary was even distributed to campers at Camp Ramah Wisconsin. Thus the Massad vocabulary was disseminated to Yavneh, Ramah, and other camps. According to Halkin, a language maven who wrote the *Forward*'s Philologos column for twenty-four years, an entire section of the edition he received was devoted to the vocabulary associated with baseball (*kadur basis*; see figure 2.4). Writing more than fifty years after he attended Massad, Halkin still recalled the idiosyncratic term *du-siluk* (literally translated as "bi-removal"), the

Figure 2.4. Vocabulary terms were routinely posted at Camp Massad for activities like baseball and swimming. (Courtesy of Estates of Noam and Nehama Shudofsky and Massad Camps, Inc.)

Massadism for "double play." "It was such a fancy expression that I didn't realize it was Hebrew at all," Halkin remembered. "Sometime after my first summer at Massad, I was in a pickup game in the park. When, playing second base, I flipped a ground ball to the shortstop covering for me, who fired it to first for the double play. I shouted out: 'Way to go! What a ducy look!' The look I got was indeed a ducy!"[55]

In their purist fervor, Shulsinger and his staff eschewed English loanwords that had fallen into the Israeli vocabulary. For example, rather than use the common Israeli word for sweater, *svedder*, Shulsinger coined the term *tsimri-yah*, from the Hebrew word *tsemer*, for wool. Few if any of these words successfully traversed the Atlantic. Indeed, Shulsinger would no doubt have been disappointed to learn that during Israel's first professional baseball game in June 2007, between the Petah Tikva Pioneers and the Modiin Miracles, Israeli broadcasters used English terminology in their play-by-play commentary.[56]

Those whose diligence flagged in memorizing the Massad Dictionary (see figure 2.5) were able to rely on numerous decorative and instructional signs and murals that adorned the camp's facilities and buildings. Many of the instructional signs included key vocabulary words for the activity at hand (see figure 2.6).

| CLOTHING | |
|---|---|
| Safety Pin | סֶכַּת בִּטָּחוֹן נ׳ |
| Sandal | סַנְדָּל |
| Scarf, shawl | סוּדָר |
| Shirt | כֻּתֹּנֶת (כֻּתֳּנוֹת) |
| Shoe | נַעַל (נְעָלַיִם, נַעֲלַיִם נ׳ |
| Heel | עָקֵב (עֲקֵבִים) |
| Shoe buckle | חֶבֶט (חֲבָטִים) |
| Shoe horn | כַּף הַנַּעַל נ׳ |
| Shoe lace | שְׂרוֹךְ |
| Toe cap | חַרְטוֹם (חַרְטוֹמִים) |
| Sole | סֻלְיָה |
| Shoemaker | סַנְדְּלָר |
| Shorts | מִכְנָסַיִם קְצָרִים |

— 20 —

| CLOTHING | |
|---|---|
| Silk | מֶשִׁי |
| Skirt | חֲצָאִית (חֲצָאִיּוֹת) |
| Sleeve | שַׁרְווּל |
| Rolled up sleeve | שַׁרְווּל מְפֻשָּׁל |
| Slip | תַּחְתּוֹנִית (תַּחְתּוֹנִיּוֹת) |
| Stitch, seam | תֶּפֶר (וּתְפָרִים) |
| Stocking | פֻּזְמָק (פֻּזְמָקָאוֹת) |
| Sock, hose | גֶּרֶב (גַּרְבַּיִם) |
| Style | אָפְנָה |
| Suit | חֲלִיפָה |
| Suspenders | כְּתֵפוֹת (כְּתֵפָה) |
| Sweat shirt | מֵיזָע (מֵיזָעִים) |
| Sweater | צַמְרִיָּה (צַמְרִיּוֹת) |

— 21 —

Figure 2.5. Sample pages from the *Milon Massad*, the Massad English-Hebrew Dictionary, c. 1950. (Courtesy of Varda Sherman Lev)

Figure 2.6. Massad campers and staff consult a placard with waterfront vocabulary in Hebrew. (Courtesy of Estates of Noam and Nehama Shudofsky and Massad Camps, Inc.)

Others highlighted famous proverbs from Zionist icons like Theodor Herzl and classical Jewish texts like *Sayings of the Fathers*.

LEARNING HEBREW THROUGH THE ARTS

If many campers were enculturated into Massad's Hebrew-speaking environment on the ball field, others found their entrée through culture and the arts. Massad's first music and dramatics counselor David Alster-Yardeni explained that "underlying the founding of Camp Massad from the outset was the perspective of Jewish culture as a central axis for all summer activities."[57] In this respect, the camp reflected the core values of Hanoar Haivri.[58] Shulsinger and Alster-Yardeni concurred from the outset that Hebrew culture, particularly the performing and fine arts, "needed to be a framework for deep emotional experiences that would draw the camper closer to the values of the nation in the most precise and direct way possible."[59] The men first met in 1941 at the 92nd Street YMHA, in Manhattan, after a performance of Alster-Yardeni's Hebrew play, *Chalom v'Hagshama* (Dream and Realization), about the life of Judah HaLevi, which was written and performed to commemorate the octocentenary of the medieval Hebrew poet's death. Shulsinger was so taken by the performance and the magnetism of its playwright that he offered Alster-Yardeni a staff position on the spot. Alster-Yardeni accepted, and for the next twenty years, the two men were partners in fashioning Massad's cultural landscape.

Alster-Yardeni adopted a deliberate approach to his selection of songs and dramatic material. Especially in the camp's early years, he favored settings of classical Zionist poems by writers such as Chaim Nachman Bialik, Shaul Tchernichovsky, Hannah Senesh, and Rachel (Bluwstein), and dramatic material that emphasized the themes of Jewish survival and the Zionist return to Eretz Yisrael, directly or obliquely alluding to current events including the Holocaust and Israel's War of Independence. He was likewise drawn to pioneering songs and marching songs from the Jewish Brigade and, later, army ensembles like the Nahal Troupe, which was known for its *Eretz Israel* songs, folk music that was designed to strengthen Jews' connection to the Hebrew language and the Land of Israel.[60] For example, in 1942 Alster-Yardeni taught his campers a popular *chalutz* (pioneer) folksong of that era, Yitzhak Livni's *Shir Shomer* (The Watchman's Song), which they performed with great gusto for the Machanaim campers.[61]

In the tumultuous mid-1940s, Alster-Yardeni's dramatic taste veered toward agitprop. In 1945, he wrote and directed a camp production that compared the camp's fifth anniversary to that of Kibbutz Ein Hamifratz, a stockade and tower settlement established south of Acre during the final gasp of the 1936–1939 Arab Revolt. In 1946, Alster-Yardeni followed up with *Hoi Ad Matai?* (O, till When?), a drama set in a railway station where Jewish displaced persons and refugees from the "four corners of the Earth" converge in search of a permanent home-

Figure 2.7. Dramatics became a vehicle for encouraging Hebrew expression at Massad. (Courtesy of Estates of Noam and Nehama Shudofsky and Massad Camps, Inc.)

land, thus enacting the biblical promise of *kibbutz galuyot*, the ingathering of the exiles.[62] Alster-Yardeni looked to Hebrew playwrights and authors like Avraham Shlonsky (*Utzi Galutzi*) and Yigal Mossinson (*Kazablan*) for romantic and comedic material. He also inaugurated the practice of translating and adapting English-language musicals and plays into Hebrew. One of the first productions of this type, a Hebrew adaptation of Gilbert and Sullivan's *The Pirates of Penzance*, was translated by Alster-Yardeni and Marnin Feinstein, the boys' head counselor in the mid-1940s and the son of Hebraist and Herzliya Teachers College principal Moses Feinstein.[63] According to multiple alumni respondents in the Camp Massad Poconos Facebook group, the translations were fairly faithful to the original material, with little or no Judaic flavor added. In the words of one, "The Jewish content was doing the play in *Ivrit* [Hebrew]."

However, in general, dramatics at Massad was a vehicle for teaching Zionist and Israeli history and culture (see figure 2.7). Reflecting on his years at Massad, Alster-Yardeni explained that he "always hoped to connect the child and the teenager in a deep and spontaneous manner to the heritage of the past. . . . I always knew in my heart that this path had an absolute advantage over appealing to the intellect and rational thought."[64] He certainly succeeded with former campers like Tzippy Krieger Cedar, a self-described drama geek who recalled that "living Hebrew culturally" was profoundly moving for herself and her camp friends. Committing to memory pages of Hebrew dialogue and "conversing on stage in Hebrew" helped her become a "fluent Hebrew speaker."[65]

In 1952, Israel hosted its first international choral festival, the *Zimriya*, which was subsequently held triennially.[66] Alster-Yardeni was enchanted by the performances and especially taken with the festival's name. The following summer he launched a music festival in Massad under the same name. Despite some misgivings, on Shulsinger's advice he introduced a spirit of competition, with campers performing in a Hebrew sing-off by age group. Each division performed a *shir edah* (a divisional song), typically written by the counselors and set to a popular American melody, as well as a ballad, handpicked by Alster-Yardeni, from the emerging Israeli songbook. In that way, the *zimriya* not only became an opportunity to solidify a sense of camp spirit; it was also a pedagogical tool to promote Hebrew artistic expression among the counselors and an opportunity for Alster-Yardeni (and subsequent music directors) to introduce a new crop of Israeli songs to the camp's musical canon.[67]

All in all, the zimriya fostered a distinctive Hebrew camp culture and a sense of shared cultural and linguistic literacy for campers and staff. Songs introduced during the zimriya were later reinforced through dining room sing-alongs. In the late 1950s, music counselor Jonathan Zak, who would later become a prominent Israeli pianist, organized a Massad Makhela (choral group; see figure 2.8). In 1960, a group of twelve counselors decided to convert the chorale into a year-round endeavor, thus becoming the first Hebrew-singing choir in North America. Under conductor and Massad tennis counselor Stanley Sperber, the Massad Makhela released two records before becoming financially and creatively independent from the camp in 1964, taking the name Zamir Chorale.[68] (A few years later, as music instructor at Camp Yavneh, a Hebrew-speaking camp in Northwood, New Hampshire, Sperber inspired a similar choral group to establish the Zamir Chorale of Boston, led by Joshua Jacobson.) By the 1970s, Massad had introduced a *Shabbat Vatikim*, an "old-timers" Shabbat, when alumni would flock to the camps for the weekend and campers and counselors who had been in the camp for longer than five years were invited to lead the singing. Years after the camps closed, many former campers and counselors could still sing these songs from memory. David Bernstein, who attended Massad Bet as a camper beginning in 1964 and rose through the staff ranks to boys' head counselor and education director, recalls "the pushing of Hebrew language and culture [at] Massad was least successful when they sat you down in a *sicha* [facilitated discussion] and tried to tell you about [the Hebrew poet Chaim Nachman] Bialik, and most successful when you would have to put on a play in Hebrew; most successful when you had a zimriya and you had to sing these songs or during *maccabiah* [color war]."[69]

Figure 2.8. The Massad Makhela (Massad Choral Group). (Courtesy of Estates of Noam and Nehama Shudofsky and Massad Camps, Inc.)

Massad's version of color war was similarly inspired in part by Zionist culture in Palestine. Shulsinger appropriated the term *maccabiah* from the quadrennial international Jewish sports competition, which was launched in Palestine in 1932 and was consciously patterned after the Olympics.[70] But the term should not obscure the all-embracing nature of Massad's five-day competition, which reached far beyond athletics. A 1950 Massad Aleph maccabiah schedule and rulebook included competitions in dance, art, dramatics, singing, publishing a newspaper, and college bowl, as well as swimming and track-and-field meets and a full menu of team sports (see figure 2.9).[71]

In 1950, Shulsinger identified three objectives of maccabiah: to "awaken the child's inner desire for creative self expression"; "to impart to the child information about his people, his land and culture"; and "to increase his vocabulary, so that he will become accustomed to the natural use of the Hebrew language."[72] These learning outcomes were as much in evidence among members of the staff as the campers. Richard Starshefsky who, as we read at the chapter's beginning, had arrived in camp a few years earlier with only broken Hebrew, recalled cowriting the Hebrew lyrics to one of his team's songs for Massad Bet's 1967 maccabiah.

Figure 2.9. Maccabiah breakout, c. 1960, in which a Torah scroll announces in Hebrew, "Maccabiah has begun!" (Courtesy of Estates of Noam and Nehama Shudofsky and Massad Camps, Inc.)

Starshefsky was later appointed *rosh pluga*, or color war captain, a coveted role at Massad that was reserved for counselors who combined leadership qualities with Hebrew fluency.

For Massad's critics, maccabiah epitomized everything that was wrong with the camp: its excessive regimentation, emphasis on competition, seeming indifference to the literature on child psychology and moral development, and placement of Hebrew rather than Judaism at the camp's spiritual and emotional core. Shulsinger could easily shrug off skepticism from external fault finders, yet he might have been surprised that some of the most trenchant criticisms came from within Massad's founding circle. In particular, Sylvia Ettenberg, who initially conceived of a Hebrew-speaking camp with Moshe Davis and had spent many summers learning the residential camping business from Schoolman at Cejwin Camps, was consistently at odds with Shulsinger while serving as girls' head counselor during Massad's first season in Tannersville. As she saw it, her primary job was counselor training—coaching her staff on how to respond to the physical, emotional, and spiritual needs of their charges. She had no patience for Shulsinger when he played the role of drill sergeant, and she resisted his entreaties to patrol her campers' use of Hebrew, particularly in their private conversations. She was vexed by his use of admonishments and incentivizing around Hebrew speaking and took strong exception to the camp's competitive spirit.

She further explained that "the whole idea of maccabiah was something that I wanted ruled out of camp," but Shulsinger would not hear of it. Where he saw motivation she saw warped priorities. She added, "This was a children's camp, and as the maccabiah was going to be developed, the staff was much more excited about it than the kids. They were the ones who stayed up until 2 o'clock in the morning. . . . It became the adults' thing." Ettenberg was sufficiently distraught that she ended up leaving camp for three days during maccabiah. She acknowledged that her sour experience at Massad played a role in how she and Davis designed the Conservative movement's Ramah camping movement, which they cofounded in 1947. Massad was a cautionary lesson: "Whatever Shlomo did, we resolved to do the opposite." In fact, as we explore in the next chapter, Ramah incorporated and adapted many Massad traditions and its customized "camp Hebrew" vocabulary. Ramah directors also followed Massad's example by incentivizing Hebrew speaking. But Ettenberg and Davis, and camp directors like Louis Newman, strove to make Ramah more educationally progressive and religiously oriented.

Starshefsky saw things differently. "Maccabiah was a tremendous educational tool because it took the principle of competition and it turned it into a medium for education," he explained. Beyond the impact that maccabiah preparation and supervision had on the counselors themselves, their deep investment in the process proved essential to nurturing total experiences for their campers. And according to Rabbi Louis Bernstein, Massad Bet's director from 1957 to 1971, the competitive nature of maccabiah fostered "a remarkable level of Hebrew speaking."[73] Indeed, judges were instructed to deduct points during each activity for speaking English, as well as for disorderliness, slovenliness, and poor sportsmanship.[74] Insiders like Bernstein readily admitted that maccabiah was concocted, in part, to address backsliding during the final week of camp. Campers' interest in speaking Hebrew flagged as they anticipated their imminent departure for home.

Perhaps, at its core, the conflict between Shulsinger and Ettenberg was about the uses and potential misuses of Hebrew. For Ettenberg, who subscribed in principle to the concept of a Hebrew-speaking camp, Hebrew was an instrument, a vehicle for promoting campers' cultural, religious, and spiritual growth. For Shulsinger, by contrast, Hebrew was a performative, a form of social action: the act of speaking Hebrew at camp created a new cultural Zionist reality.[75] Shulsinger conceived of Massad as a herald of the Jewish national rebirth, the flowering of Hebrew culture in a remote Diaspora outpost that testified to the viability of the Zionist program.

## PROMOTING JEWISH UNITY IN AN ERA OF DENOMINATIONALISM

While Ettenberg was an educator, Shulsinger was an evangelist. Indeed, in his zeal to promote Hebrew and Zionism, Shulsinger could turn a blind eye to matters he deemed ancillary, including the camps' religious culture. Except for taking care that the ritual practice of the camp satisfied the standards of his mostly modern Orthodox clientele, the religious life of the camp was never high on his priority list. Shulsinger's laissez-faire attitude was facilitated by the relatively relaxed approach to traditional observance that characterized modern Orthodoxy in the 1940s, as well as by the blurred line between Orthodox and Conservative Judaism in those years.[76] From the outset, Massad counselors were culled from the student bodies of both Yeshiva University and the Jewish Theological Seminary, as well as the cultural Zionist Herzliya Hebrew Teachers College and the liberal Jewish Institute of Religion, which gave the camp a nondenominational feel.[77] Before the launching of Ramah camps in 1947, and particularly the establishment of its camp in the Poconos (1950), Massad attracted a sizable contingent of campers from the sons and daughters of the Northeast Conservative elite. Massad also drew a small and religiously diverse group of campers from Zionist families in small Jewish communities across the United States that lacked a robust Jewish educational infrastructure. Over time, the clientele became more homogeneously modern Orthodox[78]—even though as late as the early 1970s, Massad eschewed a denominational label.[79]

In the 1960s, however, Massad administrators began responding to the demands of an increasingly self-assured and rigorous modern Orthodoxy by becoming more ritually stringent. They may have felt some pressure from the campers themselves, who were vocal about some of the discrepancies between the ritual practices at camp and those of their home congregations and schools.[80] The traditional drift was more pronounced at Massad Bet, because its longtime director, Louis Bernstein, was a Young Israel-affiliated pulpit rabbi who later served as president of the modern Orthodox Rabbinical Council of America. But both camps made innovations, including adding a prayer partition (*mechitza*), instituting mandatory afternoon and evening prayer services, eliminating swimming on the Sabbath, installing handwashing stations outside the dining halls, reciting the full Grace after Meals rather than an abbreviated version, and curtailing mixed dancing. These changes telegraphed Massad's struggle to remain a comfortable summertime destination for its modern Orthodox base.[81]

### MASSAD AS AN ERSATZ ISRAEL

If Shulsinger took an instrumental approach to traditional Jewish observance at camp, his commitment to Zionism and to the state of Israel was wholehearted and unwavering. Shulsinger referred to Massad as *Eretz Yisrael b'zeir anpin*, the

Land of Israel in microcosm. The camps' ambience consisted of a carefully curated mélange of signage, terminology, pageantry, Zionist culture, and spoken Hebrew. In both its depictions and erasure of Arabs from the Israeli landscape, Massad engaged in a kind of boundary policing and maintenance. (When the guise of the "Arab" appeared at camp it was typically in the form of a bogeyman: in the early 1970s, counselors would sometimes terrorize campers by descending on their tent encampments during overnights dressed in keffiyehs and flowing white robes and making high-pitched ululations.)

Another form of silencing took place with regard to Yiddish language and culture and, by extension, the narrative of Diaspora-centered Jewish cultural effervescence that it epitomized. Here Massad's policy was comparable to the anti-Yiddish practices of the Jewish community in Mandate Palestine and the early state of Israel. Strikingly, this suppression extended even to the commemoration of Jewish resistance during the Shoah. Jack Bloom recalled that a music teacher at Massad insisted that the campers learn Hirsh Glik's *Zog Nit Keyn Mol* (Never Say [This is the Final Road]), also known as the "Partisan Song," in Hebrew translation rather than in the original Yiddish. The song was inspired by the Warsaw Ghetto Uprising and became an anthem of the United Partisan Group during the final years of World War II. At Massad, "Yiddish was considered to be jargon," explained Jack Bloom. The unmistakable message was that "*we* sang in Hebrew while *those people* who spoke jargon sang it in Yiddish, and that's always been a little bothersome to me, the lack of respect for Yiddish [at Massad]. Maybe, it had to be done to make Hebrew the elite thing."[82]

One should not underestimate the symbolic import of substituting Hebrew for the original Yiddish in the quintessential hymn of Diaspora Jewish resistance. Massad's founders and senior staff were cultural Zionists committed to the proposition that language can enact a purer, ideal vision of Zionism. Indeed, Massad provided an optimal environment for the creation of a Hebrew community: Israeli Arabs and Yiddish-speaking refugees were absent, and there was a culture of policing linguistic hybridity, including Anglicisms, Yiddishisms, and Arabicisms. Moreover, campers and staff were free of the onus of building and defending a state.

Sociologist Dan Lainer-Vos offers another interpretation of Massad's performance of Israel in microcosm; he treats Massad as a national simulation designed to ignite within campers and staff a sense of national consciousness despite their geographic distance from Palestine:

Instead of creating a sense of undifferentiated membership, the simulation of the nation allows participants to believe that others, perhaps more centrally located members, experience a more intense sense of national belonging than themselves. In so doing, national simulations generate an interpretive schema that allows participants to treat potentially alienating internal differences (for example, between American and Israeli Jews) as an inessential matter, and to think of themselves as occupying a distinct and attenuated position within the same nation.

Massad represented Shulsinger's hope that "firsthand experience of what authentic Jewish life in Israel may feel like" would "generate strong ties of obligation to Israel," thereby ensuring that the sense of geographical distance that campers and staff felt vis-à-vis Israel did not calcify into existential alienation or indifference.[83]

Lainer-Vos's interpretive framework helpfully underscores that the engineering of an effective simulation depends on the selective deployment of realism to create the perception of reality. Summer camps like Massad are well-suited sites for simulations because of their often remote locales and deliberate efforts at cloistering. To the extent that perceptions are shaped as much (if not more) by collective imagination as by real-life conditions, the simulation may be dependent on an idiosyncratic script and a highly stylized setting.[84] This was certainly the case at Massad, where the performance of Israeliness was sui generis and intermittent. Consider Shulsinger's preference for substituting invented Hebrew vocabulary words for loanwords from other languages used commonly in Israeli parlance. At Massad, the use of *karich* for "sandwich" trumped the reality that most Israelis used the loanword *sandvich*.[85]

Similarly, Massad directors' enthusiasm for pageantry that deployed a pastiche of Zionist motifs, cultural nuggets, and iconography was born of the imperative to simulate "authentic" rituals for campers and staff (see figure 2.10). Until its final years, Massad steadfastly refused to institute formal camper learning sessions, even as they became the norm in religious movement camps like Ramah and Bnei Akiva's Moshava. Instead, the entire camp functioned as an immersive Hebrew language institute, or *ulpan*. Each season, a central organizing theme was chosen to "integrate and harmonize" the camp's educational programming. Individual weeks were dedicated to relevant subthemes that were explored through semiweekly *sichot* (facilitated discussions), art projects, skits, songs, dances, and competitions patterned after popular television quiz shows. Each week culminated with a *tekes* (ceremony), "a special pageant including a play, presented with great ceremony under the open sky." The overriding goal of the weekly Massad tekes was promoting peak experiences that heightened campers' sense of connection to Israel and Hebrew culture. Yet the tekes itself would have struck many Israelis as an incongruent mixture of decontextualized familiar and alien elements. Shulsinger and his colleagues chose topical themes. For example, during the 1945 season, which opened weeks after the German surrender and was punctuated by V-J day (August 15), the central theme was "The Reconstruction of Israel in the Diaspora and in Palestine."[86]

Figure 2.10. The 1948 declaration of the state of Israel was commemorated at Massad. (Courtesy of Estates of Noam and Nehama Shudofsky and Massad Camps, Inc.)

Another dramatic ceremony was *havdalah*, the weekly ritual marking the end of the Sabbath and the transition from holy to profane. For many years at Massad Aleph, havdalah was meticulously choreographed. The entire camp assembled in Machon Szold, the main auditorium. A procession of adolescent girls in white robes, holding aloft lit, braided havdalah candles, streamed down the center aisle to the front of the room as the camp sang Tuvia Shlonsky's haunting setting of Shaul Tchernichovsky's poem "I Believe," which begins, "*Tzachki tzachki al hachalomot*" ("Laugh at all my dreams, my dearest; laugh, and I repeat anew/ That I still believe in mankind as I still believe in you"). Against this backdrop of wistful solemnity, a male member of the senior staff recited the havdalah prayer. When he concluded, on cue campers and staff rose from their seats and joined in a rousing rendition of Massad's anthem, "*Techezakna*." Bob Hyfler, who attended the camp from 1964–1970, recalled the ceremony as a bizarre and incongruous yet moving juxtaposition of religion, politics, and sexuality. Because it is inconceivable that the ceremony was consciously designed as ritual satire or subversion, the sandwiching of the havdalah prayer (which emphasizes boundaries and Jewish particularism) between Tchernichovsky's paean to brotherhood and universal peace and Bialik's patriotic, workers' anthem is best understood as the triumph of aesthetics over ideological consistency and of realism over authenticity. Perhaps Hyfler was also correct that what saved these rituals from descending into the realm of "corny, camp shtick" was their exoticism, the fact that they were in Hebrew.[87]

Reading comprehension and written expression were also fostered. Active participation in camp life required campers and counselors alike to conduct library research into topics ranging from the names of their cabins (e.g., Merchavia, Degania) to maccabiah themes. Inspired by the top-of-the-hour *Kol Yisrael* (Voice of Israel) news headlines on Israeli radio, select campers and counselors prepared daily news "broadcasts" that were performed in the dining hall. Campers wrote Hebrew articles for the camp newspaper and the camp yearbook, *Alim* (Leaves), so named to be congruent with the camp's use of a tree as its emblem and organizing motif, and staff wrote Hebrew lyrics for zimriyah and maccabiah songs.

The importance of Israel simulation at Massad should not obscure the camp's commitment to the flowering of a vital Hebrew culture in North America. Unlike at many infusion camps, Hebrew was not merely instrumental at Massad. Shulsinger never wavered from his conviction that "the spoken Hebrew language must of necessity be the keystone for the entire camp program and the center around which all cultural, educational and recreational programmatic efforts must revolve."[88] On the bottom of Massad's emblem, on either side of the date palm tree, were the letters *ayin* and *tsadi*, which stood for the term *ivri tzair*, Young Hebrew. Although the term *ivri* is commonly understood as a synonym for Jew, the choice of this archaic identifier that posited identity as coterminous with language cannot be coincidental.[89] Even though Zionism and, later, the state of Israel were counted among the pillars of Massad's educational program, the camp preexisted the Jewish state. Hanoar Haivri, the organization that willed Massad into existence, was committed to the revival of Hebrew independent of any political agenda for Mandate Palestine.

Once Israel was established, Shulsinger strategically refused to openly endorse aliyah (emigration to Israel) or publicly adopt a negationist stance vis-à-vis Diaspora Jewry, particularly those Jews living in western democracies such as the United States. On the contrary, despite his grave personal doubts about the long-term sustainability of American Judaism, Shulsinger staked out a place for Massad within the American Jewish educational mainstream by endorsing a synthetic approach toward campers' dual cultural heritage. Only American Jewish integration would "achieve a level of fulfillment and harmony in our cultural program and in the personal life of the camper." Arguably, there was no better symbol of Massad's integrationism than Hebrew-speaking campers enthusiastically playing the quintessentially American game of baseball. Writing in 1967, Shulsinger warned that it would be "a gross pedagogical error to base a pedagogic approach to youth" on "a philosophy of pessimism" about Jewish life in North America, "particularly at a time when there is actually so much evidence of organic creativity." As a purely tactical matter, "preaching *aliyah* will not bring results. Only an educational program which seeks to deepen the young person's understanding of Judaism and of the Zionist idea may prepare the ground and create conditions for aliyah from the United States."[90]

Privately, Shulsinger and his wife were less guarded in their support for American Jewish emigration to Israel. They cited as a measure of Massad's success that more than 600 alumni chose to settle in Israel by the mid-1990s. But this was never their overt goal, even if they justified their own return to Israel after retirement on that basis. On their move, they added "Shear-Yashuv" (A remnant shall return), from Isaiah 10:21, to their family name.[91] Shulsinger fashioned Massad as a Hebrew oasis rather than a catalyst for mass American Jewish immigration to the land of Israel. Wary of alienating parents, Massad's leader proceeded gingerly when it came to promoting aliyah. Realizing the import of the Shulsingers' refusal to take a public stand on aliyah, despite their personal attitudes, Moshe Davis observed, "In a strange way, the most intensive Jewish activism in this country is led by people who could certainly be classified as 'Negators of the Diaspora.'" Massad is the perfect example. Among its founders were individuals who denied the possibility of Jewish survival in America. But their actions spoke louder than their words.[92]

## The Decline of Massad

Massad inspired a few imitators in the 1940s and '50s, including the Massad camps in Canada, and a second wave of Hebrew-speaking camping experiments were undertaken in the 1960s and early 1970s.[93] While these boutique programs did attract a modest number of campers in the late 1970s and '80s, Massad Poconos experienced a steep decline in enrollment. The proximate cause was Shulsinger's failure to groom a successor and the subsequent infighting among various factions of the board. Several of Massad's main feeder schools were approached about purchasing the camp, but their respective boards declined to assume the costs.[94] Significantly, Massad's brand of peoplehood-centered Judaism became passé as Conservative and Reform Jews migrated to their own denominational camps; Orthodox families who would have considered Massad in the 1950s or '60s abandoned it decades later for religiously oriented and strictly observant Orthodox camps like Morasha, near Lake Como, Pennsylvania, which was founded by Yeshiva University. Even as the modern Orthodox community became more punctilious in its observance of traditional Jewish law and less interested in interdenominational cooperation, Massad's administration and board remained reluctant to surrender the camp's commitment to Jewish unity and inclusivity, which they prized as one of its distinctive features.[95]

Indubitably, however, the eclipse of Massad is also linked to the decline of Tarbut Ivrit and the consolidation of the Jewish state. The most significant reason for the decline of Tarbut Ivrit was the emergence of a vibrant Hebrew culture in Israel. The rationale for a Hebrew revival program in the Diaspora became less compelling when the growth and vitality of Hebrew culture were ensured by Israel's national apparatus and its various cultural organs. The existence of the Israeli nation-state normalized Hebrew as a national language, not simply a language of Zionist cultural revival. Thus, Hebraic cultural Zionism in North America, as well as in other lands of the Diaspora, was rendered unnecessary. As the establishment of Israel absolved institutions like Massad of the responsibility to serve as vehicles for Hebrew revival, it simultaneously diminished the camp's cultural import and implicitly invited parents and communal leaders to evaluate its success or failure on the basis of more conventional overnight camp criteria. According to Frost, "The dramatic victory of Hebrew in Eretz Yisrael and its becoming the language of communication for millions of people, among them non-Jews, made Hebrew speaking a fact and no longer an ideal. It was now more difficult to excite the counselors (and campers) about the 'holiness' and stubborn devotion to that ideal."[96]

Attempts to encourage the reading of Israeli publications also met with difficulties, due in part to the reading level but also because of a cultural disconnect between American and Israeli Jewish youth. Similarly, there was a struggle over presenting American-themed programs—for example, American musicals translated into Hebrew—instead of Israeli fare. At a 1977 meeting of the leadership, Shulsinger said, "I object to Hebrew speaking if it is only the mouthing of words; Hebrew words do not signify Hebrew culture. There is a tendency in Massad Bet to concentrate on plays that are devoid of Hebrew content. We must do more in the camps with regard to Zionism."[97] Even as Massad's leaders reconciled themselves to the difficulty of creating a vibrant Hebrew-speaking diasporic culture, they were also confronted with the unrelatability of Israeli Hebrew culture, with its distinctive sensibility, to an American Jewish audience. According to members of Massad's senior staff, neither counselors nor campers were interested in deeply engaging with Israeli Hebrew culture. The theater staff was eager to stage productions like Peter Frye and Aharon Meged's *I Like Mike*, based on the 1961 Israeli film, but the campers clamored for Hebrew translations of Broadway fare, such as *South Pacific* and *West Side Story*.[98]

The challenge was especially pronounced for the music staff. Changing American Jewish tastes had elevated the popularity of neo-Hasidic and folk melodies over other Israeli music. In the 1970s, the hottest Israeli music exports were emerging from the annual Israeli Chassidic Song Festival, which debuted in 1969. Many of the songs, like *"Oseh Shalom"* (Nurit Hirsh) and *"Od Yishama"* (Shlomo Carlebach), were unabashedly liturgical. The other breakthrough Israeli music was bubble gum pop, epitomized by *"A-ba-ni-bi"* (Ehud Manor and Nurit Hirsh), which snagged first prize at the 1978 Eurovision Song Festival. Even though these and similar songs were taught at Massad, the camp's last music director Michael Berl lamented their lack of *"tochen"*—that is, content and substance—and he drew the line at "silly" love ballads. Berl found himself reaching for the "message songs" of artists like Naomi Shemer, but he admitted that it was a difficult balancing act: "I had to be very careful in the Israeli songs that I picked because I knew that [the campers] weren't too keen on singing them and it would be a hard sell."[99] By the 1970s, as the "Hebrew only" policy became laxer in the cabins, Hebrew music also competed for campers' and counselors' attention with American pop and folk rock.

If shifting musical appetites were partially to blame, young people were also reflecting the messaging in their Jewish day schools: there, Hebrew and Israeli cultural literacy were taking a back seat to classical Jewish text study.[100] As Mintz observed, in the immediate postwar era, Jewish education was the last bastion of the Hebrew movement in America. But it finally succumbed to the same pressures that felled Tarbut Ivrit more generally: rapid Americanization, suburbanization, the emergence of the synagogue as the dominant institution on the Jewish landscape and its absorption of the afternoon supplementary school, and the "eclipse of moderate Zionist Orthodoxy" and its replacement with a triumphalist neo-traditionalism.[101] By the 1970s, Ramaz and Yeshivah of Flatbush's fealty to Ivrit b'Ivrit instruction placed them in a dwindling minority of schools. The recruitment of a critical mass of fluent Hebrew-speaking campers and counselors became a progressively unattainable goal. The trend toward monolingualism in the American Jewish community also felled the Yiddishist camps. Some of the longest operating Yiddishist camps in the Northeast, including Kinderwelt and Boiberik, closed within a decade of Massad.

American Jews' widespread attainment of a solidly middle- and upper-middle-class standard of living coincided with the growing affordability of jet travel. By the 1960s and '70s, overseas tourism became a viable leisure activity for families and students, interfering with camps' ability to recruit and retain counselors and campers for an entire summer. A sign of the times was the Shulsingers' reluctant decision to institute the option of a four-week session, rather than insisting that campers attend for a full eight weeks so as to maximize the impact of the immersive Hebrew environment.

If leisure travel, regardless of destination, threatened the viability of summer camps, Israel tourism presented a particular (and ironic) challenge to Hebrew immersion camps like Massad. Whereas only about one-third of American Jews reported visiting Israel in surveys conducted in the 1970s and '80s, the percentage was far higher among the highly engaged Jews who comprised Massad's clientele.[102] For some longtime Massad campers, a first trip to Israel could feel like a homecoming. Arleen Pilzer Eidelman recalled listening to Israeli radio during her first visit to the country, in 1957, and feeling a special bond with the country because she recognized the names of people and places: "I was with other kids [who had not attended Massad], and what I was hearing on the radio seemed to have more meaning to me than it did to them." Charles Kleinhaus had a similar reaction during his first visit to Israel as a recent high school graduate, in 1959:

"It was mind-blowing to visit places which you had your bunk named after. . . . It had a relationship to your own history, in a weird way. *Degania* was a bunk, and there you go and you see Degania—it's a whole kibbutz." Eidelman and Kleinhaus were convinced that their decisions, years later, to move to Israel were related to this sense of kinship and ownership that was carefully cultivated at Massad through its promotion of linguistic and cultural fluency.

But there was another unintended consequence of the growth of Israel travel on Massad: a diminished rationale for the creation of *Eretz Yisrael b'zeir anpin*, a microcosm of Israel in the Poconos. Kleinhaus grasped this insight after further reflecting on his first visit to Degania: "It's not just a bunk when you get to see the real place," he asserted. Visiting Israel reduced Massad in some minds to child's play. Why play at living in an imaginary Israel when you could visit and relocate to the real Israel? According to Berl, this realization was also evident to parents and caused them to readjust their camp selection priorities: "The compulsive need to send your child to Massad, so that they'll have an Israel experience, wasn't necessary. If I want my kid to have an Israel experience I'll take him there myself or send him on a teen trip or a gap year program [between high school and college]."[103]

On the counselor front, the same inexpensive airfares that allowed American Jewish youth to visit Israel or backpack their way through Europe also made it possible for camps to import Hebrew-speaking counselors from Israel. Massad was among the first to bring Israeli emissaries to their camps in the mid-1960s, a phenomenon that we discuss in chapter 7, but Massad's leadership ultimately viewed this move as a mixed blessing, because it undermined the goal of creating a population of American Jewish Hebrew speakers and because it exposed the cultural chasm between American and Israeli Jewish youth.[104]

Because the challenge that Israel posed to Massad was existential, it could not readily adjust its business model. The competitive nature of the market encouraged the proliferation of the first specialty camps. For example, Camp Raleigh, a private modern Orthodox camp in Livingston Manor, New York, marketed itself as "the sports camp in a Torah environment." But Massad already inhabited a very specific niche market. Some members of Massad's board believed that the camp could staunch the camper exodus by upgrading its spartan facilities, which by the mid-1970s were in noticeable disrepair.[105] But in the final analysis, the essence of Massad was Hebrew immersion; an Olympic-sized pool or water skiing on the lake would not change that fact.

Other immersion camps took a different tack. Faced with the threat of closure, they adopted a more permissive approach to English speaking and placed greater emphasis on Jewish, not merely, Hebrew culture. Such a compromise was unthinkable at Massad in the Poconos. In the view of the Shulsingers, the senior staff, and the camp's board, Massad would scarcely be Massad without its immersive Hebrew environment. After several years of retrenchment, including the shuttering of Massad Gimel in 1972 and Massad Bet in 1980, the camp's final season at its oldest Poconos facility, in Tannersville, was held in 1981. After decades in the sunshine, immersive Hebrew camping had been eclipsed by Hebrew infusion.

A decade later, Massad's final director, Rabbi Mayer Moskowitz, reflected on the fate of the camp, relaying a favorite quip of American Hebraist Daniel Persky. Lamenting the waning interest in Hebrew among his Diaspora Jewish brethren, Persky was said to have grumbled sardonically, "Two thousand years there wasn't a Jewish state and it had to happen to me?!?"[106]

——————

Massad Poconos' early success and relatively rapid decline illuminate the immersion model with all of its possibilities and limitations. Although this camp no longer exists, its influence continues to this day. People who attended or worked at Massad went on to work at many other camps, bringing some Hebrew practices with them, such as Hebrew musicals, maccabiah, and calling the infirmary the *marp*. Perhaps the most important and enduring influence of Massad was the many camps it inspired—camps that initially made Hebrew speaking a centerpiece of their programs. Some of these camps followed Massad's lead and closed. Massad Manitoba maintains an immersive Hebrew environment but does not insist on campers using Hebrew in their informal interactions. Several others, like Yavneh, Massad Quebec, and Ramah, made the transition to Hebrew infusion. The next chapter offers a detailed case study of this transition at Ramah camps.

# Camp Ramah

## A TRANSITION FROM IMMERSION TO INFUSION

When news reached Camp Massad during the summer of 1950 that the newly established Camp Ramah Poconos was flying a flag with an emblem of the Ten Commandments alongside the Stars and Stripes, rather than the national flag of Israel, senior staff members were irate. The first camp in what became the Ramah camping network was established in 1947, in Conover, Wisconsin, as a Hebrew-speaking camp under Conservative movement auspices, but the expressed motivation for its commitment to Hebraism was knotty. On the one hand, its overseers at the Jewish Theological Seminary's (JTS) Teachers Institute, Sylvia Ettenberg and Moshe Davis, were avowed cultural Zionists who were involved in the same Hebrew youth organization that spawned Massad. Yet the seminary itself, under Chancellor Louis Finkelstein, tiptoed gingerly around the controversial issue of political Zionism, even after the creation of the state of Israel. Ramah's founders articulated the camp's commitment to Hebrew as instrumental to its ultimate goal of raising a generation of textually and culturally literate Conservative American Jewish leaders.[1]

For Massad's leaders striving to create a microcosm of Israel at camp, Ramah's failure to overtly embrace an ideology that linked Hebrew to the Zionist project and its apotheosis in the establishment of Israel seemed inexplicable. Even more infuriating to them was the prevalence of Massad alumni among Ramah's founders, senior staff, and counselor force. Ramah's ideological deviation felt like an act of betrayal because former Massad insiders had perpetrated it. Exceedingly riled, a cadre of Massad counselors and staff informally known as the "Massad mafia" raised money from their coworkers and rented a light aircraft and a pilot. Three members of their group—Abie Kraushar, Ray Arzt, and Rabbi Louis Bernstein—flew over the Ramah camp and "bombed" it with 500 leaflets excoriating Ramah for its alleged anti-Zionism. Arzt, who could recognize Ramah from the air, acted as the spotter, while Kraushar threw the leaflets out the window. As for Bernstein, the most anxious of the three, his job was to sit in the back of the plane and recite *tehilim* (psalms). Unfortunately for the Massad mafia, the wind carried all of the leaflets into the woods, and few if any at Ramah actually witnessed the strafing because it occurred while lunch was being served in the dining hall. In fact, the incident only came to their attention a few days later when a counselor came upon a few leaflets while hiking in the woods with his campers. Years later, Ettenberg was still holding onto a letter of apology for the incident from Shulsinger.[2]

The airborne leafleting of Ramah Poconos occupies a special place in Massad lore, perhaps because it encapsulates so much about Massad's Zionist values and the cultish devotion of its staff and alumni. But it is also revealing in what it conveys about Ramah and the purposes of Hebrew and Zionism at camp. In Ramah's early years, Hebrew was linked more to Jewish cultural literacy than it was to the newly created Jewish state.

Ramah aspired to be a Hebrew immersion camp, and many would argue that it came close to achieving this goal in its early years. Yet even in the 1950s, Hebrew infusion, rather than immersion, increasingly became the norm, especially beyond public spaces like the dining hall and the ball field. This trend toward infusion rather than immersion became more pronounced by the mid-late 1960s and 1970s, so that by 1989, the contributors and editors of Ramah's fortieth-anniversary volume dispensed with the pretense that Ramah camps remained strictly Hebrew speaking. This chapter explores how the leadership of a camp network that was initially committed to immersion moved toward an unenthusiastic acceptance of Hebrew infusion. We argue that the falloff in Hebrew speaking at Ramah is attributable in part to its early decoupling of Hebrew from Zionism and Israel. In making Ramah a vehicle for strengthening American Conservative Judaism, Ramah's founders were inadvertently weakening the rationale for modern Hebrew immersion.

We also document equally important factors in Ramah's reluctant capitulation, including the challenge that Hebrew immersion posed to other camp goals, such as fostering a nurturing cabin environment and teaching intellectually stimulating classes, as well as the impediment it posed to counselor and camper recruitment as the camping network (and the Conservative movement) underwent rapid growth. Although Ramah's directors viewed infusion as a concession, this shift from immersion reflected the camps' adaptability to changing American Jewish conditions, including the waning influence of Hebraists on the curricula of congregational supplementary schools and day schools. As it turned out, infusion rather than immersion was better suited to the camp's core mission of raising engaged Conservative Jews. This was especially true as the camp system expanded the number of beds in the 1960s and again in the 1990s and the 2010s. Even as it retained a commitment to leadership training, it strove to broaden its appeal by serving the needs and interests of a wider, more diverse camper population. In a sense, the evolution of Hebrew at Ramah serves as a fitting companion to the history of Hebrew at Massad. Ramah's response to the same factors that undermined immersion there enabled that camp network to adapt and endure, even as Massad declined.

## Hebrew in the Heavenly Ramah and the Earthly Ramah

When Ramah Connecticut director Morton Siegel introduced his camp to a visitor in 1955, he made a point of insisting that "our kids are not fanatics." He characterized them instead as "polite, skeptical, intelligent, well-adjusted in the American world, tolerant, and very well educated," adding, "They don't think of themselves as missionaries, certainly, nor behave like them."[3] With this quintessentially American description, Siegel effectively drew a bright line between Ramah and Massad, where apostles of Hebrew in America, true believers, were zealously engaged in their own pioneering venture.

Not animated by the gospel of *chalutziut* or a desideratum to cultivate Diaspora Hebrew culture, Ramah was instead conceived as a leadership training camp. According to Teachers Institute dean Moshe Davis, the impetus for the camp was the desire to intensify Conservative Jewish education.[4] Over the previous two decades, congregations had cut back on the number of meeting hours per week of their supplementary schools, first in response to Depression-era and wartime exigencies and later to accommodate the schedules of suburban parents and competition from other afterschool programs such as team sports and music lessons. Characteristically, JTS's response to this phenomenon was calibrated to cultivate a gifted elite.[5] Revealingly, Ramah Wisconsin's first director, Henry Goldberg, split his time between operating the camp and running the Teachers Institute's Leadership Training Fellowship, a corps of teens handpicked from Conservative synagogues nationwide and established in 1945. (United Synagogue Youth, a corresponding youth program designed for the Conservative masses, was not established until 1951 and even then was run under the auspices of the movement's congregational arm rather than by JTS.)

Goldberg identified three additional objectives that animated Ramah's program:

1. the creation of a positive, wholesome environment where the camper would see and practice Judaism at its best
2. the development in the camper of an awareness of the role he should play as a Jew living in America
3. the acquisition of certain knowledge, habits, and skills that would help the camper exercise his function as a Jew both intelligently and creatively.[6]

Insight into how Ramah conceptualized Jewish living in its ideal form can be gleaned from author Chaim Potok's description of the camp as "an attempt on the part of our movement to create a Talmudic Jewish community on the soil of twentieth-century America."[7] Potok meant to call attention to the camp's punctilious observance of Jewish law, as interpreted by the movement's Committee on Jewish Law and Standards, and the prominent role occupied by study on the schedule. In the early decades, Ramah camps reserved two 45-minute sessions per day for formal study, in this way compensating for the reduction of hours in the supplementary schools. They also had a staff position of scholar-in-residence, typically a JTS faculty member, to act as a role model and decisor.[8]

But equally important, in Potok's view, was the way Ramah cultivated an atmosphere of inquiry and debate while maintaining norms of practice. "Prayer at Ramah is mandatory, but it would not be unusual to hear its validity or particular mode of expression challenged," he explained. Similarly, although Sabbath observance was non-negotiable, "in no way would it be considered a wrong should someone question a particular method of observance suggested by the camp." Potok painted a picture of a camp environment imbued with study and ritual practice and informed by insights into group dynamics.[9] Regardless of whether the earthly Ramah always lived up to Potok's idealized description, his distillation provided a clear expression of Ramah's values.

Where did Hebrew fit into Ramah, both in theory and in practice? On paper, the answer was straightforward. From the outset, Ramah aspired to be a Hebrew-speaking camp. The guidelines as set forth by the camp directors and the Teachers Institute were clear: all official camp business, including staff meetings and public announcements, were to be conducted in Hebrew. So, too, were camp activities: Hebrew was to be the language of the dining hall and the athletic fields. All songs were to be sung in Hebrew (with the notable exception of patriotic hymns on American Independence Day), and dramatic productions were to be performed in Hebrew. Even bunk interactions between counselors and campers and among campers were supposed to take place in Hebrew.

As with Massad, observers were fascinated by the spectacle of Americanized youngsters using modern Hebrew as a routine language of communication (see figure 3.1). The Hebrew-speaking aspect of camp life was often emphasized in newspaper and magazine stories about Ramah. "Here is an entire community of close to 200 men, women and children, playing, eating their meals, living—and all in the Hebrew language," marveled a reporter from the *Chicago Jewish Sentinel* after visiting Ramah Wisconsin in 1952. He went on to share some emblematic anecdotes: youngsters chanting "*hava nelech!*" roughly translated as "let's go," to cheer on their team member at bat in a close softball game; the lifeguard in charge of free swim at the lake blowing his whistle and shouting "*Zugot!*," literally "pairs," as swimmers scurry to find their partners for buddy call.[10]

In reality, the translation of the guidelines into practice was messier than the *Sentinel* author grasped. Less awestruck visitors, even in the early years, acknowledged administrators' determination to maintain Hebrew as the public language

Figure 3.1. Hebrew was the public language of Camp Ramah, with many words borrowed from the Massad lexicon, including the term *Chanutiya* (canteen) above the takeout window. Note that the menu item are described with drawings rather than being translated into English. (Credit: National Ramah Commission)

at Ramah while drawing attention to the use of both English and Hebrew at the camps. Among the more perceptive was Morris Freedman, who wrote about his 1954 visit to Ramah Connecticut in *Commentary Magazine*. He recalled, "The counselors and many of the campers used Hebrew quite unaffectedly, and lapsed as often from English to Hebrew as from Hebrew into English." Freedman was describing language practices that scholars today call translanguaging. He also noticed that many campers and counselors, while speaking to one another primarily in English, would repeatedly and instinctively reach for and use Hebrew words when they felt that there was no English equivalent that could adequately convey their desired "shade of meaning." Freedman was effectively testifying that CHE was widely and reflexively practiced by campers and staff virtually from Ramah's inception, existing alongside the "official" Hebrew that could be heard at mealtimes and from the camp loudspeaker.[11]

The *Commentary* writer was also a discerning reader of Ramah Connecticut's abundant signage, beginning at the camp entrance, which was adorned with a large Hebrew sign reading "*Machaneh Ramah*" (Camp Ramah) and a smaller but equally emphatic sign in printed English directing that "Cars for Camp

Figure 3.2. Camps like Massad (pictured here) and Ramah, which typically used Hebrew signage, included English translations in venues like the waterfront, where safety was a concern. (Courtesy of Estates of Noam and Nehama Shudofsky and Massad Camps, Inc.)

Ramah Not Permitted beyond This Point on the Sabbath." The juxtaposition of these signs exemplified the functional versus symbolic uses of language and revealed the ways Ramah telegraphed different camp values and priorities; that is, Hebrew and Sabbath observance. The English sign was designed primarily for visitors, yet each sign in its own way served as a boundary marker between the intentional camp community and the outside world. On the campgrounds, Freedman noted that the preponderance of signage was in Hebrew. Hebrew signs operated as identifiers and frequently served a pedagogical function. For example, common mealtime vocabulary words were posted in the dining room, as were Hebrew blessings for before and after meals. Predictably, however, signs meant primarily for visitors were rendered in English or both Hebrew and English—but so were those related to safety and dietary laws. Thus, water safety rules were posted in English, in addition to Hebrew, as were dining hall labels distinguishing dairy from meat on cabinets and equipment. Similar distinctions were observed at Massad, as in figure 3.2. Recognizing the effectiveness of habituation, administrators at both Massad and Ramah did not hesitate to expose community members to less familiar Hebrew words and phrases; when context proved to be an insufficient guide to meaning, the unversed could always turn to a friend or elder for clarification. But the physical and religious welfare of the community was never endangered in the name of ideological linguistic purity.[12]

## HEBREW AS A MEANS BUT NEVER AN END IN ITSELF

Distilling more than two generations of scholarship on Conservative Judaism in the United States, historian Jack Wertheimer observed, "From the beginning, the movement was based on the marriage of an anti-Reform elite ideology to anti-Orthodox folk aspirations."[13] The place of Hebrew in the movement reflected the resulting uneasy dynamic between these conflicting impulses. On the one hand, the elites were adamant about the centrality of Hebrew. In a 1927 address before the movement's Rabbinical Assembly, Louis Finkelstein articulated seven shared principles that united Conservative Judaism's leaders. The sixth item was a commitment to the Hebrew language. Conservative rabbis were "entirely sympathetic to the establishment of Hebrew as the language of conversation, Jewish literature and learning," he declared. Aspirational as this plank was, it did not evoke controversy among Finkelstein's rabbinic colleagues, unlike his statements on the nature of God, the conception of Torah, and the adaptability of Jewish law.[14] The centrality of both textual and modern Hebrew was reaffirmed twenty years later by Teachers Institute leader Rabbi Mordecai Kaplan in a speech on "Unity and Diversity in the Conservative Movement."[15]

On the other hand, the Conservative laity, by and large, did not aspire to Hebrew fluency. Hebrew had symbolic value in that it conveyed authenticity in prayer and study and connected them with the Jewish people and Hebrew culture of Palestine/Israel. As political scientist Daniel Elazar and sociologist Rela Mintz Geffen asserted, Conservative Judaism spread because it bound second-generation Jews to tradition but made modest demands in the way of personal practice.[16] Its approach to Hebrew was exemplified by its supplementary formal educational institution, commonly known as the Hebrew school. As the name suggests, Hebrew was initially a centerpiece of its curriculum—a program that was inherited from its precursor, the modern communal Talmud Torah—and Hebraist educators in the postwar decades steadfastly affirmed its importance. In actuality, however, as the number of instructional hours per week declined and the intensity of the school's offerings waned, its curricular emphasis shifted to enculturation and the acquisition of synagogue skills. In 1969, Walter Ackerman lamented in the *American Jewish Year Book* that students were leaving the schools with "a capability in Hebrew which hardly goes beyond monosyllabic responses to carefully worded questions."[17]

As a leadership training institution designed and led by Teachers Institute officials and JTS-trained rabbis and educators, Ramah's approach to Hebrew naturally reflected the attitudes of the elites. The original motivation for Hebrew at Ramah was arguably best summed up by Seymour Fox in his discourse on Ramah's philosophy, *Vision at the Heart*: "All of us believed that if you wanted to understand and be part of Jewish history, you had no choice but to master Hebrew; *that* was how you joined the ongoing conversation with Rashi, Maimonides, and all the other great commentators and philosophers."[18] When Rabbi Judah Goldin, who led the Teachers Institute in the 1950s, was asked about the role of Israel at Ramah in 1955, he responded emphatically: "We're not a Zionist camp. Not that we exclude Israel or the subject of Zionism. It's just that our program is not one which revolves predominantly around Israel."[19] Out of the media spotlight, however, many of Ramah's counselors and some members of the leadership were far more comfortable introducing Zionist influences into camp. Fox, who directed Ramah Wisconsin in 1954–1955 and remained a guiding figure in the Ramah camping movement until his emigration to Israel in 1966, conceded that Hebraist staffers were inspired by Israel's establishment. However, the senior leadership avoided associating the camp with political Zionism, at least until the establishment of the Israel Seminar in 1962. "It must be acknowledged that [JTS Chancellor Louis] Finkelstein wasn't a Zionist at first, and neither was I," Fox wrote.[20] Finkelstein had gone as far as forbidding the singing of the Israeli national anthem *Hatikvah* at JTS's 1948 graduation exercises, which were held barely a month after the declaration of the Jewish state. Even so, during the summer of 1947, campers and staff at Ramah Wisconsin sang the first two stanzas with the original pre-state lyrics each morning (except the Sabbath) as they hoisted the Zionist flag (see figure 3.3). Camp practice, no doubt influenced by the large contingent of Massad alumni on the Ramah staff, thus diverged from JTS policy—even though, after the state of Israel was declared, the prospect of raising a foreign nation's flag became more controversial, at least at the Pennsylvania camp as we saw in the story at the beginning of this chapter. Ramah Poconos, which was about an hour's drive from many of the Catskill resorts and bungalow colonies favored by New York Jews in the summertime and within easy driving distance of JTS, often hosted Conservative movement officials.

JTS and Ramah's evasive rhetoric on the state of Israel may have reflected Cold War fears about accusations of Jewish dual loyalties. To the extent that Hebrew was valued in national terms, in Ramah's early decades it was invoked as a unifying language of the Jewish people, the cultural patrimony, and the carrier of values and spirit, from which a revivified and revitalized national culture could emerge—not primarily as the language of the state of Israel. In the final analysis, whatever Zionist convictions may have animated various Teachers Institute officials or staff members, including Ramah's primary architects, Moshe Davis and Sylvia Ettenberg, the essential rationale for Hebrew at Ramah was American rather than Israel centered: the cultivation of a homegrown Conservative leadership.

Figure 3.3. A boy in a scouting uniform at Camp Ramah Wisconsin in the 1940s holds a Zionist flag with the word *Yisraelim* (Israelis) on it. Camp Ramah adopted an ambivalent and at times contradictory approach to political Zionism during its early years. (Credit: National Ramah Commission)

To further elucidate this point, it is useful to delve into the nature of the relationship between Ramah and Massad. Shulsinger's camp exerted considerable influence on Ramah during its early years in terms of both personnel and program. Davis and Ettenberg were emigrants from Massad who were active in Hanoar Haivri and instrumental in helping Shulsinger launch the Hebrew immersion camp. Likewise, their crucial ally in the Chicago Jewish community, Rabbi Ralph Simon, was a Massad parent whose support for Jewish camping was premised on his children's positive experience at Massad. What is more, many early Ramah counselors and staff who left an indelible mark on the camp's culture were also Massad alumni.[21] These individuals were stirred by the creation of a Hebraic national culture in Palestine and probably accepted as a foregone conclusion that Ramah would be conducted in Hebrew. Shulsinger himself recognized the need for a Hebrew-speaking camp catering to supplementary school children, as opposed to Massad, which served a day school population. He declined to admit more than a sprinkling of such youngsters into Massad, fearing that their weak Hebrew backgrounds would dilute its Hebrew environment.

Davis and Ettenberg, as well as the first camp directors, embraced Massad's Hebrew-centered ethos. From its founding until 1951, Ramah Wisconsin implemented many of Massad's conventions, including the use of a reward system to promote Hebrew speaking, bestowing stars or *raish*, *mem*, and *hey* patches (the Hebrew letters that spelled Ramah), rather than Massad's coveted *ayins*. Psychology professor Arthur Elstein, who began attending Ramah Wisconsin in 1950, recalled that winning the Hebrew-speaking prize three weeks in a row entitled a bunk to the *pras meyuchad* (special prize): a day trip to Eagle River, the county seat, which contained an ice cream parlor. Ettenberg's aversion to Shulsinger's more heavy-handed tactics allowed for a more relaxed environment around Hebrew speaking. But despite her discomfort with competition at Massad, she did not interfere when Goldberg and his successor in Wisconsin, Rabbi Hillel Silverman, harnessed the youngsters' competitive energy to promote Hebrew singing, cheering, and speaking through activities like maccabiah. She was relieved, however, when Ramah Wisconsin's third director, Louis Newman, abolished these practices in 1951.[22]

Another Shulsinger import was the Massad Dictionary, which accounted for the camps' shared vocabulary. "We were asked to memorize Camp Massad's Hebrew dictionary," recalled Rabbi Shelly Switkin, who attended Ramah Wisconsin during its inaugural season. "You walked around with the [Massad] dictionary and you did the best you could," Elstein agreed. "It was a good, practical, everyday Hebrew dictionary. If you needed [to know] how to say lettuce, tomato, chopped meat. And there was this whole vocabulary made up to play baseball in Hebrew. If you think about it, on the one hand it is laughable. . . . [But] on the other hand, it shows serious commitment. And, you know, why not?"[23] Elstein's comment exemplifies how camps as ideologically grounded institutions create plausibility structures, the contexts that provide meanings for cultural practices. It also underscores how the dissemination of the Massad Dictionary contributed to the creation of the rudiments of an intercamp Hebrew dialect. Finally, Elstein's use of the term "laughable" to describe the "practical, everyday Hebrew" tacitly reinforces the proposition that this functional Hebrew was unlikely to facilitate camper engagement with biblical and rabbinic sources (or even with modern Hebrew literature), as Ramah leaders might have hoped.

The Massad Dictionary was also introduced to Camp Yavneh, the Boston Hebrew Teacher College's Hebrew study camp established in 1944 in Northwood, New Hampshire. "We used the Massad Dictionary for everything," recalled Rabbi Allan Smith, who began attending Yavneh in 1950 and later became the director of the Reform movement's camping program. "Baseball was *kadur basis*, a strike was a *hachtaa*, and a foul ball was *pasul*."[24] The osmosis between Massad and Yavneh continued well into the mid-1950s, according to former Yavneh staffer Rabbi Herbert Rosenblum. Massad, Yavneh, and Ramah drew many of their counselors from the same pool of Hebrew-speaking college and graduate students.[25] Thus, Massad's Dictionary became authoritative linguistically, if not ideologically. A shared dialect of Hebrew and then eventually CHE developed, partly through written transmission, including through the dictionary and songsters, and partly because personnel traveled from camp to camp and became agents of linguistic diffusion. Over time, an individual camp's dialect of CHE was distinguished by self-styled neologisms and the incorporation of modern or textual Hebrew words in response to new situations and the arrival of new staff, including Israelis. The fluidity of CHE and the decentralized nature of American Jewish camping ensured that a single standardized dialect never became fixed.

Over time, significant ideological and pedagogical differences developed between Massad and Ramah, despite their shared lineage. Even as they had a hand in crafting Massad's educational philosophy, Davis and Ettenberg grew to regret its single-minded focus on the Hebrew language. "A number of us felt that although Hebrew should be the language [of camp], Hebrew was only an instrument. It couldn't be *the* goal," Ettenberg recalled. The goal in her mind was strengthening American Judaism and cultivating tomorrow's Conservative Jewish leaders. Davis's and her critique extended beyond Massad's preoccupation with Hebrew to include its authoritarian approach to discipline and its alleged emphasis on orthopraxy as opposed to religiosity. Ramah positioned itself as the anti-Massad: a camp where speaking Hebrew was meant to further the ultimate goals of leadership training and individual religious and spiritual growth. Fundamentally, its initial leaders believed, the emphasis at camp should be on strengthening Conservative Judaism.[26]

Davis's and Ettenberg's critique was internalized by Ramah's senior staff who echoed it in their own writings. Potok insisted that Hebrew, "intrinsic as it has always been to Ramah, became a tool, a means, never an end in itself." For Potok, the key to Ramah was its synthesis of Jewish and American cultures: "the end was always a strange and somewhat elusive vision of a new kind of human being, sensitive, alert, keen, vital, at home simultaneously in two major cultures and able to contribute to the one or the other without forgetting either the heritage of his people or of his adopted land."[27] Rabbi Goldin made essentially the same point in 1954, but he believed that the pervasive American culture would overpower American Jewish youth unless they were imbued with "a full consciousness of Jewishness." For that reason, he wrote, "the heart of our program is in Jewish observance—daily and Sabbath prayers, grace at meals, reading and studying texts, and so on." But only Hebrew could unlock the richness of classical Jewish texts and the fullness of Jewish rituals and ceremonies. "How without Hebrew, without the language of their people, can one get to love the tradition?"[28] Conservative leaders like Goldin believed that the paradigms of Jewishness performed in the synagogue and the home were insufficiently compelling to the movement's youth. Ramah provided a more robust and gripping model of Jewish living, including countercultural practices like speaking Hebrew, that would compel American Jewish youth to adopt a hybrid or additive approach to American assimilation.

Thus the overarching goal that inspired Ramah's commitment to Hebrew in the early years was the cultivation of a textually and culturally literate Jewish elite. Neither Potok nor Goldin mentioned a Zionist motivation for speaking Hebrew at Ramah. Ramah's early complicated relationship with political Zionism exemplified the lack of coherence around its rationale for Hebrew immersion. If the argument for Hebrew was framed around textual literacy, how was this furthered by promoting the use of modern Hebrew, and particularly the mastery of camp vocabulary? Yet, if Hebrew speaking was justified on ideological grounds, as contributing to the revival and survival of the Jewish people, did not the creation of Israel as a Hebrew-speaking state render camp an inferior and even trivial place for that to happen? "Can any of our staff today believe that by telling a camper in Hebrew to finish making his bed he is contributing to the reconstituting of the Jewish people? Does anyone believe there is somehow a direct line between playing baseball in Hebrew and contributing to the wellbeing of Israel?" former Ramah New England director Robert Abramson asked rhetorically.[29]

Certainly, the lack of ideological consistency at Ramah reflected an underlying tension between the movement's leadership and the camp directors and staff. In this regard, it is useful to recall that camps were traditionally countercultural institutions, conceived as "a world apart" and designed to be transformational and not to reify the status quo.[30] Accordingly, regardless of JTS leaders' ambivalence about political Zionism in its early years, Ramah camps were suffused with modern Hebrew culture, imported directly or adapted from Israeli sources, particularly in the realms of music, dance, and dramatics. And despite the aspiration of having campers and staff converse across the generations with rabbinic and medieval personages, it was typically modern, rather than biblical or rabbinic, Hebrew that was taught and spoken.

Before 1961, Hebrew classes at Ramah were taught by the counselors rather than by trained teachers. Using materials developed in-house, they taught conversational Hebrew by focusing on practical, often camp-specific vocabulary and reading comprehension through two modern Hebrew literature series, *Lador Junior Hebrew Library* (Jewish Education Committee Press), and *Sifriah Oneg* (KTAV). In Judaics classes, the weekly Torah portion was studied in the original Hebrew along with selected rabbinic texts that were chosen to reinforce ethics and values, but the language of instruction was supposed to be modern Hebrew (although some teachers used English). The goal was to create a program that was integrated as seamlessly as possible with the United Synagogue's congregational school curriculum.[31]

## RAMAH AS A "PSEUDO-HEBRAIC" ENVIRONMENT

The challenges involved in realizing the founders' vision for Hebrew at camp arose almost immediately. A frank report on the first season at Ramah Wisconsin, in 1947, written by the camp's director, Henry Goldberg, acknowledged that many of the campers did not arrive with a sufficient Hebrew background to implement an entirely immersive Hebrew environment. Goldberg considered the presence of the weak and non-Hebrew speakers at camp to be a violation of the agreed-on admissions criteria, which stipulated that campers should have "a minimum of two years of Hebrew education for the ten year olds, three years for the eleven to fourteen year olds, and four years for the fifteen year olds and above."[32] But Professor Burton Cohen, who began attending Ramah Wisconsin in its inaugural season, observed that even children like himself who attended intensive supplementary schools were typically not Hebrew speakers. For example, the widely used and well-regarded Chicago Board of Jewish Education curriculum emphasized reading comprehension in preparation for classical text study rather than oral and writing skills.[33] From the perspective of early campers, like Cohen and Shelly Switkin, the Hebrew environment was fairly rigid. Switkin recalled that the camp's loudspeaker blasted bugle calls and Hebrew announcements beginning with "*Hakshivu, hakshivu!*" (Attention, attention), throughout the day until the camp's non-Jewish neighbors around the lake complained.[34] Recollections of the Hebrew-rich environment, which was unlike anything they had experienced previously, stuck with many campers long after they became adults, while the backsliding into English that Goldberg recalled faded from memory.

Goldberg's protestations notwithstanding, there seemed to be a tacit admission that the aspirations of the camp around Hebrew conflicted with economic imperatives. Ramah was ultimately a business that catered to a clientele made up overwhelmingly of congregational school students. The nature, quality, and quantity of Hebrew instruction at their schools varied widely. Ramah's organizers needed to walk a fine line between presenting the camps as an elite training ground and intimidating potential customers. The brochures that Ramah disseminated in its early years focused on camp facilities, athletics, and cultural activities, sometimes soft-pedaling the educational activities and Hebrew-speaking nature of the camp. A 1947 brochure included the Hebrew education requirement, but it also sought to reassure anxious parents by marveling that "campers who do not have the ability to converse in Hebrew, but who have adequate comprehension of the language and experience with it, soon acquire a facility in the everyday use of Hebrew that is almost amazing." All the more "amazing" was the fact that the claim was made before the inaugural season when there was not yet any evidence to support it. A 1948 brochure for the second (ill-fated) Camp Ramah, in Maine, reduced the requirement to "two years' education in a congregational school" without explicitly mentioning facility in Hebrew, whereas a brochure for Ramah Poconos, dating from the early 1950s, omitted the entrance requirement altogether.[35]

In addition to the inescapable financial pressures to minimize admissions requirements, Ramah's directors also had to contend with local area rabbis who balked at the notion that their congregants' children might be shut out of the camp on the basis of their weak Hebrew skills. This point was driven home at a 1951 meeting of the Camp Ramah Poconos Committee. Rabbi Leon Lang, spiritual leader of one of Philadelphia's largest congregations, Beth El, and a former president of the Rabbinical Assembly (1940–1942), insisted that "the educational program should be geared to the needs of the pupils from our congregational schools," rather than some unachievable ideal. "Promising children" should be admitted to the camp regardless of their ability to speak Hebrew. Lang's comment suggested that Poconos director Rabbi S. Gershon Levi was attempting to remain faithful to Ramah's Hebrew-speaking vision. Nevertheless, the complaint was echoed at the meeting by other rabbinic supporters of the Poconos venture and could not be ignored.[36]

An internal 1962 report, "Hebrew in the Ramah Camps," written by Ramah Poconos director David Mogilner, demonstrates that the dream of an immersive Hebrew camp remained elusive. Bitingly disparaging the prevalence of code switching and CHE, Mogilner referred to Ramah as a "pseudo-Hebraic environment." His critique may surprise contemporary Ramah staff and supporters, many of whom harbor romanticized views about the extent of Hebrew speaking at Ramah network camps during its early decades. "The general Hebrew environment at camp is from poor to middling," Mogilner began, before listing a series of generalities that he claimed reflected the situation at every Ramah camp. On the one hand, Hebrew was generally accepted as the "official language of camp" and was used for public announcements, in public spaces (e.g., the dining hall), cultural expression (e.g., dramatics, song festivals), religious worship, classes, and general staff meetings. On the other hand, Hebrew was seldom spoken by campers among themselves, and the language of the cabins was primarily English, although counselors attempted to introduce Hebrew during daily routines like cleanup. Programming on a divisional level often "paid tribute to Hebrew" before breaking down into English; instructional activities (e.g., swimming, tennis, arts and crafts) were "seldom if ever" conducted in Hebrew; education-related staff meetings were conducted in English; and general participatory activities like a baseball game or general swim were "run in English to the accompaniment of 5–10 key Hebrew words."[37] Mogilner was describing a camp environment infused with camp Hebraized English.

Significantly, many staff members, including those who worked in the office, kitchen, and maintenance, typically spoke little or no Hebrew, making an immersive environment impossible. The report singled out the counselors as the linchpin of any serious effort to make Ramah a truly Hebrew-speaking camp and observed that they often had weak Hebrew skills and lacked "the will needed" to confront "all the difficulties inherent in the situation." Moreover, most were products of Ramah and its "pseudo-Hebraic environment." They were socialized into the prevailing conditions and viewed them as normal and desirable.

Finally, Mogilner identified a tension between an ideological commitment to training campers to speak Hebrew and the desire to nurture them. The counselors were convinced that their primary role was to tend to their campers' emotional and social well-being. "How can someone be sensitive in a foreign tongue?" Mogilner, a staunch advocate of Hebrew at Ramah, asked rhetorically. "How can a counselor show that he cares for a camper if the camper doesn't understand him?"[38]

This final point is crucial to understanding how Ramah's aims were at cross-purposes. With Louis Newman's arrival as director of Ramah Wisconsin in 1951, character education and concern for the emotional well-being of the child became central to Ramah's mission. Newman began a 1953 director's report by distinguishing Ramah from Massad and Yavneh, where he had previously worked. When he first arrived, "Camp Ramah in Wisconsin was like all other Hebrew-speaking camps, concentrating on having the child learn to use the Hebrew language functionally. Practices were taken in toto" from Massad and Yavneh without "a thorough analysis of whether they fit into the philosophy of the Conservative movement in general, and the specific additional tasks of camp in particular." Newman singled out practices like destructive "raids," and an omnipresent spirit of competition, as well as the counselors' creation of a "country club atmosphere." By invoking fealty to an inexplicit Conservative Jewish philosophy, Newman obscured his own radical transformation of the camp, which was influenced as much if not more by Joshua and Leah Lieberman's nondenominational Pioneer Youth camp as any guidance from his overseers at JTS.[39]

The Liebermans' democratic and noncompetitive camping ethos excited Newman, a student of progressive education who entertained the possibility of working at Pioneer Youth camp before accepting the position at Ramah. His essential work at Wisconsin was to synthesize progressive educational ideology with Ramah's distinctive philosophy. He referred to his approach around camp as *shita ha'mitkadmit*, the progressive method.[40] According to historian Shuly Rubin Schwartz, Newman's staff often portrayed him holding the "Torah in one hand and [a book by John] Dewey in the other." Some of his innovations—allowing campers to design their own program, outside of the mandatory prayer and study components, and eliminating color war—came right out of the Liebermans' playbook.[41]

The tension between Deweyian progressive pedagogy and the commitment to teaching campers to speak Hebrew was palpable. The former emphasized a commitment to individuated development, whereas the latter emerged from a collective ideal. Indeed, the conflict between these two approaches signified a more fundamental tension between mainstream American cultural and pedagogical values and those of Zionism, whether cultural or political. Newman was committed to the Hebraic element of Ramah's program, but his director's reports reveal the challenges he faced in this area. He was keenly aware that because he was dealing with a population that was not Hebrew proficient in the main, his commitment to Hebrew was potentially at odds with his educational agenda. "The more meaningful life at camp is to the children, the more they want to discuss their personal problems of school, home, education, the more difficult it is to restrict them to Hebrew since the vocabulary acquired is one used in classrooms, the bunk, or the ball field," he observed. It became increasingly difficult for counselors to focus on campers' personal growth and character development while being compelled to communicate in a foreign language with a limited vocabulary. Newman also defended a decision to make English the language of instruction in junior counselor education and leadership training classes, presumably because of the complexity of the material. In short, Newman seemed to recognize that value tensions demanded compromise, and he argued for the balancing of priorities even as he allowed that the Hebrew-speaking imperative sometimes outweighed other concerns. He wrote reassuringly that both campers and staff felt a consistent "pressure to speak Hebrew," even more so than in previous years.[42]

Attorney and former camper Alan Silberman recalled that Newman sometimes applied that pressure through the use of theatrics and manipulative sociodramas that may have been at odds with his progressive educational principles. For example, one morning in the early 1950s, the campers were frantically awakened forty-five minutes early to the news of a crisis.

"Wake up, wake up. There's an emergency, emergency." Everybody runs, quick, gets dressed, runs to the center of the camp. There is Shirley Newman [Louis Newman's wife] . . . on top of a little hill, sitting on a chair, crying her heart out. "It's lost, lost. It's lost." Everyone said, "Oh my God, what happened? . . . What's going on?" So then . . . the little *tekes* [ceremony] goes on for another 10 minutes. "What, what?" Finally, she says: "*Ivrit* [Hebrew]."[43]

Hebrew, Shirley Newman bawled, was in danger of being lost at Ramah Wisconsin.

Despite Newman's concern about the decline in speaking Hebrew, Ramah's reputation as a Hebrew-speaking camp intimidated first-time campers like Joel Roth. Convinced that he would starve to death because he did not know enough Hebrew to function in the dining room, the boy who would grow up to become a JTS Talmud professor and rabbinical school dean ran away from camp with his cousin during the first days of the 1953 season. The boys were eventually found in the woods and reassured by their counselor that they would be fed regardless of their Hebrew-speaking ability.[44]

Roth and his cousin might have felt isolated, but their rudimentary Hebrew-speaking skills were hardly anomalous. According to Newman, more than two-thirds of the campers studied functional Hebrew during their formal lessons. "The primary goals set for the teacher were to help the children adequately express themselves in their needs at the table, in the bunk, and in their recreational activities." Grammatical accuracy was deemed a second-tier goal, as was written expression.[45] In an addendum to a 1953 report, Newman offered a window into the methods used in the teaching of functional Hebrew. Counselors used the mundane experiences of camp life to teach basic camp vocabulary and simple grammatical structure. For example, laundry day became an opportunity to teach the children the names of various items of clothing. Mealtime was likewise treated as a teachable moment. Roth and his cousin could be forgiven for being spooked as "*na l'havir et ha'melach*" (please pass the salt) was transformed from a routine act of politeness into a didactic request with ideological undertones (see figure 3.4).[46]

The extent of an individual camper's exposure to and practice with Hebrew probably depended most of all on the aptitude and whims of her counselor. But Newman and his staff worked hard to provide multiple venues and opportunities for Hebrew expression. One of the most important Hebrew innovations under Newman was the introduction of all-Hebrew camper productions of popular American musicals. Although Hebrew dramatics was also a central component of Massad's program, Shulsinger and his staff gravitated in the early years toward original productions with explicit Jewish content or adaptations of works by established Hebrew playwrights. Newman and his dramatics counselor, Leah Abrams, shared a different philosophy. Appreciating the popularity of Ameri-

Figure 3.4. To promote Hebrew speaking, Camp Ramah Wisconsin borrowed the slogan "*Ivri, daber Ivrit!*" (Hebrew person, speak Hebrew!) from the Militia for the Protection of the Language in Mandate Palestine. (Credit: Camp Ramah Wisconsin)

can show tunes, they wagered that teaching campers to sing the songs and deliver the accompanying dialogue in Hebrew would effectively build their vocabulary and demonstrate proper grammatical structure. Abrams, who was a dramatics counselor at Massad, offered to defect to Ramah with her husband Jerome Abrams if Newman would pay her to translate and direct a production of the Rodgers and Hammerstein hit *Oklahoma!* The production proved to be such a sensation that it was performed for the parents on Visitors Day. The following summer, Abrams translated and directed Irving Berlin's *Annie Get Your Gun*. Former campers maintain that the Hebrew that stuck with them over time was just as likely to be snippets of Hebrew show tune lyrics as the conversational Hebrew that was used in the dining room or at the waterfront.[47] To this day, despite the diminution of nonroutinized Hebrew at Ramah, the Hebrew musical remains a highlight of the Ramah camp season (see figure 3.5).[48]

Figure 3.5. Betsey Nodler and Jimmy Winoker performing in Hebrew as the title characters of *Hansel & Gretel* at Ramah Poconos in 1958. (Credit: National Ramah Commission)

Although Newman's tenure as Wisconsin's director lasted only three seasons, he had an outsized influence on the entire Ramah movement because he trained many of its future leaders. The value tensions that Newman identified were further magnified under the leadership of his charismatic successor in Wisconsin, Seymour Fox, and were felt to varying degrees at the camps in Pennsylvania, Connecticut, and California. But as long as counselors were doing double duty as Hebrew teachers, they felt an incentive to reinforce the formal Hebrew program by speaking Hebrew to their campers in both public and private settings. Former campers who attended Ramah in the mid- to late 1950s recalled that "Hebrew was a serious business." Although in most cases, English remained the language of communication between campers, the public language of the camps was Hebrew. Campers were encouraged to speak Hebrew even if it was riddled with grammatical errors. Ramah Poconos' educational director in the mid-1950s, Matthew Mosenkis, playfully referred to this as "*ivrit im shgiyim*" (Hebrew with errors), purposely using an incorrectly gendered plural. Among his son Robert's most amusing memories as a Poconos counselor was sitting with his bunk in the dining hall when he noticed one of his campers' faces turning green. The boy's hand shot up, and he managed to blurt out, "*Ani tzarich* [I need to], um, how do you say 'throw up' *b'ivrit*?" before he heaved his lunch.[49]

## "Vision at the Heart"

Ramah's approach to political Zionism underwent a shift in the 1960s, allowing its leaders to increasingly look eastward to help address the chasm between intent and reality regarding the place of Hebrew at camp. The most tangible expression of this shift was the creation of the Summer Shlichim (Emissaries) Program in 1965–1966 (which we discuss in greater detail in chapter 7). Its origins can be traced to a practical need for more Hebrew-speaking staff members at Camp Ramah. Along with the inauguration in 1962 of the Ramah Seminar in Israel, the establishment of the Summer Shlichim Program was designed to foster campers' sense of connection to Israel and its Jewish population. Indeed, this rationale was more central to the Israeli government's support for the initiative than the strengthening of Diaspora Hebrew education.[50]

But even as Hebrew at Ramah received a boost from the Israeli emissaries and from the expanding profile of Israel at the camps, its status as the public language of Ramah was undermined and contested by disparate forces. First and foremost, there were difficulties recruiting Hebrew-speaking American staff. By this time, many of the staff were homegrown or products of other Conservative movement institutions, not necessarily fluent Hebrew speakers. Some directors were reluctant to turn away former campers with weak Hebrew skills who applied to be counselors. Those who were unmoved by loyalty or sentimentalism were frequently swayed by a financial motive: staff often came to camp bringing along their full-paying younger siblings.[51]

When possible, staff members with weak Hebrew skills did not serve as bunk counselors, but some directors did not have the luxury of being picky. Following the growth of Conservative Judaism in the postwar decades, Ramah expanded rapidly in the 1960s, adding four new camps—Canada (1960); Nyack, New York (1961); Berkshires, New York (1964); and Glen Spey, New York (1967)— and more than doubling its capacity. By 1970, the Ramah camps boasted an enrollment of close to 4,000 campers and an annual operating budget that topped $2 million. Rabbi Simon Greenberg mused in the late 1960s that "if we can ever establish twenty Ramah camps throughout the country, we will succeed in virtually reshaping the very nature and character of the American Jewish community."[52] But in truth, the camps were spread perilously thin. Directors in the larger camps were compelled to accept virtually all applicants for counselor positions, regardless of their Hebrew proficiency. Even some of the Judaic studies faculty at the camps were not strong Hebrew speakers. Critics implored that greater emphasis be placed on quality control, even if it meant scaling back enrollment. But rising operating and renovation costs, as well as the need to make regular loan payments, prevented the national office from putting the brakes on the growth. Only a decline in applicants in the early 1970s compelled Ramah to consolidate by selling off Glen Spey and dispersing its campers to Ramah New England and Ramah Berkshires.[53]

In retrospect, it is not surprising that by the 1960s some members of the Ramah teaching staff were using English as the language of instruction in their standard-level Jewish studies classes. Rabbi Neal Kaunfer, who directed the education program in New England between 1964 and '68, explained that as the curriculum became more conceptual and learning tasks were developed around the affective as well as cognitive domains, teaching in Hebrew became untenable for all but the most advanced Hebrew speakers. Campers in Ramah New England were grouped by Hebrew ability at the beginning of the summer, which allowed the advanced track, made up primarily of day school students, as well as products of Boston's intensive afternoon school system and Philip "Shraga" Arian's afternoon school at Albany's Temple Israel, to pursue a Hebrew immersion program. In the regular track, by contrast, class conversations were conducted in English as campers dissected select biblical texts, relating to the biblical characters and discussing issues of morality and ethical behavior. "If you are going to ask kids what they think about the family dynamics in the Joseph story, that requires thought and expression. Most of the kids simply could not express themselves on that level," Kaunfer stated.[54]

Although Ramah's growth and effective transformation from an elite to a mass camping movement undermined efforts to bolster spoken Hebrew, the diminution of Hebrew at Ramah predated the growing pains of the 1960s. Fox, the dominant force guiding the direction of the Ramah camps between 1954 and 1967, never disavowed the centrality of Hebrew, at least on a rhetorical level. But in practice, Hebrew speaking was deprioritized when it was perceived to be in tension with other priorities. "From the fifties on it was clear that because our campers knew very little Hebrew and our counselors were not comfortable with the Hebrew language, Hebrew would lose in the competition with other goals of the camp."[55] Fox, whose own Hebrew skills were middling, was even more candid in his 2000 monograph about how he tried to actualize his vision for Ramah. Citing, once again, the camping movement's built-in handicaps, he also conceded that Hebrew simply was not his highest priority: "I must accept some of the blame for this failure. My attitude was: If there's a conflict between understanding ideas and learning the language, let's go for understanding."[56]

Fox's graduate studies at the University of Chicago and scholarly work in education profoundly shaped his influence on Ramah and thus on a generation of counselors and campers. When he joined the staff of Ramah Wisconsin as a junior counselor advisor in 1953, he was a rabbinical student at JTS who had completed his coursework toward his PhD in education at the University of Chicago, under the direction of Joseph Schwab. In the early years, Fox extended Newman's experiment in democratic living and self-actualization and routinized counselors' study of educational psychology and philosophy as a feature of the camp's professional development program. Ramah under Fox was summed up in an image offered by educational psychologist and former Ramah counselor Joseph Reimer of counselors struggling to "figure out how to handle campers' homesickness and aggressiveness" by sitting under a tree reading Dewey and Schwab.[57] Newman and Fox were symptomatic of a trend at Ramah to hire senior staff with backgrounds in teaching and educational psychology, which indirectly occasioned a revaluation of Hebrew's priority.

Fox gave up his directorship in 1956 when he became a JTS administrator, but he assumed an oversight role and convened a winter seminar for camp directors to discuss Ramah's educational principles and direction while parsing works of educational philosophy and social and developmental psychology.[58] During the early 1960s, he invited Schwab, a curriculum reform expert, to lead intensive seminars for camp leaders in which they debated and re-envisioned the mission and educational approach of the camps. Enticed by "a living laboratory in which to try out [his] ideas," the "friendly critic" encouraged directors to replace Newman's democratic, noncompetitive camp model with a dialectical approach whereby specialist-led interest groups provided settings for campers to hone their skills while counselors created a nurturing cabin environment or "home haven" that provided support and refuge, an experiment in character development and self-actualization.[59]

## FROM A HEBREW-SPEAKING CAMP TO A CAMP
## WHERE HEBREW IS SPOKEN

Significantly, while Fox's seminars professionalized Ramah from an educational perspective, they generally did not engage with Jewish texts and avoided discussion of pertinent contemporary Jewish issues. "In all those get-togethers, there wasn't anything dealing with *tefillah* (prayer), Talmud, Torah, any of this stuff, except indirectly," former Ramah New England director Ray Arzt recalled. "That was, on one hand, the strength because we became very serious educators, practical educators. But on the other hand, we did not enter into the *pardes*, into the labyrinth of Jewish meaning and possibilities."[60] The discussions also did little to further conversations about the place of Hebrew; in fact, the implementation of the Schwabian framework discouraged counselors from fomenting disequilibrium in the cabin by treating it as a pedagogic as opposed to a nurturing environment, thereby de facto discouraging Hebrew instruction. Former Ramah counselor Rabbi Elliot Dorff, currently the rector of American Jewish University, explained that even though the "home haven" model allowed the counselor to establish expectations, like participating in cleanup or speaking Hebrew in the dining room, "in one's home one needs to be accepted and loved for who one is as a person and as a member of the group, regardless of one's talents and abilities or lack thereof." A savvy counselor could encourage Hebrew speaking in the way she offered and withheld approval. But ultimately, she needed to give her campers unconditional love and make herself available for "moments of true dialogue," heart-to-heart conversations where campers could safely express their feelings of vulnerability.[61]

Potok, who experimented with the Schwabian framework as head of the oldest division (*Machon*) at Ramah Nyack in 1963, observed, "Outside of the dining room, spoken Hebrew had virtually disappeared from the *Machon* by the fifth week [of camp]." He and his staff were left to ponder whether "the goal of self-realization" was inimical "to any intensive dealing with solely Jewish questions." After all, "the framework was essentially a humanistic one. . . . The problem became: how do we link the moment of self-realization to Judaism?" Potok's suggestion that the challenge be addressed by introducing Jewish source material into discussions of human relations was greeted enthusiastically and affected practice moving forward. But no satisfactory answer was offered to address the perceived artificiality of using Hebrew for character education.[62] It was much easier for counselors to give directions in Hebrew than to conduct existential debates or establish deep emotional connections with their charges in Hebrew.

Also in play was the changing American Jewish zeitgeist. By the late 1960s and 1970s, much of the youthful energy in Jewish religious life was emanating from the havurah movement, which was interpreted as a reaction to the suburban bourgeois Judaism that predominated in many Conservative synagogues.

Havurah members rejected hierarchical models of Jewish organizational life in favor of a do-it-yourself Jewish ethos that emphasized autonomy, spirituality, and social justice. Ramah New England director Ray Arzt was the first to infuse his camp with this new spirit by hiring personalities like former Lubavitcher emissary and spiritual seeker Rabbi Zalman Schachter, who taught the campers to make their own colorful *talesim* (prayer shawls).

In 1968, Schachter joined a new experimental spiritual community in Somerville, Massachusetts, called Havurat Shalom, which was disproportionately comprised of young people who grew up in and had become disillusioned with the Conservative movement. Arzt brought a contingent of havurah members, including founder Rabbi Arthur Green and author Jim Sleeper, to Ramah New England during the summers of 1968 and '69. Although the havurah members were not inimical to Hebrew, it did not figure heavily in their countercultural Jewish experimentation. Internalizing the New Left's critique of Israel as an occupying power with colonial designs on Arab lands in the aftermath of the 1967 Six Day War, havurah members also did not make Israel a focal point of their Jewish identities. Indeed, the ambivalence about Israel among havurah-affiliated Ramah staff members was a source of friction between them and the Israeli emissaries, who were employed at camp largely to reinforce the Ramah movement's Hebrew-speaking ambitions. Hebrew enthusiasts were already facing an uphill battle winning over older campers who were far more interested in American countercultural currents and the antiwar movement. Ramah senior staff engaged in network-wide policy discussions around sex and drugs in the late 1960s and even enlisted Joseph Schwab's advice when setting policy. (Schwab's recommendation of forbearance was not well received by the senior staff.) In 1969, the oldest division in New England staged an English-language production of the rock-musical *Hair*, which scandalized some Ramah supporters and offered a revealing commentary about Hebrew's failure in the battle for hearts and minds.[63]

Joseph Wouk, who played Claude, one of the show's leads, recalled the production as exhilarating but unremarkable, and in many respects he was correct. The script that the Ramah actors worked from was expurgated of profanity, and the nudity that engendered controversy in the Broadway production was omitted. The show was not performed for the younger campers, and it generated little heat or open pushback in the moment from the scholar-in-residence or the teaching staff. But the show, which was thematically transgressive in its celebration of youth culture and generational rebellion, was performed in English rather than Hebrew, an unprecedented violation of Ramah tradition. If that seemed natural to Wouk and his friends, it was because very little else was in Hebrew that summer. Wouk observed that most of his bunkmates could hardly put a Hebrew sentence together and would have been lost if the play were staged in Hebrew.[64] One of Wouk's division heads that summer, Joseph Reimer, acknowledged, "Hebrew played a very minor role in our ideology. We were interested in exploring Judaism as a liberation force. We were interested in giving older kids more choice at camp. We were interested in exploring music and the spirit."[65]

It was only when the production was sensationalized by the camp's critics that it became a subject of controversy and a public relations nightmare, contributing to JTS's decision to close Ramah New England in 1971 and reopen it under new leadership in 1972. In truth, the camp administration's inability or unwillingness to clamp down on other facets of American youth culture at the camp, including marijuana use and sexual experimentation, weighed more heavily on the minds of the national leaders who felt compelled to clean house. But *Hair* was a convenient shorthand for Ramah's perceived ills: it served as a rallying cry. Both thematically and linguistically, staging *Hair* was an act of defiance, a brazen and highly public challenge to Ramah's values. The impassioned reaction of critics, including parents, Conservative movement leaders, and seminary officials, to the production underscored the symbolic role of Hebrew at Ramah. The wholesale flaunting of conventions around Hebrew usage at Ramah New England signaled a structural breakdown that was perceived by internal and external critics as a fundamental threat to Ramah as an idea and as an embodiment of a value system, in a way that rule violations around sex and drug use were not.

Arzt's assistant, Robert Abramson, who became Ramah New England's director in 1970, confided to one observer that "*Hair* contributed most to the sense of the end of Jewishness because it was the most visible thing and it broke the tradition of Hebrew plays which was the last bastion of Hebrew at camp."[66] Abramson's conflation of Hebrew and Jewishness is telling. Educational anthropologist Zvi Bekerman, who conducted fieldwork at Ramah New England during the summer of 1983, found that staff and campers alike routinely and reflexively associated speaking Hebrew with Jewishness. When he asked, "What is Jewish about camp?" his respondents were as likely to point to the use of Hebrew in calling balls and strikes at a baseball game or playing Israeli music while doing aerobics as they were observance of the Sabbath or engagement in Torah study.[67] Bekerman grasped the reductive nature of their formulation; setting and context, he observed, imbued various instances of camp Hebrew usage with a Jewish or secular valence. But it would be a mistake to summarily dismiss the ideologies of Diaspora community members—in this case, Ramah staff and campers— that using a heritage language can heighten feelings of ethnocultural belonging even when the words and subject matter are quotidian. In the case of Ramah staff and campers, this association was reinforced by the value and importance that camp leaders placed on Hebrew speaking. Their directives about Hebrew use, even when honored in the breach, elevated and coded it as a Jewish activity.

If the diminution of Hebrew at Ramah New England, particularly among the older campers, constituted an extreme case, longtime Ramah director Rabbi

Jerome Abrams identified the mid- to late 1960s as the point of no return, when immersion definitively gave way to infusion throughout the Ramah camping system, even in Ramah's public culture.[68] The trend accelerated in the 1970s and '80s. Ramah did not operate in a vacuum, and Conservative congregational school educators were increasingly reassessing their Hebrew-centered curricula, as they were confronted with damning reports about student outcomes. After twenty years of closing their eyes, they felt forced to confront the mismatch between their ambitious curricular aims and the declining number of teaching hours. By this time, Ramah was attracting a growing contingent of day school students. In an earlier generation, these youngsters would have provided a nucleus of Hebrew speakers, as they did at Massad. But the commitment to *Ivrit b'Ivrit* (Hebrew as the language of instruction in Judaic studies courses) was waning even in day schools.

Author William Novak, who attended Ramah camps in the mid-1960s, offered a trenchant critique of the place of Hebrew at Ramah camps in a 1972 *Response* magazine article:

> Hebrew at Ramah has ceased to be a language; it is merely a specialized vocabulary. A great deal of effort is spent on teaching children a series of Hebrew nouns: the words for butter, cheese, milk, water, boat, swimming, and an amazing list of specialized words: dustpan, sculpture, sandpaper, archery, diving boards, and so on. Because of the emphasis on the particular vocabulary, Ramah has succeeded only in Judaizing, or Hebraizing, a child's English vocabulary. Ramah campers learn how to do everything in Hebrew except . . . talk![69]

However derisively, Novak was describing the triumph of infusion and CHE over immersion. With the zeal of a true believer he implored Ramah's leadership to teach modern Hebrew or abandon the "legal fiction" that Ramah was a Hebrew-speaking camp. "We have a situation where children go around all day, picking up words like pennies of UNICEF and putting them in an English paper bag." Making an argument that is sometimes heard today by critics of Hebrew infusion, Novak suggested that it was better to teach youngsters to say *"Ani holech i'* [I am going to the] swimming pool" than "I am going to the *breicha* [swimming pool]." The former sentence he characterized as "more or less, Hebrew," because it was modeling language structure, whereas the latter, he complained, was essentially English. "We must remember that Hebrew is a language, not a series of words." He concluded his diatribe by noting bitterly, "And, of course, every time there is an 'important' announcement (at least twice an hour), it is in English. *Of course.* That way they'll understand."[70]

As Shandler's work on postvernacularity suggests, the presence of Hebrew vocabulary in CHE also signifies Hebrew's importance to the speakers or at least to camp leaders.[71] And Novak's critique notwithstanding, Ramah camps continued to telegraph the importance of Hebrew by maintaining its use in public spaces. In the mid-1980s, Bekerman reported that CHE was ubiquitous at Ramah New England, whereas Hebrew speaking was typically confined to senior staff meetings, public announcements, and frontal presentations at communal or unit-wide events. Hebrew also remained the language of public, choreographed, and routinized performances, including prayer, song, and dramatics presentations. In addition, Hebrew was frequently used in written communications, such as the daily staff bulletins distributed at breakfast, although security- or safety-related instructions and information otherwise deemed important were communicated in English. According to Bekerman, campers were exposed to little or no Hebrew speaking in their cabins or during activities. Even activities like wake-up and cleanup that were supposed to be conducted in Hebrew were not. Daily Judaics classes were taught in English to ensure camper comprehension and encourage participation. In the dining room, campers seldom used full Hebrew sentences at their tables unless they were poking fun at the Hebrew-only rule, in which case requests in Hebrew to pass food or drink were followed by "humorous expressions" or "giggling." As for the Hebrew announcements, Bekerman found that "campers do not pay much attention . . . for they know that if anything important is said it will be repeated in English by the counselors or division heads." In general, the counselors (even veterans who rose through the camper ranks) were dubious of the camp's official Hebrew policy.[72] To be sure, Hebrew had its champions among the senior staff, and Hebrew mastery was a point of pride and a source of cultural capital. At the same time, for many administrators Hebrew was, at best, one goal among many. Speaking Hebrew at camp was a habitual but somewhat shallow artifact of camp life. "It was part of the camp ritual," Abramson explained in 1989. But routinization can breed apathy; Hebrew at Ramah, the longtime Ramah director worried, "seems to be going the way of many rituals":

> There are those who are loyal to it out of a sense of tradition; some engage in nostalgia, remembering and wishing for the old days. Others talk about coming to terms with the present. But what is most characteristic of the time when rituals seem atrophied is that few, if any, feel the force of the original decision. Many cannot even articulate a reason for continuing such rituals as dining-hall announcements in Hebrew, non-understood daily memos in Hebrew, and Hebrew signs. They accept these facts as "part of Ramah." When rituals go unexamined, when they are not renewed and enriched in their transmittal, they become ossified. They lose their vibrancy and potency. They cease to capture commitment and to engender dedication.[73]

It is unclear whether Abramson recognized that the same critique could be made about religious rituals, like the observance of *Tisha B'Av*, a fast commemorating the destruction of the ancient Jerusalem temples and the loss of Jewish sovereignty that is observed in late July or August (the date determined by the Jewish calendar) and seemed superfluous to some in the wake of the establishment of Israel in 1948 and the extension of Israeli rule to East Jerusalem, including the Old City, after the 1967 war. In that case, rather than eliminate the fast, the camps made a concerted effort to revitalize it, expanding the observance to commemorate other historical tragedies, such as the Spanish Expulsion and the Holocaust. Of course, the abandonment of many religious rituals was deemed untenable, given Ramah's fealty to *halacha* (traditional Jewish law). This suggests that Hebrew fell lower on the hierarchy of priorities than religious observance, thus reinforcing the distinction between Ramah and Massad Poconos, where Hebrew had intrinsic rather than instrumental value. Indeed, this distinction allowed Ramah to adapt more easily than Massad to changing conditions, including the declining number of prospective Hebrew-speaking campers and counselors.

Other Hebrew-speaking camps were similarly challenged by these larger trends. By the early 1980s, even Yavneh, which had been sustained for decades by a steady influx of campers from Boston's network of rigorous Hebraic supplementary schools, was finding it difficult to attract equipped campers and competent staff. Margie Berkowitz, a Yavneh camper in the 1950s, attempted to restore the camp's Hebrew-speaking focus when she served as director from 1984 to 1986. "I came in with all the nostalgia of wanting to make it a Hebrew camp again," Berkowitz recalled. "I was trying everything: games, prizes, anything. But the bottom line was we were never going to go back to that. It just wasn't going to happen. This breaking your teeth on the Hebrew language started not to make any sense, and there was no staff to really implement it, so it gradually died away."[74]

By 1991, the camp was carrying a $40,000 debt and only operating at one-third capacity. Yavneh was at a crossroads: either close its doors or reinvent itself as a Hebrew-infused Jewish culture camp. The camp board chose the latter course and hired a director with strong fundraising and managerial skills and a deep commitment to the camp's religiously pluralistic and Zionist environment, but who was not a fluent Hebrew speaker. "I describe the camp today as a camp where Hebrew is spoken, not a Hebrew-speaking camp," explained the director, Debbie Sussman, while showing us around the camp in 2015.[75] We heard Hebrew announcements in the dining room, Hebrew songs taught for the annual *zimriya* (song festival), and Hebrew instructions from the longtime waterfront director at the lake; yet the predominant language was English, albeit a dialect thoroughly infused with what campers and counselors called "Yavneh Hebrew." Reflecting on changing attitudes toward the Hebrew language since she was a camper in the 1950s, Berkowitz explained, "It was heartbreaking, but I realize now that unlike when I was a camper, these kids can go to ulpan in Israel. We were saving the Hebrew language. That was the idea. We were the saving remnant not knowing what was going to come ahead."[76] By the 1980s and '90s,

Hebrew no longer needed "saving," and in any case, American Jewish campers and counselors were in no position to serve as saviors. Like Ramah, Yavneh's leadership reluctantly conceded that changing realities demanded shifting priorities.

Crucially, as Ramah campers and counselors were moving away from non-routinized Hebrew expression, they remained avid and reflexive speakers of Ramah CHE, a dialect that was richly studded with Hebrew nouns, expressions, and formulaic Hebrew sentences. Administrators instinctively used this camp dialect in their conversations and official communications, even as they routinely implored counselors to speak Hebrew to their charges.[77] This is the situation at Ramah camps today: it is a primarily English environment in which Hebrew is heavily infused throughout the day and session—in prayer, song, theater, (mostly routinized) announcements, and loanwords, most relating to camp referents. An additional element has endured throughout the decades: a tension between ideology and practice as leaders debate how much Hebrew to use while still maintaining a viable business model.

———

Our historical analysis, including three case studies—Reform, Massad, and Ramah camps—has shown how camp leaders have deployed Hebrew in diverse ways to serve various educational purposes and how they have adapted over time to changing circumstances in Jewish education, American culture, and Israel. Our analyses have also pointed to several themes, including ideological tensions and the role of entertainment and hybridity in Hebrew infusion. In part II, we explore these themes in greater depth, based on surveys, interviews, and observations we conducted between 2012 and 2015.

PART II

# Present

# CHAPTER 4

# A Flexible Signifier

## DIVERSITY IN HEBREW INFUSION AND IDEOLOGY

Jeffrey, an administrator at Moshava Malibu, a Bnei Akiva (modern Orthodox Zionist) camp in California, said something we heard from many interviewees in our contemporary research. In explaining how Moshava uses Hebrew, he compared it to other camps: "There are other Orthodox summer camps that don't use the Hebrew words; . . . most of the for-profit summer camps on the East Coast, in fact, don't use any of the Hebrew words. Like, they call *chadar ochel* 'dining hall' and they call *roshei edah* 'division heads.' We don't use those terms . . . because of our connection to Israel." Just as there is a spectrum of religiosity in Jewish camps from secular to Haredi Orthodox, and of Zionist orientation from no Israel content to encouraging aliyah, so too do camps fall on a spectrum when it comes to Hebrew. In some camps, Hebrew use is limited to a few words and phrases, like *Shabbat shalom* and *sheket b'vakasha*, and a few blessings or songs. At the other end of the spectrum, in the most Hebrew-rich camps, announcements and other activities are conducted in nonroutinized Hebrew, and Hebrew is used often in games and performances. But our analysis consists of more than placing camps on a Hebrew continuum on the basis of quantity. At each camp, individuals have varying understandings of what Hebrew means, and they make decisions (conscious and unconscious) about which types and expressions of Hebrew to use and when to use them. Hebrew acts as a flexible signifier—a symbol that can be tailored for diverse purposes—enabling Jewish camps to distinguish themselves and emphasize particular forms of American Jewishness.[1]

This chapter begins with ethnographic portraits of Hebrew use at three contemporary camps, based on our brief visits in 2015: Habonim Dror Camp Galil, a small, progressive Zionist camp in Pennsylvania (est. 1946); Beber Camp, a medium-sized, independent, pluralistic camp in Wisconsin (est. 1976); and Camp Sternberg, a large Orthodox girls' camp in New York (est. 1964). These descriptions touch on several aspects of infusion that are developed later in the book: the hybrid and entertaining nature of camp Hebrew use, the privileging of fragmentary and routinized engagement with Hebrew over proficiency; diverse visual displays of Hebrew dotting the camp landscape; Israeli staff members taking leadership roles in infusion; and leaders' concerns about campers feeling included. But the main intention of these descriptions is to demonstrate diversity: the three camps all use Hebrew-influenced English and other Hebrew practices, but in different ways and with different objectives.

We then show how these three camps' diverse orientations represent broader trends by presenting findings from our survey, interviews, and observations at many camps. Hebrew use varies based on the camp's network, religiosity, and orientation toward Israel and—within each camp—according to situation, topic, and speaker. In addition, we analyze how leaders and campers understand the multiple meanings of Hebrew. At camps of many types, we heard similar discourses of building Jewish identity and connections to Israel and the Jewish people. But they mobilize Hebrew in diverse ways, with an eye to aligning themselves with or distinguishing themselves from other camps or Jewish subgroups. This unity and diversity are reflective of the broader American Jewish community. Diverse Jewish groups communicate primarily in English, incorporating some Hebrew loanwords and routinized Hebrew recitation, but they do so in diverse ways, depending on their orientations toward religiosity, Israel, and other factors.

### THREE ETHNOGRAPHIC PORTRAITS
#### *Camp Galil: A Hebrew-Rich American Kibbutz*

Although Camp Galil is located in Pennsylvania, several aspects of the campgrounds evoke an Israeli kibbutz from the mid-twentieth century. The infirmary is called the *marp*, a clipping of *marpe'a*, a word used in kibbutzim, in contrast to the more common Israeli Hebrew *mirpaa*. A barn-like building is called the *refet* (cowshed), even though no animals currently live there. Four sheep graze next to a vegetable garden, which is labeled with bilingual signs ("גזר—carrots," "חסה—lettuce," etc.). The cabins and tents, known as *tzrifim* and *ohels/ohalim*, are named after Israeli kibbutzim: *Gezer, Grofit, Yizre'el*. The dining hall is labeled with a hand-painted sign in cursive Hebrew letters: *chadar ochel*, like the communal dining halls in kibbutzim. A banner draped over the railing of the dining hall identifies the camp and movement, "Camp Galil Habonim Dror," and the camp tagline: "The Spirit of Kibbutz Close to Home." In contrast to the classical Zionist notion of Israel as the Jewish home, home here refers to America. Even so, the designers of the camp have heavily infused the American terrain with Hebrew and other elements of Israeli kibbutzim. Like CHE, the space is hybrid.

As part of the Habonim Dror Labor Zionist youth movement and with historic ties to the kibbutz movement, Galil is driven by a socialist ideology. Staff strive to create a cooperative living experience in which campers share money and snacks through the *kupa* (communal fund) system and are empowered to take collective responsibility for their camp. They learn about American society, Jewish history, and the Israeli-Palestinian conflict through a progressive, social justice lens. Campers are told that some alumni of the camp and movement have made aliyah and joined both long-standing and new kibbutzim in Israel.

In addition to its kibbutz-related symbols, the camp emphasizes the importance of Israel and Hebrew with its many printed and handwritten signs in a combination of English and Hebrew, sometimes in Hebrew letters—block or cursive—and sometimes in transliteration. In the office building, rooms are called by their Hebrew names, such as *cheder chinuch* (education room). A stack of paper is labeled "Scrap Paper—נייר סקרפ" (*niyar scrap*). Cubbies for the age-based divisions are identified with their Hebrew names, without translations: *Amelim* (workers), *Chotrim* (rowers), *Tsofim* (scouts), and so on. A schedule posted on the wall lists daily activities mostly in Hebrew, such as *Hashkama* (wake-up), *Menucha* (rest), and *Aruchat Erev* (dinner). The *moadon* (clubhouse) has a banner with words in English and transliterated Hebrew and Arabic, "Shalom, Peace, Salaam," indicating the camp's interest in the Israeli-Palestinian peace process. A sign on a bathroom entreats users in Hebrew, transliteration, and English to make their presence known: "סליחה, יש מישהו בשרותים? *Slicha, yesh mishehoo basherutim?* Excuse me, is there someone in the bathroom?" On the bottom in smaller letters is a reminder for the "Hebrew" person to "speak Hebrew": "עברי—דבר עברית! *Ivri—Daber Ivrit!*" This imperative sentence, also heard in the dining hall whenever someone making announcements slips into English, originated in 1930s Mandate Palestine, where it was used in the Militia for the Protection of the Language's campaign to enforce monolingual Hebrew-language policies among the multilingual Jewish population.[2] Participants may associate references like these with Israel, whether or not they recognize them as archaic.

Although Hebrew and Israel are present throughout camp, they are central at the mini-*moadon*, also known as *cheder Yisrael* (Israel room). A dozen small Israeli flags decorate the building's entrance. Inside are more Israeli flags, maps of Israel (all identifying the Green Line separating Israel and the West Bank), a large timeline of military operations and other significant dates in Israel's history, and a poster identifying Israel's youth movements in English, Hebrew, and Arabic. There are Hebrew games, a hand-drawn Hebrew Bazooka (a chewing gum popular in Israel) cartoon, a Hebrew alphabet poster, and a bulletin board labeled *Ivrit Shimushit—עברית שימושית* (functional Hebrew), on which pink index cards present Hebrew words that Israeli and American counselors had introduced in daily humorous word-of-the-day skits involving elaborate plots, short songs like "Are you ready for *Ivrit Shimushit*?" and homophony (e.g., *boker tov* [good morning] and "broke your toes").

In addition to the written Hebrew found throughout the camp, Galil infuses its activities with spoken Hebrew announcements and loanwords. The camp handbook, sent to parents and campers before the summer, includes a glossary of sixty-nine Hebrew words and phrases used at camp with this preface: "At camp (machaneh) you will find that we use a lot of Hebrew to designate the various places in camp and the names of the various activities during the day. In addition, we use it to ask for things at meals, to make announcements, and for cheers and songs. But all of this, though it may seem strange at first, will become very natural in just a few days, believe it or not! The words are very easy to learn because we use them all the time."

Indeed, this is what we observed on a Saturday evening at Galil. When we arrived, campers were finishing a discussion in the *kikar*, an open area where many activities take place. The conversation was in English, but at the end, the leader switched to Hebrew for a routinized announcement: "*Achshav kulam na lavo la'aruchat erev* [Now everybody please come to dinner]" (translations in brackets are ours). Campers filed into the dining room and found seats at the long wooden tables. Micah, a young man wearing a purple *kipah* (which was conspicuous, because most men were bareheaded), announced the menu in English, and the campers and counselors took turns walking to the buffet to fill their plates. The conversations were in English, but as soon as dinner was over, Hebrew dominated the *hodaot* (announcements). Micah stood on a bench and began, "*Shabbat shalom, Machaneh Galil* [Peaceful Sabbath, Camp Galil]. *Acharei aruchat erev, yesh lanu chofesh* [After dinner, we have free time]." The campers cheered, and Micah continued: "*Acharei chofesh, yesh lanu kumzits* [After free time, we have a (mellow) song session]." The noise level in the room rose, and Micah complained in English, "I'm not gonna talk over you. Be quiet." After the campers quieted down, he continued in English, offering nonroutinized information: "We're gonna be in a circle in front of the mini-*mo* [short for *moadon*, clubhouse]. If it's raining, we'll be in the *moadon*." Then he switched back to Hebrew for the more routinized announcements: "*Acharei kumzits, yesh lanu medura* [After the song session, we have a talent show]" (*medura* literally means "campfire," and the camp often has its talent show around a campfire). "*Acharei medura, yesh lanu glida!* [After the talent show, we have ice cream!]." The camp chanted in response: "*Glida, glida, ani ohev glida!* [Ice cream, ice cream, I love ice cream!]."

After free time, campers formed a large circle in front of the mini-*mo* (it was not raining). They sang several mellow American English songs with a 1970s folk feel, including "Iowa," "Wagon Wheel," and "Angel from Montgomery." Amanda, a young woman wearing jeans and a t-shirt, announced, "*Achshav yesh lanu Havdalah* [Now we have the end-of-Shabbat ceremony]." The ritual began with a song in Hebrew and English. Everyone stood up, held hands, and walked in spiral formations, singing,

*Lo yisa goy el goy cherev* [nation shall not lift up sword against nation]
*Lo yilmedu od milchama* [neither shall they learn war any more].
Don't walk in front of me, I may not follow.
Don't walk behind me, I may not lead.
Just walk beside me and be my friend,
And together we will walk in peace again.[3]

When some campers became rowdy, Amanda stopped the song and said, in English, "This is a very Jewish ritual that we do every week. Don't talk."

After "*Lo Yisa Goy*," Amanda began the next part of the ritual: "Lie on a friend if they say yes." Most campers and counselors rested their heads on friends' bellies, some in clusters of five or six. Everyone seemed relaxed, and conversations ceased. Another counselor played a calm English song on an iPod with speakers— Coconut Records' "Going Back Home to the West Coast." After a few more mellow songs, someone began the Hebrew *Havdalah* blessings: "*Hinei el yeshuati*" (Behold, God is my savior). Campers and counselors sat up, put their arms around each other's shoulders, and sang enthusiastically. Before each blessing, someone shouted the object of the blessing: "Spices!" "Fire!" They sang "*Shavua Tov*" (good week), and everyone stood up and exchanged hugs. Next, they sang "*Eliyahu Hanavi*" (Elijah the Prophet), including a new feminist verse that highlights a female prophet: "*Miriam haneviah, tirkod itanu l'taken et ha'olam* [Miriam the prophetess, dance with us to repair the world]." The mood shifted from ceremonial to celebratory as they began the upbeat 1950s song "Everybody Loves Saturday Night." After the first verse in English, they sang it in several other languages and styles, beginning with a shout-out of the next language: "Hebrew! *Kol echad ohev motsey shabat* . . . French! *Tout le monde aime* . . . Spanish! *Todo el mundo* . . . Mandarin! *Renrenay shishi* . . . Nigerian![4] *Bobowaro* . . . Arabic! *Kuluwahad ohov* . . . Latin! *Quizcunotem* . . . British: Everybo'ey . . . Underwater! . . . Ironic!"

Next, they proceeded to the *medura*, at which groups of campers and counselors performed mostly improvised skits in CHE (e.g., "going on a *tiyul* [hike]," "a new *avodah* [job] of cleaning the *bet tzevet* [staff house]"). When a performer spoke too quietly, a counselor in the back shouted, "*Lo shomim!* [We can't hear!]." And when audience members made too much noise, others shouted, "*Sheket!* [Quiet!]." To congratulate performers after a good skit, the audience chanted, "*Haya tov, haya tov, haya tov meod* [It was good, it was good, it was very good]." Then, as promised, the evening's official activities ended with the much-anticipated *glida* (ice cream).

What can we learn from just a few hours on a Saturday evening about the role of Hebrew at Galil? First, we see the deployment of liturgical Hebrew in one of Galil's few instances of religious observance. Even in the absence of prayer services found at many other camps, Hebrew blessings over wine and candles bookend Shabbat. Second, modern Hebrew is an integral component of Galil's culture, representing its Zionist orientation. Whereas many activities—meals, soccer games, and discussions about Jewish history and identity—are conducted primarily in English, modern Hebrew loanwords, mostly nouns, are ubiquitous, and routinized announcements in the dining hall and between activities are mostly in modern Hebrew. Third, the singing of folk and peace songs and the occasional Arabic signs reflect Galil's left-wing politics and focus on Palestinian concerns.

Based on the use of so many Hebrew signs and full Hebrew sentences in announcements, one might conclude that Galil considers Hebrew proficiency an important educational goal. On the contrary, the administrator who responded to our survey considered strengthening proficiency in spoken modern Hebrew as only a minor goal. So why is Hebrew so central to the Galil experience? Camp tradition is part of the answer. The Habonim movement has been infusing the camp experience with Hebrew loanwords and songs since the first camps opened in the 1930s,[5] and current participants are eager to continue this and other traditions that give Galil and the wider movement their unique character. In addition, we find an answer in the goals Galil does consider primary: enhancing personal Jewish identity, strengthening connection to the Jewish people, and strengthening connection to the state of Israel. The camp sees Hebrew infusion as a means of achieving these goals. According to a Habonim movement leader we interviewed, camp Hebrew is ideally "an opportunity to link to the Jewish people worldwide, an opportunity to connect to their Jewish identities more broadly."

Notably, this connection is based not on contemporary Israeli Hebrew as a spoken lingua franca but on routinized and sometimes archaic elements of modern Hebrew infused into a primarily English environment. Galil, like other Habonim camps, is entrenched in a form of "displaced nostalgia"[6] that endows the pre-state and early years of Israel with great sentimentality, based on generations of camp tradition, not participants' memories. This nostalgia leads to some degree of temporal freezing, maintaining long-standing camp practices even when they have become anachronistic outside of camp. We see this in Galil's kibbutz orientation, use of words such as *marp*, and even the *chultzah*—the staff's blue collar shirt with a red string at the neck, similar to the shirt worn by Habonim members decades ago. The kibbutz movement is no longer primarily agricultural and no longer a central ideological or political force in contemporary Israeli society, as the socialist ideologies that created the state have ceded to individualism and capitalism. The political winds have shifted in other ways too; left-wing Israeli political parties seeking a peace agreement with the Palestinians have been sidelined as more hardline positions have taken hold. Despite these changes, Galil participants continue to venerate an idealized image of the Israeli past, even as they respond to current events with critical discourse. Living in a virtual time warp helps them maintain their Zionist stance and think of Israel in a palatable way. If the Israel they would prefer does not exist, they can at least represent it symbolically at camp. Hebrew plays a role in this representation, enabling the camp to promote a form of Jewishness and Zionism based in collectivity and social justice. The strategic use of Hebrew to underscore its progressive philosophy is most evident in Habonim Dror's decision—the year after we visited Galil—to adopt coined gender-neutral and gender-inclusive Hebrew suffixes, as we explain in chapter 8.

Through the use of English as its primary language, including for nonroutine announcements, Galil emphasizes its Americanness. Through the ample use of Hebrew announcements, songs, skits, and CHE, Galil emphasizes its identity as an American Jewish camp strongly committed to an idealized Israel. Through the absence of some words that refer to religious observance and outlook, such as *Hashem* (God) and *tefillah* (prayer), Galil emphasizes its relatively secular orientation—embracing only select religious rituals and framing them as more cultural than theological. In short, Hebrew usage at Galil is intended not to make campers proficient in Hebrew, but rather to facilitate their socialization into the Galil community and the broader community of secular (or at least not necessarily religious), progressive, Zionist American Jews.

### Beber Camp: Where Hebrew Is Associated with Religion, Israel, and Joy

While spending time at Galil might strengthen one's Hebrew vocabulary, spending time at Beber Camp will strengthen one's leg muscles: seventy-two steps lead from Lower Camp to the dining hall and office. We arrived at the office, out of breath, and immediately heard Hebrew: three counselors were engaged in individual bar/bat mitzvah tutoring sessions with 12-year-olds. The campers chanted their Torah portions, and the tutors—Jewish day school graduates—followed along. We noted the irony of hearing Hebrew upon arrival, as a Beber administrator had discouraged us from spending much time at this camp, not because of a lack of hospitality, but because she felt we would not find much Hebrew there.

Beber, a pluralistic camp in Wisconsin, was originally affiliated with B'nai B'rith and is currently part of the Association of Independent Jewish Camps (AIJC). We perused the posted schedules and notices around the office and saw more Hebrew. The three age-based camper divisions have Hebrew names: *Makor* (foundation), *Kesher* (connection), and *Ramot* (heights). Bunk names are English words for animals and foods, such as monkeys, tacos, and s'mores. Some activities have Hebrew names: *menucha* (rest), *shomer* (patrol), *oneg* (snack reception), and Havdalah. In one activity, *Mishpacha* (literally family), a gathering that brings together campers of different ages, the groups have Hebrew names for values, like *koach* (strength), and the leaders are called *ima* (mother) and *aba* (father). But most activities have English names, in contrast to Galil's use of Hebrew; for example, "hobbies" (not *chugim*), "Israeli dancing" (not *rikud*), "arts and crafts" (not *omanut*), and "evening activity" (not *peulat erev*).

As we walked around camp, Hebrew did not jump out at us as it did at Galil, but it did appear here and there. Each year, the Pioneers (pre-staff leadership division) do a camp improvement project, and a few involved creating Hebrew signage. One was a directional signpost in the middle of the large bunk area in Lower Camp pointing toward five cities from where campers are recruited. On one side, the pointers are in English letters (Cleveland, Milwaukee, Louisville, Chicago, and New York), and on the other side they are in Hebrew block letters (קליבלנד, מילוווקי, etc.). A similar project was a directional signpost pointing to locations around camp, including Restrooms (שרותים), Crown Hall (כרון הול), and Lower Camp (מחנה תחתון). Directional signposts are frequently decorative, and the Hebrew on these signs is clearly not meant for the Israeli staff members, all of whom are competent in English. Instead, the signs highlight the symbolic importance of Hebrew at camp, a hallmark of infusion. A third project serves a more practical function—giving campers and staff a visual aid for the words of the Havdalah ritual. Hand-painted wooden signs in the amphitheater present the Havdalah blessings (over fire, spices, etc.) in textual Hebrew and transliteration. Crown Hall, a multipurpose room where song sessions and services take place, features dozens of square wooden placards from past intra-camp competitions or color wars, known here, as in many camps, as *maccabiah*. As an unspoken rule at Beber, teams receive extra points for using Hebrew on their placards, and most teams have done so. Many placards have words or phrases in Hebrew like מדור לדור (from generation to generation) and ביחד כאחד (united as one). Some include both English and Hebrew, such as "להבה נצחית—Everlasting Flame."

The five Israeli emissaries, who worked that summer as bunk counselors and specialists, played a major role in the incorporation of Hebrew at Beber. They ran Israeli games with Hebrew names like *tifsuni* (catch me). They posted multilingual pedagogical labels in the dining hall, such as "קיר *kir* wall," and "מזלג *mazleg* fork." And during cabin cleanup, they ran an inter-cabin competition involving Hebrew: they put labels in each cabin with words like "דלת—delet" (door) or "מיטה—mitah" (bed), and campers earned points for posting them on the proper objects. At the end of the session, the cabin in each division with the most points won a trip to Dairy Queen.

According to an Israeli emissary, the campers seemed to enjoy these Hebrew-oriented activities. But the most popular, as many staff eagerly told us, was the lunchtime appearance of Mr. Milon (Mr. Dictionary). For a few years, Mr. Milon was performed by Asaf, a charismatic returning Israeli emissary.

Jared, a division head, began the Mr. Milon ritual after finishing the post-lunch announcements:

> JARED: After a long break, do you want to guess who's coming back? *Mi zeh?* [Who is it?] *Milon* in Hebrew means dictionary. Mr. Milon teaches us a word in Hebrew. When I say "Mr." you say "*Milon.*" Mr.!
> CAMP: *Milon!*
> JARED: *Ken!* [yes]
> CAMP: *Ken!*
> JARED: Yes!
> CAMP: Yes!

Campers cheered wildly as Mr. Milon made his grand entrance, jogging in with his fists in the air, dressed as a superhero, wearing an Israeli flag as a cape, a blue-and-white cowboy hat, and a Zorro-like black eye mask. He carried an inflatable Thor hammer decorated with an Israeli flag:

> MR. MILON: *Shalom*, Beber Camp.
> CAMP: *Shalom*, Mr. Milon.
> MR. MILON: See that wall over there? That's where we'll post the Hebrew word of the day. Are you ready for the Hebrew word of the day?
> CAMP: (Cheers).

He began a three-minute monologue by saying he "had a small appearance in the new Avengers movie." At an event like Comic-Con, Mr. Milon narrated, a boy came up and requested his signature, thinking he was Thor. He replied, "The line for Thor is over there," pointing to his left. The boy insisted, and he and Mr. Milon went back and forth. After several exchanges about the "line for Thor," Mr. Milon told the audience, "And then it hit me!," and fell to the floor dramatically. The camp cheered, knowing that "and then it hit me" introduces the ritual's climax, the Hebrew word of the day: "Line is *thor. Tor* is line in Hebrew." The camp cheered wildly, and another staff member placed a label on the "word of the day" bulletin board: "Tor—line—תור."

Asaf handed the microphone to Jared, who announced a camper's birthday. The crowd sang first in Hebrew ("*Yom Huledet Sameach*," the Hebrew translation of the English birthday song), then in English ("Happy Birthday to You"), then, "Skip around the Room," as the birthday girl joyfully skipped around the dining hall. "Now the *Birkat*," said Jared, using the abbreviated name for *Birkat Hamazon*, the post-meal blessings. "*Chaveray nevarech*," he sang. The camp responded, "*Yehi shem. . .*" During the first paragraph of *Birkat Hamazon*, campers and staff participated enthusiastically, banging on tables, performing ritualized hand motions, and standing on benches at various parts. Some campers followed along with the transliterated cards on the napkin holders on each table.

These post-meal rituals—Mr. Milon, the Hebrew birthday song, and *Birkat Hamazon*—exemplify hybridity. The combination of American, Israeli, and religious Jewish practices, including elements of English, modern Hebrew, and textual Hebrew, comprises the distinctive culture characteristic of many American Jewish camps. Mr. Milon presents Hebrew not only as an exotic foreign language but also as entertaining and as something that belongs in America, not as a full language but in hybrid English-Hebrew forms. His monologue introduces the Hebrew word of the day through English and Hebrew-English homophony—the fact that Thor and Tor sound similar (or the same, in an Israeli accent). The character's American cowboy hat decorated like the Israeli flag allows Israeliness to blend seamlessly with Americanness, as does his English-Hebrew name, Mr. *Milon* (not *Mar Milon*, as at some more Hebrew-oriented camps). The costume in effect transforms the "Hebrew man" of Zionist pioneering lore into a superhero in the American register, with a cowboy hat to cement the image.[7]

Such skits can be found at many camps around North America, as can *Yom Huledet* and *Birkat Hamazon*. A feature that distinguishes Beber from a majority of camps is that about 15 percent of its staff are not Jewish.[8] Beber Camp had trouble finding Jewish American college students with the requisite skills in sailing, art, horseback riding, and the like, so they turned to international hiring programs like Americamp, and they fly in non-Jewish staff from England, Australia, Latin America, and elsewhere. Such a contingent of international staff may enable the non-Jewish staff to gain knowledge of and friendships with Jews, but it can make it harder for a camp to integrate Hebrew and other Judaic content into daily activities. Administrators do not see this as a problem, because Beber intentionally compartmentalizes Judaics into specific periods, especially morning flagpole (where *Hatikvah* is sung), meals, and Shabbat—which includes Friday challah baking, evening and morning Shabbat services, Israeli dancing, song sessions, *mikud* ("focusing"—a cabin discussion session), and Havdalah. Although Israeli counselors occasionally teach Hebrew words or use fragments of Hebrew in their informal interactions, there is little or no Hebrew or Jewish content in most activities. One exception is the two Israel Days each session, when Beber incorporates Israel content into "hobbies," such as making and wearing Maccabi Tel Aviv soccer team jerseys in sports, using Israeli army commands at the ropes course, and cooking Israeli food in outdoor cooking. At camps that infuse Hebrew throughout their daily activities, like Galil, staff members are expected to learn CHE and routinized announcements. At Beber, the only people expected to have any Hebrew knowledge are the song and prayer leaders, bar/bat mitzvah tutors, and Israeli emissaries. Other staff members might learn select words, but Hebrew is less central to their jobs.

When we asked a Beber administrator about the desired camper outcomes regarding Hebrew, he said, "I don't think you have to have a working knowledge of Hebrew as a living language to be a good Jew. . . . For us, it's about exposing them to something that is very, very meaningful as a Jew." It is clear that Beber, like Galil, is using Hebrew practices as a means not to campers' Hebrew proficiency, but to Jewish community. Hebrew songs and prayers, Mr. Milon, and Hebrew signs are intended to encourage campers to associate Hebrew with American Zionism, Jewish religious observance, and the entertaining traditions of Beber Camp.

### Camp Sternberg: Orthodox Jewish English, Not CHE

Sternberg, in New York's Catskill Mountains, is the largest of the three camps profiled here, with more than 800 campers in the largest session, compared to 300 at Beber and 180 at Galil. An Orthodox all-girls camp, Sternberg attracts campers from all over the country, but primarily from the Northeast. The vast majority of campers attend Orthodox Jewish day schools during the year, compared to only a few day school students at Galil and some at Beber.

Sternberg has more Jewish content than Galil or Beber, but it is limited primarily to certain times of the day and week. Most activities have English names, like wake-up, cleanup, and night activity. But a few have (Ashkenazi) Hebrew or Yiddish names, which campers would most likely also use at home and school. Campers *daven* (pray) twice on weekdays—*Shachris* (morning) and *Mincha* (afternoon)—and attend a daily *shiur* (religious learning session). *Shabbos* (Shabbat) includes more *davening*, Friday night *seudah* (festive meal), Saturday afternoon *seudah*, and the Saturday evening *shalosh seudos* (the third meal). On weekdays, in post-meal song sessions, girls stand on chairs, singing and dancing to recorded Hebrew music. Some songs combine English and Hebrew, and songbooks include some inserted Hebrew-letter words (e.g., "daughters of 'ה [*Hashem*—God], בלב אחד [*b'lev echad*—with one heart] again. . . . We're on our way back home, ירושלים [*Yerushalayim*—Jerusalem]!").

During our visit to Sternberg, we observed several activities: a heated match of *machanayim* (literally two camps, a variant of dodgeball), painting, sewing, musical chairs to a Maccabeats tune ("Smart Ways to Live"), girls in long skirts and leggings making their way up and down a giant climbing wall, lunch, and the (English) Happy Birthday song. Aside from the long skirts, the name *machanayim*, the kosher food, the blessings, and the choice of music, these activities might have been conducted at any camp, Jewish or not. The Hebrew and Judaic content at Sternberg is mostly compartmentalized to certain times of the day and week. An exception is color war (notably not called *maccabiah*). In addition to sports, color war includes a *chidon* (quiz) that focuses on Bible and other topics of Judaic knowledge, as well as artistic placards known as teams' "everlasting contributions." The placards, posted around camp, mostly feature Hebrew quotes from the Bible and liturgy, and they are labeled with team names, always in Hebrew without translation and always pairs or opposites, like שמש, ירח; ישן, חדש; ארץ, שמים (heavens, earth; old, new; sun, moon).

Most locations around camp have English names (bunk, infirmary, dining room) or camp-specific acronyms (POKA—Pioneers' Outside Kitchen Area), with two exceptions: the *shul* (Jewish English for synagogue) and the creative blend *Shmakolet* for the canteen. SHMA (Listen) is a Hebrew prayer and the acronym for three camps/divisions—Sternberg, Heller, and Magen Av; *makolet* is modern Hebrew for a small market common in Israel; and this word evokes the dismissive Yiddish-origin reduplicative *shm-* prefix, as in "money, shmoney." Most of the divisions have English names, like Pioneers, or are named after people, like Heller, but the special needs divisions have Hebrew names: *Migdal* (tower) and *Kesher* (connection, which is also a division name at Beber). Bunk names combine letters and numbers, like P2 and S7. We found occasional modern Hebrew words and phrases written around camp—for example, on bunk H9: "רק להלר? למי" (For whom? Only for Heller)—but fewer than at Galil and Beber.

Because the administrators at Sternberg limited our visit to a few hours, we were not able to observe Shachris, Mincha, or the Shabbos rituals. But we did observe the blessing after lunch (*Borei Nefashos*, rather than *Birkas Hamazon*, because no bread was served). The girls chanted this blessing with American Ashkenazi Orthodox pronunciations—for example, *rabos* and *haolamim* (ending rhymes with "him")—in contrast to most other camps, which tend to use more Israeli-influenced pronunciations: *rabot* and *haolamim* (pronounced *meme*). Finally, we observed the lecture (*shiur*), which was influenced in almost every sentence by Hebrew and Yiddish.

To prepare for the late-morning lecture, about 60 tenth-grade girls found their seats on wooden benches in a multipurpose room decorated with Hebrew placards from past years' color wars. Rivky, a woman who appeared to be in her forties, welcomed the girls and asked, "How late did you stay up last night?" The girls giggled and murmured about how little sleep they got. Rivky introduced the visitor, a well-known educator, Rabbi Mandelberg. The girls stood up to honor him, and for the next half-hour, Rabbi Mandelberg captivated the room. His charismatic lecture encouraged the girls to conquer their inner struggles and to recognize that everyone has challenges. To connect with the girls, Rabbi Mandelberg incorporated a few Jewishly tinged references to American pop culture, including the band One Direction ("even though they broke up, *nebech* [what a pity]") and the song "Let It Go" ("That song is pure 100% *apikorsus* [heresy], but that's your life—the struggle of your generation"). Except for a few giggles, the audience was completely quiet, rapt in attention.

Rabbi Mandelberg lectured in what linguists call Orthodox Jewish English, a variety of English used by American Orthodox communities that incorporates many loanwords and other influences from Hebrew and Yiddish.[9] Because of these distinctive features, Rabbi Mandelberg's language would be difficult for the average American to understand. To give a few examples, his Yiddish words included *frum* (religious), *gezunt* (health), and *shul* (synagogue), and his Hebrew words, which also appear in Yiddish, included *shiduchim* (marriage matches), *kavana* (focus/intention), and *Klal Yisrael* (the Jewish people). He pronounced most of these words in an American Orthodox Ashkenazi way—for example, *tsníes* and *hachnásas órchim*—compared to Israeli Hebrew *tsniút* and *hachnasát orchím*. Rabbi Mandelberg's English also included other distinctive Orthodox features, like the Yiddish-influenced "by," as in "*Halevay by* all of you" (you should all experience [the aforementioned]); sentence-initial verbs indicating narrative progression, as in "Said a girl"; and chanting intonation contours highlighting important points. As is the norm in language directed toward girls and women, the lecture lacked some of the more scholarly phrases and Yiddish grammatical structures common in male varieties of this language, known as Yeshivish.

This half-hour lecture included more Hebrew loanwords and other distinctive features than we heard throughout our entire (longer) visits at most camps. This type of language is not unique to Rabbi Mandelberg. At Sternberg, we heard many of these and other features of Orthodox Jewish English in the informal speech of young female staff members and campers, including the Yiddish-influenced *by* ("They make the plaques *by* color war"), the Yiddish-influenced *already* ("They've been here for thirty-five years *already*"), the Israeli Hebrew-influenced *so* ("When *shul* is not in use, *so* they have . . ."), Yiddish-influenced preposition absence ("*Motzei Shabes* [Saturday night] we'll have Pioneers Got Talent"), the old-fashioned English word "supper" (dinner),[10] and dozens of Hebrew and Yiddish loanwords ("Men *daven* [pray] in the *beys medresh* [study center], and there's usually a *minyan* [prayer quorum]"; "I went to *tuvel* [ritually immerse] silverware in the *kelim mikvah* [ritual bath for utensils]"). Some of the distinctive features we heard in the lecture are used primarily by men in study contexts, such as chanting intonation and starting a sentence with a verb, and we did not hear these from women or girls at Sternberg. The gender differences are striking in contrast to the gender-neutral CHE introduced at Galil.

When Galil and Beber campers go to camp, they encounter Hebrew games and skits and Hebraized English that differs from what they hear at home or school. But at Sternberg, campers are surrounded by the same language they hear September through June. Almost all of the girls at Sternberg live in Orthodox communities where they likely hear male teachers lecture like Rabbi Mandelberg. They would probably consider *by, so,* and *tuvel* not "distinctive features," but simply part of the language they hear and use every day with their friends and relatives. The Hebraized/Yiddishized English spoken at Sternberg is not unique to camp and is not intended to strengthen campers' connections to Israel or the Jewish people. It is simply the native language variety common in (English-speaking, Ashkenazi, non-modern) Orthodox American communities. Sternberg does use some elements of infusion, such as routinized Hebrew prayers and songs, and these may be performed with a more entertaining orientation at camp than at school or home. But infusion at Sternberg lacks the pedagogical orientation of Galil and Beber, found in skits, games, and other metalinguistic interactions.

Sternberg also differs from the other camps in its administration's rationales for Hebrew use and pedagogical goals. Their most important rationales are that Hebrew allows campers access to the Jewish religious and textual tradition and to connect to Jews around the world and throughout history. Strengthening knowledge of Hebrew prayers and blessings is a primary goal at Sternberg, whereas it is important at Beber and not a goal at the more secular Galil. Sternberg rates strengthening connection to the state of Israel as only a minor goal, whereas Galil and Beber consider it primary. Sternberg leaders pursue their pedagogical goals not by using CHE and other camp-specific Hebrew practices, but by using Orthodox language in ways similar to the campers' home communities and to Orthodox Jews throughout North America.

## INTER-CAMP DIVERSITY

Hebrew is a common thread in all three of the camps profiled here. Participants sing Hebrew songs, recite Hebrew blessings, see visual representations of Hebrew on signs and placards around camp, and use Hebrew words for some divisions and activities. In all of the camps, Hebrew is associated with fun and entertainment, whether that manifests in playful names for locations, theatrical skits, or banging or dancing on tables. Hebrew is also associated with Americanness, as fragments of Hebrew are woven into the primarily English environment. None of these camps offers formal Hebrew classes, and none is interested in fostering linguistic proficiency. Instead, the Hebrew practices are intended to accomplish educational goals regarding campers' imagined connections to other Jews, sometimes specific types of Jews. We see this in the camps' survey responses regarding the relative importance of various goals: at all three camps, Hebrew proficiency goals are less important than goals regarding Jewish identity and connection to Israel and the Jewish people.

At the same time, the three camps differ greatly in the types of connections they wish to foster and the types of Hebrew they use to accomplish those goals. At each camp, the amount and type of Hebrew used help define its unique Jewish character—secular, progressive, Zionist; pluralistic; or Orthodox—potentially contributing to campers', parents', and staffers' selection among many camp options. In other words, Hebrew serves as a flexible signifier. Participants at Sternberg, Galil, and Beber may never encounter each other or even be aware of the existence of the other camps or camps like them. But outside observers can clearly see both the differences and the common message: Hebrew is an important part of being Jewish.

Such commonalities and differences are evident in Jewish-identified camps across America today. In response to our survey, all camps report using at least some Hebrew songs or prayers/blessings and at least some Hebrew loanwords, but camps differ greatly in their adoption of other Hebrew practices. Hebrew murals and location signs, Hebrew names for activities, and skits teaching Hebrew words are common, whereas spontaneous announcements, classes, and theatrical productions in Hebrew are rare.[11]

A few camps, such as Massad Manitoba and the short-lived Israeli American Council's Machaneh Kachol-Lavan, are (or were) conducted primarily in Hebrew. Massad Manitoba, founded in 1953 and inspired by Massad in the Poconos, recruits most of its campers and staff from the Jewish community in Winnipeg. As a Massad Manitoba administrator indicated, "Hebrew is why we exist." Whereas participants at most Hebrew-rich camps encounter a collection of Hebrew nouns, participants at Massad Manitoba encounter many Hebrew sentences, both routinized and nonroutinized, including in announcements and theatrical performances—what Massadnikim call *shtik*. But the Hebrew at Massad Manitoba diverges from Israeli Hebrew in lexicon and, especially, grammar. One Massad Manitoba alumnus was placed into third-semester Hebrew at an Ivy League university, based solely on the Hebrew he acquired at Massad. But his instructor reportedly said, "I've never met someone who has such good vocabulary and such bad grammar." Although most Massad Manitoba campers speak English at home, many of the campers at Kachol-Lavan came from Hebrew-speaking homes. The camp (whose name means "blue-white," the colors of the Israeli flag) was geared toward Israeli Americans and was conducted primarily in Hebrew. Campers translanguaged, using Hebrew and English to varying degrees, depending on topic and audience, as we might expect in any bilingual setting. The camp only operated for a few years; the summer we visited was its final summer.

Aside from Massad Manitoba and Kachol-Lavan, most of the camps with many Hebrew practices belong to one of four networks: Ramah, Young Judaea, Bnei Akiva, and Habonim Dror; others include OSRUI and Kutz (both URJ camps), Yavneh (historically Hebraist), and Camp JRF (Reconstructionist, now Havaya). Camps with fewer Hebrew practices include those affiliated with no network (especially for-profit camps), with AIJC, and with JCCA. Orthodox camps recite Hebrew prayers and blessings regularly, have Hebrew quote placards, and use Jewish life words, but they tend not to engage in Hebrew practices like performing skits that teach Hebrew words and using Hebrew names for activities and roles (Bnei Akiva is an exception). Hebrew practices correlate with a camp's orientation toward Israel, reflected in whether its leaders consider connection to Israel to be a primary goal and whether the camp has many Israeli emissaries. Another factor is how much Hebrew non-Israeli staff members know. Camps at which the director and the typical (non-Judaic) specialist are proficient in Hebrew tend to have many Hebrew practices. At camps that integrate Hebrew throughout camp life, even specialists tend to have Hebrew ability.

Camps differ not only in how many Hebrew-related practices they have but also in which Hebrew loanwords they use. We distinguish between "Jewish life words," the Hebrew loanwords used in Jewish English in year-round communities, and "camp words," the Hebrew loanwords used primarily at camp (including both those with camp-specific referents, like *tzrif* [cabin], and those that do not have camp-specific referents but are not generally discussed with Hebrew words in American contexts outside of camp, like *schiyah* [swimming]). Jewish life words come from textual Hebrew and modern Hebrew (and Yiddish), whereas camp words come primarily from modern Hebrew. Some camps use only Jewish life words, some use primarily camp words, and some use many from both categories (see figures 4.1 and 4.2) Among the words used by the most camps are Jewish life words like *Shabbat shalom* and *ruach*. Camp words are less commonly used overall but occur frequently at Ramah, Bnei Akiva, Habonim Dror, Young Judaea, and, for some words, URJ and Hashomer Hatzair.

No matter which Jewish camp people attend, and no matter what their Jewish and Hebrew background is, when they spend time at a Jewish camp, they usually encounter a set of common Hebrew words referring to aspects of Jewish religious and communal life. These words have the potential to make them feel connected to Jews of many backgrounds, with or without camp experience. If their camp is part of a Zionist network, they usually encounter a separate set of common Hebrew words referring to aspects of camp life. These words have the potential to make them feel connected to Jews who attended similar camps if they discuss their common summer experiences using the same specialized vocabulary. In addition, each camp network, and each camp, has its own distinctive Hebrew loanwords and abbreviations. Understanding and using this local terminology can make participants feel connected to each other, the camp, and perhaps its wider network. In short, CHE serves as social and cultural capital on multiple levels.

INTRA-CAMP DIVERSITY

In addition to diverse Hebrew practices among camps, we also found diversity within each camp. The use of loanwords and full Hebrew sentences varied depending on the situation and the speaker.

### *Distinctions by Situation*

Camps were far more likely to use Hebrew for routinized announcements than for announcements with spontaneous wording. For example, at Ramah California, as at Habonim Dror Galil and the historical Ramah camps discussed in chapter 3, announcements about where groups should go after meals tended to be in Hebrew, but when staff members explained camp rules, instructions for an activity, or anything related to safety, they tended to use only English. We never

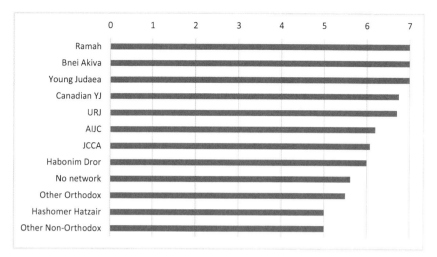

Figure 4.1. Average number in each camp network of these seven Jewish life words: *Shabbat shalom* (peaceful Sabbath), *Birkat Hamazon* (Grace after Meals), *boker tov* (good morning), *tikkun olam* (repairing the world), *ruach* (spiritedness), *tefillah* (prayer), and *sheket b'vakasha* (quiet please).

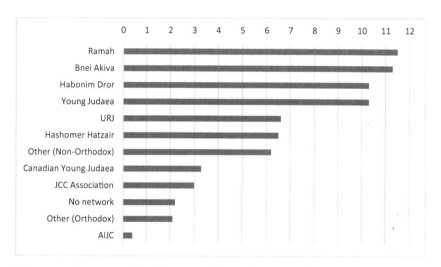

Figure 4.2. Average number of camp words in each network from among these thirteen words: *chadar ochel* (dining hall), *nikayon* (cleaning), *machaneh* (camp), *mirpaa* (infirmary), *marp* (infirmary nickname), *omanut* (art), *hodaot* (announcements), *tzrif* (bunk), *hakshivu* (attention), *schiyah* (swimming), *edah* (division), *zimriya* (song festival), and *shekem* (canteen).

heard Hebrew at the ropes course, for instance, even though several of the staff members operating it were Israeli. One day, after lunch, the division head who was making announcements had trouble getting the campers to be quiet. She started in Hebrew, saying, "*Machane Ramah, b'vakasha* [Camp Ramah, please]," mentioning various divisions by their (Hebrew) names, and counting down from ten to zero in Hebrew. After about five minutes, she said, "I'm gonna say this in English. We've been here a week. It shouldn't take this long to get quiet." Campers finally stopped talking, and she switched back to Hebrew for her more routinized announcements. At Camp Stone, a Bnei Akiva camp, according to a former staff member, the beginnings and endings of activities were marked by Hebrew announcements on the loudspeaker, such as "*Peula alef nig-mera achshav* [activity #1 is done now]." But security-related instructions were generally in English, as were announcements calling campers to the office. This is similar to the routinized Hebrew announcement at Galil ushering campers to dinner: "*Achshav kulam na lavo la'aruchat erev* [Now, everyone, please come to dinner]." These transitional announcements serve as "framing" devices, also found in some Native Americans' ceremonies and events.[12] In both Jewish and Native American settings, most interactions are in English, because many participants cannot function solely in the group language. However, the framing phrases serve to reinforce participants' connections to the language and the group.

Although OSRUI's Chalutzim is an immersive Hebrew division, its use of Hebrew also varies by activity: Judaic classes and (nonlinguistic) educational programs are conducted in English. Once, near the beginning of the session, in introducing an evening activity, Ami, a counselor, switched to English after having spoken Hebrew all day. A few campers were surprised: "English?" they inquired. Ami explained, "It's in English because it's an educational program." OSRUI leaders know that most Chalutzim campers will not know Hebrew well enough—even by the end of the session—to have high-level Hebrew conversations about philosophy, history, and identity. Although understanding is not as crucial as with matters of health and safety, these conversations are deemed important enough to conduct in English. As at Ramah camps historically, Hebrew acquisition is only one of Chalutzim's educational goals.

## Distinctions by Speaker

Another distinction we observed at some camps is that senior staff tend to use more Hebrew than lower-level staff and campers.[13] At Ramah and URJ camps, upper-level staff members used loanwords somewhat consistently, and counselors and campers used some loanwords but also their English equivalents. At JCCA and other pluralistic camps, administrators, counselors, and campers rarely used loanwords, except for certain locations and activities, and they only used a few Jewish life words; most Hebrew loanwords we heard there were from rabbis, Judaic educators, and Israeli emissaries. At most Zionist movement camps, we did not notice significant differences according to speaker.

At some pluralistic and Reform camps, we found a related aspect of differentiation: official documents like schedules and maps used a Hebrew word for an activity or a location, but most people used only its English equivalent. As a staff member who showed us around at URJ Newman said, "Everything has a Hebrew name, but we don't always call them that." Similarly, during maccabiah at URJ Jacobs, some of the signs and cheers used the teams' Hebrew color names, but in most conversations participants used the teams' English names. Because of this variation, our survey gave multiple options when asking camps if they use particular Hebrew words: "used frequently by both staff and campers, used frequently by some staff but not by most campers, used only in a few contexts (e.g., on a sign or schedule), or rarely or never used." Respondents embraced these options. For example, an independent camp in the South responded that *tikkun olam* is used frequently by staff and campers, *kehillah kedosha* is used only in a few contexts, and *rikud* is rarely or never used. Both our observations and survey demonstrate that there is no unified way of speaking CHE, even within a given camp.

## Why Hebrew?

Another area of unity and diversity involves rationales for Hebrew use. When we asked camp leaders and participants why their camps used varying types and degrees of Hebrew, five associations came up repeatedly but in differing orders of importance: Israel, Jewish texts and religion, Jewish collectivity, distinguishing camp from the rest of life, and camp tradition. In some camps, one or two associations were central, and in others all five were equally important.

### Israel

As would be expected, Israel was a common rationale for using modern Hebrew at Zionist camps. A Habonim Dror national leader said, "Hebrew is the connecting language between us and Israel, so we certainly want everyone to speak it, to be familiar with it, to be comfortable with it, to love it." But as a staff member at Gilboa (a Habonim Dror camp in California) pointed out, the goal of wanting "everyone to speak it" is an ideal. The more realistic outcome is what many camp leaders refer to as "connection," meaning that American Jews should increase their feelings of personal attachment to Israel, and leaders hope that Hebrew infusion plays a role in that affective socialization.

Even camps that are not primarily oriented toward Zionism still consider Israel an important motivator for Hebrew infusion. A JCCA leader said that at JCC camps, where religion is not central, Israel is important: "We learn [some] Hebrew because that's the language they speak in Israel, and we're connected to Israel, and our connection to Israel is how we express our connection to the totality of Jewish life, history, and thought." A URJ national leader said he wants URJ camps to teach campers Hebrew words so they will view Hebrew as a living language of Israel and eventually be motivated to travel there. In this sense, Hebrew infusion can also be seen as one of the ways that camps prepare American Jews to visit Israel, not primarily as tourists learning cultural norms and how to say "thank you" and "where is the bathroom?" but as Jews with a sense of personal belonging to Israel and its language—albeit with a surface understanding of both.

A Zionist orientation does not necessarily entail intensive Hebrew use; several camps have significant Israel programming but little Hebrew. A leader at a JCCA camp attributes this to campers' limited Hebrew knowledge. But even at Lavi—a private modern Orthodox camp where many campers have strong Hebrew skills and there are dozens of Israeli staff members and Israel-oriented programs—only English names are used for camp locations, activities, and roles, and their Hebrew loanwords are limited to Jewish life words and the names of divisions.

Although most camp staff members we interviewed emphasized the role of Hebrew in fostering connections to Israel, some focused on the skill of speaking Hebrew with Israelis. Several staff members at Ramah camps talked about camp Hebrew enabling campers to function better in Israel when they later visit. Some of the campers we interviewed at Ramah, OSRUI, and Young Judaea camps shared this stance. Many planned to visit Israel, some hoped to do a gap year there or serve in the Israeli army, and a few were considering making aliyah. Some campers in OSRUI's Chalutzim immersion program aspired to converse in Hebrew with Israelis, including, for some, Israeli relatives. One OSRUI fourth-grader said, "I think most Jews go to Israel, and that's probably going to be a major part of our lives. And if you know it's going to be a major part of your life, you probably want to communicate." A Ramah ninth grader told us her exposure to Hebrew at camp was already paying off. She had learned the numbers in Hebrew school, but hearing them in the announcements of page numbers during prayers at camp solidified them in her mind. When she visited Israel, she was able to barter at the *shuk* (open-air market) in Hebrew.

Most of the Israeli staff members at American Jewish summer camps have strong English skills. Even though campers do not need Hebrew to communicate with them, some emphasized that learning elements of Hebrew gives them a window into the lives of their counselors and other Israelis. A Tel Yehudah camper said she likes that some of her counselors use Israeli slang and encourage campers to do so as well: "It's really capturing the essence of an Israeli, and when an Israeli counselor talks to you and you're trying to speak to them in Hebrew . . . you're getting who they are a little bit." Even when campers are not physically in Israel, some feel a bond with Israel and Israelis in part because of the Hebrew they encounter at camp, especially at Hebrew-rich camps. However, most campers, even at Hebrew-rich camps, do not become proficient enough to have advanced Hebrew conversations with Israelis. Their linguistic connections are mostly on a symbolic level.

### Judaism

Although Israel was a common response when we asked, "Why Hebrew?" most interviewees also answered by mentioning some aspect of Judaism as a religion. For example, a program officer at a foundation that supports many camps noted, "Hebrew gives an insider's access to not just Israel, but to the history of Jewish people—all the texts. . . . We don't believe that it's the same to access these texts in a language other than Hebrew." Many camps want campers to feel like insiders when it comes to Jewish observance, and textual Hebrew loanwords and prayers provide a small step in that direction. At some camps, Hebrew is limited primarily to liturgical contexts: blessings before and after meals, Shabbat services, Tisha B'Av, and bar/bat mitzvah tutoring. In these camps, the rationales for Hebrew tend to be religiously oriented. Leaders at JCCA camps and other camps where participants arrive with minimal Judaic and Hebrew knowledge are often careful not to use too much Hebrew even in liturgical contexts, to avoid overburdening campers. As an educator from Alonim (a pluralistic camp in California) characterized it, they focus on "exposure without alienation." This reflects a tension between socializing campers into particular models of Jewish religious practice while maintaining camp as an attractive option in a consumer market.

Another aspect of Judaism that camp staff, especially at Reform and pluralistic camps, mentioned in relation to Hebrew was Jewish values. Many values are presented to campers as Hebrew loanwords, often accompanied by translation: for example, *bikkur cholim* (visiting the sick) and *bal tashchit* (do not waste). During staff week at a URJ camp, we observed a conversation about whether the "value of the day" should be presented just in English or also in Hebrew. In some cases, a Hebrew word was well known, such as *tikkun olam* or *kehillah kedosha*. But a few educators debated whether to use certain words in Hebrew or English— *middot* or "values," *simcha* or "joy." One educator felt the value of the day was a good opportunity to introduce more Hebrew words. Another argued that using a Hebrew word does not necessarily make a value Jewish, especially if that word is from modern Hebrew and has no foundation in biblical or rabbinic literature. At a pluralistic camp, we heard conversations about how to pronounce Hebrew words for Jewish values, including Jewish counselors correcting non-Jewish counselors' mistakes (like *jimilut hasádim* for *gemilut chasadím*—kindness). In this case, campers were being socialized not only to embody specific Jewish values but also to feel comfortable with their Hebrew terminology. Although Hebrew was rarely named as its own Jewish value, the use of these loanwords and the conversations surrounding them conveyed the importance of Hebrew— and its correct articulation.

## Jewish Collectivity

Related to the Israel and religiosity rationales, many interviewees also spoke about Hebrew as a Jewish language that fosters Jewish identity by connecting Jews around the world. A Beber administrator said, "The idea that everywhere across the world on Friday nights, people are saying the same prayers in the same language, regardless of their native language or where they are—it's very powerful." Beyond liturgy, several camp leaders identified Hebrew ideologies and practices that "connect" Jews in far-apart locations, including awareness of Hebrew as Jews' special language and knowing a few modern Hebrew words. Some staff members at camps that are less Israel oriented, including Ortho-dox camps, mentioned that Hebrew has little to do with Israel and much more to do with Judaism and Jews. But even camps that are strongly oriented toward Israel are also interested in Hebrew as a/the language of the Jewish people. A URJ Newman leader who is comfortable with the Zionist emphasis at his camp said, "Hebrew does not only belong in Israel. It's not just Israeli, but it's a Jewish lan-guage." Sentiments like this, which we heard from several camp leaders, point to Hebrew infusion at American camps as a practice that claims Hebrew as a Jew-ish, rather than primarily Israeli, product.

Multiple Habonim Dror leaders mentioned Jewish collectivity. One said, "The Zionist vision is not separate from the Jewish . . . Hebrew is very much at play in both of those." Even in the absence of regular prayer at Habonim camps, Hebrew is seen as connected to Jewishness; using or knowing it provides an opportunity to "be connected as cultural Jews" and thus to the Jewish people. We found similar sentiments at more religiously oriented Zionist camps. A Moshava Malibu admin-istrator said, "Hebrew is . . . just the means to the ends. The ends is that nationalis-tic pride and that sense of 'I'm proud to be a Jew.' The language is just a means to that. It's one of the ways that we bind together, right? We all speak the same lan-guage, no matter where we are." In actuality, not all Jews speak Hebrew, and Ameri-can Jews are most likely to communicate with Jews around the world in English. Even so, these leaders reference an imagined metalinguistic community[14]—a col-lectivity of Jews around the world who view Hebrew as the shared language of their sacred texts and their old-new homeland. They intend Hebrew infusion at camp to foster participants' connections to this imagined community.

## Distinguishing Camp from Year-Round Life

Many Jews in and beyond summer camps understand Hebrew as related to Israel, religiosity, and Jewish collectivity, yet two ideological associations are unique to camp: Hebrew making camp distinct from the outside world and camp tra-dition. Several interviewees pointed to the role of Hebrew in making camp feel like an "island" in time and space, or a "bubble" experience.[15] A Gilboa admin-istrator said that Hebrew is "part of creating this insular world that's only ours, that's completely detached from the outside." Even as Hebrew connects camp participants to Jews throughout the country and the world, it also distinguishes them through camp-specific lexicon, especially at Hebrew-rich camps.

This distinguishing effect, which other scholars of summer camp highlight, could take place through any activity, in any language, and at any camp, Jewish or not. Many camps' special English terminology, including acronyms and abbreviations, serves a similar purpose, whether deliberate or not. Some Jewish and non-Jewish camps, especially in the early and mid-twentieth century, used Native American words for their divisions and bunks.[16] The fact that most Jewish camps today select Hebrew as their primary distinguishing language indicates the importance of Hebrew in the creation of Jewish imagined communities—not as a unifying language of communication like in European nationalism, but as a unifying idea and source of lexical enrichment.

The campers we spoke with attached great meaning to Hebrew as a differentiating mechanism. A ninth grader at Ramah California said Hebrew is "what makes camp so special, because it's a separation from every single other day." In response to a question about the abundant Hebrew words used at camp in contrast to those used in his hometown, Miami, a Camp Judaea camper responded, "If these words were used all the time in Miami, they wouldn't be fun or special anymore." At Hebrew-rich camps, Hebrew is so central to the distinguishing culture that campers cannot imagine the camp without it. A Massad Manitoba camper said, "Massad without Hebrew would be another camp. It wouldn't be Massad, because we couldn't do any of the things that make it Massad."

The distinguishing effect was particularly noticeable for campers coming from year-round experiences in which Hebrew was less present. A ninth grader at Ramah California who attends public school contrasts herself with her many campmates who attend day schools: "It's a lot easier for them because . . . they know so much more Hebrew. But . . . it's not as special then because they speak it at home, at school. . . . But for me, when I come here it's the only time when people speak Hebrew to me." For many campers, the distinguishing effect is not just linguistic. At camp, Jewishness is normative and no longer marked or minoritized, in contrast to their year-round lives.

Some leaders criticize the distinguishing effect, worrying that campers will view Hebrew only as the enriching language of camp and not as the language of Jews, Judaism, and Israel. As we can see from the interview data discussed above, campers at Hebrew-rich camps do seem to perceive these connections. Additional research is necessary to explore the views of campers at camps with less intensive Hebrew infusion, such as JCC and private camps, especially campers who do not engage with Jewish communities outside of camp. It is possible that they view Hebrew, including Jewish life words, solely as an enriching language of camp. Another critique of the distinguishing effect is that CHE is only useful in the camp setting. In general, this is accurate, but CHE does sometimes serve as a bonding force or even a secret code among people who attended the same camp or different camps that used similar words. An example is a commercial for JDate, a Jewish online dating service, that portrays a man rejecting a woman who does not know the word *maccabiah* and then becoming more serious with a woman who does.[17]

## *Camp Tradition*

A few camp staff members answered our question of "Why is there so much Hebrew here?" with responses like "It's been part of the culture for many years" or "That's the way it was, and that's the way it still should be." Traditions are particularly strong at long-standing camps where many staff members are former campers. Hebrew loanwords were likely initially introduced for ideological reasons by a Hebraically oriented staff member, or perhaps because camp leaders heard them at another camp they attended or staffed. The original ideological valences of the phrases might not be clear to camp participants today, and they might have different semantic meanings for different people, especially in the absence of translations and metalinguistic explanations. We see this in the changed usage in certain words. For example, at one pluralistic camp, leaders introduced announcements with *hakshivu* (attention), but they sometimes shortened it to *hak* and used it as a transitive verb, as in "*Hak* those counselors up to the lodge."

For some camp staff, "camp tradition" was enough of a rationale for using many Hebrew words, but others disagreed. An administrator at Beber called for greater intentionality in Hebrew use, as with other aspects of Judaics at camp. He changed the tradition of calling the lake *agam* because it did not seem intentional to him, and (in the opposite direction) he changed the name of the middle division from TC (Teen Connection) to *Kesher* (connection) to align with the other divisions, *Makor* and *Ramot* (however, the pre-staff leadership division still has an English name, Pioneers). A 2006 Ramah report critiqued the reliance on tradition as an impetus for Hebrew use: "Division heads and other top specialists or teachers could not articulate a clear rationale for Hebrew usage at camp. Most claimed that they had not heard any rationale in camp, but rather just 'received the tradition' that Ramah was committed to Hebrew for historical reasons, and followed it as part of their loyalty to camp practice."[18] The report framed this as something to fix, articulating several rationales for Hebrew use. Some Ramah camps addressed this report by discussing rationales for Hebrew use at staff trainings. The centrality of tradition at camp not only makes camp leaders less likely to articulate rationales but can also make change contentious, as we elaborate in chapter 8.

## *Comparisons and Connections among the Five Rationales*

Although we discussed the five rationales of Israel, Judaism, Jews, distinctness, and tradition separately, in practice they overlap and carry various weights at various camps. Many camps operate on the basis of several or even all five of them. Some camps see one rationale as much more important than others, and some camps avoid or "erase"[19] one or more of them. Shomria (Hashomer Hatzair, New York) foregrounds Zionism and avoids Judaism; Eden Village (Eco-Judaism, New York) emphasizes Judaism and has little to say about Zionism. Gesher (Russian-American, California) and Bechol Lashon (Jews of Color, California) highlight Jews around the world, but such a focus is rare at most camps. Some camps foster additional ideological associations with Hebrew, such as environmentalism at Eden Village, Russian Jewish identity at Gesher, or Sephardic heritage at Sephardic Adventure Camp.

When interviewees discussed the Israel and Judaism rationales, a few did so through what we consider a parallel distinction between two types of Hebrew: textual and modern. For example, a Yavneh administrator said that in the 1960s, Yavneh taught both "biblical Hebrew and modern Hebrew," and a Sprout Lake (Young Judaea) educator said she wants her campers to use "modern Hebrew, not only *Birkat Hamazon* and *tefilot* [prayers]." Others distinguished between different types of Hebrew without labeling languages. A Ramah New England administrator said he wants campers to be able to order in a restaurant and ask for directions in Hebrew and to acquire "*tefillah* skills . . . which is a different kind of Hebrew, I understand, but still it's sort of linked to me." Indeed, textual Hebrew and modern Hebrew share much of their grammar and vocabulary, and learning one helps in learning the other, but only to a limited extent.[20] Despite exceptions like these, most interviewees did not explicitly distinguish between modern and textual Hebrew, and we never observed camp staff members teaching about this distinction. In fact, some younger campers at Ramah and OSRUI felt that the (modern) Hebrew words they were encountering at camp would help them understand prayers and Torah and prepare for their b'nai mitzvah. An OSRUI Chalutzim camper said she was starting to figure out the meanings of more of the prayers based on her immersion in modern Hebrew.

We also observed some campers and staff members making connections between textual and modern Hebrew. In a Hebrew class of sixth to eighth graders at OSRUI, the teacher asked, "How would we say 'we are wearing shoes'?" Max began to answer: "*Anachnu-*," and Joey interrupted, "*korim umishtachavim* [bend the knee and bow]." Joey recognized the word *anachnu* from the bowing part of the Aleinu prayer, and he said the two words that follow. At Moshava Indian Orchard (IO), the religious Zionist orientation sometimes leads to blurred lines between textual and modern Hebrew. One year, the curriculum involved teaching "biblical slang of the day," phrases from the Tanach that campers could use in everyday conversation. For example, educators taught, "*Ish hayashar b'einav yaase*" (every man did what was right in his eyes), the final line in the biblical book of Judges (21:25), which they translated as "everybody do whatever they want." As one of the educators told us, the staff would use it when kids were

| Rationale | Very Important | Important |
|---|---|---|
| Hebrew allows campers to connect to Israelis and the state of Israel. | 51% | 32% |
| Hebrew allows campers to connect to Jews around the world and throughout history. | 47% | 31% |
| It's camp tradition. | 42% | 33% |
| Hebrew allows campers access to the Jewish religion and textual tradition. | 34% | 37% |
| Hebrew distinguishes camp from the outside world. | 20% | 42% |

Figure 4.3. Relative Importance of Rationales for Hebrew Use at North American Jewish Camps.

running around, and eventually "kids actually picked up on it and would start saying it randomly to their *madrichim*." Through a deliberate act of language planning, a biblical phrase became part of contemporary spoken parlance (at one American camp), just as Eliezer Ben-Yehuda and other modern Hebrew revivalists had hoped. This creative example demonstrates how emphasizing the connection between textual and modern Hebrew can be useful. Yet the two types of Hebrew can also present complications. We observed a few instances where Israelis were asked about textual Hebrew and gave incorrect responses because they were unaware of differences between textual and modern Hebrew.

All five of the rationales for Hebrew use are important or very important at a majority of camps, as our survey found. Our question about rationales echoed interviewees' verbiage by using "Hebrew" as an umbrella term (as well as the word "connect"): "Camps have different rationales for incorporating Hebrew words, songs, and so on. How important are the following rationales to your camp?" As figure 4.3 indicates, Israel ranked highest, then Jewish people, camp tradition, Judaism, and distinguishing camp.

Camps in Zionist networks—Bnei Akiva, Ramah, and Young Judaea—tended to indicate connection to Israel and Israelis as very important; Chabad and Ramah camps were most likely to emphasize access to the religious and textual tradition; and camp tradition was most often selected as very important by Habonim Dror and Young Judaea camps. This diversity relates to the broader goals of these camp networks: socializing campers to be connected to Israel, competent in religious observance, and/or feeling ensconced in a particular movement.

Each of the rationales is associated with particular Hebrew loanwords used at camp. The religion rationale can be seen in Jewish life words in the domains of religious observance, like *Shabbat shalom, tefillah,* and *maftir* (additional Torah reading), as well as words for Jewish values, like *chesed* (kindness), *tikkun olam,* and *tzaar baalei chayim* ([concern for] animal suffering). The Israel rationale relates to words like *kibbutz, aliyah,* and *mishlachat* ([Israeli] delegation), as well as words associated with the Israeli army, such as *toranut* (turn of duty), *mifkad* (gathering), and *amod dom* (stand at attention). The camp distinctness and tradition rationales relate to camp words like *chanichim, tzrif,* and *peulat erev,* some of which come from youth movements that predate the summer camps. And some leaders see the Jewish people rationale in many of the shared words, because they give camp participants a shared vocabulary with participants at other Jewish camps and, in the case of Jewish life words, with Jews around the world.

In addition to these connections, some camp participants understand any Hebrew word as related to Israel. There are several possible reasons for this. First, camp participants generally know that these words are Hebrew, and they understand Hebrew to be the language of Israel. Second, Israeli emissaries are prominent in camp Hebrew practices like Hebrew word skits. Third, campers might hear some of the words they learned at camp if they visit Israel, such as *boker tov* (good morning), *b'teavon* (bon appetit), and *misrad* (office). Some camp Hebrew words, like *marp* and *chadar ochel,* have changed in Israeli Hebrew since they were adopted at American summer camps. Camp participants may not be aware of these differences and still tend to associate the words with Israel. Hebrew words are also associated with Jewishness, as are songs, cheers, and prayers. For example, a Ramah ninth grader said, "Whenever someone says something in Hebrew, it reminds us that this is a Jewish camp."

These multiple ideological links are evidence of a broader sociolinguistic phenomenon regarding individuals' associations with linguistic variables (particular ways of saying things): "The meanings of variables are not precise or fixed but rather constitute a field of potential meanings—an indexical field, or constellation of ideologically related meanings, any one of which can be activated in the situated use of the variable."[21] In our case, Hebrew words are associated with a "constellation of ideologically related meanings"—Judaism, Israel, and camp (including tradition and distinctness)—all of which are associated with each other and with Jewishness (including Jewish peoplehood and smaller Jewish collectivities). Figure 4.4 represents this constellation of ideological links. Judaism, Israel, and camp are connected to Hebrew through mediated levels of associations: Israeli society, Jewish ritual and text, and camp roles, locations, and activities.[22]

Although a given word is often associated primarily with one of the meanings, in certain instances secondary associations can be more strongly activated. Imagine an arrow connecting words to a category illuminating temporarily. For example, the word *maftir*—normally associated with Judaism—may also be

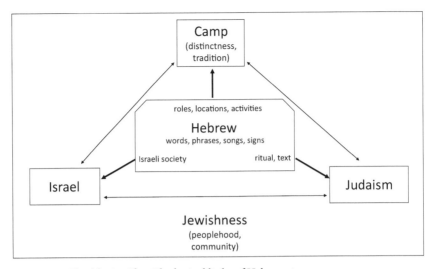

Figure 4.4. Flexible signifier: Ideological links of Hebrew at camp.

temporarily connected with Israel if an Israeli staff member chants the *maftir* Torah portion or speaks about it. *Omanut* (modern Hebrew for art) may be temporarily associated with Judaism if campers make *challah* covers. All of the words may be associated with camp, especially in the minds of participants who encounter little or no Hebrew in their lives outside of camp. At camps that emphasize Israel and not Judaism, "Israel" may be illuminated most brightly. When a staff member talks about Hebrew as a Jewish language, "Jewishness" may flash. This neon-sign image illuminates the diverse and malleable associations of Hebrew at camp and its role in group identity.

———

This chapter has demonstrated how Jewish camps mobilize Hebrew in diverse ways. A few camps make spoken Hebrew their centerpiece, but most selectively use elements of Hebrew as a way of emphasizing their particular brands of Jewishness. This diversity is influenced by—and helps constitute—camps' religious, political, and other identities. Of course, Jewish sociolinguistic variation is not limited to summer camps. A similar study in Jewish day schools, supplementary schools, synagogues, or homes of different Jewish orientations would also find linguistic diversity. A 2008 survey found that American Jews differed in their reported use of Hebrew and Yiddish words. For example, Orthodox Jews were more likely to pronounce the Festival of Booths as "SUK-kiss," whereas non-Orthodox Jews were more likely to say "soo-COAT." Jews of all different orientations used some Hebrew (and Yiddish) words, but they used different words and pronounced them differently.[23] We see similar diversity in the routinized Hebrew sung and chanted in ritual contexts. Hebrew plays an important role both in the similarity of Jews (Jews of many backgrounds use elements of Hebrew) and in their diversity (Jews of different cultural, religious, and national backgrounds use different types and elements of Hebrew). At summer camps, this diversity may be even starker than in other Jewish settings because of the increased use of Hebrew words, songs, signs, and other practices. Based on their leaders' policies and practices regarding Hebrew infusion, summer camps socialize participants to perceive connections to specific Jewish collectivities, both reflecting and enhancing the diversity in other Jewish communal settings.

Although our research highlights linguistic diversity, language exists within a broader cultural constellation. Hebrew infusion is only one of the many ways camps have distinguished themselves from each other along various Jewish continua. A camp might have more or less prayer or educational time, more strict or lenient *kashrut* (dietary rules) policies, or more or fewer Israeli staff members. In conjunction with these and other domains, camps decide how and when to use Hebrew based on how they want to present themselves and how they want their campers to understand the role of Hebrew in American Jewishness. Because of its many associations and uses, Hebrew has been a particularly flexible signifier. Hebrew would not be as malleable if it were used as the camp's vernacular. It is precisely because camp leaders infuse Hebrew selectively—during certain activities, in certain parts of camp, by certain staff members, to refer to certain referents, serving certain ceremonial functions—that Hebrew's diverse associations are highlighted.

# CHAPTER 5

# The Building Blocks
# of Infusion

On a sunny day in Oconomowoc, 10-year-old Lily climbed the spiral stairs to OSRUI's water slide. Excited and a bit nervous, she finally reached the platform. There she found Iddo, an Israeli counselor, who was not only patrolling for safety but also infusing some Hebrew into the activity. He pointed to her earrings and taught her their Hebrew word, *agilim*. He would not let her slide down until she repeated it. The next day, Lily recalled this interaction in a focus group with other young campers, responding to a question about how their experiences with Hebrew at OSRUI compared to Hebrew learning in their religious schools. She offered Iddo's water slide password as an example of how camp "makes Hebrew more fun," even if she had to learn something before sliding down. Lily also pointed out that she had already forgotten the word for earrings, attributing this to the setting: she did not write the word in her notebook like she does in religious school.

Some might see this kind of engagement with Hebrew as watered down (whether or not it takes place at the pool) and potentially harmful to language acquisition. It only focuses on isolated words, not the structure of the language, and the campers do not generally retain the words they are taught. If acquisition of Hebrew is the goal, this pedagogical interaction must be considered a failure. However, as this chapter shows, such interactions are generally geared not toward language acquisition, but toward affective and communal goals: creating a distinctively American Jewish camp culture that places a positive value on Hebrew. Lily may not have retained the word, but she remembered this as a fun exchange with an Israeli counselor involving Hebrew. Iddo infused one more element of Hebrew into the primarily English environment, adding to the Hebrew word skits, songs, and other activities Lily experienced at camp. Activities like these use English-Hebrew hybridity and a fun, entertaining orientation to construct campers' ideologies about Hebrew as an important, positively valent dimension of the American Jewish camp experience, even though English is the primary language of interaction. With these affective goals in mind, Iddo's Hebrew password might be considered a success.

All of the practices described in this chapter involve Hebrew-English hybridity in a primarily English environment, demonstrating that Hebrew is part of the American Jewish camp experience. Some of the practices are impromptu and not necessarily entertaining, such as using loanwords and initiating pedagogically oriented metalinguistic (talk about language) exchanges, in which staff members discuss and translate Hebrew words with individuals or small groups. But many of the activities analyzed in this chapter are entertaining and occur in group settings as part of the camp routine: they include Hebrew word-of-the-day presentations, games, songs, theatrical productions, jingles, liturgical insertions, and call-and-response routines. Like other activities and rituals, camp staff members initiate these practices every day, week, or session, and campers participate in varying ways, demonstrating their engagement and amusement. These practices have much in common with forms of entertainment in the broader society. Most are intentional and top-down; that is, staff members initiate them, and campers experience them, just as most forms of entertainment are intentionally created by professionals and experienced by the public. In forms of entertainment in the broader society, there is a continuum of participation; for example, video gaming requires user participation, but people can watch television with only a click and minimal attention. Similarly, campers are expected to participate in some Hebrew infusion practices, such as games and call-and-response routines, but their consumption of skits can be more passive. Despite the entertaining orientation of many Hebrew infusion practices, they are not frivolous or corrosive, as some have posited regarding television within the broader society.[1] They serve an instrumental, educational purpose, just as play does in other contexts:[2] Hebrew infusion practices socialize participants to hold positive ideologies about Hebrew and Jewishness.

Research on foreign- and second-language education has found that games, songs, and other entertaining practices can lower students' anxiety and sustain their motivation throughout the difficult task of language learning.[3] However, most of the Hebrew infusion practices we observed at camp lacked an important element of the games used in language classrooms: the opportunity for students to practice speaking the target language in spontaneous ways. Some of the Hebrew infusion practices at camp, such as announcements and skits, give campers opportunities to practice the receptive skill of listening. Those infusion practices that involve campers producing the language, such as songs, call-and-response, and theatrical performances, do not involve spontaneous Hebrew speech; rather, campers use only routinized Hebrew sentences (as well as Hebrew loanwords in their CHE). In addition, in a language classroom, students are accountable for language acquisition through tests, report cards, and, for younger students, parent-teacher conferences. Camp leaders intentionally avoid such assessment to differentiate camp from school and increase camper satisfaction, an important outcome in a consumer model where families have many summer options.[4] In fact, camp staff expressed concern that some practices—naming a Hebrew word activity "Hebrew class," requiring campers to use Hebrew, or even Hebraizing their English too much—could cross the tipping point from fun to tedious or anxiety inducing.

Of course, language learning happens in many settings, not only classrooms. As research on language socialization has found, children and adult novices are socialized not only to speak in certain ways but also to be part of various collectivities with particular views about language.[5] A number of language socialization studies have focused on communities that use two or more languages, highlighting the roles of families, social networks, schools, churches, and other institutions in socializing community members to value specific languages differently and to use the group's ancestral language for certain purposes—or to avoid it as much as possible.[6] Jewish camps, like other contexts of ethnolinguistic infusion, present a special case of language socialization. The novices (campers) are socialized to acquire certain language ideologies, but they are never expected to use most of the language practices they hear from leaders, such as words they are "taught" in skits and games. They may be expected to use some of the CHE they hear from camp leaders, but only those who go on to particular staff positions are expected to initiate word teaching and other top-down Hebrew practices. However, at some Hebrew-rich camps, campers are expected to understand and produce more Hebrew. At the end of the chapter, we outline how these Hebrew-rich camps facilitate a progression of learning.[7]

## LANGUAGE CONTACT AND CHE

A primary building block of Hebrew infusion is language mixing, which is, of course, a broader phenomenon. In our world of increasing migration, transnationalism, and technological innovation, many people have access to more than one language. The results of this language contact have been the subject of myriad studies within linguistics, anthropology, and education.[8] A relatively new approach is analyzing the results of language contact as "translanguaging," defined as "the deployment of a speaker's full linguistic repertoire without regard for watchful adherence to the socially and politically defined boundaries of named (and usually national and state) languages."[9] In other words, what some see as mixing two languages others see as simply speaking. Translanguaging is a subversive notion because it disrupts concepts that have underpinned language education for years, including a "monolingual orientation": a belief that languages have distinct boundaries and should not be mixed.[10] Although some Jewish leaders critique CHE and other forms of English-Hebrew hybridity, the translanguaging lens reframes them as the expected result of a group using two languages—as a natural form of American Jewish linguistic creativity.

However, the ways that camp participants combine Hebrew and English differ from what occurs in other situations of language contact. When people have at least moderate ability in more than one language, they are able to mix them spontaneously. But when they have limited proficiency in a language, as at most Jewish summer camps and other situations of ethnolinguistic infusion, they use mostly routinized fragments within the matrix of their primary language. To analyze this language mixing, we draw on a concept from formal linguistics: loanwords. A loanword, also called lexical borrowing, is a word or phrase from one language routinely used within another language, whether or not the speaker is bilingual, and it is generally integrated into the phonological system of the matrix language.[11] Like in the translanguaging of Spanish-English bilinguals, for example, Hebrew infusion involves speakers deploying a combination of elements—some from Hebrew and most from English—without flagging the Hebrew elements as foreign. But infusion offers a unique perspective on translanguaging because many camp participants are not competent enough in Hebrew to create spontaneous Hebrew sentences, and they use only a limited repertoire of Hebrew fragments—loanwords and routinized sentences. This contrasts with some research on translanguaging, which eschews the distinction between loanwords and (what was traditionally called) "code switching," because when speakers have competence in multiple languages it does not matter if some words are codified as loanwords.[12]

Jewish camps of all types use Hebrew loanwords. They also use routinized Hebrew in prayers and songs and sometimes in announcements with set phrases in limited contexts. Only the camps that are most committed to Hebrew and have many Hebrew-proficient participants use Hebrew in nonroutinized announcements. Israeli staff members and Hebrew-proficient Americans at camps of all types may use nonroutinized Hebrew, but generally not in official contexts. In some cases, nonroutinized Hebrew is interspersed with English, as in other situations of translanguaging in bilingual communities around the world. For example, an Israeli krav maga (martial art) instructor at Ramah California said, "I want to see three lines. [Zack], *kach* line *achora* [take the back line]. *Atsor!* [stop]. Everybody in a *chet* [the shape of the Hebrew letter]. First I take my left leg and punch . . . *Achad, shtayim, shalosh* [one, two three] . . . *Meuleh* [excellent]. *Yefeh meod* [very nice]. *Yala, kadima* [OK, continue]. *V'ready* [and . . .]." He mixed English and Hebrew (once within a word, using a Hebrew prefix with an English word, *v'*ready) and used several words that are not common in CHE. In another instance of translanguaging, we heard an Israeli mother say to her son, "*Yalah, bou la*'cabin [Come on, let's go to the cabin]." It does not matter whether "cabin" is a loanword or not, because the speaker and her son are both proficient in Hebrew and English. This contrasts with a parallel sentence common in CHE, "Come on, let's go to the *tzrif*." Here, *tzrif* must be considered a loan-word because it is routinized (used frequently within English sentences in a Jewish camp context), integrated into the phonological system of English (the consonants and vowels are rendered with an American, not Israeli, accent), and said by people who cannot necessarily utter spontaneous Hebrew sentences. We can analyze the utterances of the krav maga instructor and the Israeli mother as textbook cases of bilinguals translanguaging, but the *tzrif* example must be seen as a CHE sentence in which only loanwords are used.

Routinized Hebrew and loanwords have been important in Jewish communities historically. In antiquity, Hebrew was the spoken language of Jews in the land of Israel. After various conquests and migrations, Jews shifted to other language varieties as diverse as Aramaic, Judeo-Arabic, Yiddish, and Ladino. In most of their communities, Jews maintained routinized textual Hebrew for prayers and blessings. (Although many boys and men studied texts in Hebrew, only the elite could use textual Hebrew in nonroutinized ways.) The regular use of routinized textual Hebrew led Jewish communities around the world to incorporate hundreds of Hebrew loanwords into their everyday speech, particularly referring to religious observance, communal matters, and euphemisms, as well as secretive language regarding business and non-Jews.[13] Contemporary Jews in the United States and other English-speaking countries continue the tradition of using routinized textual Hebrew prayers and incorporating textual Hebrew loanwords into their primary language. "Jewish English" is an umbrella term that scholars use for the many varieties of English spoken and written by Jews: it incorporates hundreds of words from textual Hebrew and has other distinctive features in contrast with other varieties of English.[14]

Since the rise of modern Hebrew and especially the establishment of the state of Israel, Jewish English has been enriched not only by textual Hebrew and recent ancestral languages like Yiddish and Ladino but also by modern Hebrew.[15] The same is true for other contemporary Jewish language varieties, like Jewish Swedish and Jewish Latin American Spanish.[16] In addition to textual Hebrew loanwords such as *etrog* (citron for Sukkot) and *shiva* (seven-day mourning period), Jewish English now includes modern Hebrew loanwords like *kipah* (skullcap) and *kol hakavod* (well done, lit. all the honor), as well as nonlexical influences from modern Hebrew. CHE is a specialized register of Jewish English, incorporating (often dozens of) additional loanwords from modern Hebrew.

In sum, leaders and participants at American Jewish summer camps mix Hebrew and English in multiple ways, ranging from spontaneous translanguaging to routinized Hebrew in songs, prayers, and announcements; and to Hebrew loanwords within CHE. At most camps, routinized Hebrew and loanwords are the norm because of the low levels of prior Hebrew skills of most camp participants and staff. Some critique this fragmentary use of Hebrew, but we see it as a valid cultural product of American Jewry, aligned with other situations of ethnolinguistic infusion. For example, a Miami/*myaamia* language and culture camp mixes language in similar ways. The goals of this camp and broader "language reclamation" efforts, as tribe member and researcher Wesley Leonard characterizes them, include "fostering a positive and informed *myaamia* identity, a connection to the larger Miami community, a cultural understanding of the language, and some linguistic proficiency. The goal is not full linguistic fluency by 100 percent of the Miami population."[17] Similarly, the goal of Hebrew-English hybridity at most camps is not Hebrew proficiency but fostering positive Jewish identities and connections. In short, CHE and the infusion practices described below are distinctly American Jewish phenomena, but they share commonalities with other situations of language contact, especially in historical Jewish communities and contemporary language reclamation.

### HEBREW WORD-OF-THE-DAY SKITS

One of the first practices that many people mentioned when we asked about Hebrew at camp was "Hebrew word of the day," and most camp directors who responded to our survey reported having such presentations at their camps. In some cases, the presentations we observed were simple and straightforward. At one JCCA camp, for example, a counselor presented the Hebrew word, *glida* (ice cream), and campers guessed its meaning and briefly discussed its history—all in English. This is a top-down, pedagogically oriented practice that highlights the importance of Hebrew. However, in most of the cases we observed, the word-of-the-day presentation was more entertaining, involving jingles, songs, skits, and wordplay.

At Alonim, an Israeli emissary taught the word, *naknikia* (hot dog), in anticipation of the cookout later that day, using a call-and-response song called "*Shigaon*" (Crazy):

> LEADER: I'm gonna tell you how to say how to say "crazy"
> CAMPERS: Tell us how to say how to say "crazy."
> LEADER: "*shigaon.*"
> . . . tomatoes: *agvaniot*
> . . . hot dog: *naknikia*
> . . . the song is over: *nigmar hashir.*[18]

We heard this song at a few camps and learned that it was taught as part of Cornerstone, a Foundation for Jewish Camp fellowship that trains returning counselors from several camps to enhance their programming, including incorporating more Jewish content. In this case, a top-down practice performed by camp staff was initiated by leaders of the American Jewish camping infrastructure.

A common technique in Hebrew word presentations is to point out homophony between English and Hebrew: a word or phrase in one language that sounds similar to a word or phrase in the other. We saw this with Thor and *tor* during the Mr. Milon skit at Beber described in chapter 4. While this skit involved only one character, many Hebrew word skits portray homophony leading to miscommunication among two characters, one Israeli and one American. Then, a hero, with a name like Hebrew Man, *Ish Ivri* (Hebrew man), or *Mar Milon* (Mr. Dictionary), often wearing an Israeli flag as a cape, comes to the rescue by explaining the homophony. At Tel Yehudah, two counselors, Yair and Seth, began such a skit. They were discussing their ropes course experience, and Yair mentioned a *tik*, meaning bag. Seth thought Yair was talking about a tick, a bug that could transmit disease, and became visibly anxious. Hebrew Person, played by Alon, entered the room wearing an Israeli flag cape and explained that *tick* in English was a parasite and *tik* (pronounced *teek*) in Hebrew was a bag.

These top-down, pedagogical, and entertaining presentations that highlight homophony serve a few purposes. First, they offer mnemonics for English speakers to remember the meanings of the Hebrew words. If a camper first encountered the word *mazleg* in a skit involving "a fork in ma's leg," when she later hears the word *mazleg* she might recall the skit and remember what the word means. However, words are selected not because they are useful for communication with Israelis (which is concerning for those interested in acquisition), but because of their similarity in sound to an English word or phrase. Second, the homophony highlights for English speakers that their language has something in common with Hebrew—words that sound similar. In fact, these homophones are "bivalent," meaning that a linguistic element belongs to two linguistic systems simultaneously.[19] At the same time, the skits emphasize differences between the languages, sometimes involving miscommunication. Although this emphasis may lead camp participants to feel distant from a language so distinct from their native English—or give voice to the distance they were already feeling—it can also help bridge that gap by giving them mnemonics. Finally, the use of bilingual wordplay, jingles, and other entertaining aspects of these presentations is intended to highlight the importance of Hebrew and to associate Hebrew with the joy of camp.

At OSRUI's Chalutzim Hebrew immersion program, the word of the day served a different function than at English-speaking camps. The words selected tended to be useful for communication, such as *hatchala* (beginning), *rega* (moment), and *kef* (fun), and then counselors (and, they hoped, campers) would use the word in their Hebrew conversation many times throughout the day. Sometimes when the word of the day was introduced, it was accompanied by special intonation (high-low-high-fall pitch [fall means beginning on a high tone and swooping to a low tone] for *MEyuCHAd*—special),[20] a gesture (jazz hands for *chadash*—new), or an action (pushing someone for *asur*—forbidden). Whenever someone used the word, he or she used the accompanying intonation, gesture, or action. This incorporation of performance uses multiple modalities and appeals to multiple senses, making it more entertaining and helping language learners remember the word—an objective much more important in an immersion than infusion setting. In fact, this program contrasts with most camps in its expectation that campers will use the words taught in these presentations throughout the day and session.

At Hebrew-rich Massad Manitoba, the word-of-the-day ritual also incorporated multiple modalities, as well as competition. During our visit, the word was introduced at breakfast with an elaborate Hebrew jingle: "*Ze shigaon. Osim kol yom. Tikach milon. Po b'massad, baboker lomdim milat hayom. B'bidika mishtamshim b'mila . . . V'milat hayom ze . . .* [This is crazy. We do it every day. Take a dictionary. Here at Massad, in the morning we learn the word of the day. At [cabin] check we use the word . . . And the word of the day is . . .]." A counselor drew a paper from the word box that said *balagan* (mess, chaos). After breakfast, campers went back to their bunks for *nikayon*. In addition to cleaning, each bunk had to prepare a skit around the word *balagan*. Administrators went from bunk to bunk to check the cabins (*bidika*—checking) and to judge the skits. At the end of the summer, the bunk with the most points got to pour a bucket of ice water on a popular counselor. Campers appreciated this entertaining, competitive engagement with Hebrew, as well as the other Hebrew use that is so common at Massad. One girl told us, "Hebrew at camp is much different than at school. At [my Jewish day school] we don't do plays. It's like work there. And Hebrew here is much more about using the language to have fun and be creative."

Hebrew word skits have the potential to engage camp participants not just during the skits themselves but also at other times. At Ramah California, during an art activity, an American counselor said to her campers, "Who knows how to say marker in Hebrew? *Toosh!*" She pointed to her rear (*tush*), indicating the near-homophony. "Marker, *toosh*, [singing the Hebrew word jingle:] *Ivrit, Ivrit, Ivrit, daber Ivrit.*" Then she and two Israeli counselors joked about past skits while a few campers watched, smiling in recognition at this shared repertoire of entertaining Hebrew infusion practices.

Among the campers and alumni we interviewed, the near-universal response was that the skits are fun and, as a 10-year-old OSRUI camper said, "really useful" for helping them remember the words. A woman who worked at Habonim camps several years ago told us that she retained the words of the day, even though they were not common in conversational Hebrew, because of the humorous ways they were presented. She recalled the "Super Ivrit Ninja Turtles" theme song used when she was part of the Ivrit presentation team, and she remembered the lyrics of many lengthy songs from the skits. Whether or not campers remember all or even some of the words presented, the skits have the effect of associating Hebrew with the fun, communal orientation of camp activities. When performed in a non-immersive setting, the skits also send the message that Hebrew is not central enough to the community's existence to conduct all activities in the language.

BILINGUAL WORDPLAY

Combining and playing with Hebrew and English words are common not just in skits but also throughout camp culture. Some instances are in informal references, such as *Amitzimers* and *Yesodlings* (campers in the Amitzim and Yesod divisions), and joking references, such as *Kallah-lipops* (campers in the Kallah division, combined with lollipop). But we also find wordplay in more official contexts initiated by camp leaders. We encountered Hebraizations/Judaizations of English words using the [ch] sound in place of [h], such as *Chaiku* (Jewish haiku) and *Challahween* (an activity involving candy). One camp Hebraizes/Judaizes the chapel—a usually Christian prayer space in the YMCA site they rented—as "*khapEL*," using the Hebrew [ch] and moving the stress to the final syllable, emulating many modern Hebrew words, and perhaps evoking theophoric synagogue names like Beth El. Several blends involve the word *Shabbat*, such as *Shabbox* (a box from which campers pick a piece of paper listing their Shabbat job) and *Shabbat-o-grams* (notes exchanged before Shabbat), and a few involve the English word "Jew," like *Jumba* (Jewish Zumba).

Some of the camps we visited have developed a particularly thick culture of wordplay. Eden Village campers make "*lev* potions" (love potions playing on the Hebrew word for heart) and *Lev-i-Tea* (a local blend—herbal and lexical— presented with love notes), and they can spend alone time in the *Hitbota*Booth (a place to be alone and talk to God, from the Hebrew word for that solitary spiritual practice, *hitbodedut*). The URJ Newman schedule includes *p-nik* (personal *nikayon*—showering), *t'floptions* (options during *tefillah*—prayer—involving storytelling, art, or hiking), and *frolfillah* (<u>F</u>risbee <u>g</u>olf te<u>fillah</u>, also known as "mindfulness and the disc"). Several of Newman's bunk nicknames involve alliteration, puns, or blends with division names, such as *Hevracados* (Hevra division, avocados) and *Kallah Koalas* (Kallah division). The Avodah division has an *Avodauction* (Avodah auction), and the Avodah girls are nicknamed the *Avodolls* (Avodah dolls). Camp Alonim uses many blends involving the "Alo" portion of the camp's (Hebrew) name, such as *Alo-options*, *Alo-stage*, and *Alo-tweets*. Other terms combine Jewish life words with English words, such as *T'filawn* (*tefillah* lawn), *Havdalawn* (*Havdalah* lawn), and *Havdavening space* (*Havdalah* / *daven*ing). On a poster in the office, staff members had penciled in dozens of ideas for the theme of that week's staff *oneg* (reception), including *Marilyn Monroneg*, *Broneg* (to which someone responded "Feminismneg"), and *Bring Your Own Egg*. Habonim Dror Camp Gilboa has a *chug* (elective) called "<u>Chug</u>s and Kisses," during which campers practice random acts of kindness. And at Gilboa's morning and evening gatherings when each division is supposed to say the formulaic "*kulanu po*" (we're all here), groups prepare punny alternative responses that combine the Hebrew phrase with English words, like "*Kulanu pogo sticks*" (jumping) and "*Kulanu posting Shabbat selfies on Instagram*" (holding up pretend phones). These instances of wordplay combine Hebrew and English in fun ways and contribute to the distinctive culture of each camp.

Another locus for wordplay and homophony is prayers and blessings. A service leader at Hilltop, a Reform camp, introduced the <u>*Barchu*</u> prayer with a joke: "Knock knock." "Who's there?" "Bar." "<u>Bar who</u>?" "Please rise for the *Barchu*." Such bivalent jokes add a bit of humor (and perhaps eye-rolling) to prayers and may serve as mnemonics for campers to remember liturgical words. At many camps, we observed English words or hand movements inserted into Hebrew blessings and prayers based on sound similarity.[21] Whether initiated by staff or by campers, these insertions are performed by campers, and they often become routinized. For example, in *Birkat Hamazon*, campers point to their <u>ears</u> at the phrase "<u>*ir*</u> *hakodesh*." In the Aleinu prayer, campers do a karate chop at "*haya*" in "*v'ne'emar v'<u>haya</u> adonay*," and they say "<u>who</u>" with palms upturned and shoulders shrugged as if asking a question at *bayom ha<u>hu</u>*? or, in a high-falling pitch, emulating an owl (*bayom haHU*). At one camp, this phrase involves a humorous English grammatical "correction": "*bayom ha*-WHOM!" A few insertions—likely initiated by campers—border on vulgarity, such as "I swear I saw her bra" instead of "*asher asher bara*" and emphasizing *kaka* (poop) or "cock" in "<u>*kakatuv*</u>."

Homophonous liturgical insertions serve three purposes, similar to the punny Hebrew word presentations. They create shared local ritual, enhancing the sense of community at camp; they bring entertainment into an activity that is generally serious (prayer); and they allow campers to connect a foreign language to a familiar one, enhancing their sense of personal connection to Hebrew. In the liturgical cases, the frames are Hebrew sentences, whereas in the skits they are English. But in both instances, participants are emphasizing the similarity in sound between words or parts of words in Hebrew and English and adding more entertainment to the camp experience. Perhaps this is why many administrators allow such insertions, even if they would generally be discouraged in a more decorous, adult-centered prayer context. However, some administrators do criticize and even suppress ritualized insertions and gestures, especially vulgar ones, because they obscure the Hebrew words and dilute the sanctity of the liturgical act.

The debate about whether such practices are appropriate during prayer goes beyond homophonous insertions. It includes questions about the acceptability of bouncing up and down during part of the *Aleinu*; clapping, snapping, and banging on tables during *Birkat Hamazon*; making Macarena-like hand motions at "*Oseh shalom*"; and shouting specific words that are part of prayers ("*Shabbos!*" in *V'shamru* and "*Mashiach!*" and "*U'mfarnes!*" in *Birkat Hamazon*). At URJ Kalsman, staff members ended the popular practice of banging on tables by instituting a hand motion for each word of *Birkat Hamazon*, such as drawing an air circle for *olam* (world) and miming a crown for *melech* (king).[22] We observed elements of this practice at other camps, such as holding up one finger at *echad* (one) and making a snipping motion with two fingers at *brit* (covenant) because of its association with circumcision. But Kalsman was the only camp where we observed an entire prayer that was gestured and where this tradition was taught formally and done consistently. This practice differs from the "ear/*ir*" and "haya/*haya*" examples described earlier in that the hand motions align with the meaning, rather than the sound, of the Hebrew words. Whereas homophony, table banging, and clapping have the potential to foster joy and connection, Kalsman's routinized gestures are intended to enable campers to internalize the meaning of the Hebrew prayers.

When camp leaders and participants play with Hebrew and English in these ways, they are demonstrating that Hebrew is not owned solely by Israeli society but is also a valued possession of Diaspora Jews. They are also enabling camp participants, many of whom are monolingual, to engage with Hebrew in fun, creative ways. By voicing similarities in sound between English and Hebrew, punny skits, blends, and prayer insertions send a message that the two languages are connected and that Hebrew is part of American Jewish culture. Such bivalent wordplay is common in situations of language contact around the world—in literature, song, commercial signs, advertisements, conversation, and language classrooms.[23] It can be an especially important aspect of ethnolinguistic infusion, because it gives monolingual participants an opportunity to have fun with the group's special language and to see the language as something that belongs to them, even if they are not proficient in it.

### HEBREW RITUALS: JINGLES, CALL-AND-RESPONSE, AND INSERTIONS

Another common infusion practice is to use Hebrew phrases in routinized ways. A common example is a quieting ritual used at many camps, religious schools, and other Jewish communal settings: A staff member says, "*Sheket b'vakasha*" (quiet please) and children respond, "Hey!" Several camps use "*Hakshivu, hakshivu*" (Attention—plural command form of "listen") to introduce announcements over loudspeakers and in dining halls, even when they have little Hebrew elsewhere at camp. "*Na lakum*" (please stand up) and "*Na lashevet*" (please sit down) are often said during prayers at many Hebrew-rich camps. In addition, individual camps have initiated unique instances of ritualized Hebrew. For example, at a Bnei Akiva camp, the prayer leader said before each service, "*Daka b'sheket lifnei tfilat [arvit]* [a moment of quiet before [evening] prayers]." Sometimes the leader then immediately began the prayers, indicating that the ritualized Hebrew sentence was more important than the moment of silence it supposedly heralded. At Bechol Lashon, they "visited" multiple Jewish communities. After each clue about the country they would be visiting that day, campers said in unison: "*Eifo Eliyahu baolam?* [Where in the world is Elijah?]." This refrain infused a bit of Hebrew into an otherwise English activity.

Sometimes ritualized Hebrew took the form of call-and-response routines, as in this Friday-evening exchange at the flagpole at Camp Gilboa, led by staff members Michael, Jessica, and Sarah:

> LEADERS: *Shabbat shalom, Machane Gilboa.* [Good Sabbath, Camp Gilboa.]
> WHOLE CAMP: *Shabbat shalom,* [Michael] *v'*[Jessica] *v'*[Sarah]. [. . . M and J and S]
> LEADERS: *Nitsanim, kulam po?* [Nitsanim [group], is everyone here?]
> NITSANIM: *Kulanu po.* [We're all here.]
> LEADERS: *Sayalim, kulam po?* [Sayalim [group], is everyone here?]
> SAYALIM: *Kulanu po.* [We're all here.] . . .

No matter what language they are in, call-and-response exchanges are a fun part of the camp routine. When the exchanges are in Hebrew, campers may not understand exactly what they are saying, but they learn that Hebrew is important in the camp setting. As several alumni told us, they sometimes remember these exchanges well beyond their time at camp. And when they later encounter some of these words in Israel or elsewhere, the words sometimes trigger memories of camp, like Proust's madeleine.

During announcements (*hodaot*) at Solomon Schechter, a Conservative-oriented camp near Seattle, staff members and campers often interject translations with playful intonation (high-low-fall-rise pitch).[24] Here are two examples from the first breakfast of a session (Max and Jake are both administrators):

> MAX: I have a few announcements.
> CAMPERS: *HOdaO-oT!* [high-low-fall-rise] . . .
> MAX: Bring closed-toed shoes and a water bottle . . .
> JAKE: *BAKbuk MAyiM!* [water bottle] [high-low-fall-rise]

Jake told us that he often makes similar interjections, especially at the beginning of a session, because "the kids love it, it makes it fun," and it fosters a culture of inserting translations, engaging campers in vocabulary acquisition. He said the campers "catch on and start doing it themselves." Sure enough, within a day or two, individual campers were spontaneously inserting Hebrew and English translations beyond the routinized word *hodaot*:

> MAX: Someone found a white bag.
> CAMPER: *laVaN!* [white] [low-fall-rise] . . .
> MAX: After that we'll have *zman tzrif* [cabin time].
> CAMPER: *CAbin tiME!* [fall-rise] . . .
> MAX: I have another announcement.
> CAMPERS: *HOdaO-oT!* [high-low-fall-rise]

In the last insertion, a plural Hebrew word was used to translate a singular English word, indicating some campers' weak Hebrew knowledge. The fact that there was no correction or explanation of singular and plural morphology suggests that the insertions were more oriented toward affective ties than accurate acquisition.

In addition to intonation patterns, we observed several instances of Hebrew jingles used in routinized contexts. For example, Gilboa campers sang a jingle to introduce the announcement of which campers were on *toranut* (kitchen duty), using only the word *toranut*, repeated with two snaps, to the tune of the Addams Family theme song. Using popular tunes (contemporary or decades old) to sing Hebrew words not only brings an element of entertainment to daily camp activities but also has the potential to make camp participants think of the words when they hear those tunes in noncamp contexts. At Massad Manitoba, counselors and campers sang songs with original Hebrew lyrics for several aspects of camp life, including entering the cabin, dropping something in the dining hall, and delivering mail: for example, *Yesh lanu doar* [We have mail] to the tune of the Israeli song "*Yesh Lanu Tayish* [We Have a Goat]." Camps could perform these jingles in English, but the fact that they are in Hebrew serves both symbolic and pedagogical purposes: emphasizing the importance of Hebrew and teaching some words in memorable ways.[25]

## THEATRICAL PRODUCTIONS AND SONGS

In 2016, Naomi, a friend of one of the authors of this book, posted on Facebook a brief video about "Sergeant Pepper's Lonely Hearts Club Band," marking the Beatles song's forty-ninth anniversary. Naomi said it reminded her of Camp Ramah in the Berkshires, which she attended in the 1980s. "I still have all these lyrics in my head, probably taking up valuable real estate." Then she sang part of the song, a loose Hebrew translation of Sergeant Pepper: "*Ze haya lifney esrim shana. Sergeant Pepper v'halahaka. Hem yatsu mitachat kol signon, ach asu et ze tamid nachon. Az bo v'natsig lachem halahaka shel hazmanim: Sergeant Pepper v'habodedim.* [It was twenty years ago. Sergeant Pepper and the band. They went under every style, but they always did it right. So come and we'll introduce to you the band of all time: Sergeant Pepper and the lonely ones.]" This video demonstrates the powerful potential of Hebrew songs, especially renditions of popular English songs. Naomi and her campmates have likely heard the English version of "Sergeant Pepper" many times since the Ramah production thirty years earlier, and it may remind them of their entertaining camp experience with Hebrew. By translating popular songs into Hebrew—or using alternative lyrics in CHE—camps emphasize a contemporary American Jewishness in which Hebrew plays an important role.

A more intensive variant of this practice is the production of (often abbreviated) Hebrew versions of English-language musicals. This tradition began, we believe, with *The Pirates of Penzance* at Massad Poconos in the 1940s and continues at a few Hebrew-rich camps today; recent examples include *Hairspray*, *Frozen*, and *The Lion King* at Ramah camps. This practice made headlines in 2016, when Ben Platt, Ramah California alumnus and star of *Dear Evan Hansen* on Broadway, sang *"Hey lady tni li mazal"* ("Luck Be a Lady Tonight," lit. "Hey, lady, give me luck") on *Late Night with Seth Meyers*, which he remembered from his starring role in his camp's Hebrew rendition of *Guys and Dolls*.[26] Although Hebrew song and Israeli dance are found at most Jewish camps, Hebrew theatrical productions are rare. Only 12 of the 103 camps we surveyed reported having them, and that number included 7 Ramah camps. This is not surprising; in a camp where most campers do not speak Hebrew, producing a play in Hebrew is much more labor intensive than producing a similar play in English. Even if many campers have moderate Hebrew proficiency, someone must translate the play or abridge an existing Hebrew script, and performers must be coached not only on singing, dancing, and acting but also on Hebrew pronunciation and intonation. Despite these difficulties, a play offers an opportunity for performers to use the language, albeit routinized language, and for audience members to hear the language. A Ramah national administrator said that the theatrical production has "been one of the most impactful ways of teaching" Hebrew. "Even if the kids are going out of their minds trying to rehearse, and drama specialists are freaking out that they have no time to do it, at the end, this is what they retain."[27]

Indeed they do. Often when we spoke to Ramah alumni about our research, they fondly recalled Hebrew plays from long ago, including many of the lyrics. A woman who attended Ramah Poconos in the late 1950s and early 1960s never performed on stage, but she remembers the musicals performed by the staff or the oldest division, sometimes based on existing American musicals, sometimes original, always in Hebrew. She sang us snippets of songs from *Annie Get Your Gun*: *"Bachur lo tofsim b'roveh"* ("You Can't Get a Man with a Gun," lit. "One does not catch a young man with a rifle") and *South Pacific*: *"Leil aviv maksim hu"* ("Some Enchanted Evening," lit. "It's a delightful spring evening").

Some camps not only translate plays into Hebrew but also adapt their plots to incorporate Hebraist or Zionist themes. At Tel Yehudah in the 1980s, *A Chorus Line* was about Hebrew letters auditioning for a play. In *Bye Bye Bernstein*, their version of *Bye Bye Birdie*, the main character made aliyah instead of joining the U.S. Army. In *Hakosem m'eretz oz* (*The Wizard of Oz*, lit. "The magician from the land of Oz"), Dorothy searched for her homeland, which turned out to be Israel. The Wicked Witch of the West was the only character who spoke English, and she was ultimately "melted" not by water but by Hebrew letters. In other words, Hebrew was not only the medium of the performance, but it also played a prominent metalinguistic role. The more recent shows we observed or heard about were Judaized not thematically, but only linguistically—through their use of Hebrew.

Even though plays involve the rote memorization and recitation of routinized Hebrew, they offer teaching opportunities surrounding vocabulary, grammar, and pronunciation. At a Ramah California rehearsal for *Annie*, a girl recited her line to a boy with the word *bata* (you [masc.] came). The boy asked the Israeli director, "Do I say *bata* too?" The director replied, "No, she's a girl, so you say *bat*" (you [fem.] came). Some musicals incorporate Hebrew phrases from liturgy and other aspects of Jewish life. At Ramah Poconos, the seventh-grade Hebrew production of *Joseph and the Amazing Technicolor Dreamcoat* included the line "*Im tirtzu ein zo agada*" (If you will it, it is no dream), a well-known quote about Zionism by Theodor Herzl. In the song "One More Angel in Heaven," when Joseph's brothers told their father that Joseph died, they said "*Zecher tzadik livracha*" (may the memory of the righteous be for blessing) and "*El male rachamim*" (God full of mercy), phrases common in rituals and discourse surrounding death in American Jewish communities. During rehearsal, the musical director told the performers, "These are actual words used at funerals. They're part of our liturgy." This connection may have helped Jewishly knowledgeable campers memorize their lines and helped others absorb these textual and modern Hebrew phrases.

Hebrew creativity in song goes beyond theatrical productions. Several Hebrew-rich camps include original or translated Hebrew songs in maccabiah or inter-division competitions, often using the melodies of popular American songs. For example, in Moshava IO's 2015 maccabiah, Team *Shamayim* (sky) wrote and performed a mostly English version of Jason Mraz's "I Won't Give Up" with one Hebrew verse. Hebrew musical creativity has even extended to romance. At Ramah Wisconsin in the late 1960s, a bunk of 16-year-old boys wrote Hebrew versions of popular romantic songs and sang them to girls. A current Ramah leader told us, "That, I think, is reflective of tremendous success. When [Hebrew] becomes part of the prank culture, you know the kids have completely embraced it and adopted it." However, even this prank culture was relatively top-down because it was initiated by a counselor.

Such productive Hebrew song translations are feasible only in camps with a rich Hebrew culture, where many counselors and campers have deep Hebrew knowledge. In contrast, singing pre-written Hebrew songs has a relatively low bar. All but one of the camps we surveyed reported singing Hebrew songs, and most do so "a lot." Hebrew songs offer a vehicle for camp tradition, creative expression, and entertainment, and they connect Hebrew with the communal feel of being Jewish at camp.[28] To sing and enjoy a Hebrew song, one does not need to understand the lyrics completely. At most of the Hebrew song sessions we observed, there was little or no discussion of the meanings of the songs. But we did observe several instances of song leaders teaching Hebrew lyrics, especially when a song was first introduced. At Tel Yehudah, when song leaders were teaching the Israeli song "*Shavim*" (equal), they recited the words and campers repeated them. The song leaders asked campers what several of the Hebrew words meant, and a camper who had lived in Israel translated them. At URJ camps, where song sessions are frequent and song leader is a coveted staff position, song leaders often explain songs before singing them, sometimes teaching some or all of the lyrics. We witnessed one such occasion at URJ Kalsman, where Nina, guitar in hand, said, "We already had one Hebrew lesson today. We're gonna have another. Does anyone know the Hebrew word for 'hand'—who's not Israeli?" Someone yelled, "*Yad!*" Nina asked for a few more: foot (*regel*), right (*yamin*), left (*smol*), head (*rosh*), and body (*goof*). Then, with those six words projected (transliterated) on the screen behind her, she taught a song using them.

Songs can help with word retention, as research on language education indicates.[29] We asked a Ramah California ninth-grader if she ever uses camp Hebrew words outside of camp. She said she sometimes does. "If I'm with my [camp] friends and we're going to the pool, I'm like, let's go to the *brecha*, 'cause in the Ramah song it's '*schiya ba'brecha v'shabat b'kehila*' [swimming in the pool and Shabbat in community]. So I'm like, let's go to the *brecha*, and it just sticks in my head, and then we'll start singing the song." She also said she encountered the word *gibor* (hero) in Hebrew school a few months after she was a camper in *Giborei Yisrael* (heroes of Israel), the seventh-grade division. Whenever she heard the word, she would think of the division song, *Giborei Yisrael Kadima* (heroes of Israel forward). She said, "If I didn't use the word *giborei* at camp, it'd just be another word, but whenever I think of *giborei* I think of camp and I remember when I was in *Giborei*, and it makes the words have so much more meaning." These are just a few of many examples of camp Hebrew words, especially in songs, fostering community and positive engagement with Hebrew both at camp and beyond.

## Hebrew Announcements Using Mostly Routinized Hebrew

A regular aspect of Hebrew infusion at Hebrew-rich camps is routinized Hebrew announcements. Routinized and nonroutinized Hebrew lie on a continuum, and the difference between them depends on context. "*Safsalim al hashulchanot* [(put the) benches on the tables]," heard after meals at some Ramah camps, is clearly routinized. It is a set phrase used frequently, and participants can quickly learn what it means when they observe veteran or Hebrew-proficient campers putting the benches on the tables. Many camps' use of "*Yom huledet sameach l'*[Mikayla] *v'*[Jonathan] [Happy birthday to Mikayla and Jonathan]" is also routinized. Participants with limited Hebrew knowledge can quickly learn what it means when it is followed by the Happy Birthday song and Mikayla and Jonathan skip around the room. In contrast, some Hebrew announcements are clearly nonroutinized: they combine words in novel ways, convey new information, are uttered only by people with high Hebrew proficiency, and require some degree of receptive Hebrew competence to be understood. An example is this announcement by a counselor at OSRUI's Chalutzim immersion program: "*Kol mi sherotse laasot shtik hayom, lashevet im [Tal]* [Everyone who wants to do *shtik* [performances, in this case, a song] today, sit with Tal]." Similarly complex Hebrew announcements are made at only a few camps, such as Massad Manitoba, Yavneh, and some Ramah camps.

Outside of these rare settings, some Hebrew-rich camps use announcements that are in the middle of the routinized—nonroutinized continuum, such as this announcement after a meal at Ramah California indicating each group's next destination: "*Acharei Birkat Hamazon, Solelim l'Beit Keneset Ramah, Adat Shalom l'Migrash Kadursal . . . Todah. Birkat Hamazon* [After Grace after Meals, [eighth-grade division] to the Ramah synagogue, [sixth-grade division] to the basketball court. . . . Thank you. Grace after Meals]." This may seem like a nonroutinized announcement because the words vary from day to day. However, campers hear similar sentences on a routine basis, and they can generally understand them without prior Hebrew knowledge. With the exceptions of the word *acharei* (after) and the morpheme "*l'*" (to), all of the words—the prayer name and various divisions and locations at camp—are loanwords that participants at this camp would recognize from hearing them (and using them) in their local variety of CHE. Hebrew verbs are absent. Campers must merely listen for their group name and their next destination. We heard a less routine announcement at Ramah in the Rockies, when a staff member introduced us to the campers: "*Chaverim, yesh lanu orchim:* Sarah Benor *m'*Los Angeles *v'bat shela* [Friends, we have guests: Sarah Benor from Los Angeles and her daughter]." Even though this exact sentence was not uttered any other time, similar sentences may have been said, and campers could easily guess the meaning from the context: a woman and young girl, both of whom are unfamiliar and currently waving at the crowd.

The classification of an announcement as routinized or not can change over time. On the first day, Hebrew announcements are not yet routinized from the perspective of newcomers, and most camps offer translation for those with limited Hebrew proficiency. After an announcement is repeated several times, it becomes routinized. Context is also important. If the routinized announcements discussed earlier were uttered once at a camp with little Hebrew, they would be properly identified as nonroutinized. A higher percentage of camp directors reported that their camps make Hebrew announcements using "set phrases" than "full sentences with spontaneous wording," although both were limited primarily to Hebrew-rich camps.

Different types of routinized Hebrew involve different competencies. For prayers and songs, speakers must only know how to pronounce the words or be able to approximate them; comprehension is not necessary to participate in this communicative act.[30] For announcements with set phrases, some comprehension is expected. Those with more advanced Hebrew may feel they are fuller participants in this speech act, but others can become full participants, even if it requires a period of adjustment. They will likely acquire some receptive Hebrew skills involving the limited input they receive. At camps that use complex non-routinized Hebrew announcements, those with limited Hebrew proficiency may often feel incompetent and left out. Even so, they will likely end the summer with strengthened receptive Hebrew skills, which is a goal for a few of these camps. However, the only people likely to significantly strengthen their *productive* Hebrew skills are those making the announcements—usually staff members but occasionally select campers. Compared to Hebrew songs and skits, announcements may require more Hebrew proficiency for full participation, and they may be less overtly entertaining. Even so, they serve a similar purpose of fostering camp community and conveying the value of Hebrew.

## Hebrew Loanwords in CHE

Although Hebrew announcements are found at only the most Hebrew-rich camps, the vast majority of Jewish camps use at least some Hebrew loanwords. To determine how common this phenomenon is and which loanwords are used, we created a database of the Hebrew loanwords we heard at twenty-four of the camps we visited, representing diverse orientations and levels of Hebrew use. We found a total of 1,006 unique Hebrew loanwords (phrases were counted as one word), as well as hundreds more taught, posted, or used as names of divisions or bunks. Of the 1,006 Hebrew loanwords, 114 were biblical or rabbinic phrases (e.g., *V'ahavta l'reecha kamocha* [you should love your neighbor like yourself]) or proper nouns, like names of holidays, books, songs, or prayers. If we exclude these quotes and proper nouns, we find 893 Hebrew loanwords, two-thirds of which were used in at least two camps. This large number indicates that the phenomenon of Hebrew loanword use at Jewish camps is quite significant. Unlike many of the other practices described in this chapter, loanword use is portable and flexible and can happen at any time of day. Loanwords can pervade camp culture, and at Hebrew-rich camps, they do.

Are the Hebrew words in CHE really all nouns, as complaints from Jewish leaders claim? In our database of 893 loanwords, eighty percent are nouns. Yet we also found a surprisingly high number of other parts of speech, especially at Hebrew-rich camps: 46 interjections (e.g., *sababa* [cool], *gam ani* [me too]), including 17 greetings/closings (e.g., *boker tov* [good morning], *l'hitraot* [goodbye]) and

8 evaluations (e.g., *yafe meod* [very nice], *nachon* [correct]); 40 adverbs (e.g., *bichlal* [at all], *bilvad* [alone]); 38 verbs (e.g., *hakshivu, hevantem?* [did you understand?]); 35 adjectives (e.g., *asur* [forbidden], *kosher*); and 4 prepositions (e.g., *acharei* [after], *neged* [against]). Thus, CHE is far more complex than a sprinkling of Hebrew nouns into English. The frequency of the parts of speech at camp aligns with research on loanwords around the world that was conducted in bilingual contexts: nouns tend to be borrowed most frequently, followed by adjectives, verbs, and prepositions.[31]

We also looked at whether the Hebrew words used in CHE refer mostly to camp-specific referents—activities, locations, and roles that people encounter primarily at camp, such as *madrich* or *tzrif*. If this were the case, we could characterize Hebrew use primarily as a "nominal" phenomenon, with the sense of "naming" things. In fact, of the 893 Hebrew words, only 17 percent refer to camp-specific referents, and 38 percent are Jewish life words—used in Jewish English outside of camp, including many textual Hebrew words referring to religious life (e.g., *minyan* [prayer quorum/group], *shavua tov* [good week]), as well as several modern Hebrew words that do not refer to religious life (e.g., *b'teavon* [bon appetit], *sheket b'vakasha*). At many camps, the majority of Hebrew loanwords are Jewish life words and camp words that name activities, locations, and roles. But this is not the case at Hebrew-rich camps. Of the remaining 403 words—which do not have camp-specific referents and are not used in Jewish English outside of camp—a large majority were used only at an individual camp (any one of several Hebrew-rich camps). About one-quarter were used at two to four camps, and only a few words were used at five or more camps. Aside from *ken* (yes), all of the words used at five or more camps are nouns referring to things discussed at camp (but not exclusive to camp, because these were considered camp words), such as *rosh* X (head of X), *aruchat erev* (dinner), *omanut* (art), and *bakbuk mayim* (water bottle). The vast majority of the words that were used at two to four camps are also nouns referring to things that may be discussed at camp (e.g., *geshem* [rain], *banot* [girls]), but there were also some other parts of speech (e.g., *smol* [left (in dance)], *achshav* [now]).

In contrast, many of the words used at only one camp may be heard in the Hebrew-English translanguaging of any Israeli American family, including adverbs, interjections, and other parts of speech (e.g., *barur* [clear], *lo matim* [not appropriate]). We observed many of these at Hebrew-rich camps where nonroutinized Hebrew is more common, such as Ramah and Bnei Akiva camps, OSRUI, and Yavneh. Their use indicates a more productive interaction between English and Hebrew at certain camps and illustrates the blurry distinction between loanwords and code switching in translanguaging contexts where speakers have moderate or advanced proficiency in multiple languages.[32]

Even at camps with very little nonroutinized Hebrew, we sometimes observed a few Hebrew words that we did not hear at other camps. Many of these were locations, such as *desheh* (lawn) and *nof* (vista) used at URJ Newman. These and many similar instances of Hebrew use must be analyzed as loanwords because most of the participants have little or no proficiency in Hebrew. Even so, they point to the value placed on Hebrew at the camp using those words. At some time in the camp's history, one or more staff members thought Hebrew was important enough that the camp should use these Hebrew words, even if they are not common at other camps. And they had the resources to find the appropriate Hebrew word (knowledge of Hebrew, a dictionary, or an acquaintance who knows some Hebrew), as well as the cultural capital at camp to incorporate the word into the camp's variety of CHE.

Around the world, the pronunciation, word order, and meaning of loanwords are often influenced by the primary language. For example, most English speakers do not pronounce "burrito" with the trilled [r] and unaspirated [t] of Spanish. And two ostentatious women might be characterized as "nouveau riche," rather than the French *nouvelles riches*. At camp we found similar integration of loanwords. Most native English speakers pronounced Hebrew words with English norms, with the addition of [ch], which was sometimes [h] among speakers with less Hebrew exposure. We found a mixture of English and Hebrew plurals: *brachas* and *brachot* (blessings)—and other pronunciations at Sephardi and Orthodox camps—and *chugs* and *chugim* (electives). Another type of English influence is calques: direct translations of a phrase from one language into another, sometimes yielding an unusual word order. We found several English-to-Hebrew calques, such as *Shabbat shira* (Sabbath song, rather than *shirat Shabbat* or *shirei Shabbat*) and *tzevet peula* (staff activity, rather than *peulat tzevet*). Some calques were one-off jokes, such as counselors calling hot dogs *klavim chamim* ("hot dogs" rather than *naknikiot*) and, at a different camp, calling catsup *chatul l'mala* ("cat up" rather than *ketshup*) (perhaps barbecues encourage wordplay?). We also found many instances of Hebrew phrases with Hebrew syntax, such as *peulat erev* (evening activity) and *migrash kadursal* (basketball court). We even found rare, tongue-in-cheek instances of English words with Hebrew plurals, such as the masculine plural suffix *-im* in "co-songleaderim." These and many other examples indicate the hybrid nature of American Jews' Hebrew use and, more generally, of translanguaging. Whether intentional or unintentional, serious or meant as a joke, forms like *chugs* and *klavim chamim* enable American Jews to use elements of English and Hebrew simultaneously.[33]

More generally, the use of loanwords within English sentences sends a message about the importance of Hebrew at camp and gives campers an opportunity to use elements of Hebrew. In contrast to skits and announcements, CHE is not necessarily performed by staff and consumed by campers: it is available for campers to use. Some campers may say loanwords, like *tzrif* and *madrich*, and others may say only their English equivalents, bunk and counselor. Although CHE encourages productive, rather than only receptive, engagement with language, it incorporates only select words, not the structure of Hebrew. Instead, it teaches that English-Hebrew hybridity is a valid and valued American Jewish practice.

## CLASSES

Compared to most other Hebrew practices, classes are rare at camp. Several camp directors and educators told us that their camps used to schedule Hebrew classes but recently dropped them, or they had tried them briefly but considered them a failed experiment. They realized that campers were not able to make much progress toward proficiency in the brief time allotted to Hebrew each day or week. And many interviewees expressed concern that campers would be turned off by school-like activities. When camps do offer a period of Hebrew instruction, these sessions are generally geared more toward exposure and amusement than grammar or conversational proficiency. In other words, camps are using Hebrew instruction as part of their broader program of language infusion. For example, Habonim Dror Camp Miriam dedicated a block of the day to Israeli culture, including cooking and Hebrew slang. As one staff member said, it was decidedly not about grammar, and they called it *zman Ivrit* (Hebrew period), avoiding the word "class."

OSRUI has one of the most in-depth Hebrew programs. While the Chalutzim immersion division has intensive Hebrew classes, other divisions have a period called "Ivrit" daily. Even though these sessions are framed and perceived as language instruction, they can also be understood as an entertaining infusion practice. The sessions use games, art, and other activities to teach vocabulary in a few domains, such as body parts, animals, and vegetables. They are led by American counselors, partly to model Americans feeling comfortable with Hebrew. However, their comfort is with symbolic Hebrew use, mostly nouns, rather than sentence structure or conversation. Nobody at OSRUI expects campers to become proficient in Hebrew after four weeks of Hebrew relay races and fashion shows, even after doing similar activities six summers in a row. Rather, these classes are intended to expose campers to elements of Hebrew, create an experiential link between Hebrew and fun, help them view Hebrew as a component of American Jewishness, and ideally interest them in pursuing further Hebrew study—in the teen Chalutzim program and beyond.

When we observed OSRUI's Ivrit sessions, campers appeared to be engaged and happy. In focus groups, several campers said the sessions made learning Hebrew more fun than their religious schools. However, a few told us that "Hebrew" was their least favorite activity at camp or recalled having learned the same words multiple times. "I was like, we know the colors!" On the other hand, an OSRUI alum who eventually became a Jewish educator looked back fondly on Ivrit class in the 1980s: "I remember that . . . being a highlight of my day because the language really felt like a living language to me. And it wasn't just something that we studied through prayer, like we did back in my home synagogue." Though she did not attain fluency, she said, "There are still words to this very day that I know in Hebrew because I learned them at camp." Whether or not campers come away from these sessions retaining Hebrew words (beyond colors), they send the message that Hebrew is a fun and important part of camp life.

Although most of the Hebrew instruction we encountered at contemporary camps was oriented toward infusion, we found more immersive instruction oriented toward proficiency in OSRUI's Chalutzim program and at a few Ramah camps. Ramah Darom, for example, refashioned its required Hebrew classes as a series of Hebrew immersion *chugim* (electives), such as cooking, art, sports, and Zumba. The offerings of electives were based on the interests and skills of the Israeli emissaries who led them, so they had different options each year. In the Zumba class, campers did more than just dance as the instructor called out moves in Hebrew; they also discussed the dancing and other topics in Hebrew through opening and closing conversations. This sort of language immersion enhances learning by contextualizing the language within a kinesthetic activity, a common technique in language instruction.[34] An administrator at Ramah Darom considered this innovation a success: "Instead of trying to skip *Ivrit* every day, kids love it and go to it, and it's really been fantastic." In addition, he said that the Hebrew *chugim* made campers more open to using Hebrew in other contexts at camp. In contrast to most of the practices described in this chapter, Hebrew immersion electives are oriented toward strengthening proficiency by giving campers an opportunity to practice productive language skills. However, they share some features with infusion practices; they are top-down, pedagogically oriented, and, significantly, entertaining. They offer a fun, camp-appropriate alternative to school-based language instruction.

## INCENTIVE, COMPETITION, AND GAMES

Whether in "classes" or in other activities, playful competition and incentives are important aspects of Hebrew infusion at many camps. This is only part of a broader culture of competition, including in sports, singing, and quieting. We observed a great deal of competition and use of incentives at OSRUI. The Chalutzim immersion program pitted bunks against each other in *Olimpiada* (Olympics), a competition to speak only Hebrew all day. In a daily ritual involving chants and movements, campers were encouraged to participate in this competition, and each week one bunk won a coveted prize, such as eating breakfast on the lake or throwing pies in counselors' faces. Outside of Chalutzim, OSRUI campers earned "*Ivrit Plus*" points by playing a Hebrew game, reading a Hebrew book, or doing a puppet show in Hebrew. They could trade in their points for items at the *chanut* (store/canteen), including candy and t-shirts. On a more informal basis, the *Rosh Ivrit* (head of Hebrew) handed out stickers when she heard a camper use a Hebrew sentence or ask an impressive question about Hebrew. Such incentives appealed to children's appreciation of competition and rewards to encourage engagement with Hebrew and positive associations surrounding it.

Ramah camps also made ample use of competition, especially based on their Daber (speak) fellowship, a funded initiative that trained counselors to increase Hebrew use at Ramah camps, partly through fun incentives. At Ramah Poconos, the Daber fellows organized a *shuk* (market), where campers could buy treats. The only currency accepted at the Daber *shuk* was "Daber *shkalim*" (Israeli currency), which campers could earn the week before the *shuk* by using Hebrew in any activity. As one administrator reported, "The kids go crazy during the week when they're able to earn these little pieces of paper. It's so funny. You'd think that they were, like, a million dollars." The culture at Ramah Poconos is so oriented toward rewards for Hebrew use that when a girl received a green sticker for winning a game, she asked her counselor, "If I say it in Hebrew, can I get the color I want? *Ani rotsa kachol* [I want blue]." Her counselor said no, and she responded playfully, "But I said it in Hebrew!"

In the summer of 2015, when we visited Ramah Poconos, the most salient manifestation of rewards and competition was #*MeahMilim* (100 words). The director explained to colleagues in a pre-summer email: "The concept is to go back to basics; what are the 100 words that should ONLY be spoken in Ivrit. Starting with Shavua Hachanah [Training Week], and using our Daber Fellows, we will explain the concept to tzevet [staff], encouraging them to study the list and practice using (and correcting others when they do not use) these words in Ivrit . . . Madrichim [counselors] who are observed using these Meah Milim on a consistent basis will get a T-shirt." The list was divided by category: words used in the *tzrif, chadar ochel, omanut*, etc. Anyone could nominate a staff member who made a special effort to use these words. The coveted t-shirt had a Hebrew logo that said, "אני מדבר מאה מילים" ("I speak 100 words," a not-quite-idiomatic Hebrew sentence), "100 words," and the Hebrew-English Ramah movement logo. The thinking behind #*MeahMilim* was that offering prizes would encourage more Hebrew word use, and by all accounts, the program accomplished this goal. Counselors used many of these words and even corrected each other when they used their English equivalents. At first, the competition was only for staff; it was made exclusive so campers would want to participate (they did). As one administrator told us, "People in this camp will do anything for a t-shirt, even speak Hebrew." When rewards are tangible, Hebrew use serves as more than cultural capital; it is explicitly commodified. Ironically, in introducing a spirit of competition they (inadvertently) rejected a key element of Ramah's progressive educational philosophy dating back to the 1950s and reverted to an earlier model inherited from Massad Poconos.

We also found competition in short-term games involving Hebrew, especially in Israel culture sessions and maccabiah. At Beber, groups of campers received poster boards with the lyrics of *Hatikvah* (the Israeli national anthem) scrambled, and they had to put the words in order and sing the song. At Perlman, a pluralistic camp in Pennsylvania, campers played Hebrew Twister, using Hebrew words for right, left, foot, hand, and the four colors. Most of these activities involved modern Hebrew, but we also observed games highlighting textual Hebrew. At Eden Village, campers participated in an elaborate role-playing game called Midbar Quest (*midbar* means desert or wilderness), where players gave their characters and actions Hebrew names from biblical and rabbinic literature, sometimes using a dictionary or asking a text-savvy staff member.

Games and competitions are a hallmark of the camp experience in many camps. When the games include Hebrew, they send a message about the importance of Hebrew—as well as certain varieties of Hebrew and specific Hebrew words—in the camp setting. This is just another way that camps infuse their primarily English environments with Hebrew-centered entertainment and socialize campers to have positive feelings about Hebrew.

### Informal Teaching and Other Metalinguistic Conversation

Several of the practices discussed thus far involve metalinguistic conversation (talk about language). In a situation of ethnolinguistic infusion, such talk brings attention to the group language and emphasizes particular ideologies. In addition to official activities like classes, games, and skits, we found instances of impromptu pedagogical conversation about Hebrew at many camps, like the water slide password that opened this chapter. Staff members spontaneously taught or reinforced Hebrew words, often by asking campers "Who knows what [Hebrew word X] means?" or "How do you say [English word Y] in Hebrew?" At Hilltop, longtime counselor Josh was giving new campers a tour. When they reached the HIPO—Hilltop Indoor Programming *Ohel*—he initiated a metalinguistic exchange: "Who knows what *ohel* means?" One camper responded, "Food." Josh explained the difference between *ochel* (food) and *ohel* (tent). At OSRUI, a popular sports instructor taught some Hebrew as he divided up young campers for a game of "matzah ball": "I'm gonna say one of two Hebrew words: *po, sham. Po* means here, *sham* means there." These staff members were not appointed as Hebrew teachers and had limited Hebrew ability. Their use of Hebrew words and metalinguistic conversation had the potential to associate Hebrew with the charisma of young American counselors. Such interactions may not be as entertaining as some of the other infusion practices, but they similarly engage campers and highlight the importance and pervasiveness of Hebrew in this American Jewish context.

Some of this informal teaching happens in frontal discourse directed at a group of campers; other such interactions are one-on-one. For example, as a boy at Solomon Schechter ate watermelon, Ben, a staff member, asked him, "Do you know how to say watermelon in Hebrew?" He didn't, so Ben told him: *avatiach*. Like the water slide password, such one-off instances of Hebrew teaching may not lead to word retention, but they link Hebrew with the fun (and, in this case, sweet taste) of camp activities. Sprout Lake formalized this practice with their "*Ma ze b'Ivrit?*" (What's this in Hebrew?) initiative, spearheaded through the Cornerstone Fellowship. When someone used an English word that has a CHE equivalent, like bunk or counselor, a staff member would ask, "*Ma ze b'Ivrit?*" and the person was expected to respond with the appropriate Hebrew word.

We observed such impromptu Hebrew teaching at camps of all types, but it was most common at Hebrew-rich camps. At Ramah Poconos, Noga, a long-time returning Israeli emissary, frequently included metalinguistic conversation in her swim instruction, in addition to Hebrew-English translanguaging. Sometimes she connected vocabulary to other words campers were likely to know, especially from liturgy, such as "*lishmoa* [to hear]—you know, like *Shma Yisrael* ["Hear, Israel" prayer]." Other times she used translation, gestures, and metalinguistic questions, as in this excerpt:

> NOGA: Now we're gonna do it [swim] *al hagav*—on the back. *Eynaim l'mala* [eyes up] (pantomimes backstroke). Listen, don't forget to exhale through your *af* [nose] (points to her nose). If you don't, you'll get water in your nose . . . *Ken* [yes]. *Mispar shalosh, kadima* [number three, forward]. *Od* [more]. *Yofi* [nice], *yafe* [nice]. *Tistaklu aleha* [look at her] (points to girl). *Yafe meod* [very nice]. What's *yafe meod*?
>
> GIRL: Good job?
>
> NOGA: Very nice. What's "wall" in Hebrew?
>
> BOY: *Kir.*
>
> NOGA: Who said *kir*?
>
> BOY: Me.
>
> NOGA: *Kol hakavod* [well done].

Noga's metalinguistic questions engaged campers with Hebrew vocabulary in a nonclassroom setting, even when that was not the main skill being taught.

At several camps, leaders used prayers as an opportunity to discuss the meanings of liturgical words. During services at Hilltop, Kevin asked, "Anyone remember what *Amida* means? The Hebrew root *ayin-mem-daled*—what does it mean?" After several seconds of silence, a girl replied, "Stand." After affirming this response, Kevin taught about a different word for "stand": The prayer *Mi chamocha* "has a clue for when we're supposed to stand. Who can find it? If you can find it in the Hebrew, even better, but English is OK too." A girl responded, "Rise." Kevin said, "Great. In Hebrew the word is *kuma*." Kevin acknowledged that Hebrew is difficult for some campers ("English is OK too"), but his multiple mentions of Hebrew and the phrase "even better" emphasized that he—and by extension the camp—values Hebrew.

Several of the campers we interviewed said they had learned Hebrew words from such interactions. However, when we asked for the Hebrew equivalents of the relevant English words, campers often reported that they forgot. Some interviewees explicitly said they did not learn words well from such overt attempts to teach them but did retain words that were used as part of camp life (CHE). When staff members initiate metalinguistic conversations about particular Hebrew words, they generally do not expect campers to remember those words, and they certainly do not expect such interactions to lead to Hebrew proficiency. These conversations serve the same purpose as other Hebrew infusion practices: socializing young Jews to be members of a community that values, talks about, and uses elements of Hebrew, even as English is the primary language of communication.

### Translation and Progression of Language Exposure and Use

With so much Hebrew infusion, some camp leaders worry about alienating campers, especially newcomers. As a 2006 Ramah report concluded, "This can easily be avoided by training staff to be aware of those whose Hebrew levels are quite low, and providing for numerous opportunities for learning and translations."[35] Indeed, Ramah and other Hebrew-rich camps we observed did offer translations in several contexts. At Ramah California, prayer choreography and page numbers were announced in Hebrew in all age groups. But in the youngest division and the special needs division, such phrases were often translated, especially near the beginning. At the first prayer service of a two-week session for young campers, the leader translated most camp words (e.g., "*chanichim*—campers"), all page numbers ("Start on *amud shtem esrey*, page twelve"), and all instructions ("*Tishvu b'vakasha*. That means sit down please."). She even translated certain words that are part of Jewish English or liturgical Hebrew, such as: "We have all different kinds of *nigunim*, which means ways of singing tunes" and "*amen* means to agree, by the way." However, several words that are common in Jewish English went untranslated: *tefilot* (prayers), *sidurim* (prayer books), and *balagan* (mess).

Many camps translate on the first day but quickly phase out the English. At the beginning of a session at Solomon Schechter, staff members used CHE with translations of loanwords; for example, "Make new *chaverim*, new friends," "Then we do *nikayon*, clean-up" (in addition to the inserted translations with the special intonation, described earlier). Some of the translations were offered through metalinguistic questions: "Raise your hand if you've heard of a *toranut* [someone on dining hall duty]" and "Anyone know what *chadar* [dining hall] means in English?" Such interactions do not explain how these words are used differently in the camp setting than in Israeli Hebrew. They are intended to ensure that campers understand the words for the purpose of their participation in camp; they socialize campers to be proficient not in Hebrew but in CHE.

At OSRUI, a common translation practice was what they called "the sandwich method," Hebrew-English-Hebrew, often followed by a clap, miming a sandwich. For example, a counselor said, "*Kibui orot*, lights out, *kibui orot* (clap)." In a Hebrew class about animals, a teacher said, "We're gonna make another sandwich: *kivsa*, sheep, *kivsa* (clap)." This was so frequent that it became the object of satire. One skit included counselors giving each other high fives and saying: "*Kif*, high five, *kif* (clap)." Whenever someone uses the sandwich method, it highlights a particular Hebrew word. And the frequency of its use conveys a symbolic message about the importance of Hebrew at camp.

In addition to translation, sometimes there is explicit orientation about language use early in a session. At the first *tefillah* at *Taam shel Ramah* (Taste of Ramah), a week-long session for young campers at Ramah Poconos, Amber, a counselor, coached the newcomers in a greeting exchange: "We're gonna try this out. When I say "*Boker tov, Taam shel Ramah*," you say "*Boker or,* [Amber]!" After the service, Amber made more announcements that involved translation ("*Acharei aruchat boker*, after breakfast, the first *peula*, the first activity") and metalinguistic comments about these translations ("We're teaching you some *Ivrit*, some Hebrew"). When a camper asked a question about the "counselors," Amber socialized him and all present to use the Hebrew word: "Counselors! Who knows how to say counselors in Hebrew? *Madrichim*. Next time I want you to say *madrichim*." New campers learn from these interventions that Hebrew loanwords and routinized exchanges are ubiquitous and highly valued at this camp. And if some campers are overwhelmed by the Hebrew infusion, these language socialization practices ensure that they do not feel completely left out.

Beyond session-initial socialization, some Hebrew-rich camps provide a long-term progression of exposure and use of CHE and other Hebrew practices over the course of a participant's many years at camp.[36] In their first several years at OSRUI, campers are exposed to CHE, Hebrew word skits, Ivrit classes, and Hebrew announcements of page numbers for prayers. If they join the high school Chalutzim immersion program, they are expected not only to be receptive listeners but also to produce Hebrew themselves. If they stay at OSRUI as counselors, they are expected to produce some loanwords and routinized Hebrew announcements, and even more if they become division heads and administrators. The few Americans who become Chalutzim staff are expected not only to speak Hebrew but also to teach and inspire others to do so. We see a similar progression at Ramah camps, without the pinnacle of the immersion program. After several years at camp (or, for campers who start as teenagers, right away), they are expected to understand the Hebrew words for prayer choreography and page numbers without translation. Counselors and specialists are expected to use heavily Hebraized CHE, and division heads are expected to make Hebrew announcements. Head staff are expected to interact with Israeli emissaries and run some meetings in Hebrew. At Ramah, we also see a process of gradual Hebrew exposure and expectation regarding ritual participation. Older campers take on roles in services, like reading Torah, having an *aliyah* (chanting the blessings surrounding a Torah reading), and leading prayers. The gradual exposure to various aspects of Hebrew infusion leads to a hierarchy based not only on seniority but also on linguistic skill. At least moderate Hebrew proficiency plays an important role for leadership in Ramah's elite brand of Jewish life.

Another progression of language socialization and hierarchy is the transition from learner to teacher among campers. Newcomers to a camp will often ask veterans for help with the Hebrew words that are new to them. By their second summer, or even a few weeks into their first summer, these same campers may find themselves helping others. One morning at Ramah California, Nora, a ninth-grade first-time camper, did not understand when the prayer leader said, "*Shva esrey*" (17). She turned to her peer Zoe and asked, "What page?" Instead of answering in English or showing her open book, Zoe repeated the number, *shva esrey*, and then said more familiar versions of the component numbers: *sheva* (7), *eser* (10). Nora knew these numbers and found the page. Zoe may have once been in Nora's shoes, and now she was acting as the teacher, not only answering her question but also socializing Nora to understand the Hebrew numbers and the local importance of Hebrew. This is a common phenomenon in situations of language socialization: novices learn not only from those above them in the community hierarchy but also from their peers.

We also see the progression of learning and teaching in interactions between campers and their parents, siblings, and others who did not attend their camp. When they write letters home or talk about their camp experiences, they may use CHE and then find themselves in the role of translator and teacher. Although we did not analyze post-camp interactions or campers' letters, we found evidence of this progression in blog posts written by Gilboa campers. They used many camp Hebrew words and sometimes translated them. These translations may have been inserted by an adult editor, but sometimes they seem to be written by the children, as in this sentence by a seventh grader: "We do something called Avodah. Avodah is work in Hebrew, and we help camp Gilboa with it."[37] Campers are socialized to understand and use CHE and may later serve as socializers themselves, sharing their knowledge with parents and others. Whether they are learning or teaching, they are engaging with Hebrew in ways that they would not if it were not for Jewish summer camp.

————

Creativity surrounding Hebrew infusion happens at camps of many types, as the large number of camps featured in this chapter indicates. Some of the songs, skits, and games have circulated via people who worked at multiple camps or through funded initiatives from FJC and other camp networks. In some cases, infusion practices are initiated by Israeli emissaries, who learn them in their pre-summer training. But as the repeated mentions of a few camps in this chapter suggest, Hebrew infusion practices are not evenly distributed. When we told people we were researching Hebrew at Jewish summer camps, many suggested we visit OSRUI and Ramah camps, which are known for their commitment to Hebrew. Indeed, those are the camps where we spent the most time and con-ducted camper interviews to gain a more in-depth understanding of how Hebrew infusion works.

Allie, a ninth-grader at Ramah California, demonstrated the positive effects of her camp's intensive Hebrew infusion. She explained why she and her friends like that Ramah's musical is in Hebrew: "I think a lot of people really enjoy it because it makes them feel, like, oh, we understand this and not everybody else in the world does. So it's interesting and really fun." She has absorbed the mes-sages of Hebrew infusion. Although she "understands" Hebrew only at a rudi-mentary level, she characterizes it as "our language," demonstrating her sense of ownership over it and her feeling of belonging to the Jewish people. And her use of the word "fun" indicates the pleasure she takes in being exposed to elements of Hebrew. The entertaining ways that her camp infuses Hebrew into a primarily English setting—including singing, performance, and competition—emphasize collectivity and joy. Because of her summer camp experiences, Allie—like many other young American Jews—feels part of a Hebrew-oriented metalinguistic community: one that talks about Hebrew, values Hebrew, and feels personally connected to Hebrew, even as they speak English.

In some ways, the metalinguistic community that encompasses Allie and her fellow participants at Hebrew-rich camps is similar to other metalinguistic com-munities, such as Yiddish enthusiasts who purchase Yiddish souvenirs, attend Yiddish festivals, and join Yiddish clubs. In both cases, participants are engag-ing with the language in postvernacular ways, in which the symbolic function is privileged over the communicative function. And in both, participants have an ideological connection with the language without the ability to converse in it.[38] However, Jewish summer camps are not primarily oriented around language, in contrast to Yiddish clubs. Hebrew is only one of many tools Jewish camps use to socialize participants to be members of American Jewish communities. They use games, skits, and songs—many of which use little or no Hebrew—also to teach about Jewish values, holidays, lifecycle events, and Israel. Like Hebrew infusion, these activities are often entertaining, and they may involve hybridity between American and Jewish identities. In addition, many non-Judaic activities, such as horseback riding, art, and eating popsicles on a hot afternoon, bring campers joy and entice them back each summer. Combined with the Hebrew infusion practices described in this chapter and the Hebrew-English signage described in the next chapter, these practices help make Jewish camps a place—to borrow Camp Solomon Schechter's tagline—"Where Judaism and Joy are One."

# CHAPTER 6

# "Sign" Language

## VISUAL DISPLAYS OF HEBREW AND JEWISH SPACE

"Let's go, *kachol* [blue]!" Dan's rallying call was greeted with enthusiasm from his fellow 16- and 17-year-old campers at Tel Yehudah. Secretly gathered during their afternoon free time in a building far from the center of camp, they were preparing for the camp-wide color war event, *maccabiah*, scheduled to begin the following day. Their immediate and pressing mission was to prepare the blue team's signs and banners for the color war "breakout" (surprise introduction) at the next morning's flagpole gathering. After rolling out an eight-foot sheet of butcher paper on the floor and quickly painting it with a light blue background, they discussed what should be written on the sign. They knew that blue was *kachol* in Hebrew, but as another camper, Brian, started to sketch out the letters on a piece of paper, he was unsure whether, in Hebrew, the word was spelled with a *chet* or *hey*. Dan, who had learned Hebrew at a Jewish day school, gave the correct answer: *chet*. Once they agreed on the spelling, there were other orthographic decisions to make, all influenced by the diverse literacy levels of the campers who would see the signs. Should they use block letters (כחול) or cursive (כ) בחול)? Should they include Hebrew "vowels" (i.e., *nikud*)—a system of dots above and below letters that indicate the sounds between the consonants (כָּחוֹל)? Should they include transliteration, and if so, was the correct English spelling *kachol, kahol,* or *cahol*? Finally, they wondered, should they also translate it into English? After some back and forth, they decided that it was, in fact, important for them to write the words in Hebrew because this was part of camp tradition. And they opted to use block letters with no vowels, no transliteration, and no translation, reasoning that the blue paint would denote the team color and thus would be obvious to everyone, even to those who could not read the Hebrew.

Preparing for color war may seem like a mundane camp activity, but when analyzed as an instance of ethnolinguistic infusion, it emerges as a site of rich symbolic negotiation. If Dan and his friends were using only their primary language, English, they would not have discussed how to write it. Although they had varying degrees of Hebrew knowledge from other Jewish educational settings and from past summers at this Hebrew-infused camp, their Hebrew-writing skills were only rudimentary. They were also aware of similar limitations in other campers' Hebrew-reading skills, as was evident in their decision to use block letters rather than cursive. At the same time, they recognized that it did not matter whether all campers could read the Hebrew letters on the signs. The inclusion of Hebrew served a symbolic, rather than communicative, function—a reminder that Hebrew is part of this Jewish camp's past and present. But if the use of Hebrew writing was solely symbolic, random Hebrew letters would have sufficed. The signs also served a pedagogical function, exposing campers to select words written in Hebrew letters. Moreover, they served to constitute local hierarchies of Hebrew literacy expertise: those at the top level can demonstrate that expertise by producing and consuming (viewing) Hebrew signs, as well as by producing and consuming (hearing) spoken language. Conversely, those with limited Hebrew literacy might feel—and even express—alienation, or they might use the presence of signage as an opportunity to strengthen their Hebrew skills. In short, choices and interactions regarding orthography highlight and perpetuate ideologies about who should read and write Hebrew and the relationship between Hebrew and English within the camp landscape.

Orthographic choices highlight hierarchies not only among participants at a given camp but also among camps of diverse orientations toward Judaism, Zionism, and Hebrew. On one end of the continuum, at the least Hebrew-rich camps, only English is present, and at camps with a bit more Hebrew, transliteration is used in addition to or instead of Hebrew lettering. Most participants at either of those types of camps do not have the Hebrew skills that the Tel Yehudah campers demonstrated, and leaders regularly negotiate the concern that using more Hebrew will alienate participants. On the other end, at a Ramah or Bnei Akiva camp, where half or more campers have strong Hebrew literacy skills from attending Jewish day schools, color war signs are mostly in Hebrew, using a combination of print and cursive. In such environments, campers with lower Hebrew literacy skills may feel inferior or left out. Thus a reliance on Hebrew to enhance the Jewishness of a camp is not only an asset but can also be a liability, potentially alienating prospective or current camp participants.

Whereas the previous chapter focused on Hebrew infusion in spoken discourse, this chapter explores written Hebrew on signs, banners, plaques, song sheets, and other material objects, as well as on websites. Some visual displays are handwritten, and others are typed, artistically rendered, or commercially produced. Some Hebrew signs are created for long-term, widespread viewing; others are posted temporarily or are targeted to specific viewers. In this chapter, we analyze physical displays of Hebrew as a unique category of Hebrew infusion, and we "read" all of this signage to understand how visual expressions of Hebrew reflect and create varying forms of Jewishness. Hebrew signage, in conjunction with English writing and other visual cues, helps constitute camp as an American Jewish space, in contrast to other American spaces and in contrast to Israeli spaces. As campers, staff, and others view these visual cues, they are summoned to think of themselves in particular ways within the shared space and social reality of camp.[1]

## THE LINGUISTIC LANDSCAPE

There is a long tradition in the social sciences of analyzing visual displays of language(s), focusing on how they represent, organize, and give meaning to space and social structure.[2] Studying the "linguistic landscape" or "semiotic landscape," this field investigates which languages are used on signs, billboards, and posted notes, as well as the orthography and the size and placement of the letters, to analyze how space takes on social meaning. The presence of languages other than the dominant one (e.g., Chinese or Spanish in American cities, where English dominates) often serves communicative purposes by conveying information about businesses and locations to immigrants and tourists. However, the use of such minority languages also serves symbolic purposes, indicating to in-group and out-group members that people who speak that language have a presence in that neighborhood and that their language has value or a purpose.[3]

In situations of ethnolinguistic infusion, such as in immigrant and indigenous community centers and educational institutions, the communicative and symbolic functions of visual displays of language are flipped. Few if any participants need signs to understand what happens in a particular place or how to get to a specific building; their primary function is to emphasize the importance of the language in the group setting. Additionally, those who post signs often intend them to have a pedagogical function: they want group members to learn select words or phrases from reading the signs.[4] Even if many or most community members cannot understand the signs, they serve as "passive linguistic input"[5] and play an important role in building community and fostering an ethnolinguistic ideology that the language is central to group identity, although the primary language is English. Similarly, at Jewish summer camps, most Hebrew signs do not convey denotative meaning the way English signs do. Participants who know little Hebrew may be able to guess the meaning of Hebrew words on signs based on other visual cues, such as their location or their accompanying illustrations. However, the signs convey that Hebrew is important for the camp community.

While Hebrew infusion at Jewish summer camps has much in common with infusion in other groups, the stakes are different. Hebrew use is not stigmatized as many immigrant and indigenous groups' languages are. And, in contrast to endangered indigenous languages, American Jews do not have the burden of keeping Hebrew alive, because it is thriving in Israel. Among American Jews and immigrant groups, the linguistic landscape can help create a visual tie between the homeland and the diasporic enclave and can teach some of the ancestral language to group members who use English as their primary language. American Jews differ from other groups in that Hebrew writing symbolizes not only the (ancient-modern) homeland of Israel but also the sacred textual tradition. Both modern Hebrew and textual Hebrew are found in camps' visual landscapes.

In both immigrant and indigenous communities, signs featuring their group language can represent rupture and reclamation. The language was not always represented in the current location, either because the group came from somewhere else or because external forces led to the endangerment or dormancy of the group language.[6] When community members post signs in their group language, they are laying claim to both the language and the space and emphasizing the links among language, space, and group. Historically, the Diaspora that was created after various expulsions and migrations of Jews from the land of Israel represents rupture, and the modern revernacularization of Hebrew represents reclamation. Mid-twentieth-century camps' use of Hebrew signage was part of the reclamation of Hebrew as a modern language in the American milieu. This trend continues today, even as leaders no longer feel the burden of contributing to the revival of Hebrew. When camp leaders post Hebrew signs, they are marking camp space as Jewish and highlighting the links among Hebrew, the camp, and Jews in America.

Another insight of the research on semiotic landscapes is that language intermingles with other visual symbols of the group, including flags, maps, and artistic styles.[7] At Jewish camps, Hebrew coexists with other Jewish images, such as Torahs, menorahs, and maps of Israel, which mark bunks, dining halls, chapels, and multipurpose rooms as Jewish spaces. Although most participants can easily interpret these visual symbols, not everyone can understand Hebrew words. At the same time, most people just as easily recognize Hebrew letters as a Jewish symbol. In addition to Jewish visual displays placed around camp, many participants bring clothing, hats, jewelry, and bags that include both symbols like Stars of David and Jewishly valent words in Hebrew and English, such as names of schools, synagogues, and youth groups. All of these displays combine to point to the particular Jewish orientation of the space and the people who populate it.

Finally, focusing on the linguistic landscape at camp means attending to the ways in which multiple languages are represented simultaneously in signage. Like the hybrid Hebrew-English games, songs, and sentences described in the previous chapter, signage is an infusion practice that draws on hybridity and linguistic creativity. Visual multilingualism not only ensures that a sign can be read by various populations, but it also exposes a community's competing ideologies. Even when governmental institutions have a prescriptive policy that requires the display of multiple languages, tremendous variation and creativity in wording and design sometimes undermine the "parallel" intention of these bilingual signs. For example, bilingual Welsh and English signage in Wales draws from diverging language ideologies that not only elevate the status of Welsh to a legitimate language alongside English but also turn it into a cultural curiosity that suffers from tokenization.[8] Put simply, a bilingual sign does not necessarily mean language equality or entail that both languages are being used for identical purposes. At Jewish camps, if Hebrew is more prominent than English in placement or size, or if English is absent altogether, this certainly does not indicate that Hebrew is the camp's primary language of communication, nor does it indicate that the camp values Hebrew over English.

In sum, American Jewish summer camps present a special type of linguistic landscape. Rather than serving a primarily communicative function, visual displays of Hebrew demarcate group space, indicate the symbolic importance of Hebrew for Jews, and offer passive linguistic input for Hebrew learners at camp.

## LINGUISTIC LANDSCAPE IN OTHER JEWISH SPACES

As we analyze visual displays of Hebrew at camp, we must contextualize them within the broader landscape of American Jewry.[9] In some neighborhoods with high concentrations of Orthodox or Israeli Jews, visitors can see Hebrew writing in signs on the street, often alongside an English translation: on kosher markets and restaurants, Judaica shops, synagogues, yeshivas, and school buses. Hasidic and other Haredi (ultra-Orthodox) neighborhoods are dotted with posters featuring announcements or advertisements in Yiddish (written in Hebrew letters) and textual Hebrew.[10] These displays serve communicative functions for people proficient in Hebrew or Yiddish, but they also announce to outsiders the presence of a Jewish community and highlight the importance of Hebrew and Yiddish for particular groups of Jews, even within the primarily English milieu of America.

Most American Jews, however, do not live in Jewish enclaves. There may be some Hebrew lettering on the exterior of synagogues and other communal buildings, but most of the visual Hebrew that American Jews encounter is inside these buildings. Synagogues of all denominations feature decorative Hebrew letters and textual Hebrew quotes on sanctuary walls, Torah arks, donor walls, and memorial plaques. Such displays mark the space as Jewish and sacred, highlight particular values or orientations, and emphasize the role of Hebrew in Jewish religious life. In Jewish schools, visual displays of Hebrew often serve similar symbolic functions, but some displays, such as Hebrew alphabet charts and labels of items around the classroom, also play pedagogical roles.[11] If campers have attended synagogue, they will probably find the decorative Hebrew quote on the Torah ark at camp familiar. If they have attended a Jewish school, they may feel right at home when they see a Hebrew alphabet chart or pedagogical labels at camp. But most who attend Hebrew-rich camps will encounter much more written Hebrew there than in their year-round communities (except those who live in Israeli-American enclaves or attend Hebrew-rich schools with similar signage). Because of their enclosed and constructed nature, summer camps can and often do take more opportunities to highlight their Jewishness with visual displays of Hebrew.

### Creating the Camp Bubble

With their clearly delineated session dates, camps are by definition "places" that happen not only at particular locations but also at specific times of the year. In addition, camps engage in a wide array of actions to create what some interviewees called the camp "bubble." Many camps restrict the use of mobile devices and have limited or no cellular reception or Wi-Fi access, so campers cannot connect electronically with friends and family back home or go online to find out what is happening beyond camp borders. Camps are highly regimented spaces in which time and movement are purposely controlled: campers are told when to get up, what to do (e.g., cleaning cabins, brushing teeth), how to dress (e.g., wearing a kipah, closed-toe shoes), and what to say (e.g., participating in a cheer, saying blessings before a meal). Few things represent camp regimentation more than some camps' practice of turning the clocks back one hour. Creating "camp time" allows extra time for a night activity, especially after Shabbat, facilitates an earlier bedtime for younger campers, and makes campers feel like they are entering a different time zone, even if their travel to camp was a quick drive. Hebrew infusion through signage contributes to the isolated and ephemeral nature of camp, as well as to its regimentation.

### *Welcome Signs*

A common way that Hebrew signage constitutes spatiotemporal boundaries between camp and noncamp contexts is the initial sign that people encounter when they arrive at a camp's entrance. A welcome sign may include the camp's name, its logo, a greeting (e.g., ברוכים הבאים—*bruchim habaim*—Welcome), and information about the camp (e.g., year of founding, organizations it belongs to). Any of these can be written in Hebrew (Hebrew letters or transliteration or both), English, or both. In addition to Hebrew letters, many signs include other visual symbols of Judaism, such as a Star of David or menorah.

A particularly rich example is the welcome sign at Moshava IO in figure 6.1. This sign features the camp name and founding date in English and Hebrew and the Hebrew logo of the Bnei Akiva youth movement. This information is overlaid on an image of the hills, bunks, trees, and Israeli flags that constitute the camp landscape, which may also represent or evoke an Israeli landscape. This

Figure 6.1. Welcome sign at Camp Moshava IO. (Credit: authors)

sign encapsulates central principles of Bnei Akiva, as emphasized by its mission statement: "Basing ourselves on the principles of Torah v'Avodah, we encourage aliyah, love of the Jewish people, and love of Israel"[12] (*avodah,* work, refers to building up the land and state of Israel). This mission is reflected in the logo: the tablets of the Ten Commandments symbolize the sacred texts of Judaism, the wheat and pitchfork represent working the land, and the Hebrew letters *taf* and *ayin* stand for *Torah* and *Avodah.* Bnei Akiva is written in Hebrew letters under the tablets. The positioning of Moshava IO in Jewish history is further emphasized by the presentation of the founding date not only according to the Roman calendar (1969) but also to the Jewish calendar (תשכ"ט) The Hebrew letters are presented in two fonts: one emulating the Torah and one more modern. As a whole, this visual display reflects the camp's linguistic environment: it is a mélange of English, textual Hebrew, and modern Hebrew that collectively underscores the links among Torah, Israel, and camp.

A different type of English-Hebrew hybridity can be seen on Camp Lavi's welcome sign (figure 6.2). The *L* in Lavi is also the ל in לביא (*lavi,* a literary word for lion), the Hebrew rendering of the camp name, which also forms part of the lion image. This kind of written bivalency (a linguistic element belonging to two languages simultaneously) is rare, perhaps because letters that represent similar sounds in Hebrew and English look very different.[13] Lavi, a private, modern Orthodox, coed, sports-oriented camp, is not Hebrew-rich. Locations, roles, and activities have English names, and most Hebrew words are ones heard in year-

Figure 6.2. Bivalent welcome sign at Camp Lavi. (Credit: authors)

round modern Orthodox communities. However, divisions have Hebrew names related to the camp mascot, the lion, including *Gurim* (cubs), *Kfir* (young lion), and *Aryeh* (lion). These names and the image on the sign tap into a long history of the lion as a religious Jewish symbol, stemming back to the biblical tie between the lion and the tribe of Judah. The welcome sign offers a glimpse of the camp's emphasis on the lion—and of the camp population, mostly modern Orthodox Jews whose Hebrew literacy is high enough to appreciate the bivalent use of Hebrew and English.

Camp welcome signs with no Hebrew are also indicative of the creation of Jewish space. Some camps mark the main entrance with only enough information for people to know they have found the right camp and forgo Hebrew in any form, perhaps reflecting concerns about antisemitism and attracting unwanted attention. A more elaborate welcome sign might be found after the main gate or guard station. In these cases, the boundary between camp and non-camp space is that much more pronounced; only inside the camp space do participants see Hebrew writing and other Jewish iconography.

### Decorative Plaques and Murals

Even though some camps do not have Hebrew on their entry signs, nearly all have some Hebrew writing inside the camp. At some camps, Hebrew is limited to spaces in which explicitly Jewish religious activity, like prayer and study, occurs. As in synagogues and day schools, the Hebrew writing is often relevant to those activities, such as Torah arks emblazoned with עץ חיים היא (it [the Torah] is a tree of life) or with the first ten Hebrew letters representing the Ten Commandments. In some cases, this written Hebrew has a practical function; for example, the blessing over a handwashing station or the blessings recited before and after meals in a dining room. In addition, many camps feature plaques or murals with textual Hebrew quotes that represent a particular value they wish to emphasize, such as the importance of community (הנה מה טוב ומה נעים שבת אחים גם יחד [How good and pleasant it is for brothers to dwell together—Psalms 133]), respect for others (ואהבת לרעך כמוך [Love your neighbor as yourself—Leviticus 19:18], and nature (ההרים תרקדו כאלים [The mountains danced like rams—Psalms 114]). Some camps use textual Hebrew to educate about Judaism's ancient agricultural roots and its relevance for contemporary environmentalism and sustainability; examples include Eden Village's "Peah [corner] Garden," which teaches about leaving the corners of the field for poor people to harvest, and JCA Shalom's garden in the shape of Israel that features talmudic and liturgical quotes and Hebrew and English labels of the biblical "seven species."

Campers may or may not be able to read and understand the Hebrew quotations, and staff may or may not use them as opportunities to teach about values, texts, or language. Even so, these decorative plaques and murals beautify the camp space, adding color to (often dingy) dining halls and multipurpose rooms. In addition, they become part of camp folklore, thereby strengthening the sense of local community. Many plaques and murals—with phrases in textual and/or modern Hebrew—are created as part of the color war competition, as is evident by the team name and year at the bottom, or as service projects by particular divisions or leadership groups. Campers return year after year—including as staff and alumni—and proudly find the plaque they created, pointing it out to the next generation of campers. In this way, signage not only infuses Hebrew but also inserts itself into the discursive traditions of the camp. Campers may gaze at the plaques regularly, looking forward to the summer when they will make their own. In addition to building community and camp tradition, the plaques serve symbolic functions, emphasizing the importance of the Jewish textual tradition, particular values, and the Hebrew language. Even plaques and murals in English, which are found at many camps, still have most of these same functions: infusing elements of the Jewish canon, highlighting values, teaching quotes, and perpetuating camp tradition. Yet the choice to use Hebrew in these camp artifacts conveys that Hebrew, too, is a value of the camp.

### Location Signs

At many camps, especially Orthodox and private camps, Hebrew signage is limited to decorative, mostly textual Hebrew plaques and murals. At more

Figure 6.3.  Decorative bilingual location sign at URJ Jacobs Camp: *chadar ochel*—dining room. (Credit: authors)

Hebrew-rich camps, an additional type of written Hebrew is prevalent: Hebrew signs marking buildings or areas. In some cases this signage is professionally printed, and in others it is created by art specialists or groups of campers. Though there is nothing inherently Jewish about swimming laps, making a three-point shot, or threading lanyards, Hebrew signs marking pools, basketball courts, and art rooms infuse Jewishness into these locations and the activities that occur there, reinforcing the notion that camp is a Jewish space. Like the plaques discussed earlier, these signs are often decorative and infuse not only Jewishness but also beauty, as seen in the mosaic Hebrew-English dining room sign at URJ Jacobs Camp in Mississippi (see figure 6.3). In these ways, Hebrew signs are reminiscent of the *mezuzah*, which marks the entrance to a Jewish home and each room within, often beautifying the space as well.

Camps turn "secular" space into Jewish space through Hebrew signage, but they also do so with relevant Jewish symbols or references, such as an English translation of the talmudic quote about fathers teaching their children to swim, an Israeli soccer team jersey, or, at one camp, benches in the shape of trope (cantillation) marks.[14] However, Hebrew is always available as a resource for marking Jewishness: any location name can be translated into Hebrew. In contrast to Hebrew songs, skits, or loanwords, permanent location signs are a relatively easy way to infuse camp with Hebrew. To create such a sign, the camp needs only one person who can write Hebrew (or a dictionary or online translator), and anyone else can copy the letters onto a plaque and post it. Creating Hebrew signage does not require ongoing staff time or skill, but it does entail an ideology that Hebrew is important and should be visible in multiple locations at the camp. That

Figure 6.4. Bilingual pool sign (*breicha*—pool) alongside monolingual English sign explaining pool rules at Sprout Lake. (Credit: authors)

is why Hebrew signage in secular spaces differentiates Hebrew-rich camps from camps with little investment in Hebrew.

When location signs are only in Hebrew, they do not serve much of a communicative function for camp participants with limited Hebrew literacy; most can figure out where they are when they see the pool, the basketball court, or the art supplies. The Hebrew signs, however, may serve a pedagogical function, teaching particular words to campers who see them day after day. In addition, they convey symbolic meaning, highlighting not only the Jewishness of the space but also the importance of Hebrew in it. The symbolic function is underscored when Hebrew signs are placed alongside English signs that convey additional information, such as the bilingual POOL sign next to the monolingual English POOL RULES sign at Sprout Lake (see figure 6.4). As we observed in chapter 3, even in the most Hebrew-rich camps, it is rare to see signs regarding health, safety, or rules posted in Hebrew—another instance of Hebrew being limited to particular functions and spaces.

### Directional Signposts

Many camps have signs—in English, Hebrew, or both—pointing to multiple locations at camp, which can serve a useful navigational function for newcom-

Figure 6.5. Bilingual directional signpost at a Reform camp in Arizona. (Credit: Camp Daisy and Harry Stein)

ers and visitors. In addition, although camps seek to create a closed environment, many of the signposts point to external locations: synagogues affiliated with the camp, other camps in the movement, cities where campers live during the year, and cities around the world, especially in Israel. For example, figure 6.5 shows the bilingual signpost from Camp Daisy and Harry Stein, a Reform camp in Arizona, which points to various cities in Israel (with distances in kilometers, according to the Israeli system) and to the camp office (with distance in steps). Like signposts in many cities that point toward sister cities across the globe, international signposts at camp do not serve a navigational function; campers do not intend to walk to Ramat Gan in Israel. Instead, they highlight cities this camp considers important, thereby locating the camp within a world geography, often a Jewish geography. The direction of the signs is of little import. Indeed, some signposts are inaccurately situated; one even had multiple signs for cities in Israel (all of which are east of this camp) pointing in opposite directions. Some reflect inaccurate copying, like the ך (final *chaf*) that is so short it looks like a ר (*resh*), or an incomplete knowledge of Hebrew-writing conventions, such as לודג for "lodge," missing the apostrophe. These mistakes might raise the eyebrows of Hebrew-literate viewers,[15] but they do not interfere with the signs' semiotic function: situating the camp as an important Jewish space within a broader Jewish world. If signposts featuring Israeli cities were only in English, they would still serve this function; the presence of Hebrew adds an additional reminder that Hebrew is a shared resource of Jews around the world.

*Signs of Israel*

Although signposts pointing to Israeli cities situate Israel as far away geographically, other signs infuse a symbolic element of Israel into the camp landscape.
Any Hebrew signage could potentially conjure associations with Israel, because
the Israeli landscape is dotted with Hebrew (along with English, Arabic, Russian, and other languages).[16] Many camps post visual representations of Israeli
products, such as El Al airlines and Bamba (a popular snack food), featuring
Hebrew letters. Another common practice is to create signs that resemble Israeli
street signs. Camp JRF did this for each bunk, featuring the bunk name in
Hebrew, Arabic, and English (see figure 6.6). Like the Camp Daisy and Harry
Stein signpost shown in figure 6.5, this was a project of the Goodman Initiative,
a program that mentors and provides funding for camps that want to incorporate more education about Israel. Leaders of Camp JRF felt it was important to
include Arabic, reflecting many Israeli street signs, because of their progressive,
inclusive political orientation.

Of course there are ways to represent Israel visually that do not use Hebrew,
including through maps, flags, and posters with facts about Israel, all of which
are common at camp and are sometimes posted by Israeli emissaries. However, when Hebrew is included in displays of Israel, campers are reminded of
the ideological link not only between Israel and the camp but also between
Israel and Hebrew.

Figure 6.6. Oren bunk sign in Hebrew, Arabic, and English at Camp JRF (now
Havaya), resembling Israeli street signs. (Credit: Camp JRF)

## Pedagogical Labels and Word Lists

In Israel, everyday objects like doors, chairs, and trees are not generally given Hebrew labels, except perhaps in a language classroom for visitors and new immigrants learning Hebrew. The same can be said about the lack of labeling items in English in the United States. Yet Hebrew labels like these are ubiquitous in some American Jewish summer camps. When we asked camp staff about their purpose, they indicated that their pedagogical function is primary: the staff use them to teach Hebrew words. At the same time, the pedagogical function also becomes symbolic; when campers see that camp leaders wish to teach Hebrew words, they recognize Hebrew as a value of the camp. Another instance of pedagogical signage is bilingual word lists—a practice that dates back to the earliest American Zionist camps. Some word lists are placed in particular domains, such as food words in dining halls or cleaning words and chore wheels in bunks. At Gilboa, the (gender-neutral) bathrooms had different Hebrew vocabulary lists in each stall, including basic words like "yes," "no," and "I need." These lists were placed alongside articles about progressive topics, such as white privilege and Women of the Wall. The (briefly) captive audience may learn some Hebrew phrases and some progressive ideas, and they may be reminded that Hebrew, Israel, and social justice are all valued in this camp.

At the same time, word lists can also serve a practical function: teaching newcomers the Hebrew words used in each camp's variety of CHE. We see this, for example, in the *Meah Milim* (100 words) list at Ramah camps or the sign at URJ Newman listing 18 "Jewish words on schedule" with their English equivalents. At Shomria in New York, a word list (see figure 6.7) was posted in a bathroom near the *ched* (dining hall—short for *cheder ochel*). The list, explicitly framed as "Mosh [Camp] Words," rather than Israeli or Hebrew words, enumerates some differences between the words in Hebrew and in Shomria lingo; an example is *machane*, which means "cabin area" at Shomria but "camp" in Hebrew. Although this list reflects at least some desire to teach Israeli Hebrew words, it also indicates that camp leaders are aware—and perhaps unapologetic—that they have changed the form and meaning of Hebrew for use in the American camp setting. Word lists like this not only highlight the importance of Hebrew at camp but also enable participants to strengthen their CHE, which can be crucial for participation in the camp community.

## CAMP HEBREW ONLINE

While visual displays of Hebrew construct spatiotemporal boundaries and provide nuance to a camp's particular Jewish character, they also play a role in how camps extend these boundaries beyond the physical camp site and beyond summertime. Using Hebrew letters or CHE on a website or Facebook page helps

---

**<u>Mosh Words!</u>**

Mosh—Camp

Kvutzah (kvootzah)—Age group

Shirutim (sheetoteem)

[sic]—Bathroom

Ched—Dining Hall (short for
Cheder Ochel)

Tzrif (tzreef)—Cabin

Zman Kvutzah—Group time

Zman Machane—Upper and lower
camp activity

Schiya (scheeya)—Swimming

Zman Mosh—All camp activity

Chugim—Electives

Shira (sheera)—Singing time

Erev—Evening activity (Hebrew
for evening)

Mishpacha (Meeshpacha)—Family

Rikud (reekood)—Dancing

Machane—Cabin area (Hebrew
for camp)

Chultzah—Hashomer Hatzair
Working Shirt (Hebrew for shirt)

Mipa'ah—Infirmary

Chava—Farm

Shomrim (shomreem)—People in
Hashomer Hatzair

Tiyul (teeyool)—Hiking trip

Refet—Barn

Havdallah—Camp fire singing time

Seder Yom—Schedule

Machbesa (machbaysa)—
Laundry room

Mirpeset (meerpeset)—Porch

Hagshama—Self actualization

---

Figure 6.7. CHE word list posted in a bathroom at Shomria

conjure up the Hebrew-infused practices of the physical camp, even for someone at home in Chicago in the middle of winter. In addition, it gives a taste of
camp culture for non-camp-attending family members and prospective participants. Not surprisingly, the camps' diverse approaches to Hebrew come through
in their online presence. Analysis of updates sent to parents by emails and blogs
during the summer of 2015 from a sample of six camps—Beber, Galil, Modin,
Moshava IO, Ramah Poconos, and Yavneh—reveals the way these camps use
Hebrew online to position themselves Jewishly. Modin and Beber, pluralistic
camps that compartmentalize their Jewish content, used only a few Jewish life
words in their online communications (e.g., *Shabbat, Havdalah, bar mitzvah*). In
contrast, the other four camps, Hebrew-rich institutions that incorporate Jewish
content into many activities, used not only Jewish life words but also many camp
Hebrew words like *toren* (flagpole), *shichva* (age group), and *peulot* (activities).

These texts also reveal assumptions that camp leaders make about the parents
who will be reading the updates. Camps like Galil, which had the most distinctive terminology for camp referents, translated most Hebrew words; for example, "*tiyul* (a hiking trip)," "*kvutsa* (small, united community)." In contrast, many
Jewish life words and some camp words in other camps' updates were rendered
only in (transliterated) Hebrew, such as Yavneh's *Rosh Banim* [head of boys],
Moshava's *tzevet* [staff], and Ramah's *Yom Yisrael* [Israel Day]. Only Yavneh and

Moshava included any Hebrew lettering, and the latter did not transliterate the Hebrew, reflecting an assumption that parents could read Hebrew. Whether in parent email updates or on websites, visual displays of Hebrew are a means of portraying a camp's brand—how it sees itself and wants to present itself to current and prospective families. The amount and type of Hebrew used in these digital communications signal a recognition that camp is a particular type of Jewish space, even when that space extends beyond camp boundaries into the online world.

Camp websites can also help prepare newcomers for the Hebrew they will encounter at camp. This tradition predates the internet; as we saw in chapter 2, Massad Poconos prepared campers for the immersive Hebrew environment by distributing a 271-page hardbound English-Hebrew dictionary. Even at camps not geared toward Hebrew immersion, participants benefit from learning that camp's specific CHE traditions in advance. Today, several camp websites offer glossaries, ranging from a few to hundreds of words, which include not only Hebrew words but also English words used in specialized ways. For example, URJ Camp Coleman, in Georgia, provides an online glossary of thirty-three phrases, including *meltzarim* (waiters) and *nikayon*, but also "letter lotto" and "mandatory optionals."[17] Habonim Dror Tavor sends a link to its sixty-two-entry online glossary in advance, "so that everybody has the same language," as an administrator told us.[18] A JCCA leader explained that such glossaries help create an "an ethos of pluralism and hospitality." To decide whether they need a glossary, he said, camp leaders should ask, "What is it that people need to know to be a member of your community, and how easy do you make it for them to access that?" Glossaries serve a practical function: creating a public of readers who can engage in the specific register of CHE and feel competent performing camp language. But they also serve a symbolic, status-raising function: like any dictionary, glossaries codify CHE, sending a message that using Hebrew words within English sentences is a valid form of speech.

## The Impacts of Signage

When camp leaders speak CHE or lead Hebrew songs and prayers, they make camp sound distinctly Jewish. When they use CHE or Hebrew quotes in visual displays, they make camp *look* distinctly Jewish. Whereas spoken language is ephemeral, written language lasts as long as the signs are left in place, allowing campers to interact with Hebrew words when they are ready—and at multiple times throughout the summer and over the years. Our interviews show that, at least at Hebrew-rich camps, campers engage with signs in diverse ways. Several campers spoke positively of the Hebrew signs. An 8-year-old OSRUI camper who was growing up in an area with very few Jews said that the Hebrew signs made camp feel "welcoming" and served "to let you know that you're not the only

Jewish person." Yet not all engagement is positive. Campers with little Hebrew-reading background found the signs off-putting or overwhelming, at least at first. A few, however, appreciated the challenge. A 9-year-old Ramah camper with little Hebrew background taught herself the word for "water slide" by reading the Hebrew label during her many visits to the pool.

Despite the mostly positive reception of Hebrew signage, there are debates about how much Hebrew to use. At a staff meeting at a Reform camp, a staff member suggested adding Hebrew translations for the English words on the lists of tasks posted in the bunks. Yet one educator expressed her reservations: "If the counselors aren't using the language, what's the point of having Hebrew on there? It's like having Braille on the elevator." By comparing the use of Hebrew to a tactile writing system used only by the blind, this educator was articulating a belief that, unless campers needed to know or use the Hebrew words for some purpose, they would ignore them. An administrator at a private camp expressed a similar concern about Hebrew as a superficial signifier. He felt it was problem-atic that camps "lean on" Hebrew location signs as a quick fix to "do Jewish." "If you walked in, how would you know it was a Jewish camp? Well, because you see Hebrew words, you know." Such critiques highlight concerns common in situa-tions of ethnolinguistic infusion: If the language is not used for communication, why represent it visually at all? For most camp leaders and participants, however, the symbolic and pedagogical functions are not only sufficient but also important for creating a Jewish environment and socializing young Jews to be part of a col-lectivity that appreciates Hebrew, even if they cannot use it proficiently.

Hebrew signage bonds campers and creates Jewish space, but as mentioned, it also alienates or divides. This sentiment is captured in one professional's remarks about his work at FJC: when "we looked at issues of how to make camp more Jewish, the question of . . . signage and the semiotics of camp—of the space—came up. . . . There's a concern on the part of some camp directors about making camp too Jewish or making it feel formidable or off-putting—assuming that many of the campers really have no background." As the arbiters of how Hebrew-rich a camp should be, administrators strive to find the right balance in using visual displays of Hebrew. If they use too little, their camp may not appear as Jewish as they wish; if they use too much, they may alienate prospec-tive campers with low Hebrew literacy. Whenever camp leaders commission, cre-ate, post, allow, or reject a sign, they are negotiating this tipping point and entering into a broader conversation about what Jewishness means in their camp. One director was enthusiastic about using more Hebrew signage, but the camp's board was concerned that "it looked like a kind of Judaism they didn't want to associate with." The director found a creative solution: she posted detachable signs for the summer but removed them before the winter board retreat. We see here a conflict among diverse constituencies within a given camp regarding Jew-ish practice and the symbolic meaning of Hebrew. The director's stance stems from an ideology that Hebrew signage is an important aspect of Jewish summer camp, and the board's stance reflects a concern about campers' comfort and belonging; if they encounter little or no Hebrew during the year, they may feel that a summer camp filled with Hebrew signage is not intended for them.

## Bilingual Signage

One way that camps attempt to prevent this alienation is by including English translations alongside Hebrew writing. Bilingual signage sends an unambiguous message about the acceptability of both Hebrew and English as camp languages and reinforces the role of Hebrew and English in American Jewishness. Using bilingual signs (rather than Hebrew alone, even where a degree of Hebrew knowledge is assumed) facilitates comprehension for participants with low Hebrew literacy, including non-Jewish staff members. As some camp directors, including the early directors at Ramah, recognized, bilingual signs in kosher kitchens reduce the likelihood of diners, cooks, and cleaners inadvertently bringing milk items into the meat side. And as we saw earlier, Hebrew-English labels on objects or locations can explicitly teach Hebrew words. Bilingual signs also reduce the friction that Hebrew-only signs may cause. At a JCCA camp, an art teacher created and posted an artistic sign that said ברוכים הבאים [*bruchim habaim*—welcome] in Hebrew only. Concerned that campers would not understand the sign, the camp director asked the art teacher to create a similarly artistic English equivalent. One Reform camp received feedback that its website had too many Hebrew words to attract prospective families with little Judaic knowledge. The administration, however, felt that, without the Hebrew words, the website would not accurately represent camp life. Therefore, they retained the Hebrew words but made sure each was translated (e.g., *Mifkad Boker*—Morning Wake-Up Session, *Breicha*—Pool).

When a visual display of Hebrew also includes English, the size and placement of each language can be symbolic and can sometimes lead to conflict. The leadership of a Zionist camp grappled with the relationship of Hebrew and English in the camp logo, particularly how the placement and size of the two languages would portray the camp. After much back and forth, they decided to remain true to the camp's core Zionist ideals and reverse a previous decision to decrease the size of the Hebrew lettering.[19] Believing that the use of Hebrew and its relative font size "say something," the director felt that the visual representation of Hebrew in the new logo would not only indicate to prospective families that it was a Jewish camp but would also distinguish it as a camp with a strong Israel-centric educational mission. This negotiation underscores the tensions that can arise in bilingual visual displays.

Camps also convey a symbolic message when they use English or transliteration in some contexts and Hebrew lettering in others. At OSRUI, signs related

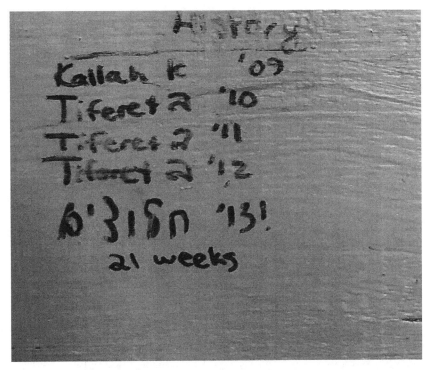

Figure 6.8. Graffiti in the Chalutzim (Hebrew immersion division) activity building at OSRUI demonstrates orthographic differentiation by division. (Credit: Rabbi Rachel Sabath Beit-Halachmi, PhD)

to the Chalutzim immersion program tend to have the most Hebrew lettering. In the office, each division's mailbox is labeled in transliteration (e.g., Kallah, Moshava, Tiferet), except Chalutzim, which is only in Hebrew letters: חלוצים. Even graffiti sometimes carries this distinction between Hebrew and transliteration. On walls and benches in the Chalutzim activity building, many campers have written their names and the years they attended OSRUI by division and session. Many used Hebrew letters for the sessions (ב, א) but distinguished the division names by lettering: all were in transliteration except צולחים [Chalutzim] (see figure 6.8). A few weeks into their Hebrew immersion summer, campers are generally able to write "Kallah" and "Tiferet" in Hebrew letters. Their choice to render those words in transliteration and "Chalutzim" in Hebrew letters indicates their different orthographic associations with each session.

### WRITING HEBREW: CHOICES AND RISKS

Visual displays of Hebrew involve assumptions about who the readers are, as well as what type of writing they should be (or become) accustomed to reading. Analyzing the varying ways to write Hebrew—the typographic choices, vowel markings, and transliteration—on Hebrew signage shows how written Hebrew works as both an inclusionary and exclusionary device in the camp context.

### Block or Cursive

In Israel, Hebrew is generally rendered in cursive (script) on handwritten materials and in block letters (print) on professionally produced signs and published materials, although some commercial signs, logos, and apparel are in cursive. In the United States, synagogues generally feature only block letters in prayer books and decorative plaques. In contrast, Jewish educational institutions are divided in their approaches to teaching Hebrew reading and writing: Jewish day schools generally teach both block and cursive letters, but most synagogue-based supplementary schools—where a majority of American Jews learn Hebrew—teach only block.[20] Therefore, cursive is associated with Israel and with high Hebrew literacy, and block letters are associated with the American religious domain and lower levels of Israeli Hebrew fluency.[21]

This diversity is reflected in visual displays of Hebrew at camp. On the one hand, some non-Orthodox camps that are not Hebrew-rich and compartmentalize Judaic from other activities use only block Hebrew. Most of their campers attend supplementary schools or have no Jewish education outside of camp, and there is no expectation that they can read cursive. On the other hand, at Orthodox camps and Hebrew-rich non-Orthodox camps, both block and cursive letters are used. Block letters are generally found on song sheets, projected lyrics, prayer books, decorative plaques, and professionally produced signs, whereas cursive is generally used on temporary handwritten notes and posters. For example, at Moshava IO, a posted note directing campers to a color war rehearsal had the team name in cursive Hebrew, but a team banner displayed at the event itself was in block letters. Similarly, figure 6.9 shows the sketch and artistic final draft of a Hebrew banner at OSRUI. An Israeli staff member wrote the sketch in cursive and directed a young American staff member to use stencils to cut out block letters from red paper for the banner itself.

Cursive Hebrew handwritten notes are often written by and for Israelis, such as a request by an Israeli emissary for a ride to the bus station at a camp with many Israeli staff members. American Jews also generally use cursive when they insert Hebrew words into handwritten English notes, like בס"ד (with God's help) in the top right corner and ברכות (blessings) and בלי נדר (without a vow) within English sentences. Notes like these are especially common at Orthodox camps (as in year-round Orthodox communities), and they are generally written by and for American Jews with high Hebrew literacy who are accustomed to writing Hebrew only in cursive. One genre of temporary handwritten signs is generally

Figure 6.9. Cursive sketch (top) and block final draft (bottom) of banner in the OSRUI dining hall: *Ivri, daber Ivrit!* (Hebrew person, speak Hebrew). (Credit: Authors and Rabbi Rachel Sabath Beit-Halachmi, PhD)

rendered in block letters: pedagogical labels intended for Americans with low Hebrew literacy (but see an exception in figure 6.10C).

At Ramah California, decorative signs, location signs, and pedagogical labels are in a combination of block and cursive letters. Cursive is used not only on temporary, handmade signs but also on more formal ones, such as a series of professionally produced bilingual banners highlighting *midot* (values). This suggests that Ramah administrators expect campers to come with or develop high levels of Hebrew literacy. Indeed, Ramah campers are required to participate in Jewish education during the year. About half attend day schools, and most of the rest attend synagogue supplementary schools. In focus groups, Ramah campers expressed diverse opinions about the presence of cursive. For campers who attended Jewish day schools, cursive was natural and desirable. For those who did not, the cursive signs were off-putting, at least initially; a few said they simply ignored them. Like the presence of Hebrew more generally, cursive works on a symbolic level, sending a message about the type of camper the camp is seeking to attract, as well as the value the camp puts on high levels of Hebrew literacy. It also contributes to hierarchies of expertise. Some campers may respond to these hierarchies with a desire to learn more Hebrew, but others may be alienated, feeling the camp is not intended for them.

### Vowel Markings

Like the choice between cursive and block letters, the presence or absence of "vowels" stems from and contributes to hierarchies of Hebrew expertise. "Vowels" is how many American Jews refer to *nikud* (applying points)—the diacritical markings that indicate vowels or alternative pronunciations of consonants. Unlike English, the Hebrew alphabet is consonantal; there are no separate letters for most vowels, though the consonants *vav* (v), *yud* (y), and *hey* (h) some-

Block

Nikud

No *nikud*

Cursive

Figure 6.10. Typology of handwritten Hebrew at camp. A: *Hamotzi* blessing in Hilltop's dining hall; B: *Gan Alonim* (young children's building) sign at Alonim; C: Bilingual chair label at Gilboa; D: Note in Beber ladies' room (Credits: authors).

times represent vowels. Over time, a system of dots and lines was added above, below, or in the middle of consonants to indicate the vocalization (/ə/, /i/, /o/, etc.) and pronunciation of certain consonants (/p/ or /f/, /s/ or /sh/, etc.). In Israel, modern Hebrew writing generally lacks nikud, because native readers can determine the pronunciation of a given word from its consonants based on the context. There is a reliance on nikud within the Israeli context in specialized texts, such as dictionaries, poetry, prayer books, children's literature, and material for Hebrew learners. Nikud is used in much of the Hebrew reading material that American Jews encounter, which is primarily religious or pedagogical in nature. Although Torah scrolls are handwritten in a distinctive Hebrew calligraphy without nikud, most printed prayer books and Torah study books use nikud.

At camps, nikud is common in writing with pedagogical functions, such as Hebrew word labels, and in writing with practical functions, like the prayer books, plaques, and projected song lyrics that facilitate the recitation of prayers and songs. Hebrew signs whose primary function is symbolic are less likely to have nikud; they include decorative plaques, quotes on Torah arks, and location signs. In any of these contexts, Hebrew without nikud can reinforce hierarchies of Hebrew knowledge, engaging some participants while alienating others.

The collage of signs in figure 6.10 captures the range of choices involved in writing Hebrew at camp, ranging from easiest to read (A) to hardest (D). Sign A—textual Hebrew, written in block letters with nikud—is intended for practical use: for campers to follow along as they recite the *Hamotzi* blessing before meals. B is a location sign that serves a primarily symbolic function alongside the transliteration that most people will read. Nikud is not necessary for comprehension, and block writing is preferred because it is a permanent sign and many participants cannot read cursive. C serves a pedagogical function, teaching the Hebrew word for chair. The writer assumed that viewers would have the ability to read cursive (or perhaps did not consider using block letters) and offered nikud to convey the pronunciation. D, in cursive and without nikud, serves a communicative function, requesting particular behavior from Israeli women: disposing properly of sanitary products.

### Transliteration

In addition to typography and vowel marking, choices regarding transliteration also affect access to Hebrew signage and differentiate between camps and individuals along the hierarchies of Hebrew expertise. Transliteration is a case of digraphia—the same language written in two different scripts; it involves the conversion of a text from one script into another for pedagogical, marketing, or communicative purposes.[22] Because Hebrew and English are written in different orthographic systems, transliteration marries the phonetics of Hebrew with the orthography of English, making Hebrew accessible to those who read English more easily than Hebrew. It allows Hebrew and English to be represented simultaneously—another instance of bivalency. Synagogues and educational institutions have long used transliteration to enable non-Hebrew-literate Jews to participate in prayers and Jewish discourse. Denominational leaders' approach to transliteration has varied and evolved over time, ranging from embracing it as a means of inclusion to expressing concern that transliteration might discourage people from learning Hebrew. In either case, transliteration is often positioned as a "faux" or a lesser form of Hebrew. However, even in institutions that discourage transliteration in prayer settings, Hebrew words in English sentences are often transliterated.

There is no universal standard or set of guidelines for Hebrew transliteration. Hebrew words have many spellings (take, as a well-known example, Chanukah vs. Hanukkah vs. its many other spellings, and the myriad transliterations of the *Shma* prayer in different prayer books). Although particular publishing houses in America standardize and enforce transliteration practices in the religious books they produce,[23] their reach does not extend to other contexts. The diversity in Hebrew transliteration hints at its ideological complexity. Transliterators need to decide which Hebrew pronunciation tradition to represent: Ashkenazi, Sephardi, or Israeli, for example. Then, there are many decisions to make, including when an apostrophe indicates morphological and phonological boundaries (*l'chaim* vs. *lechaim*; *mirpa'a* vs. *mirpaa*); when consonants are doubled (*Sukot* vs. *Sukkot*); and when an "h" represents word-final *hey* (*menuchah* vs. *menucha*). In some cases, particular spellings reflect more experience with Hebrew literacy conventions. The decision, for example, to represent the letter *kaf* with "c" and not "k" in the word *Bircat Hamazon* may annoy some transliteration purists, because *kaf* is generally rendered as "k." For the transliterator, the lack of standardization means that even everyday spellings are fraught with a minefield of decisions.

Transliteration also demands a lot from the reader. Transliteration conventions do not indicate stress patterns, which makes reading it aloud daunting. Moreover, readers of transliteration must often demonstrate their linguistic know-how in real time, especially when participating in prayers, blessings, and songs. Despite these challenges, there seems to be an assumption within the American Jewish community that an English speaker can automatically—or at least, easily—use transliterated Hebrew. For instance, we are not aware of any classes on writing or reading transliterated Hebrew. Indeed, given the diversity and even chaos in the transliteration of Hebrew, it would be difficult to teach such a class effectively, separate from teaching either Hebrew itself or the performance contexts in which the transliteration is used.

In addition to the challenges involved in writing and reading transliteration, camps are immersed in competing ideologies about the acceptability of its very use. Despite its practical utility, transliteration was sometimes critiqued as a substandard form. Several Israeli staff members called transliteration "Hebrish," and Americans sometimes picked up on the term, their tone and usage implying that it was not just a portmanteau combining "Hebrew" and "English," but an inferior form of language. In addition, some leaders perceived transliteration as having a deleterious rather than positive effect on pedagogical goals, giving "both kids and adults an excuse not to learn to read Hebrew," as one URJ camp leader said. A Ramah national administrator agreed: "We do not like using transliteration. We'd rather have kids—even if they're pre-Hebrew readers—hold a text with Hebrew letters, even if we know that they are just listening and beginning to do a whole-word approach, so that they'll be able to recognize *Shma*, even if they do not know a *shin*, a *mem*, and an *ayin*."

A URJ camp administrator included the use of Hebrew letters among the guiding principles behind the camp's many murals: "It's got to be mission-appropriate, and there needs to be some Hebrew in there—actual Hebrew, Hebrew, not just a transliteration." This administrator is conveying the ideological position that authentic Hebrew must be rendered in Hebrew letters. Nonetheless, many of this camp's murals and other visual representations of Hebrew did include transliteration.

In many cases, transliteration was considered a linguistic compromise—not as good as using "real" Hebrew lettering, but necessary because not all campers were able to decode Hebrew letters. An administrator at Solomon Schechter said the camp used transliteration, especially in the siddur: "I get that question sometimes by parents when I'm recruiting campers—if there is transliteration. 'My kid can't read Hebrew. I'm worried that, you know, can my kid go to Schechter?'"

Parents' concerns are another indication of how Hebrew letters can be alienating and how transliteration can be important for camp recruitment and branding efforts. Strict anti-transliteration policies run the risk of alienating campers who cannot read Hebrew letters, and transliteration can help facilitate a sense of belonging. This is important not only in prayer and song sessions but also in theatrical performances at Hebrew-rich camps. At Massad Manitoba, a parody of the Broadway play *The Book of Mormon* took advantage of transliterated Hebrew (what Massadnikim called "phonetics"). Campers with more Hebrew knowledge helped others by modeling the pronunciation and translating into English. Ironically, this parody of a satirical play about improving the world through the spread of the written word (the Mormon scripture) used transliteration as a vehicle for inclusion and group cohesion.

At Tel Yehudah, preparations for the Tisha B'Av ceremony used transliteration to address diverse levels of Hebrew literacy. Seven teenage campers worked with three Israeli music specialists to learn the contemporary song *"Or Gadol,"* a haunting piece by Israeli singer/songwriter Amir Dadon about loss, regret, and acceptance. Campers were given a paper that had the lyrics in block Hebrew and transliteration on one side and the English translation on the other. As at Massad, some of the campers needed the transliteration, and others could read Hebrew letters. During rehearsals, campers who required the transliteration added apostrophes and circled stressed syllables to make the transliteration more comprehensible and remind them how to pronounce words (as in *ktzat* [a bit], a cluster of letters that does not exist in English). As in the rehearsal of *The Book of Mormon* at Massad, learning the song was perceived as a group achievement; transliteration enabled not only an artistic performance but also a performance of inclusion. It enhanced the Jewish programming at the camp, turning this commemorative ceremony into an opportunity for campers with diverse Hebrew backgrounds to perform Jewishness through Hebrew.

Yet if transliteration has transformative capacity, it is still mired in ideological calculations of authenticity. After the Tisha B'Av rehearsal at Tel Yehudah, a 15-year-old camper was still struggling with some of the transliterated lyrics and was nervous about performing her solo. Although she was proud of herself for being able to sing a song in Hebrew given the fact that she had no "real Jewish education," she also saw her reliance on the transliteration as a marker of inauthenticity. She expressed trepidation that more knowledgeable Hebrew speakers at camp, including Israelis, would hear her mistakes and know that she was not "good at Hebrew," and she feared that her use of the transliteration would "give [her] away" as an inauthentic Hebrew speaker—that is, not a native Hebrew speaker or one who does not understand the words she is singing. Her insecurities reflect the dual nature of transliteration: if it is pronounced well, a camper can pass as a legitimate Hebrew speaker; when pronounced incorrectly, the camper is exposed as a Hebrew-speaking fraud. As this episode demonstrates,

Hebrew transliteration functions as both inclusionary and exclusionary. It shapes the construction of diasporic identity in relationship to Israeli identity, as native Israelis with Hebrew literacy skills do not have these concerns about the authenticity of their Hebrew articulation. Transliteration both dissolves and highlights the distinction between those who know Hebrew and those who do not, and it therefore becomes an expression of the complexity of Jewish collectivity.

———

Visual displays of Hebrew are an important site of Hebrew infusion. Although some displays communicate messages and others serve pedagogical functions, most offer symbolic reminders of the importance of Hebrew in the camp setting. In addition, they represent a multilayered sociolinguistic negotiation involving ideologies of identity, community, tradition, and authenticity. The orthographic choices that leaders and campers make reflect broader questions about what a Jewish and Israel-infused space looks like and the importance of visual Hebrew in materializing these understandings. The decision to use Hebrew to signify and reinforce Jewish identity runs the risk of alienating campers and their families with low Hebrew literacy. Like spoken Hebrew, written Hebrew thus has the capacity to welcome, differentiate, and repel. Through choices about and experiences with typography, nikud, transliteration, and translation, camps and individuals articulate ideologies and exert forms of Jewish expertise and knowledge. These linguistic decisions are wrapped up in social-ideological considerations of nativeness and authenticity, of values and priorities. These issues are explored further in the next chapter, through the experiences of Israelis at camp.

# CHAPTER 7

# Bringing Israel to Camp

## ISRAELI EMISSARIES AND HEBREW

During our visits to camps, it was not uncommon to hear the Israeli song "Golden Boy" on the loudspeaker and see campers excitedly singing the lyrics and doing choreographed movements to the song. Some investigation revealed that in most cases, the Israeli delegation (*mishlachat*) had introduced this song as a way of bringing Israeli culture to the camp. In addition to its contagious beat and its catchy lyrics, "Golden Boy" was chosen because it represented Israel on two levels. Literally, it was the nominated song representing Israel at the 2015 Eurovision, the preeminent international singing competition.[1] Symbolically, it portrayed Israel as a cosmopolitan (and secular) place with lyrics about romantic breakups and Israeli nightlife ("Mama, someone broke my heart again, now I'm gonna ease my pain, dancing on the floor"). The campers' embrace of the song meant that it quickly became an essential part of the camp soundscape. Omer, a first-time Israeli emissary, felt that the perceived excitement was a clear indication that he had succeeded in "bringing Israel to camp"—a task he identified as central to his responsibility as part of the Israeli delegation. Yet for the astute listener, this success belied a set of complications. Although "Golden Boy" is a bona fide Israeli product, its lyrics are completely in English.[2] And while the song was chosen to represent Israel in a European song contest, it is only tangentially about Israel. The only time Israel is even mentioned is in the chorus: "I'm a golden boy, come here to enjoy, and before I leave, let me show you Tel Aviv." It is a far cry from the 1991 Israeli Eurovision submission, *"Kan"* (Here), a self-referential and nationalistic song that captured the singers' emotions about establishing a Jewish home "here" after "two thousand years." In contrast, "Golden Boy" can be heard more as a tribute to globalization than patriotism. Hebrew ideologues may lament that a song entirely in English is being used to infuse Israeli culture into American camps. However, "Golden Boy" represents an Israel that speaks (or sings) to the camp audience, precisely because it is in English.

The performance of "Golden Boy" raises fundamental questions about the representation of Israel at camp, the role of Israeli staff at American camps, the portability of Israeli culture, and the role of Hebrew in navigating these terrains. Caught up in the ongoing tensions regarding the role of Israel in American Jewish life, Israelis sent to work at camps are situated within two contradictory perspectives that have deep historical and cultural roots: (1) the tenet of classical Zionism that dichotomizes Jewish life between the center in Israel and the periphery in the Diaspora and (2) the value of Jewish peoplehood, stressing the democratization of global Jewish life.[3] This tension has profound implications for Hebrew at camp because it underscores the question of which variety of Hebrew (Israeli Hebrew vs. CHE) is endowed with linguistic authenticity. Even though American camp leaders value and seek out emissaries' Hebrew expertise and see it as a proxy for educating about Jewish nationalism, they generally prefer their own language infusion traditions and relegate Israeli Hebrew to particular spaces and times at camp. Hebrew usage, then, is a window that reveals the complexity of the transnational project of teaching American Jewish youth about Israel. Parenthetically, it is crucial to remember that bringing Israel to camp is almost always defined as Jewish Israeli culture, not Arab and other non-Jewish cultures.

Much like festivals' and amusement parks' stagings of foreign sites or historical environments,[4] camps use Israeli staff and other semiotic resources, such as music, dance, and imagery, to conjure up or simulate aspects of Israeli culture, both its past and present forms. Unlike trips to Israel, in which the physicality of being there evokes a heightened affective response, camp staff cannot rely on what sociologist Shaul Kelner refers to as "site rituals," such as standing in reverent silence at Mt. Herzl or putting a handwritten note into the cracks of the Western Wall.[5] Nor can they (re)create a dialogic relationship among Israeli iconic sites, like travelers experience when they move through their carefully constructed itineraries.[6] Instead, under the aegis of what is referred to as "Israel education," camps turn to emissaries to act as Israel-experience surrogates and materialize aspects of Israel in the camp setting. For the emissaries, this means bottling up the homeland tour experience, taking it on the road, and meting it out in experiential ways that are both enjoyable and educational. In essence, they have to be curators and performers in an itinerant Israel show. As this chapter shows, Hebrew lends itself to this portability and performance and serves as one of the central means by which emissaries transport an understanding of Israel to the camp setting. Nonetheless, disparities in notions of Israeliness between emissaries and camp leaders also get entangled in ideologies of Hebrew authenticity.

First, a few notes on emissaries/*shlichim*. Technically, *shlichim* refers to those who are part of an official, government, or movement program of emissaries whose members, as a group, comprise the "*mishlachat*" or delegation. Not all of the Israeli staff members at camp are brought in through the Jewish Agency for Israel; some are brought in through other organizations or are hired directly by the camps. However, we bundled these groups together, because their way of being hired has little influence on how they are perceived by campers and other staff members as representatives of Israel. A large majority of American Jewish camps (87 percent of the camps that responded to our survey) have Israeli staff members, but the number of emissaries sent to each camp varies considerably. Most camps have only a few, but some have forty or more. One final note is that emissaries have different levels of experience. Some are experiencing American camp for the first time, others are returning, and still others are considered veteran emissaries, because they have returned to camp summer after summer.

## THE BIRTH OF THE CAMP ISRAELI EMISSARY

The use of emissaries to educate Diaspora Jews about Israel is a long-standing phenomenon. Individual emissaries began visiting American Zionist summer camps as early as the 1930s, but a formal emissary program for North American Jewish summer camps was not organized until the mid-1960s, when it began at Ramah. From there, the use of emissaries quickly spread to Massad, the Union Institute, and other Jewish cultural and educational camps, including many JCC and federation camps. From the outset, the emissaries program was designed to increase young North American Jews' awareness of and connections with the land, Hebrew culture, and Jewish citizens of Israel through direct contact with Israelis.[7] Yet this connection was not always predictable or easy to establish. Tamar "Timi" Mayer, for example, arrived as an emissary at the Union Institute in 1972 and was shocked by the campers' ignorance about Israel. She and her fellow emissaries sought to replace these misconceptions with an alternative narrative: "It was my mission to get them to understand that the language and the land are connected, and it's all about renewal. It's all about everything new."[8] Using Hebrew was part of that renewal project.

As Mayer's statement underscores, emissaries were the bearers of language and culture. That job varied depending on how each camp approached Hebrew. In JCC and federation camps they tended to be Israeli ambassadors, and any Hebrew-language teaching was bound up in this larger purpose. In camps with a mission of Hebrew speaking, like Ramah and Massad, directors looked expectantly to emissaries, hoping they would assist in furthering this goal. Israeli emissaries became the anchors of Hebrew-speaking programs at Jewish culture and Zionist camps, like Chalutzim at the Union Institute and the Ulpan at Young Judaea. After the initial trial year of 1965–1966, even Massad (which preferred relying on homegrown staff and handpicked Israeli or Israeli American specialists) joined the emissaries program, because it faced its own shortage of qualified Hebrew-speaking staff with the opening of a third Massad Poconos camp in 1968 and the general decline of Hebrew education in American Jewish day schools around that time.[9] But even in the early years of using emissaries, there were tensions regarding the number of Israelis in comparison to American staff and the larger question of finding the right balance in Hebrew usage. According to Rabbi Hillel Gamoran, one of the prime movers behind the Chalutzim program at the Union Institute, finding the right ratio between Israeli- and American-born staff was key to that program's success. His "Goldilocks" rule posited that if more than half of the program staff were emissaries, campers would conclude, consciously or unconsciously, that Hebrew was fundamentally an Israeli rather than a Jewish activity. Another camp, Yavneh, initially resisted joining the emissaries program because its director believed that American-born Hebrew-speaking staff members were more relatable role models. However, many emissaries and camp directors, particularly in non-Hebrew-speaking camps, did not view the promotion of Hebrew as part of their portfolio. On the contrary, in many emissaries' minds, Hebrew functioned as a barrier in their Israel public relations efforts. It exoticized emissaries in non-Hebrew-speaking camps, preventing them from forging substantive relationships with campers and staff.[10]

If the origins of the summer camp emissaries program can be traced to a practical need for more Hebrew-speaking staff members at Camp Ramah and as a way of fostering campers' sense of connection to Israel and its Jewish population, having Hebrew-speaking staff also proved to be the decisive selling point for the program when it was extended to federation and JCC camps in 1967. The program expanded exponentially in the aftermath of the Six Day War, at a time when Israel was elevated to a cardinal tenet of American Jewish civil religion[11] and the Israeli government undertook strategic and purposeful efforts to engage in *hasbara*[12] (propaganda) to shape its national image and narrative on the local and international stage. In 1978, only twelve years after the program was established, 283 emissaries and 68 camps were participating in it. However, the growth did not translate into a stronger focus on Hebrew at camps that were not already Hebrew-rich. A 1979 article about summer emissaries did not even mention Hebrew. Instead, the author quoted the program's U.S. coordinator, who made the case that "using shlichim in camp strengthens the ties between the U.S. and Israel, enhances cultural and religious programs, and introduces American Jewish youth to Israel and its people."[13]

During the second intifada in the early 2000s, the Jewish Agency for Israel (JAFI) invested heavily in training an unprecedented number of camp emissaries. Amos Hermon, the head of international education at JAFI, put it this way: "If American youth don't come to us, we will send our best people to them." This policy of bringing exemplary Israelis to America appealed to two complementary vectors: a strong connection to Israel was believed to be the *sine qua non* for maintaining and strengthening the local identity of diasporic Jews, and strong American Jewish support for Israel, it was argued, could help maintain and strengthen the state of Israel. In 2001, with more than 6,000 applicants to choose from, the numbers climbed to 923 emissaries serving a variety of camps spanning the gamut from private Jewish-owned camps to institutional camps, and from Zionist movement camps to religious denominational camps.[14] Sixteen years later, in 2017, there were more than 1,400 emissaries in 96 overnight camps, a significant increase in just a few decades.[15]

Although the number of emissaries has grown tremendously in recent decades, questions remain about how to represent Israel to American Jews, how to build relationships between Israeli and American Jews, and the role of Hebrew in these processes. As much as the role of emissaries has changed over time, what has remained constant is that they arrive at camps and encounter local varieties of Hebrew practices. Even for the vanguard emissaries in the mid-1960s, CHE proved vexing. Some everyday camp words, like *chadar ochel* and *mirpaa*, were reminiscent of kibbutz or other communal living situations and thus made sense. Others, like *kadur basis* (baseball), were American inventions and entirely foreign to the Israeli Hebrew speaker. And still others, like *beit kiseh* (bathroom), were archaisms that had long ago fallen out of use. Many of these words were introduced into camps like Massad by European-born Hebrew speakers or emigrants from British Mandate Palestine who were part of the Jewish Enlightenment, an intellectual movement committed to a cultural and moral renewal of Jewish life throughout Europe. As we have seen, Hebrew words were canonized in the *Massad Dictionary* and subsequently brought to newer camps like Ramah and Yavneh by staff members who were Massad alumni. Even if camps were not hermetically sealed off from Israel, emissaries discovered that camp Hebrew often developed in (relative) isolation from it. Massad senior administrator Rivka Shulsinger opined in 1978 that she preferred to employ emissaries rather than Israeli residents living in North America because of their idealism and vivacity. But she neglected to consider that Massad's Hebrew was likely more intelligible to longtime American Israelis than it was to twenty-something Israeli natives fresh out of the army. "The Hebrew at camp—it was like a museum piece," marveled an Israeli who worked at Massad in the 1970s.[16]

## ISRAELI JEWISH AND AMERICAN JEWISH DIFFERENCES

Fast forward to the 2010s, and the same bewilderment is still at play, as Israeli emissaries (as well as some American staff) derisively label CHE "Hebrish" or "not legitimate Israeli Hebrew." In contrast to the emissaries of the 1960s who were recruited to serve as Hebrew specialists at Ramah and the Union Institute and to those with similar roles at Ramah and OSRUI today, the current JAFI Summer Shlichim Program puts no special emphasis on Hebrew. Indeed, the program's website states that emissaries "strengthen understanding of Jewish and Israeli culture and customs" by working as specialists in Judaic arts and crafts, sports, Israeli culture, and dance; Hebrew is not mentioned even once.[17] The orientation seminar that takes place in Israel several months before the emissaries depart for their respective camps reflects these priorities.[18] It includes very little professional development for teaching Hebrew; emissaries do not learn about informal language pedagogical practices, nor do they leave the workshop with a folder of implementable language-teaching ideas. This lack of pedagogical training also reflects camp leaders' attitudes about emissaries' role in teaching Hebrew. Emissaries' ability to teach Hebrew is a very low priority for most camp administrators, and relatively few consider it an important factor in their hiring decisions regarding particular Israeli staff members. By contrast, most administrators consider emissaries' English fluency to be very important.[19] Indeed, most camp directors conduct the qualifying interviews in English to ascertain the applicants' proficiency.

Even before they leave Israel, emissaries begin to understand that Israeli Hebrew and the Hebrew used at camp differ in content and purpose. One of the first times that emissaries come into contact with CHE is at the orientation seminar when they do simulated activities that mimic a typical day at camp. This initial exposure gives them their first taste of CHE's status and durability. Not only do they need to learn which Hebrew words are used at their assigned camp, but they are also exposed to clippings, blends, and other Hebrew words that have different forms or meanings than they do on the Israeli street. For example, for emissaries, many of whom were recently discharged from the military, it was strange to hear the word "curfew" (which they knew as a Hebrew word—a loanword from English—referring to a military ban) with its camp meaning being the time to return to bunks after the evening activity. When they were told that "once a week you're going to do a *shmira* task," they had to recalibrate their understanding of the word *shmira* to mean making sure campers do not leave their cabins after bedtime, not guarding military installations. There were also phonological differences. *Mazál tov* became *mázel tov* and *chéder ochel* became *chadár ochel, cháder ochel, hadar ochel,* or just *hadar.*[20] Not waiting for summer to start to practice these linguistic changes, by the end of the four-day seminar, many of the emissaries began displaying increasing CHE proficiency, pronouncing Hebrew loanwords with phonology closer to American English.

In addition to presenting differences in language, the orientation seminar also showed emissaries that the American Jewish camping experience fosters a distinct form of Jewish identity—one that is both American and diasporic and at times is wholly at odds with their own experiences with Judaism in Israel. Many of the Israeli emissaries define their Jewish identification as *chiloni,* or secular, a term that categorizes Israeli Jews by religious observance. Whereas religion, even when it is only symbolic, often plays a significant role in American Jews' conceptions of their Jewishness, Jewish identity among secular Israeli Jews is more nationalistically grounded and bound up in civil religion. This difference was already palpable in the 1960s, when many camps compelled emissaries to take part in prayer and rituals. Some Israelis experienced this as a burden, but for others, like Ruth Katon, who worked at Massad Aleph in 1969, the exposure was a revelation. A completely secular Israeli who had previously ignored the fast day of Tisha B'Av, Katon was moved after taking part in the highly choreographed and dramatic service. "Suddenly it became clear to me how the living spark of the Jewish nation remains aglow in the Diaspora," Katon remarked.[21]

JAFI training leaders now purposefully introduce emissaries to American Jewish religious practices, which rely on textual Hebrew, giving them, in the words of one JAFI administrator, the opportunity to "meet a different kind of Judaism." Another JAFI staff member explained that when the emissaries arrive at camp they are "landing on a different planet, a world away" where "the whole Jewish thing is different." American Jews, they are instructed, see Judaism as a matter of choice and degree. JAFI staff encourage Israelis to "shed the part of their Israeliness that won't let them be Jewish" or, in other words, to discard their biases against the hegemonic position of religious Judaism in Israel. Emissaries are required to participate in all religious activities and events at their host camps, regardless of their own feelings, beliefs, or knowledge of Jewish ritual.

During their orientation seminar, emissaries are socialized into American liberal Judaism. They are exposed to the importance of liturgical Hebrew, learning and participating in daily prayer services and food blessings. They hear traditional prayers, such as *Modeh Ani*, set to contemporary melodies, often with the accompaniment of a guitar or tambourine to increase the affective dimension of the songs and the group experience of singing together. It is a new experience for many emissaries to be asked, in keeping with the Reform tradition, to stand and say the *Kaddish* collectively, a prayer that in Israel is mostly recited only by mourners and people observing a loved one's *yahrzeit* (the Yiddish term for the anniversary of the Hebrew calendar date of a person's passing) and is widely associated with the burials of fallen Israel Defense Forces (IDF) soldiers. What becomes clear even at the orientation seminars is that, even though emissaries are ostensibly sent to camps to model Israeliness, including native Hebrew fluency, they are socialized and inducted through camp Hebrew ritual practices into American Jewish (camp) culture.

### Negotiating Expertise

Although the ability to explicitly teach Hebrew is not a top priority in the selection of emissaries, camp leadership looks to Israeli staff to be Hebrew infusers; that is, to serve as resources who can organize and implement a wide variety of Hebrew infusion practices, including posting Hebrew signage, performing word-of-the-day skits, teaching Israeli songs, and promoting emblematic Hebrew words or sayings. Being labeled "Hebrew experts" puts them in positions where they are expected to perform the role of the Hebrew educator. However, as they quickly realize, being native speakers of Hebrew does not endow them with the metalinguistic knowledge about the structure of the language needed to explain it, nor does it help them facilitate American campers' ability to understand their fast-paced Israeli-accented Hebrew. Paradoxically and perhaps intuitively, emissaries often recognize the need to remove themselves from the position of Hebrew educator and just present themselves as Israelis.

Once at camp, Israelis' lack of comfort with textual Hebrew and religious practices also challenges their positions as Hebrew experts. Emissaries may have, in the words of a Ramah administrator, a "linguistic heritage," but many are "ignorant of the liturgical elements" that make up a significant component of American Judaism. At camps with daily prayer services, this lack of expertise in textual Hebrew has stood out and exposed fault lines between Israeli and American Jews' knowledge sets. One American Ramah leader cheekily recounted how one of her "most entertaining aspects of being at camp" was "seeing all the secular Israelis . . . have to sit through *tefillah* all the time" and especially when "they have no idea what anything means." However, when emissaries do participate in services and read Torah on Saturday morning, campers and American staff often interpret their Hebrew agility as better and more authentic than American Jews' linguistic competency, even if they lack a deep grasp of the text's content or religious significance.

Key to this tension regarding expertise is the emissaries' lack of awareness of the importance to American Jews of textual ritual language, both in terms of use and symbolic value. Although emissaries may recognize their dearth of knowledge regarding liturgical practices, this reflexivity regarding their own deficiencies does not seem to help them fully comprehend how American Jews could be so attached to a language they do not understand. A Ramah emissary expressed her struggles with this paradox, stating, "Maybe it's because I know Hebrew, like perfectly, but it bothers me that they [American campers] say prayers every day. They pray every day. And they can read in the Torah perfectly. They can read it better than I do. . . . But they have no idea what they are saying." Even though she was not religiously observant, this emmisary questioned a bedrock of American Judaism that decoding sacred texts without full comprehension is an acceptable form of religious practice. In addition, she tacitly asserted her expertise by claiming that campers are at a disadvantage because they do not know what the words mean when they pray. "I feel a little bad for them that they don't know the power of words"—a power that she claimed for Israelis by dint of their nativeness in modern Hebrew. What is missing in her lament is an awareness that textual Hebrew in the American context is not only important for its sacred functions but that it also serves as a critical community identity marker whose main function is symbolic.

In addition to textual Hebrew, emissaries grapple with the varying levels of campers' modern Hebrew proficiency. Although campers can speak CHE fluently, emissaries learn very soon after their arrival that most campers cannot construct a full sentence in Hebrew. One camp director said, "It just seems so strange to them that these American kids can sing all the stuff and yet they can't say, 'I have to go to the bathroom.'" Emissaries have to navigate what they call the "invented" Hebrew that makes up the local camp discourse. Recognizing the discrepancy between Israeli Hebrew and CHE, some camps have tried to minimize the inevitable confusion. At Galil, for example, a staff document called "Ivrit" suggests that American staff members should "explain to Israeli staff members the particular words we use at *machaneh* and help them bastardize the language." Implicit in this directive is the tacit recognition (and pride) that not only is camp Hebrew different from Israeli Hebrew but that it also represents an inferior variety.

Overwhelmingly emissaries adopt CHE, even when it deviates from Israeli Hebrew's syntactic, semantic, morphological, and phonological norms. They quickly understand that Hebrew use at camp is largely symbolic and that Israeli Hebrew is restricted to token expressions, often for entertainment value, some of which do not exist in vernacular Israeli Hebrew. Though they may joke about it, emissaries have taken on the Americanized (Ashkenazi) pronunciation *mázel tov*, in contrast to *mazál tov*. They sing Israeli Hebrew songs with gusto, knowing full well that these tunes had been off the Top 10 lists in Israel for years, if not decades. In the words of one veteran emissary, Israelis disassociate camp Hebrew from Israeli Hebrew, recognizing that when it comes to the former, "some parts lose all trace of actual Hebrew." In performing Israel through Hebrew skits, songs, cheers, and signage, they become the creators and sustainers of many Hebrew infusion practices. Not seeing it as Israeli Hebrew, emissaries accept CHE for what it is—a wholly American innovation. And with few exceptions, emissaries learn to effectively translanguage. As they become more acquainted with the vicissitudes of camp life, more often than not, they choose fitting in over holding firm to rigid definitions of what "actual" Hebrew is.

What might appear to be a complete and successful socialization to CHE, however, masks fissures regarding the limits of the acceptability of CHE and Hebrew infusion practices. As emissaries learn to move between Israeli Hebrew and CHE, they become entangled in ideologies of authenticity, which determine their integration into the camp community and their differentiation from it. They grapple with their participation in infusing images, songs, and narratives of Israel that are "stuck in the past" and that portray Israeli society in a mythic status or idealize its chalutzic (pioneering) origins. Some uses of Hebrew test emissaries' ability to play along, ignore incorrect or nonsensical Hebrew, or go beyond a perception of CHE as a form of faux Hebrew. For example, an Israeli at Yavneh did not like that the sections of the lake were referred to as *arisa alef* (crib A) and *arisa bet* (crib B), because he associated this word with a baby's crib. An emissary at Alonim worried that campers might think that "Shabbox" is actually a Hebrew word. At Ramah Poconos, an emissary said "*notzetzim*ers" (campers in the Notzetzim division) and then laughed, "It's so strange to take a word and make something else from it." "I'll say with respect," another pointed out, "the Hebrew of Camp Ramah is not necessarily *Ivrit*." Rather, he stated, "they are creating a Ramah-like reality which is nostalgically relating to a language that, you know—*lo muvan* [not understood], is not understood by Hebrew speakers." All of these metalinguistic comments underscore how emissaries reaffirm difference through ideologies of authenticity by reinforcing boundaries between vernacular Israeli Hebrew and camp Hebrew. They also suggest that emissaries feel the need to define and defend their Israeliness through Hebrew legitimacy when they are in the Diaspora. They may not explicitly talk about Israeli Hebrew as an "authentic" form of Hebrew, but when they talk about the need to "dumb down our language" for American camp consumption, the dichotomizing discourse of *ours* and *yours* gives voice to these boundaries and reasserts the hierarchical relation of Israeli Hebrew over American Hebrew.

### Conflating Hebrew and Israel

Ideologies of authenticity are entangled in ideologies of Hebrew culture and Jewish nationalism. The repeated trope of speaking Hebrew and building familiarity and affection for Israel brings into stark relief the close association between the two categories. When a Moshava IO leader touted, "I always tell kids and staff it couldn't be a camp that talks about Israel and didn't have authentic Israelis who speak the authentic language," what he cements in the minds of his listeners is the impervious bond between Israel, Israelis, and Hebrew, as well as the emphasis on vernacular Israeli Hebrew as the standard. In rhetoric and in practice, teaching about Israel and modern Hebrew go hand in hand, as the latter becomes a signifier of the former. Celebrating Israel Day, a festival-like event at many camps, for instance, often includes ramped-up modern Hebrew use. Even on "regular" days, educating about Israel is often done through the use of Hebrew as a means of giving a camp a "contemporary Israeli vibe," as one staff member suggested. Yet this vibe more often than not erases the role of other languages used in Israel, such as Arabic, Russian, Yiddish, Amharic, and the languages of foreign workers. As a result, "authentic Israel" is presented as monolingually Hebrew and Jewish.

Nowhere was the conflation of Israel and Hebrew made clearer than during the 2015 Goodman Camping Initiative and Bringing Israel to Camp Spring Workshop—a three-day seminar run by iCenter and FJC for about 125 participants from twelve camps, including some emissaries, that took place at Capital Camps in Waynesboro, Pennsylvania.[22] This program identified modern Hebrew as a primary means of bringing Israel to camp in both subtle and explicit ways. During the icebreaker that started the workshop, camp staff members were asked to come up with a Hebrew word that in some way captured the essence of the camp and then were told, "Through Hebrew language, we bring Israel into camp, so remember those words and use them in camp." Throughout the three days, participants were asked to do a wide range of activities that triggered discussions about integrating content about Israel into camp activities, and often the solution was to do this through Hebrew. For example, while mapping out the physical layout of a camp to determine where Israel could be added, an iCenter staff member told Tamarack participants that "Israel education is everywhere there is Hebrew." When the conversation turned to how places at camp could be redesignated with Hebrew names, a Tamarack counselor's question, "Is Hebrew education the same as Israel education?" was met with nods of agreement and a comment, "Why not?" The ease with which Hebrew usage was connected to programming about Israel reveals the taken-for-granted nature of this relationship. When iCenter staff discussed using Hebrew to talk about swimming strokes at the pool or labeling *kadur* (ball) on inflatable pool balls, they were also promoting a model for teaching about Israel through Hebrew infusion activities.

Linking modern Hebrew to Israel also leads to disparate notions about what qualifies as Jewish knowledge. Because emissaries' Hebrew indexes only Israel, and not other Jewish practices, emissaries are often isolated from Jewish educational programming. One emissary at an independent camp lamented that her activities were siloed to the Israel hut and were not coordinated with the Jewish educational staff. Other emissaries felt that American staff members, particularly former campers who were deeply invested in the camps' traditions, were hesitant to let emissaries do any serious educational programming that was not about Israel for fear that they did not have the pedagogical know-how or content knowledge to do it successfully.

### (Re)presenting Israel

Israeli staff members not only mobilize Hebrew in spoken interactions, but they are also expected to evoke an emotional attachment to the country through displays of visual and material representations. Much like the producers of simulations of remote places at festivals or amusement parks, emissaries depict Israel in the campscape and, in the process, hope to position campers as a certain type of tourist: those who stay in their home space and experience a new, unfamiliar, and exotic place that has been imported for their consumption. At its core, performances of Israel, often done through varying Hebrew infusion practices, set out to transcend the distance between campers and the Jewish community in Israel.[23] To construct this subjective space and create Israel imagery, emissaries engage in "banal nationalism"[24]—hanging up Israeli flags, displaying advertisements for popular Israeli candy bars and snacks, and posting maps of Israel and images of Israeli leaders and celebrities. All of this material culture is critical in establishing ideologies of nationalism. Emissaries also plan the program for many camps' Israel Day, a cultural performance in which part of the regular camp schedule is replaced by multisensory events, including making pita, eating falafel and Israeli snack foods, learning contemporary Israeli songs and dances, creating tickets with Hebrew and English wording that campers use to get into the festivities, and bartering at the *shuk* (market) using Hebrew phrases and fake shekels with Hebrew lettering. Thus, Israel Day programming not only distills Israel into a concentrated time during the camp calendar but also defines what Israeliness is.

Through these linguistic material resources, emissaries create a portrait of Israel in which they can perform Israeliness in noncontroversial and entertaining ways. An administrator at a URJ camp told us, "Having Israeli staff members here is great just so kids can be exposed to Israeli culture. The kids also think the Israelis are really cool because they've come from Israel. . . . On Israel Day, Israelis sold absolute crap at the *shuk* (market). Kids went nuts for total crap. Kids thought it was cool to get things with Hebrew written on it." This comment expresses a favorable opinion about having Israelis at camp while being dismissive of the enterprise. It also taps into a sentiment that exposing campers to Israel remains on the superficial level, in which its history and culture can be reduced to Hebrew-inscribed baubles. Hebrew, in this sense, has become an atomized manifestation of Israel.

Campers' reactions to Israel Day may have been favorable, but as part of the deliberate staging of Israel as entertainment, Hebrew runs the risk of being perceived as lacking seriousness and depth. The URJ leader's sentiment also underscores the coupling of coolness with Israel and, by extension, Hebrew. A Lavi staff member told us, "All the cool places in camp like the dune buggies and the ziplining and all that type of really cool stuff are run by Israelis." The cool factor of Israelis and Hebrew is a repeated trope. At URJ Jacobs, this came up in a discussion about the presence of lemon juice on every table in the dining room, which started because Israelis requested it for their salad. A camp leader thought about the social potential this culinary addition would have on her Mississippian campers: "They'll try it, I guarantee, because anything the Israelis say is cool; it's great." Israeli coolness was also extended to Camp Judaea's color war experience, in which the four teams representing Israeli "military triumphs" (1948, 1967, 1973, and 1982) made up cheers, performed (often humorous) skits, and put up posters that combined the Hebrew names of the teams' colors with the historical events of each war. Working with American staff, emissaries successfully attached Israeli battles to coolness, often through the use of Hebrew words and images, and presented a partial, sanitized version of Israeliness that avoided any discussion of the casualties of war for both sides.

This sanitization could also be seen as a mandate to stage positive images of Israel, when Israelis and American staff know that the actual country is more complicated. At several camps, campers sang and danced to a 2004 recording of "*Shirat Hasticker*" (The Sticker Song) by the popular Israeli hip-hop group

Hadag Nahash. However, campers did not always know, and the emissaries did not always tell them, that this song's popularity was a function not only of its catchy beat but also of its lyrics that quoted political slogans appearing on car bumper stickers in Israel at the time. The lyrics of "A strong nation makes peace" and "Allow the IDF to hit them hard" represent a collage of slogans (themselves full of wordplay and cultural references) that underscore political and cultural tensions in Israeli society. However, much of this nuance was downplayed or ignored at many camps. Emissaries were aware of the dilemma that if they discussed the controversial meaning of the lyrics, it would distract from the enjoyment of singing and dancing to the song. We observed such a negotiation regarding the song *"Tootim"* (Strawberries), made famous by the Israeli group Ethnix in 1992 in the optimistic days leading up to the signing of the Oslo Accords in 1993. A veteran emissary and music specialist at Tel Yehudah taught this song to a group of 15-year-old campers. After performing the song with the other music specialists, he presented the campers with the lyrics written in Hebrew, transliteration, and English and discussed how the lyrics about strawberries ("Come on, let's buy only strawberries, instead of the machines of war") were a political commentary on the futility of war. What lightened up this heavy discussion was not only the catchy melody of the chorus and the brevity of the explanation, but also the dance moves campers were taught to accompany their singing.

Portraying military aspects of Israeli society is particularly tricky because of the desire to laud patriotic army service and Israel's military triumphs without glorifying violence or discussing the historical conditions or the perspective on these "successes" among those on the other side of these fights. The military is still a strong presence in the lives of many of the young emissaries, who were either recently released from mandatory service or are still doing reserve duty. Their military experience is a common topic of discourse. As one OSRUI camper summed up, "If the American counselor gives an introduction, they'd say their name, how old they are, what college they go to . . . their siblings and family. If you ask an Israeli counselor, they'll tell you their name, their age, and then immediately after that, they tell you what they were in the army." In many ways, Israeli staff bring aspects of their military experiences into camp through Hebrew-infused games. Israelis performing the role of drill sergeants have campers do relay races while saying the numbers in Hebrew. At Ramah California, one emissary told campers, "I'm *Mefakedet* [officer] [Maya.] . . . When I say *pol*, it means get down. When I say *matzav shtayim*, it means like this [push-up position]." With the help of Hebrew, American campers are able to perform a sanitized Israeli army duty that combines combat with entertainment, much like the programs set up for tourists in Israel who spend a few hours or even a week going through a simulated basic training course in a real IDF uniform and have the experience of shooting a military firearm.[25] Like other aspects of Jewish Israeli life, military service takes on valences of coolness without a deeper and critical engagement regarding the effects of ongoing military conflict on Israeli society and on the people in the territories it occupies.

More often than not, when Israelis talk to Americans about their military experiences they do so in generalities and do not relate their individual actions or their opinions about Israeli politics, including the occupation of the West Bank. Whereas the use of Hebrew army slang and lingo downplays the seriousness of war and its effects, ironically, the gravity of topics such as terrorist threats and military operations dictate the need for Israelis to talk in English, which in turn has implications for how some Americans come to see their relationship with Hebrew. An OSRUI camper talked about how Israeli army service was a motivating factor in her decision to try to learn Hebrew: "They [Israelis] are the ones who have done all the, you know, they went and served their country. And we're just sitting here doing things. And I feel like if we—once we learn Hebrew, we can kind of even it out a little." Though not a commonly heard sentiment, this camper's logic presupposes that if Israeli Jews can sacrifice their lives in the defense of the Jewish state, American Jews can at least learn Hebrew. What this equivalency tacitly points to is that, like being in a war, learning Hebrew is not fun and games, but represents a sacrificial act that Diaspora Jews can do to serve the Jewish state. This idea of learning Hebrew as service can also be detected in the prayer for the security of the state of Israel, common in American synagogues and camps. One administrator revealed that reciting this Hebrew prayer was seen a way of getting campers to go beyond themselves and recognize the struggles that Israelis are undertaking to defend Israel and Jews everywhere. In this sense, modern Hebrew and prayer ritual are joined to perform patriotism to Israel, the campers' ancestral homeland. Thinking about Hebrew as a form of Israeli patriotism is especially provocative, because it endows American Jews with a form of Israeli nativeness despite their lack of birth citizenship or their claim to Israeli citizenship through the Law of Return, all without having to renounce their allegiance to the United States. In this postmodern form of patriotism, acquiring and using Hebrew link modern Israeli culture, religious tradition, and American Jewish identity.

Expressing solidarity with and patriotism to Israel is, however, also subject to American-driven calculations. Though some camps are eager to talk about the founding of Israel and its military victories, many camp leaders express reluctance about dealing with current events. Part of this calibration is the result of a sensitivity to the range of camp participants' political leanings, as well as fear of parental complaints if camps become too political. Camp leaders tread gingerly when discussing the Israeli occupation or avoid addressing it at all. In the summer of 2014, when three Israeli teenagers were kidnapped and killed and a seven-week conflict ensued between Israel and Hamas in Gaza, camps sought out ways of addressing this crisis that were aligned with their particular pro-Israel perspectives, while not appearing too political or dampening the fun spirit at camp. Although some camps chose not to address the issue at all, others programmed concentrated and affectively intense performances of solidarity. For Solomon Schechter this included having the whole camp community say *Kaddish* together. Surprise Lake initiated an activity called "We Stand with Israel," which included a moment of silence and singing the Israeli national anthem, *Hativkah*. URJ Harlam wrote letters of support to IDF soldiers, and URJ Eisner created a whole-day program, which culminated in the entire camp going out to the field, forming the shape of Israel, and taking an overhead photo to be sent to Israel to show their support. Habonim Dror Gilboa made a banner in English, Hebrew, and Arabic that read, "Only peace will bring peace." Other camps held moments of silence, a compelling commentary itself that speaks volumes on the limits of language to express sorrow and solidarity.

Events like the Gaza conflict in 2014 directly challenged camps' hermetically sealed borders and their ability to curate Israel representation. *In loco parentis*, camp leadership had to calibrate their response to controversial topics according to the age and maturity of the campers, while also weighing the risks they ran in depressing the effervescent atmosphere that campers expected. When they faced a situation about portraying Israel in crisis, modern Hebrew was widely absent from the programming, but interestingly retained its position in noncontroversial daily Hebrew-infused activities like Hebrew word skits and singing. Hebrew could continue to function symbolically in the campscape without the staff having to confront Israel in reality.

For Israelis, the avoidance of or minimal engagement with controversial topics during the 2014 crisis reinforced symbolic boundaries between themselves and American Jews. Emissaries felt that American staff and campers were not really interested in knowing much about Israel and displayed indifference when more serious topics were brought up. They were surprised that staff members, even those who had spent time in Israel on various homeland and educational programs, did not know details of Israel's history or the reality of life in Israel beyond the sentimental and the symbolic. Despite the strong personal relationships they established with campers and colleagues over the summer, emissaries felt isolated, especially during the Gaza invasion and particularly at camps that chose not to address the news at all and at camps with few emissaries. Though camp leadership at many camps offered their Israeli staff more frequent opportunities to check email, make phone calls home, and read the Israeli press, camp life went on in its traditional fashion. One American counselor recalled being taken aback by the emissaries' preoccupation with events in Israel and their lack of participation in camp rituals that summer, given their centrality to the overall camp experience.

As much as camps attempt to display solidarity with Israel and imbue the camp experience with a discourse of Jewish peoplehood, the compartmentalized role of Hebrew brings to the surface the realities of Israeli and American Jews' differences. For example, at the height of the 2014 conflict, emissaries at camps with large Israeli delegations took solace in being able to speak Hebrew with each other, knowing that most English-speaking staff and campers could not understand their conversations. Paradoxically, Hebrew became a refuge, which enabled them to separate themselves, reaffirm their own bonds as Israelis, and deal with the existential anxiety that they felt as the conflict dragged on over the course of the summer. Although Israelis were in a Jewish space at camp, in the words of one emissary, they were "not home," which made it hard for them to continue in the camp routine. If Hebrew was perceived as a way to make connections between Israeli and American Jews and reinforce notions of Jewish peoplehood, its limits were tested when Israelis reclaimed it for their own social and psychological needs.

Israel as imagined by American Jews has taken on a reality of its own, with camps being perhaps the most extensive manifestation of this phenomenon. Camps' reluctance to deal with the complexity of contemporary Israeli issues results in a nostalgia for the "good old days"—manifested by singing classic Israeli songs, celebrating historical figures on the Israeli timeline, and using archaic Hebrew words. However, these yearnings for a different time are a displaced nostalgia. Campers and staff members are not evoking or longing for their direct personal memories, because they were not alive during the state's early years. Nor are they longing for the real Israel of the late 1940s and early 1950s, with its food ration cards, immigrant transit camps, recurrent border conflicts, and lack of television. Freezing perceptions of Israel through words and images and relegating modern Hebrew to tokenism and entertainment engender nostalgia by erasing the reality of contemporary Israel, thereby giving Americans access only to symbolic, positively valent elements. Israeli and American Jews produce and perpetuate this nostalgia, raising the question if what is being brought to camp is eretz Yisrael or ersatz Israel.

––––––

The increasing numbers of Israeli emissaries and the proliferation of Hebrew at camps represent two sides of the same nationalistic project: educating American Jews about Israel in the service of building affective ties between these communities. However, the reliance on modern Hebrew exposes an unresolved tension implicit in this aim. Emissaries arrive at camp prepared to "bring Israel to camp" only to find that, rather than being agents of change, they themselves become the objects of transformation. That is, they become more like American Jews. Emissaries set out with the goal of mobilizing Israeli Hebrew and Israeli culture but instead find themselves speaking mostly English, participating in religious practices unfamiliar to them because of their secular upbringings, acquiring CHE, staging Israel activities that are often siloed from other camp educational activities, avoiding political topics deemed off-limits, and performing the Israel of the American Jewish imaginary. Their Hebrew nativeness is both a resource and a limitation as they discover that Israel as imagined by American Jews takes on a reality of its own at each camp. Specifically, CHE, with its hybridity and creativity, directly challenges Israeli language ideologies that perceive modern Hebrew as the authentic Jewish language. Imported to camp to perform Israeliness in part through their fluency in Hebrew, emissaries nonetheless must defer to camp norms, including its Hebrew infusion practices. Questions remain unanswered as they negotiate meanings of authenticity as applied to language, patriotism, and homeland.

# CHAPTER 8

# Conflicting Ideologies of Hebrew Use

On a Sunday night, about 200 staff members gathered for one of their regular meetings at Ramah Poconos. As counselors and specialists sat on long benches enjoying ice cream sandwiches, Aaron, an administrator, discussed some of the camp's "core values" and other issues that staff members should think about, including ensuring campers' safety, keeping the camp clean, and "being a *dugma* [role model] for the *kayitz* [summer] experience." He engaged in what he called "*hakarat hatov*—the recognition of good" by praising a few staff members' "amazing *sipurim* [stories] of *hatzlacha*, success." Although most of the meeting was conducted in this kind of heavily Hebraized CHE, Aaron sometimes also used nonroutinized Hebrew in translingual ways, such as "First, *kama milim al hapegisha hazot bichlal* [a few words on this meeting in general]" and "teaching other *madrichim ech l'lamed* [counselors how to teach]." The meeting was also filled with metalinguistic conversation, including Aaron translating less common words and phrases, explaining the difference between the words *betichut* (safety) and *bitachon* (security) and discussing the importance of using certain words only in Hebrew. At one point a counselor asked a question about the "boys' area." Aaron responded, "I believe you mean *migrash banim*, but that's OK, you're new here." A few other staff members interjected jocularly, "*Meah Milim!*" referring to the Ramah movement's program encouraging staff members to say certain words only in Hebrew (ironically, *migrash banim* was not on the list). A minute later, another counselor made a comment including the word "bunk," and several staff members corrected him to *tzrif* (which was #1 on the *Meah Milim* list). The atmosphere was playful, and nobody—including the two counselors who made the "mistakes"—appeared upset by the corrections.

The next morning at prayer services, most of the division head's announcements were in nonroutinized Hebrew, such as "*Meltsarim, atem yecholim l'sayem et hatefilot shelachem v'lalechet lachadar ochel* [Waiters, you can finish your prayers and go to the dining hall]." A *Yahadut* (Judaism) teacher gave a short teaching in English about the *Shma* prayer. Then a camper who was leading part of the service made a brief announcement in English, and another camper said, "*Ivrit!*" reminding her that all announcements during services should be in Hebrew, an interjection we also heard a few times in the dining hall. At services in a younger division, the counselor calling page numbers corrected herself for using an English word: "Also on pag- *amud shtayim* [page two]—*Ma Tovu* [name of the prayer]."

These snapshots from our observation in the Poconos represent broader trends at Ramah and other Hebrew-rich camps. English is the primary language of conversation at camp, but staff members are expected to use Hebrew in certain contexts. When people stray from these expectations, superiors or peers sometimes correct them, or they correct themselves. This language policing, in combination with the many infusion practices, reminds everyone present of the importance of Hebrew in the camp setting, but it can also reflect or engender conflicting language ideologies: beliefs about how language should be used, by whom, when, and to what degree. Such tensions are not limited to Hebrew-rich camps and are even found at camps with very little Hebrew.

One overarching tension that affects all the others is caused by conflicting and underarticulated Hebrew-related goals. Although a few camps are interested in campers attaining spoken Hebrew proficiency, even those camps see their immediate goal as teaching select elements of Hebrew and fostering a desire for further education.[1] The primary goal of Hebrew infusion is not mastery of the language, but an emotional attachment to Hebrew, which is intended to strengthen campers' connection to the Jewish state, the Jewish religion, and the Jewish people. However, because camp leaders rarely discuss such goals explicitly, staff members have diverse understandings of how Hebrew should be used and what it represents; sometimes their understandings are influenced by their perceptions about how Hebrew was once used at their camp or other camps, which may or may not be accurate.

Debates about Hebrew use are an age-old Jewish pastime. In antiquity, the translation of the Bible into Greek and Aramaic provoked controversy in some Jewish circles. The rabbis of the Mishnah discussed whether certain prayers and the Scroll of Esther should be recited in Hebrew or the vernacular. In the Middle Ages, Sephardi Jews debated whether Hebrew or Arabic was more appropriate for expressing secular ideas. Hebraists in the Italian Renaissance argued that biblical Hebrew was superior to mishnaic Hebrew and to medieval *piyyut* (liturgical poetry), which incorporated some foreign influences. In the eighteenth and nineteenth centuries, German maskilim (enlightened Jews) championed Sephardi Hebrew pronunciation as the most pure and enlightened, as aligned with their preferences in art and architecture. Reform leaders avidly debated the proper balance of Hebrew and the vernacular in their prayer books and temples.

Zionist leaders deliberated whether to endorse Hebrew or another language and, once they settled on Hebrew, policed its use heavily. And at various points in history, purists have criticized Jewish languages as corrupt versions of their non-Jewish correlates, including their hybrid use of Hebrew words.[2]

In America today, debates about how much and which type of Hebrew to use are found not only at camps but also in synagogues, schools, and other Jewish institutions.[3] As we and others have argued, these debates are now influenced by two new factors: the existence of Israeli Hebrew and the presence of Israelis in American Jewish communities.[4] Before the twentieth century, Jewish students (generally boys) learned textual Hebrew through their study of biblical and rabbinic literature. Today Jews (male and female) can continue this practice, but they can also learn modern Hebrew as a vernacular by interacting with native speakers, consuming Israeli media, and visiting Israel. This historical change led to many of the conflicting ideologies discussed here, not only because of Israelis' comments but also because of sociolinguistic projection—Americans seeing their language through Israelis' eyes, even if the Israelis in their midst do not share their critical stance. In other words, the debates are fueled by the existence of modern Hebrew as a spoken language alongside the Hebrew of sacred Jewish texts, as well as CHE, which draws from both.

Jews are not the only group that debates which language(s) should be used and how much language mixing is acceptable. Such ideological conflicts are common around the world, especially in situations of language contact.[5] Often these situations involve power differentials: colonized or immigrant groups gain access to a language associated with status and power (especially English, French, or Spanish), and speakers mix elements of that with their communal language.[6] In religious communities, this mix often includes a sacred language as well.[7] Such instances of language contact can lead to conflicting ideologies about language purism and mixing and about which languages should be used for which purposes.

An example can be seen in complementary schools in the United Kingdom.[8] These institutions meet on weekends and teach immigrant heritage languages, including Turkish, Mandarin, and Bengali. Although the students in these schools hear their heritage languages at home and American Jews generally do not, many of the Hebrew-related phenomena we found at Jewish summer camps are also present at these complementary schools. Teachers and students mix English and the communal language in the same conversation, the same sentence, and occasionally even the same word—akin to the English-Hebrew translanguaging in Hebrew-rich camps. Just as we found a hierarchy of Hebrew use, complementary schools feature "unreciprocal code-switching": teachers speak primarily Bengali, Mandarin, and the like, and students speak primarily English. Like Jewish camp leaders who have conflicting language ideologies, complementary school teachers and students follow two different approaches: "separate bilingualism," meaning that speakers should keep English and the communal language separate for different situations, and "flexible bilingualism," meaning that translanguaging is acceptable. Students tend to practice flexible bilingualism, whereas teachers tend to prefer separate bilingualism, believing it will improve students' language proficiency and increase the chances of communal language maintenance. Like injunctions to speak Hebrew at camp, teachers in these schools sometimes remind their students to speak the communal language when they speak too much English. Although the students—generally immigrants and children of immigrants—tend to have more solid ability in these languages than American Jewish campers have in Hebrew, the phenomena of translanguaging and conflicting ideologies are comparable.

When a language is used sporadically in symbolic ways, rather than as a language of instruction or primary communication, it has the potential to engender more emotional responses.[9] For example, in Sri Lankan communities in the United States, Canada, and the United Kingdom, locally born children use Tamil loanwords in English sentences and are taught to recite Tamil chants and speeches, despite their limited comprehension. Older community members sometimes criticize such emblematic uses of Tamil and consider these language practices inauthentic.[10] Conservative stances not only critique language mixing but also favor older forms of language over innovative forms. Such attitudes, ironically, can hinder language revitalization efforts, as found regarding several endangered indigenous languages.[11] If these languages are to have a chance of survival, linguists recognize, they will necessarily be in simplified forms or intermingled with the colonial or other dominant language.[12] In the cases of Hebrew and immigrant languages, the survival of the language is not at stake as it is with endangered languages. Even so, in all of these communities, the distinctive identity of the ethnic group is intimately bound up with language. As our and others' research suggests, in many contexts group members are more likely to use loanwords than full conversations in the group language. If young people are not willing or able to use traditional forms of the language but are happy to mix elements of it into their dominant language or use innovative forms, purists might be fighting a losing battle.

When people express views about language, they are also expressing views about personal and group identity. The tensions we discuss later in this chapter concern Hebrew, but they are part of broader debates about the desired outcomes of American Jewish experiential education. When camp leaders consider how much Hebrew to use or whether to correct clippings or blends, they are also debating what competent participants in American Jewish communities should know, feel, and do—and how camps should support those aims. Are camps socializing campers to be proficient in Hebrew or just to gain some exposure? Should the Hebrew used at camp foster participants' feelings of membership in the camp community or in a broader imagined community, like American Jewry, world Jewry, or Zionists, or in a particular subgroup like Sephardim or eco-Jews? Should American Jews think of their communities as a major center of contemporary Jewish life or as a satellite that looks to Israel as the center of world Jewry? Camp leaders may not discuss these questions on a day-to-day basis, but they underlie the conflicts regarding Hebrew.

## GOALS OF HEBREW USE

One of the central ideological debates has to do with the goals regarding Hebrew at camp. Our survey asked directors to rate the importance of ten educational goals (figure 8.1), and we found that the most important goals were ones related to Jewish connection: enhancing Jewish identity and strengthening connection to the Jewish people and Israel.[13] Working toward these goals does not necessarily involve language, but as our interviews indicated, the Hebrew used at camp is seen as playing a role in attaining them. Goals regarding Hebrew infusion—strengthening the connection to Hebrew and knowledge of Hebrew songs, prayers, blessings, and select words—were important in about half of camps, but they generally were not primary aims. Among the infusion goals, knowledge of Hebrew songs and prayers/blessings was more important than connection to Hebrew or knowledge of select Hebrew words. Goals regarding proficiency in Hebrew speaking and reading were important only to a few camps. These findings were mirrored in interviews with camp staff.

### Connection

Several interviewees emphasized the relative importance of affective connection over linguistic skill, even at Hebrew-rich camps. A Moshava IO educator said that, even though Hebrew pervades camp life, language education is not a central goal. The staff want campers to learn some Hebrew, but more importantly, "we want kids to walk out with a love for Israel, a connection to Israel." Similarly, a Camp Solomon Schechter administrator felt that Hebrew infusion allows him to "accomplish my goals of getting kids to be excited about being Jewish and loving Israel . . . in a way that is nonpolitical"—avoiding potentially contentious debates about borders, settlements, and military actions.[14] A Galil staff member also emphasized Hebrew as a means: campers should "feel a sense of belonging and responsibility for the Jewish people through our language." These quotes suggest that campers' connections to Israel and the Jewish people are not to be taken for granted: they must be cultivated, and leaders see camps as playing a role in that cultivation. Theoretically, one could love Israel and feel a sense of belonging to the Jewish people without any Hebrew knowledge, but these camp leaders' comments indicate their belief that Hebrew should play a role in Jewish collectivity. One might expect camp leaders whose primary interest is connection to promote Hebrew proficiency, because Jews in America, Argentina,

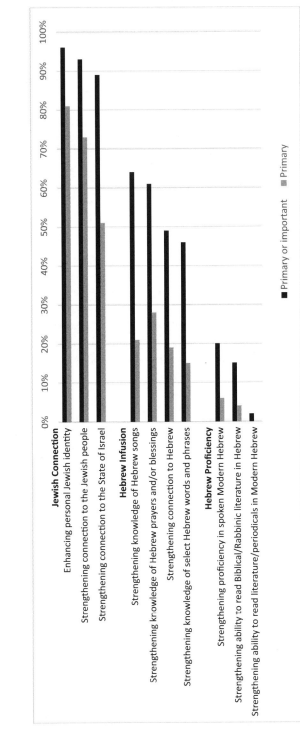

Figure 8.1. Survey data showing the percentage of camp directors who consider each goal to be primary or important.

France, and Israel could then "connect" on a more intimate level by conversing in a shared language. However, camp leaders focus instead on the symbolic role of Hebrew infusion—the use of select Hebrew phrases and a metalinguistic orientation toward Hebrew—in fostering campers' belonging to the imagined community of world Jewry.

## Proficiency

Twenty percent of camps did report proficiency in spoken modern Hebrew as an important or primary goal. In interviews, administrators at some Hebrew-rich camps expressed a desire for campers to become more proficient, but their specific aims were realistic. A Ramah Darom administrator said his goals for the camp's Hebrew immersion electives include some functional conversational Hebrew and themed vocabulary lists. "Proficiency and comfort is a goal," he said. "Fluency is not a goal." An OSRUI administrator expressed a similarly ideal yet realistic orientation regarding staff: "My fantasy is that if we ever got really good at it, all of our staff meetings would be in Hebrew. Now that's a fantasy more than a reality." Even among camp leaders who would like to see more Hebrew proficiency, expectations are relatively low.

If proficiency is not a goal, staff could still intend for campers to improve their language skills. A few camp leaders mentioned such goals. When we asked a Moshava IO leader to describe a successful camper with regard to Hebrew, she replied, "Somebody whose Hebrew has improved significantly. . . . If they come back from a vacation in Israel and they say, '[Miriam], we had the best time, we understood everything that the tour guide was saying,' that's a success for me." A Yavneh administrator reported that a goal is to raise each child's Hebrew level: "That means if they come in with 10 words, they leave with 25." She relayed that Hebrew school principals have told her that "they can always tell the kids that went to Yavneh because their Hebrew is definitely improved. And they're more interested in Hebrew, and they're more comfortable with Hebrew." Here we see a focus not only on increased Hebrew skill but also on affective goals, as we elaborate later.

Although some camps hope to increase vocabulary and comprehension, they generally do not create lists of words that campers should learn, and if they do, they do not test campers on them. Ramah's *Meah Milim* (100 words) program rewards the use of particular words, but campers are not formally assessed. A URJ Kalsman administrator said, "We have what I believe are realistic goals, which is to have an exposure to Hebrew. . . . We try and teach kids some nouns, some verbs, some phrases. But there's no grammatical structure-based education system. There is no actual curriculum of here are the 30 words they should learn their first year, and 20 words their second, and 40 words the next." Several camp directors rejected the idea of assessing campers' vocabulary acquisition or other language skills, because that would feel antithetical to the informal culture of summer camp and too similar to school.

At Hebrew-rich camps, some of the campers we interviewed reported increased proficiency as a personal goal. They did not expect to be fluent by the end of the session, but they hoped to learn some Hebrew. Indeed, several campers told us about hearing a Hebrew word in Hebrew school or on a trip to Israel and understanding it because they had learned it at camp. For example, a Ramah California ninth grader said she understood the word *makom* (place) in Hebrew school because every morning during the previous summer she had heard, "Go to your *makom tefilla* [place of prayer]." She also heard the word *ochel* (food) on a trip to Israel and recognized it from *chadar ochel*.

Many of the alumni we spoke with from Ramah, Habonim, and Young Judaea camps (of various ages) attribute much of their Hebrew knowledge to their time as campers. One alum and current staff member at Ramah Poconos said, "I certainly learned more Hebrew here, even in two months out of the year, than I did at Hebrew school, and I went to Hebrew school through 12th grade." A woman who attended a Habonim camp in the 1970s and subsequently emigrated to Israel found that she knew more Hebrew than she expected, even though she had a minimal Jewish education outside of camp. Although alumni of less Hebrew-rich camps did not relay such success stories, they sometimes reported making connections later in life. A URJ camp alum reported having a "lightbulb moment" in a modern Hebrew class in rabbinical school. Studying the verb *l'nakot* (to clean), he recalled the word for cleaning at camp: "Oh my God! *Nikayon*— cleaning! I understand how it works now!" The fact that this moment of realization came only in a Hebrew class many years later indicates the limited benefit of Hebrew loanwords at camp for Hebrew learning. He knew that *nikayon* meant cleaning, but knowing that word did not help him understand the structure of the language.

### Lighting the Hebrew Fire

Several camp leaders said they wanted campers to come away from camp with a desire to learn more Hebrew. This notion was especially common at camps with little Hebrew or Jewish content. A Surprise Lake staff member said the staff want to give campers "a sampling or tasting [so] that they can learn and try more in the future." A Kibbutz Max Straus educator characterized his job as "opening doors": "When you're dealing with kids who are so secular at home and in their communities, [the idea] is to give them at least the cultural Judaism . . . you know, throw in Hebrew words, and give them some songs. And . . . then they go off and explore." Hebrew infusion can ignite campers' interest in future Hebrew study. This kind of affective kindling was even a goal at camps with intensive Hebrew education. A Ramah Darom administrator said, "We know full well that in the 28 days that we have campers, we are not going to achieve fluency. So . . . our goal is very much to teach *Ivrit*, but it is even more than that: get kids to love *Ivrit* and get excited about *Ivrit* and instill in them a desire to learn more."

What does further Hebrew study look like? A URJ national leader said he wanted camp alumni to be motivated to take Hebrew courses in college and engage with Jewish texts.[15] Other leaders focused on Israel. A Hebrew educator at OSRUI said, "We measure our success by the number of kids who go to Israel and learn more Hebrew." Whether the intended educational domain is Judaism, Israel, or both, this concept is highlighted by a hand-painted sign in the OSRUI garden with a quote by poet W. B. Yeats: "Education is not the filling of a pail, but the lighting of a fire." Notably, the sign's focal point is the Hebrew word אש (fire) in large block letters. Yet fire can be both beneficial and dangerous. A Sprout Lake educator mentioned a risk: if "they come out of here saying, 'Ugh, enough Hebrew,' then we missed. It doesn't matter if we just did nouns; if we did too many nouns or we did it the wrong way, we missed." Therefore, she said, "The ultimate goal is . . . about children leaving here with an appreciation of Hebrew and with curiosity about Hebrew and a comfort." If the goal is lighting the Hebrew fire, Hebrew must be infused in a relatively controlled and nonthreatening way.

Some camp leaders felt they had been successful in lighting the Hebrew fire, pointing to campers and alumni who reported taking Hebrew classes because of their exposure at camp. Some pointed out that this is a long-term goal, as are many goals of Jewish camps, and therefore cannot be measured each summer. This long-term perspective is evident in a Ramah California leader's comment: "Camp is not so much, how does it change their life in October; it's, how does it change [their] life 25 years later? And so if somebody chooses to take a Hebrew class in college because of the Ramah experience, that's going to impact their life later. You know, they choose to spend a semester or a year in Israel. That's going to fundamentally change the outcome of how they speak Hebrew and who their *chevre* [friend group] is and everything else." This perspective emphasizes the mutually reinforcing relationship between language and community. Hebrew at camp is seen as encouraging future Hebrew engagement, which leads to Jewish communal connections and more Hebrew engagement.

### Lack of Measurable Goals

Although most interviewees were able to articulate theoretical or ideal goals, very few told us about explicit benchmarks for Hebrew acquisition, even in camps that emphasize proficiency. Immersion programs at OSRUI and Ramah New England test students' Hebrew levels before and after the program, but we did not find similar assessments at any other camps. We also did not see any documents regarding Hebrew-related outcomes, except for Ramah's *Meah Milim* list, which is operationalized via camp-wide competition, not individual assessment. Even a survey conducted by the National Ramah Commission—with responses by 5,260 alumni—did not measure linguistic outcomes.[16] Of the seventy-six questions, several related tangentially to Hebrew, including items about text study,

Israel visits, and Israel attachment, but none asked directly about Hebrew proficiency, use, connection, or even continuing education. This suggests that the use of Hebrew at Ramah camps is, in practice, more a means to other educational goals than an end in itself. Similarly, a Ramah Poconos leader said that campers and parents fill out surveys after each summer, but they are not asked explicitly about Hebrew, and the questions about educational programs tend to focus on how much campers enjoyed them, rather than how much they learned. This is evidence of consumerism trumping ideology in a competitive market. Even if leaders would like campers to improve their Hebrew skills, they consider it more important to focus on camper satisfaction to maximize return rates and positive word-of-mouth publicity.

At Ramah in the Rockies, we observed an exchange regarding the lack of measurable goals. The staff handbook stated, "*Chalutzim* [campers] will increase their knowledge of and connection to the Hebrew language. This will be accomplished through daily use of Hebrew by *chalutzim* and *tzevet* [staff], increased Hebrew signage, and commitment to Hebrew songs." In an interview, Carol, a visiting Hebrew educator, criticized this statement as vague and pointed out that it was not accompanied by concrete goals about what campers should be able to do by the end of the summer. A few staff members overheard our conversation and chimed in that, to them, the affective goal (increased connection to Hebrew) was more important than gaining linguistic skill (increased knowledge of Hebrew). Avi, a division head, asserted that "connection" is a concrete goal but should not be measured, because "I don't think that's what summer camp is for." Carol countered that camps assess other skills, like swimming, with the goal of tracking improvement throughout the session. Avi admitted he approaches Hebrew differently because he thinks of Hebrew as something one learns in school, and "I just associate a classroom with something really negative." According to Avi, articulating and assessing goals for Hebrew skills would bring an unwanted reminder of school into the pristine camp setting. Although many people learn second languages (including Hebrew) outside of classrooms, the association between schools and language learning is common around the world, as we see in the predominance of school-based language revitalization efforts.[17]

The reluctance to set measurable goals is not limited to Hebrew or to summer camps. In venues of informal Jewish education, like JCCs, youth groups, and Hillels, goals are not consistently articulated or measured.[18] A prime reason is that, like Avi, leaders want to distinguish their venues from formal educational settings, which give tests and grades. While some informal educators assess participants' progress through observation and other means, many avoid overt assessment, hoping to maintain their programs' identities as providing fun, entertaining experiences.

## INFUSION OR IMMERSION

How do these diverse articulations of goals play out in language policy and planning decisions? At several camps, especially those with an interest in proficiency, we found tensions surrounding Hebrew infusion. Some staff members feel that using Hebrew nouns in English sentences (what we call CHE) does not meet their educational standards, because it does not lead to proficiency in Hebrew. An Israeli woman involved with Ramah's Daber program expressed a desire for campers to use full Hebrew sentences: "Instead of 'Now we're going to the *agam*' [lake], it's better to say *'Achshav holchim la'agam'* [Now we're going to the lake] or even *'Achshav holchim l'*lake.'" If campers are exposed only to Hebrew loanwords, she felt that they will not learn the structure of Hebrew. Another Daber educator, an American woman, shared these concerns: "A language is not just a noun. . . . When you learn a language, you learn how it behaves. And you can only learn how it behaves in different situations if you hear its flow, if you hear its intonation, if you hear its rhythm. And if you say, 'I'm going to the *breicha* [pool],' what is that? . . . They're giving camp a flavor." Of course, this tension between infusion—giving camp a flavor of Hebrew—and immersion is not new: it goes back to the early days of Ramah camps.

Although critiques of infusion were most pervasive at Ramah camps, we also encountered them elsewhere. According to a Tel Yehudah administrator, a funder told him that using words like *chadar ochel* in English sentences was bad for campers' Hebrew-language acquisition. Although that worried him, he was still proud of the many Hebrew words campers learned through infusion at Tel Yehudah. A Beber administrator was comfortable with an Israeli staff member telling campers that *agam* is Hebrew for lake or *degel* for flag, but he did not want camp participants to use those words in English sentences. This concern seems to be influenced by an ideology of language purity, but for leaders interested in building vocabulary, it may be counterproductive. Telling learners about a word once or twice is less effective for lexical acquisition than having them hear and use it as a loanword multiple times a day in context.

Individuals sometimes expressed conflicting views. An OSRUI leader characterized his camp's Hebrew infusion as intentional. Throughout the camp, except for the Chalutzim immersion program, Hebrew nouns are used for activities, roles, and locations, and campers are exposed to few Hebrew sentences beyond routinized announcements and basic sentences in Hebrew classes. This leader wanted campers to come away from camp feeling that "Hebrew is the language of the Jewish people, no matter how much they speak or don't speak." Even so, he criticized the use of CHE: "I woke up one day, and I said, 'We're teaching Yiddish; we're not teaching Hebrew,' because if we teach you *shulchan* [table] and *ritzpah* [floor] and *me'il geshem* [raincoat] and *sefer* [book], we've only done the same thing that is probably the extent of your Yiddish—you know *kop* [head] and a variety of other random words that . . . have no connection to each other. So, now our big push is to teach you verbs." Such critiques of Hebrew loanwords stem from a desire to foster Hebrew proficiency, even when the critics realize that proficiency is an unlikely outcome, and indicate the commonly held belief that verbs are where the "real" language resides. They also reflect an ideology that Hebrew is a pure or valid language and that hybrid language varieties like Yiddish and (although not explicitly named) Jewish English or CHE are not—exactly the kind of ideology contested in scholarship on translanguaging.[19]

Although we encountered several camp leaders with a stance favoring full Hebrew sentences, many expressed positive feelings about CHE—which is not surprising, because most camps take precisely this approach. A Ramah Poconos administrator wrote in his letter to staff introducing the *Meah Milim* project: "In 2015 Ramah is not likely to be a place where the majority of our *madrichim* are using full and flowing sentences in *Ivrit*," implying a contrast between the contemporary situation and his understanding of Ramah's early years. "But rather," he continued, "Ramah should be a place where <u>EVERY</u> *madrich* is expected to use *Ivrit* in every sentence," in the form of loanwords, as the *Meah Milim* program encourages. A Gilboa administrator pointed out that infusion does offer some benefit for language learning: "Nouns are vocabulary. Vocabulary is important." An Israeli staff member at Yavneh agreed, saying that increasing campers' Hebrew vocabulary, even if mostly nouns, is a legitimate goal in and of itself.

Several interviewees emphasized the affective, connective potential of Hebrew infusion as more important than language pedagogy. A JCCA leader said, "If you agree that the use of the language is serving primarily a symbolic function, then anything about language theory and language learning is irrelevant." Those who share this stance would likely have no problem with Hebrew words that diverge from Israeli Hebrew, like *chadar* (short for *chadar ochel*). One administrator felt that policing language could "cause some campers to retract." We did observe this effect at OSRUI's Chalutzim immersion program in an exchange during *tefillah* between Evan, a tenth grader, and Rabbi Kleiner, a Hebrew and Judaics teacher:

> RABBI TO CAMPERS: *Lama anachnu omrim, "Baruch ata Adonai"*? [Why do we say, "Blessed are You . . . ?"]
> EVAN: Because we—
> RABBI: *B'ivrit.* [In Hebrew.]
> EVAN: *Ani lo yodea.* [I don't know.]

Evan was willing and able to answer Rabbi Kleiner's question in English, but as soon as she reminded him to speak Hebrew, he withdrew. By the end of the summer, Evan may have been better able to answer questions like this in Hebrew.

But such interactions point to one reason why immersion programs are rare, revealing a dilemma that we saw Ramah administrators struggling with as early as the 1950s: if it is difficult for beginning Hebrew learners to conduct basic activities in Hebrew, it is virtually impossible for them to have age-appropriate conversations about Judaica and philosophical issues without resorting to English.[20]

But this is far from the only reason why most camps favor infusion over immersion or instruction. The administrators we spoke with offered other reasons, which we sorted into three categories: priorities, campers, and staffing. A Habonim national leader pointed out that acquisition-oriented language instruction would be time consuming: "For that to be meaningfully impactful in terms of the language pedagogy, in terms of the kids developing Hebrew language in a serious way, I think that needs to be the sole function of the educational content." A Moshava IO administrator agreed: "If we were going to make it a real educational straightforward goal to really teach Hebrew language, we just wouldn't be able to accomplish what we wanted from a Zionist programming point of view, which we felt was our real raison d'être. . . . [So] we made a conscious decision many years ago that trying to also focus in on the teaching of Hebrew language would be too difficult for our staff. . . . It's really an issue of choosing your priorities."

A Ramah Poconos leader explained that campers—and finances—play a role in this issue:

> It's one of the big tensions at camp right now in trying to implement a Hebrew-language program. On the one hand, you have to deal with the kids, who are so much happier in this kind of informal, project-based, more relaxed atmosphere. They're so much happier, and camp enrollment is good, and all of that. But we also have the old-timers who are kind of like rending their garments and saying, "*Oy vey* [Yiddish exclamation of dismay]." . . . But holding onto some of those lofty ideals doesn't necessarily fill the bunks.

This quote suggests that even for Hebrew-rich camps, filling beds trumps the ideal of a Hebrew environment. The "old-timers," mostly parents and grandparents who attended Ramah decades ago, romanticize the past and nostalgically bemoan the reduction in Hebrew use. But as we explained in chapter 3, even Ramah's early leaders (who themselves were not immune to market forces) debated how much Hebrew to use, and they ultimately settled on (Hebrew-rich) infusion over immersion.

Concerning campers' comprehension of Hebrew, another staff member at Ramah Poconos pointed out that even the basic announcements that are currently in Hebrew sometimes lead to confusion. She related incidences of campers not knowing where their next activity was and sometimes asking counselors, especially Israelis, for translations. Campers' confusion and resistance to immersion can lead to a reduction in Hebrew use among some staff members.

As for staffing, a national Ramah leader explained that it would be difficult to find staff members capable of creating an immersive environment, given the other priorities for what constitutes a good counselor:

> We're always excited to have Hebrew speakers apply. I think that once we start placing staff members in different *edot* [divisions], it's one of the things that we're looking at, to make sure that there are, in fact, strong Hebrew speakers in each *edah*. But I think every director in any camp across the country would say our first priority is to find an amazing *madrich* who takes safety, and nurturing of kids, and serving as a role model—and a Jewish role model; those are the things that we must have. So, it's not like Hebrew is up there in that top three or four.

If a camp is unwilling to make Hebrew a central priority, it is unlikely to create an immersive environment. For these reasons, infusion has been and continues to be much more common than immersion at American Jewish camps.

The tension between immersion and infusion is about the desired outcomes of summer camp. Should campers gain the ability to function in Hebrew, perhaps in an Israeli context, or should they mainly feel strengthened Jewish connections via Hebrew infusion? This question relates to a broader ideological debate about the relationship between American Jews and Israel. If Israel is the center of global Jewish life, then perhaps Israeli Hebrew is a necessity for living Jewishly, and American Jews should know it. If America and Israel are both centers of contemporary Jewish life, then proficiency in Israeli Hebrew may be a welcomed addition but not a necessity. The former stance would favor Hebrew immersion at camp, and the latter stance infusion. Although we did not hear camp participants articulate these two positions overtly, and they are certainly ends of a continuum rather than binary alternatives, they seem to underlie the debate about Hebrew at camp.

## How Much Hebrew to Infuse

Related to the tension regarding immersion and infusion are competing ideologies about the amount of Hebrew to infuse. Leaders at camps of many types discuss whether they are offering too much, too little, or just the right amount of Hebrew for their specific missions and populations, reflecting the "tipping point" dynamic.

### More Hebrew

On one side of the debate are those who argue for more Hebrew use. A staff member at a Habonim camp said, "We have a complex about not knowing and using enough Hebrew." This "complex" led her and others to incorporate more Hebrew loanwords, signs, and announcements. In some cases, the Hebrew "complex"

stems from a feeling that the camp once used more Hebrew, but that it has gradually diminished over the decades. This discourse of nostalgia is especially prevalent at Ramah camps. Several interviewees joked that at Ramah in the past, the
lifeguard would not save drowning swimmers unless they called, "*Hatzileni!*"—
an archaic, formal Hebrew way of saying "Save me!" One staff member who
attended Ramah in the 1980s deadpanned, "We have no Hebrew here." When
we pointed out the Hebrew sign behind him and the fact that the announcements
a few minutes earlier had been in Hebrew, he replied, "It's nothing compared to
what it was." Ramah staff have been complaining about Hebrew decline at least
since the 1950s.[21]

At Ramah in the Rockies, Carol, a visiting Hebrew educator, and Matan, a
staff member, debated how much Hebrew should be used in the *ohel ochel* (dining tent). Carol said that mealtimes offer a perfect opportunity to use more
Hebrew. "*Ma ochlim hayom? Salat. Ma yesh basalat? Yesh agvaniya, yesh melafe-
fon* [What are we eating today? Salad. What's in the salad? There's tomato,
there's cucumber]. You do this every single day. . . . It's not hard to do." Matan
pointed out that they do use Hebrew for routinized announcements in the *ohel
ochel*, but he worried that "90 percent of campers" are sometimes lost during
nonroutinized Hebrew announcements. Carol replied, "If you use pictures and
you use pantomime, believe me, no child is going to leave camp because they
don't know what's going on." During our visit, we found that Matan's approach
was common. Routinized announcements included "*Od chamesh dakot* [five
more minutes]" and "*Safsalim al hashulchanot; meltsarim na l'hishaer* [benches
on the tables; waiters please stay]." But announcements that carried new information were mostly in English. One evening, the chef was introduced with routinized Hebrew: "*Haerev yesh lanu siur ochel me'*[Jillian] [This evening we have
a "food tour" by Jillian]." Jillian then described the (restaurant-worthy) galettes
she had made, featuring kale from the camp garden, all in English.

### Less Hebrew

In line with these concerns about too much Hebrew making camp less attractive or comfortable for campers with little Hebrew facility, several camp leaders
were reluctant to use more Hebrew. One reason given was that it was simply not
necessary. A staff member at Camp Bechol Lashon said, "My goal is to have the
kids feel that who they are is Jews and that they belong in the center of the Jewish community. And you can do that very well in North America without any
Hebrew." Although most Jewish communal settings do include varying degrees
of Jewish life words, quotes like this point to the exceptionally heavy use of
Hebrew loanwords and announcements at many Jewish summer camps, which
some leaders deem unnecessary.

Another argument against using too many Hebrew words, as in the discourse
about immersion, is the concern about camp being associated with the negativity

of religious school (sometimes referred to as "Hebrew school"). A Yavneh administrator told us that some Hebrew-fluent counselors resist using Hebrew when they discipline campers because they do not want to foster negative feelings about Hebrew. An Israeli staff member at Yavneh had a related concern regarding Israel: "At a certain point, too much Hebrew will turn the kids off from Israel, making them feel that there is a barrier between Israeli Jews and American Jews." He, like many Israeli counselors, stuck to English when trying to be empathetic and connected, because he saw Hebrew as a barrier to establishing an emotional bond in a situation of nonfluency. We see here the centrality of affective goals, as well as a tension among Israeli staff members at Hebrew-rich camps between their roles as Hebrew teachers and Israel ambassadors.

Leaders at several camps mentioned that debates about Hebrew were part of broader discussions about how much Jewish content to incorporate. Some parents decide not to send their child to a particular camp—or not to send them back after their first summer—because the camp is "too Jewish." Although they may be thinking of religious rituals or educational content, Hebrew infusion can also play a role in this characterization, and therefore camp leaders are sometimes resistant to incorporating more Hebrew (an example is the board members objecting to Hebrew signage, discussed in chapter 6). Campers' and staffers' language abilities are also a concern. Even at Moshava Malibu, where many campers are proficient, a staff member felt that using more Hebrew words would be an added burden. And a URJ Newman leader reported that administrators encountered "pushback" when they asked staff to incorporate more Hebrew words. He paraphrased their response: "I'm having trouble with my kids just with English. My plate is full; please don't ask me to do one more thing."

### Hebrew as Alienating and Bonding

As a parent of a Ramah in the Rockies camper told us, "Language separates people." She worried about newcomers feeling left out because they do not know the Hebrew words used at camp, especially those who are reluctant to ask for clarification: "They say if you hear it, you'll understand the context, but not everybody does." She was concerned that linguistic confusion might make campers decide that they "hate camp" and want to go home. We expected to hear concerns like this from the campers we interviewed at Ramah California, OSRUI, and Tel Yehudah, but not one camper expressed views that strong. A few campers who came in with little Hebrew education mentioned feeling a bit lost at first, and some said they asked their day school friends or counselors, especially Israelis, questions about specific words or signs, but all of them quickly acculturated. On the other hand, although we interviewed new and veteran campers of diverse Hebrew backgrounds, we did not interview former campers; it is possible that some were so turned off by the Hebrew that they did not return.

Camp leaders do recognize the potential for Hebrew to exclude. A staff member at Ramah in the Rockies mentioned as one of their goals that campers will not feel alienated when they hear or see Hebrew. If campers are put off by Hebrew, that can defeat the purpose of Hebrew infusion: to foster connection to Hebrew and, through Hebrew, to Jews, Judaism, and Israel. As we might expect, this concern was also present at camps with less Hebrew. A Beber administrator said, "In the Jewish community, we're so good at mixing Hebrew phraseology into English words in casual settings. If I don't know that word, how does that make me feel as a part of the community or the experience you're creating? Not good." He is not opposed to using some Hebrew, but he is wary of alienation. As we saw in chapter 5, camp staff do their best to gauge campers' reactions and offer translation and other metalinguistic practices to increase comfort among newcomers.

The issue of alienation goes beyond the spatiotemporal boundaries of camp. One woman—a Hebrew-fluent Orthodox day school alumna and scholar of rabbinics—told us, "When friends of mine who went to Ramah or Moshava talk about camp, I have no idea what they're talking about." Even when camp alumni use solely English words to discuss camp-specific experiences, those who did not attend (that) camp may feel alienated. But Hebrew words (or any special camp language) add an additional layer of exclusivity. This is the flip side of Hebrew infusion creating a camp bubble.

Despite concerns about alienation, several interviewees spoke positively of the potential for Hebrew to serve as an insider wink or a secret language.[22] A Ramah ninth grader said, "It's our language, which . . . is really awesome, because to other people it's like . . . what's Hebrew? All of my non-Jewish friends are like, it's so weird. . . . It makes me feel like I have this connection to this whole other community—that brings us together." A tenth grader at OSRUI, likewise, said that one of the reasons she enrolled in Chalutzim was to speak Hebrew to her brother so their friends and parents would not understand—a reversal of the immigrant trope from a few generations back when parents spoke Yiddish *az di kinder zoln nisht farshteyn* (so the kids would not understand). These sentiments highlight how language use constitutes an "act of identity."[23] By using a certain word, grammatical construction, or language, an individual aligns herself with some people and distinguishes herself from others. What can be exclusionary for some people (non-Jews, noncampers, or newcomers) can lead to a positive connection for others (experienced campers, Jews with Hebrew knowledge). Shared knowledge of a particular Hebrew word may serve as a bond between Jews who have attended a particular camp; for instance at a Major League baseball game a Ramah Wisconsin alumnus heard a man behind him shout "*Hachtaa!* [strike]" and turned around to ask when he had attended Ramah Wisconsin. Shared knowledge can also connect Jews who have attended different camps (e.g., maccabiah in the JDate commercial), a Jew who learned a Jewish life word at camp and a Jew who never attended camp but learned that word in synagogue or school (e.g., *tefillah, b'teavon*), or an American Jew who learned an Israeli Hebrew word at camp and an Israeli Jew (e.g., *madrich, boker tov*).

### These Debates in Action

Debates about how much Hebrew to use surfaced not only in our interviews but also in exchanges we observed at camp, especially at Hebrew-rich camps. In many cases, these exchanges were instances of language policing. An OSRUI administrator told us that at division head meetings, when people say "counselor," she corrects them to use *madrich*. She also corrects *chugs* (electives) to *chugim*, because "*chugs*" "sounds wrong." At Moshava IO, an educator reported, "When we're writing our *choveret* [booklet] or our map, I'll write it in English and [Miriam, an administrator] will remind me those key words should be in Hebrew."

Generally, such language policing applied to staff members, but sometimes it extended to campers. At Moshava Malibu, we were sitting in the bleachers during a maccabiah meeting with team Red/*Gevurah* (Strength). One of the team captains told the hundreds of campers on the team, "When we say, 'Who are we?' you answer *Gevurah*, not Red." A boy near us said to his friend, "Red is easy. I don't speak Hebrew." Exhortations to use Hebrew reveal both that there are linguistic expectations and that not everyone is following them. At Galil, an administrator told us that all announcements should be in Hebrew, even if a camper is saying she lost her water bottle. If someone violates this rule, she said, "We'll start the song *Anu Galil, Machane Galil. Anu b'Galil, machane Ivrit* [We are Galil, Camp Galil. We are at Galil, a Hebrew camp]. It's this whole song and dance to tell a person they have to do their *hodaa* [announcement] in Hebrew." When we visited, we did not hear this jingle, but we did hear "*Ivrit!*" when someone began an announcement in English in the dining hall, even though many of the nonroutinized announcements were in English. At camps like Galil, Hebrew use is part of the camp routine, and so is correcting English use. At times, language policing is even more important than whatever message is being communicated, such that interrupting is not only acceptable but also encouraged. The symbolism of using Hebrew trumps the substance of the message.

The most common venue for such metalinguistic interactions was Ramah camps. In fact, the name of Ramah's *Daber* program is an imperative—"Speak!"— as is the jingle sung during the Hebrew word presentations—"*Ivri(t), daber Ivrit* [Hebrew (person), speak Hebrew]." In addition to the *Meah Milim* program, we also observed several instances of staff members correcting others for using English, including those described at the beginning of this chapter. At a Ramah California staff meeting, Rachel, a division head, said, "The counselors were-." Dalia, an administrator, interjected, "The who?" Rachel corrected herself, "Oh sorry, the *madrichim*," and then continued her sentence. Dalia offered a more explicit correction in a learning session with third-grade boys. She asked each *chanich* (camper) to say, "One *maase tov* [good deed] that I did this week . . ." A boy said, "One good thing I did—"; she interrupted him and asked him to say *maase tov*, and he did. Dalia may have intended this correction not merely to enforce the linguistic culture of the camp but also to encourage the campers to use this phrase so they would more likely remember it.

In addition to corrections for the "inappropriate" use of English, we observed positive reinforcement when campers and staff members used Hebrew. During an activity at Ramah Poconos, the activity leaders used many of the *Meah Milim*, plus additional Hebrew words, including team names. Afterward, Aaron (the administrator who led the meeting that begins this chapter), approached Gabby, a counselor who had led much of the activity:

AARON: *Yasher koach* [nice job, common Jewish English phrase of praise].
GABBY: *Todah* [thank you].
AARON: *Meah Milim—samti lev* [100 words—I noticed (lit. I put heart)].
GABBY: *Ma*? [what?]
AARON: (points to heart) *Ani samti lev* [I noticed].
GABBY: *Todah* [thank you].
AARON: I noticed.
GABBY: *Hevanti* [I understood]. (smiles)

Aaron not only praised Gabby's use of Hebrew but also did so in Hebrew. When she appeared not to understand his praise, he switched to English to translate the idiomatic phrase for "I noticed." This reinforced his positive message about Hebrew use, even if it constituted a brief diversion from his own Hebrew use. Despite his switch, Gabby continued the conversation in Hebrew, demonstrating not only her Hebrew skills but also her sense that Hebrew was an appropriate language for this conversation.

Corrections, praise, and other metalinguistic interactions like questions not only shift attention from semantic content to linguistic form; they also emphasize the value of Hebrew at the camp.[24] When anyone interrupts an activity or conversation to remind someone to use Hebrew or to correct Hebrew mistakes, everyone in earshot perceives that Hebrew is important. This message is amplified when it happens repeatedly throughout the summer. Yet correcting can also be a form of shaming. Along with praise and teaching, it helps establish and reinforce one type of unofficial hierarchy at Hebrew-rich camps. People who have more Hebrew knowledge or are more concerned about Hebrew use at camp are sometimes in a position of power or authority, especially Israelis, Israeli Americans, and Americans who have spent time in Israel or attended rabbinical school. This hierarchy sometimes conflicts with other hierarchies, especially those based on age, staff position, and camp experience. Israeli or Israeli American campers, especially new campers, may not have much power in the official hierarchies at camp, but Americans sometimes turn to them as experts when Hebrew questions arise. In other words, Hebrew knowledge can serve as cultural capital.

## TRANSLATION

As we explained in chapter 5, many camps translate Hebrew loanwords or announcements, especially near the beginning of the session, to minimize newcomers' feelings of alienation. But some staff members believe this actually makes it harder to learn the words. A Ramah in the Rockies administrator said translating every Hebrew announcement is "the worst idea ever, because then nobody actually listens to [the] Hebrew . . . , even if you know it, because you just wait for the English." A man who directed a few Zionist camps said, "If you call everything by a Hebrew word, and you don't mention the English words, they'll all get it. And then they'll feel proud, too. . . . Kids are not stupid. If you make an announcement in Hebrew and then give them the translation, why do they need to work? I mean, it's obvious." Some campers echoed this sentiment. A ninth grader who had little Hebrew background before starting Ramah California said she used to listen for the English page numbers during services, but in her age group this year they announced page numbers only in Hebrew. She said, "It kind of makes you learn the numbers." A Chalutzim camper at OSRUI agreed that translation is counterproductive: "It just makes us feel better if we can figure it out on our own [rather than] having someone help us and tell us what it is."

We found this approach in a Galil document called "Ivrit" that appears to be from the 1990s: "All *hodaot* should be in Hebrew. Do not translate (with the exception of the first day) because there will always be someone who let[s] the kids know what is going on." In other words, official discourse should be in Hebrew, but unofficial discourse can include English, such as a counselor or camper translating for a newcomer. We observed this practice at several camps. At Massad Manitoba, all announcements were in Hebrew. Even when a toilet was clogged and temporarily off-limits, this announcement was made in untranslated Hebrew. The announcer said it slowly and repeated it a few times, and then some staff members translated at their tables. At Gilboa, fewer announcements were in Hebrew, but they similarly avoided official translation and encouraged informal metalinguistic interaction. One Friday night, a counselor started a chant, beginning an Israeli dance session: "A big *maagal* with everybody in it." Mia, a counselor looking after some third graders, turned to a first-time camper and said, "Let's make a big circle. *Maagal* means circle." She was socializing the camper to have receptive competence in CHE.

The decision whether to translate relates to the goal of Hebrew use at a given camp. If the goal is language acquisition, then repeated translation may hinder that goal. If the goal is fostering feelings of connection to Hebrew, then translation can support it, especially for newcomers. It may disrupt the flow of conversation and even become the source of satire, but it is precisely the "inorganic" use of language that highlights the importance of Hebrew at camp—not as a language of free-flowing communication but as a means of enriching the primarily English environment. In addition, translating may make some participants feel more welcome and less alienated, which is beneficial in the competitive, consumer-driven camp market.

## WHICH TYPE OF HEBREW TO USE

Hebrew has had multiple, overlapping historical forms (e.g., biblical, mishnaic, modern, Ashkenazi, Sephardi), and Israeli Hebrew has changed significantly over the past several decades. This diversity, combined with the lack of explicit rationales and goals regarding Hebrew at camp, results in tensions about which variants of Hebrew to use, including the choice of loanwords and pronunciations. Two camps had unique debates regarding this issue: Eden Village and Sephardic Adventure Camp.

With its focus on eco-Judaism and "earth-based spirituality," Eden Village brings together Jews who share that commitment but come from diverse religious and political orientations: from secular to Orthodox, from radical left to far right. The camp addresses its religious diversity by offering multiple prayer options and its political diversity by avoiding potentially contentious conversations, especially about Israel. Some staff members felt that this stance should extend to language. An administrator told us, "I had people saying, 'If we are speaking Hebrew, because we're not focusing on Israel, it should be biblical Hebrew.' And other people say, 'Well, why would we do biblical Hebrew? That's not really even helpful.'" This debate relates to the rationale for Hebrew infusion. Is it intended to be "helpful" in campers' Hebrew-speaking abilities? Which of the associations with Hebrew should be stronger, Israel or Judaism?

Eden Village has settled on a Hebrew infusion geared less toward Israel and more toward biblical and rabbinic concepts, especially those surrounding the land. The "*peah* garden" teaches about the biblical injunction to leave a "corner" of the field for charity. They sing and speak about *adama* (earth, ground), *shemesh* (sun), and *geshem* (rain), all biblical Hebrew words regarding nature. They learn about medieval rabbinic concepts like *sefirot* (kabbalistic spheres) and *hitbodedut* (solitary spiritual practice). They call a goat *seir*, a biblical Hebrew word, rather than the modern Hebrew *ez* or *tayish*. The dining hall is called *beit shefa* (house of abundance), a coined phrase using biblical Hebrew words. And, like most camps, they use textually based Jewish life words, such as *bracha* (blessing), *Havdalah* (end of Shabbat ceremony), and *gemilut chasadim* (kindness). They do use a few words that appear in modern Hebrew and not textual Hebrew (or whose meanings mirror those of modern, not textual, Hebrew), like *l'hitraot* (goodbye), *teva* (nature), and *chugim* (electives), but the vast majority of their loanwords are textual. (In a similar analysis at Ramah California, we found that about half of the loanwords were textual and half modern.) Linguistically, Eden Village lives up to a line from its song: "We're trying new ancient things." Just as classical Zionists created an old-new Hebrew in an old-new land, Eden Village is creating a unique contemporary CHE, influenced primarily by ancient textual Hebrew. Even so, the camp cannot avoid some elements of modern Israeli Hebrew, because they have become central in Jewish English and especially in the CHE repertoire shared by many camps.

As a practical matter, the metalinguistic debates about which type of Hebrew to use at Eden Village were peripheral. Most participants likely did not think about whether they were using words from modern or textual Hebrew. In contrast, at Sephardic Adventure Camp (SAC, near Seattle), such conversation was common. In a class about blessings, a teacher said, "Some of you might know it as *bráchas*," which is the common American Orthodox pronunciation of the Hebrew word for blessing, influenced by Ashkenazi Hebrew and Yiddish. "But here at Sephardic Adventure Camp we call them *berachót*," the Sephardi pronunciation of the same word. A different teacher corrected a girl for using a similar common American Orthodox form with the English plural. The girl said, "You say *bráchaz* on the food you eat," and he responded, "You say *berachót* on the food you eat." In this "corrective recast,"[25] the teacher confirmed the content of the girl's statement but also corrected her pronunciation.

The Sephardi Hebrew issue came up repeatedly during announcements at SAC. One evening, Ofira, an Ashkenazi woman in her first year on staff, used the common Ashkenazi American Orthodox word for evening prayers, *máriv*. A teacher and a few other staff members and campers playfully interjected the Sephardi word for evening prayers: *Aravít*! Ofira apologized, smiling: "Sorry, *Aravít*." Tzvi, a counselor who had *peyos* (sidelocks common among Haredi Ashkenazi Jews), jokingly shouted the Haredi Ashkenazi form: "*Máyriv*!" Their demeanors suggested that they had had similar exchanges before. In previous years, we learned, a staff member taught campers to chant, "*Kal, kal, kal*, not *shul*" whenever someone said *shul*, the Yiddish-origin word for synagogue, which is common in Jewish English in American Orthodox communities of many ethnic backgrounds. *Kal* is Ladino and Sephardi Jewish English for synagogue, from the Hebrew word *kahal* (community). These SAC staff members were pushing back against the hegemony of some Yiddish and Ashkenazi Hebrew influences within (Orthodox) Jewish American English.

Such corrections are common at SAC because one of the camp's primary objectives is to foster Sephardic identity and connect campers to the language and culture of their elders, most of whom immigrated to Seattle from Rhodes and Turkey. The practice of inserting corrections crystallized in a tongue-in-cheek song a few years earlier, sung to the tune of a well-known Ladino song,

"*Kuando El Rey Nimrod.*" It listed several statements favoring Sephardi Hebrew or Ladino words over Ashkenazi Hebrew or Yiddish ones: *kal*, not *shul*; *Arvit*, not *Mayriv*; *bivaz* (life), not *gesundheit* (health—response to a sneeze); *Judezmo*, not *Yiddishkeit* (Jewishness). Despite the exhortations in the song, we heard many staff members using the Ashkenazi forms—including some of the same people who corrected others' usage. *Shul* even appears on an official SAC schedule. As one SAC educator told us, "We are a Sephardic community, which is a minority in a largely American Ashkenazic world. So, therefore, it's normal that things like *míncha* and *brácha* will slip in," in contrast to Sephardi *minchá* and *berachá*. When outside influences are changing the linguistic norms of a community, metalinguistic conversations become important for maintaining a sense of communal identity and distinctness.[26] Even if people continue to use the non-preferred form, the corrections themselves serve as a reminder of the importance of the group's ancestral language. Such conversations are a common and important aspect of ethnolinguistic infusion.

At most camps, we found combinations of two or more types of Hebrew: some Ashkenazi forms and some Israeli forms, some Jewish life words from textual Hebrew and some camp words from modern Hebrew. Although we observed a few complaints and corrections, most of the time the coexistence of multiple variants did not lead to metalinguistic debate. However, we did observe debate about whether certain camp words are archaic and should be updated to more contemporary modern Hebrew. Some Habonim and Bnei Akiva camps refer to art with the stilted phrase *malechet yad* or *melechet yad* (handiwork), rather than the more common contemporary term *omanut*. The phrase *chadar ochel* (dining hall), common at many camps (and influenced by older kibbutz language), can be seen as archaic, because Israeli Hebrew has changed since American Jewish camps started using this word several decades ago; many young people in Israel, including many of the emissaries, now say *cheder ochel*.

One Ramah administrator characterized the way Hebrew is spoken at Ramah as "*Ivrit shel Shabbat*"—fancy Hebrew, literally Shabbat Hebrew. He explained, "It's Americans that speak with a thick American accent and *Ivrit meduyeket* [precise Hebrew]," including formal words and phrases like *anu* (we) and *na lashevet* (please be seated), in contrast to contemporary *anachnu* and *shvu/tishvu b'vakasha*. The *hatzileni* joke presented earlier (formal Hebrew for "save me") provides a classic, albeit apocryphal, example. When fancy or formal Hebrew is used in informal contexts, it has a similar effect to archaic Hebrew: Israelis and others with strong Israel connections may view those who speak it as out of touch with contemporary Israeli society and language. We see here conflicting ideologies regarding what Hebrew is or should be: a formal, artful language stemming from sacred texts or a colloquial language of contemporary Israeli life.

Some leaders have attempted to update the Hebrew used at camp. One Habonim camp changed *malechet yad* to *omanut*, because "everyone said that is a term from like the 1950s." Ramah Wisconsin leaders said they updated scripts for their Hebrew theatrical productions "so we're not speaking the pseudo-biblical Hebrew of the 1950s." Often it is Israeli staff members who suggest or execute these changes. Other times it is American staff members who see the Hebrew used at their camp through the eyes of Israelis (sociolinguistic projection), thinking they might find it archaic or otherwise different from Israeli Hebrew.

## Ideologies of "Correct" Hebrew

Another manifestation of sociolinguistic projection involves Hebrew-English blends, such as *Shabboptions* (Shabbat options), and clippings like *meltz* (wait tables—from *meltzar*). From a linguist's point of view, any new word, pronunciation, or construction that has become part of a community's language is considered an innovation, not an error. However, most people are not linguists. In many societies, especially literate ones, elite individuals resist language change: grammarians, teachers, and parents devalue forms that diverge from standards, a process with detrimental effects on minoritized language groups.[27] Similarly, in language-contact situations, some community members resist language mixing, favoring purism.[28] When community members identify a particular form as an error, they are expressing ideologies not only about language but also about the people who use it, reflecting and reinforcing social hierarchies. We encountered several critiques of "errors" at camp that delegitimized the hybridity of CHE and validated and extolled Israeli Hebrew purism. Other commentators conveyed positive reactions to language mixing. Whenever someone expresses an opinion about Hebrew at camp, they are taking a stance about Hebrew "correctness" or "authenticity." These linguistic determinations reflect broader understandings regarding the relationship between American and Israeli Jews.

### Critiques

The most common critique we encountered was that the words used at camp differ in form or meaning from Israeli Hebrew, with the harshest criticism coming not from Israelis (see examples in chapter 7), but rather from Americans. Sometimes their reactions were obviously affected by the presence of Israelis, as if the Americans were viewing camp language through their eyes. At Hilltop, when the service leader told a knock-knock joke involving English-Hebrew homophony: ("Bar who? Please rise for the *Barchu!*"), an American counselor turned to an Israeli counselor behind him and said quietly, "You came all the way from Israel for that?" This sarcastic comment may have been a critique of the humor, but because it was directed to an Israeli, it likely reflected an ideology that Israeli Hebrew is more authentic than the hybrid Hebrew-English practices of American Jews.

Several Americans critiqued camp Hebrew words that do not exist in Israeli Hebrew, like *marp* (infirmary) and *chanutiya* (canteen), as well as words with innovative meanings, such as *hashkava* ("bedtime ritual" at camp, vs. preparing a corpse for burial). As one Ramah leader said, words like those are "not going to help you when you go to Israel, except get people to laugh at you. Like, *'eyfo hachanutiya b'vakasha*? [Where's the canteen please?].'" Another joked that words like this "should be a criminal offense. . . . As long as we are teaching Hebrew words, let's teach correct Hebrew words, and if not, let's forget about it." This extreme judgment reflects an all-or-nothing approach and excludes non-Israeli forms of modern Hebrew.

Even some who see connection as the primary goal of Hebrew infusion critiqued hybridity and innovation. A JCCA leader distinguished between "legitimate," "authentic" Jewish life words like *chesed* (kindness) and "invented" camp words like *mo* (clipped from *moadon*—club house). *Chesed*, he said, "connects you to Jews all around the world today because that's a word that has been part of the Jewish conversation since the beginning. The weird word that got invented in your camp, that nobody else uses, doesn't connect you to anybody other than your camp community." Whereas many campers and leaders praised the distinguishing effect of camp Hebrew (as we explained in chapter 4), here we see a negative reaction. Such critiques were common not only among camp leaders but also among other Jewish communal leaders. If the goal of using Hebrew at camp is to connect camp participants with Jews more broadly, using Hebrew words that no other Jews know seems to defeat the purpose.

Another area of debate is morphology. Some people criticized Hebrew words with English plurals as indications that the speakers are not aware of the word's Hebrew derivation or are not knowledgeable about the Hebrew morphological system. Many campers did use *chug*s and *rosh*es (heads), and some likely did not know the Hebrew forms *chugim* and *rashim* (or *rashei edah/edot*). But a few campers indicated that they use the English plurals despite their Hebrew knowledge. A tenth-grade boy in OSRUI's Chalutzim program said, "Really the plural of *chug* would be *chugim*, but almost everybody says *chug*s, because . . . we think of it as the English." Camp participants exert ownership over Hebrew words by integrating them morphologically into English, even when they know the "correct" Hebrew forms. When camp leaders critique English plurals on Hebrew loanwords, they are advocating for a more Hebraized version of CHE, which exposes campers to Hebrew morphology, in addition to Hebrew lexicon. At the same time, they are delegitimizing the morphological integration of loanwords into the English matrix, an organic process common in situations of language contact around the world.

### Positive Reactions

We also encountered positive reactions to neologism and hybridity. At URJ Newman, several staff members, including rabbis, told us with smiles about their culture of wordplay. A few even felt that unusual blends, such as *p-nik* (personal *nikayon*—hygiene) and *t'floptions* (*tefillah*—prayer—options), help campers connect to and remember the Hebrew words, just as creative prayer options, such as singing prayers to Disney tunes and drawing images from the prayers with sidewalk chalk, help them connect to and engage with the prayers. The entertaining, hybrid Hebrew-English forms both reflect and enable campers' positive engagement with and ownership of elements of Hebrew. A Tel Yehudah administrator said he is comfortable with camp participants using "errors" in their Hebrew words: "Whichever way they use it, thank God they're using it. And if they feel excited about it, when they get to Israel, they'll really learn the language." This stance evokes the goal of campers wanting to learn more based on the positively valent Hebrew infusion they encounter at camp.

An educator at Alonim called blends like *Havdalawn* (*Havdalah* lawn) and *broneg* (bro *oneg*) "fantastic," characterizing them as "code speech": "If an inside joke or an inside treasure . . . you-have-to-be-in-our-community-to-get-it thing is connected to Judaism or Hebrew, to me that's a very high sign of success." Why? Because "it portrays a sense of ownership and love. . . . I feel a part of something, and that thing that I feel a part of also uses made-up words that are drawn from Hebrew." She recognized that camp participants do not necessarily know what these words mean and that the Alonim-specific Hebrew-English blends are not easily transferable to year-round Jewish communities. She compared this to the special *Birkat Hamazon* that Alonim created to level the playing field between campers who come to camp knowing the traditional version and those who do not. Campers will not find much use for these blessings outside of camp, but like the playful language blends, they make camp special and give participants one more thing in common—one that is Jewishly valent. The unique, playful Hebrew infusion practices found at camp are appreciated for their power to build a Jewish camp community that values Hebrew.

### Mixed Stances

A few staff members expressed conflicted stances about innovative Hebrew forms. A counselor at Sprout Lake said she is aware that camp participants tend to "Americanize pluralizations," like *eidah*s (divisions) instead of *eidot*. She said she tries not to do this, suggesting that she considers this hybrid morphology to be undesirable or perhaps incorrect. Despite her efforts, she acknowledged that she and her colleagues still use such mixed forms. Similarly, an administrator at Solomon Schechter said, "I do aspire to people not calling it the *chadar* but calling it the *chadar ochel*." However, he himself sometimes still calls it the "*chadar*," and that name is on a few official signs. He also expressed a positive stance about innovative forms, like *peulat sababa* (lit. activity of coolness), the euphemistic term that replaced *limmud* (learning) when they made their Jewish study sessions more experiential. "I think that the made-up words are helpful, because they add fun, they add excitement, and they eventually do lead to a kid, I think, potentially learning Hebrew because it excites them about Judaism. . . . Camp has got to be fun, and these words are fun." Even as innovative forms are critiqued, they are associated with the goals of campers enjoying Hebrew and eventually pursuing further Hebrew study.

In critiquing innovative forms, some interviewees distinguished among different types. An American Hebrew educator who has consulted for a few camps pointed out that acronyms, clippings, and blends like *motzev* for *moadon tzevet* (staff lounge) actually emulate Israeli slang, such as *dash* and *chul*, acronyms for *drishat shalom* (greeting of peace) and *chutz la'aretz* (outside of Israel). However, she criticized words that do not exist in Israel and stray from Israeli linguistic practice, such as *chanutiya*, *chadar*, and *hashkava*: "If we want to show them how Hebrew behaves, we can't make it incorrect." This is another example of Israel influencing American Jews' language ideologies; her model for "Hebrew" is solely Israeli, and she considers Israeli linguistic innovations acceptable but American innovations inauthentic.

### Should Mistakes Be Corrected?

Ideologies about correct Hebrew and hybridity sometimes lead to attempts at change. For many years, CITs at Solomon Schechter were called *odedim* (encouragers). After repeated complaints from Israelis and Hebrew-knowledgeable Americans that *odedim* was not used this way in modern Hebrew, the administration tried to change it to *ozerim* (helpers) in the 1990s. Most *ozerim* and others resented the change and continued to use *odedim*. Within a few years, the camp formally reverted to *odedim*. Similarly, an administrator at URJ Kalsman said she was trying to change "Morning *Mifkad*" (gathering) to "*Mifkad Boker*," "because if we're using a Hebrew word, why not make it all in Hebrew?" But campers and staff were reluctant, and even she had trouble remembering to use the new name. "The culture sucks you back in," she said. When Israeli Hebrew is in tension with camp tradition, tradition often wins. The difficulty of making changes was a common trope—and not just regarding Hebrew. One administrator said, "God forbid we change anything; it would take at least four years." He said that "tradition consciousness" starts around age 12 or 13: campers become invested in camp traditions and do not want them altered.[29]

However, change is possible. At Solomon Schechter, the art activity was formerly called *amanut*. Israeli staff members often corrected people to *omanut*, the more common Israeli Hebrew pronunciation. Jake, an administrator, told us how he changed the name to *omanut*—with some difficulty. The word appeared in the camp song, in the line "*Amanut v'limudim, ruach, sport, v'rikudim* [art and (Jewish) studies, spirit, sports, and dance]," and Jake would sing <u>o</u>manut loudly into the microphone. Campers quickly picked up on it, but some of the staff resisted, preferring the pronunciation they were accustomed to. Staff members finally gave in when Jake and some other camp musicians recorded the camp song and shared the recording with the camp community. Another Solomon Schechter administrator told us that changes like this are generally not taken up so quickly: "It takes three years to change something. The first year, you introduce it. The second year, they realize they're doing it. And the third year, it's always been that way." As we heard from staff members at several camps, the best way to get changes to take hold is to get buy-in from the counselors; then campers tend to follow suit.

Changing deeply entrenched words comes at a price; it involves correcting multiple people multiple times a day, which is tedious and can lead to discord, especially at camps lacking a thick culture of language policing. A rabbi at a URJ camp expressed a desire to change some "mistakes": "I want to get these kids not to say 'The *Hamotzi*' [redundant because "the" appears twice] and 'The *Birkat*' [clipped from *Birkat Hamazon*]. They use these phrases, and they don't know what it means, and it's such a teachable moment." Even if she eventually embraced the "teachable moment," it is unlikely that campers would stop using these forms because they are so entrenched in camp culture. However, her proposed metalinguistic conversation would further socialize campers to understand the importance of the Hebrew words at camp, as well as the prevailing view of which forms are correct.

Although we did hear some corrections, some staff members said they avoided this role. A Ramah director said he tells staff members, "I'd rather have you use your Hebrew, even with the mistakes you are about to make, than to shy away, waiting for perfection." Another Ramah director is careful about whom he corrects: "If a kid is enthusiastically referring to the downtime after lunch as *shaat* [a clipping of *shaat menucha* (rest hour)], I'm not going to make it my mission to correct their *dikduk* [grammar]. At the level of *madrichim*, and especially *rashei edah* [division heads], once they are speaking in front of the whole camp and making announcements, then there's a little more training and care to make sure that they are speaking correctly." The differentiation according to camp hierarchy appears to apply not only to the language use that is expected but also to calculations of when metalinguistic exhortations are justified.

Why would staff members not police mistakes, even mistakes by campers? A Ramah report highlighted the issue of self-confidence in language learning: "Ramah camps emphasize the need for everyone to use Hebrew to the extent they can, in a warm and supportive environment where no one will be laughed at. Indeed, our North American population, including the director, Judaic educators and other top personnel make many mistakes in Hebrew, yet this is all part of the educational enterprise."[30] Thus fostering an environment of self-confidence is more important than fostering an environment of perfect Hebrew. The report also pointed out an ironic development. Many Ramah leaders "feel that the increased level of Zionism at all our camps, including the higher number of shlichim, can have a negative impact on Hebrew usage among North Americans.

Hebrew language becomes, for many, the language of the shlichim exclusively. North Americans can become intimidated using Hebrew 'when there is always an Israeli listening,' and can be less likely to go 'out on a limb' to make a mistake in a language when not everyone around them is in the 'same boat.'"[31] This provides yet another example of how Israel and Israelis have an impact on the ideologies surrounding Hebrew use at camp, based not only on their comments but also on Americans' sociolinguistic projection—evaluating their own Hebrew use through Israelis' eyes.

### What Language Is That Word?

Another concern expressed about using innovative Hebrew loanwords was that campers might not even realize they are Hebrew. Staff members were especially worried about this with words that campers would not encounter elsewhere, like *marp* and *chadar*, but some also expressed this concern about Hebrew loanwords in general. A Moshava Malibu staff member said, "Sometimes, when you use the word *mitbach* [kitchen] enough times to a third grader, they're not necessarily understanding that you're using a Hebrew word."

Although the campers and staff members we interviewed did express awareness that their camps used many Hebrew words, a few demonstrated that the concern about campers not recognizing words as Hebrew is well founded. We found examples that were reminiscent of the Massad camper in chapter 2 who interpreted *du-siluk* (double play) as "ducy look." For instance, a Ramah California counselor said, "You don't really notice that words like *marp* and *chadar* are Hebrew. I [originally] just thought that's what they named it." One OSRUI camper initially assumed *chadar ochel* was just another name, like "Port Hall" (a camp building), and another thought the dining hall was named after someone named *"Chadar."* An OSRUI administrator told us that a camper said his favorite part of the summer was "Edgar." He misinterpreted the Hebrew name of the ropes course, *etgar* (challenge), as an English name. When a camper assumes that a Hebrew word is English, Hebrew infusion is not fostering that individual's connection to Hebrew. But, as most of these examples suggest, participants do tend to learn that the words are from Hebrew—eventually. When they make that discovery, it is likely through metalinguistic discourse—another camper or staff member explaining the word's origin. Such interventions bring yet more attention to Hebrew.

We also found the inverse process: "Sometimes kids assume that words they don't know—buildings [named after] people, for instance—are just more Hebrew words," as a parent at OSRUI told us. For example, Tel Yehudah has a building called the Mel Center, named after the legendary Young Judaea leader, Mel Reisfield. We heard from administrators that many campers assume Mel is a Hebrew word. This also happens with acronyms. A counselor at Moshava IO thought that "RML" was an unfamiliar Hebrew word, *aramel*, until she learned it was a hybrid acronym, using the first letters of the transliteration for *rosh mosh lishka* (head of camp office). Similarly, some alumni at (the now defunct) Camp Swig thought that "GABUAP" was Hebrew, but they eventually learned it was an acronym for "grassy area behind the *ulam* [auditorium] and pool." These examples demonstrate the contextual nature of Hebrew as a flexible signifier.[32] If the Moshava counselor encountered the letters *RML* on a storefront or heard them spoken by an American newscaster, she would surely assume it was an English abbreviation or word. But because she heard it at a Hebrew-rich camp, she assumed it was yet another Hebrew word. The fact that even non-Hebrew words are sometimes seen as Hebrew points to the ubiquity of Hebrew at some camps and demonstrates that many participants absorb the message of Hebrew's importance at camp.

## Hebrew Gender

Another area of linguistic innovation involves gender. In English, it is possible— and increasingly common—to speak to or about someone without specifying their gender, as long as one avoids gendered third-person singular pronouns. This is not the case in Hebrew (like many other languages), which marks all nouns, adjectives, and verbs (except infinitives) for gender. When speaking to or about a group of women, Hebrew speakers generally use the feminine plural, but when speaking to or about a mixed-gender group, even including many women and just one man, they generally use the masculine plural. Additionally, Hebrew uses the masculine singular form for unspecified gender (e.g., *madrich* can refer to a male counselor or a counselor of unspecified gender)—although many contemporary Israelis use both forms when the person and their gender are not yet known (e.g., in an advertisement seeking a *madrich/a*).

In a Hebrew infusion setting, this gender marking can be useful. Some camps distinguish between girls and boys in a particular division by using the masculine and feminine plural suffixes (*-im* and *-ot*). For example, one bunk at Galil had a sign that said, "Welcome Bogrot," meaning girls in the Bogrim division. At OSRUI, we heard *madrich* and *madrichim* used to refer to both male and female counselors. But sometimes people specified: "Find a *madrich* [-MASC] or *madricha* [-FEM]" or "Who is a *mitnadevet* [volunteer-FEM] or *mitnadev* [-MASC] who wants to begin?" This use of gender marking has the potential to make camp participants think more than they would in a purely English environment about the grammatical structure of Hebrew, as well as about gender.

Hebrew gender marking makes it difficult for a nonbinary or genderqueer individual to avoid being classified by gender in a camp that uses Hebrew words for roles. At one URJ camp, a counselor named Alex identified as genderqueer and preferred to go by "they." However, because the camp used *madrich* and *madricha* for counselors, people had no choice but to refer to Alex's gender. Because Alex identified more as male than female, they decided to be called *madrich* rather than *madricha*. If the camp were conducted solely in English, this would not have been an issue (although the camp would still need to make decisions about bunk assignments).

In 2015, the progressive Habonim Dror North America movement formally addressed this issue with a resolution. They coined a new gender-neutral singular noun suffix, *-ol* (based on the Hebrew *kol* [all] or *kolel* [inclusive]), to refer to a camp participant with nonbinary gender or to use when the speaker does not wish to specify gender. The resolution also introduced a gender-inclusive plural suffix, *-imot* or *-otim*, which had already been used sporadically in some feminist and queer circles in Israel. Like many other aspects of Hebrew at camp, these moves drew from Israeli Hebrew but also introduced innovation.

Research on feminist, gay, lesbian, and transgender language in Israel describes several linguistic innovations designed to right the perceived wrongs of past sexist language, to avoid indicating gender, or to highlight gender ambiguity.[33] Some feminists address mixed-gender groups with the feminine plural, similar to using "she" for gender-neutral references in English. Some transgender Israelis mix forms, like *hachaverim osot* (the friends-MASC do-FEM). The *-imot* suffix is rare but is attested in transgender communities, as in *chaverimot* (friends-MASC-FEM) and *transimot* (transgender people-MASC-FEM).[34] Despite these innovations, Hebrew remains a language with heavy gender marking, and changing it in Israel, even within a particular community, is a herculean task.

In contrast, the Habonim Dror movement was more easily able to address these issues because they use CHE, rather than Hebrew, and due to their status as a small community with a clearly stated commitment to inclusivity. In the summer of 2016, all Habonim camps adopted the "suffix revolution," as one staff member called the use of *-imot* and *-ol*, and most camp participants responded enthusiastically. Staff and campers alike often used the neutral singular suffix (e.g., "Go find a *madrichol*," or "We have a new *chanichol* in the *tzrif*"). Divisions were renamed with the inclusive plural: Chotrim became Chotrimot; Bogrim, Bogrimot. *Chanichimot*, rather than *chanichim*, became the default when referring to or addressing mixed-gender groups of campers. Single-gender suffixes were still used when referring to single-gender groups. For example, at Gilboa, we heard a counselor announce, "The winning *tzrif* of the clean *tzrif* competition: It's a tie between the Sayalot and the Sayalim," meaning the girls' and boys' bunks of the Sayalimot division. At Galil, a girls' bunk in the Bogrimot division would have normally been called Bogrot, but because one of the campers was female-to-male transgender (but preferred to remain in the girls' bunk), the bunk was called Bogrimot. A girls' bunk in Bonimot had a nonbinary camper who went by *they* and *chanichol*. Instead of Bonot, this group was called the Palace Dwellers, based on this *chanichol*'s suggestion to use the bunk's nickname ("The Palace"). Using an English rather than Hebrew name avoided having to mark the group's name for gender.

Like many linguistic modifications, the suffix revolution has had its critics. Some parents and others worried that campers would be confused by the new Hebrew suffixes or would learn Hebrew incorrectly; their worries echo concerns about *chadar* and *marp* discussed earlier. Some felt the suffixes "sounded ridiculous" and said things like "This isn't real Hebrew," "You can't just change a language," "This is such an insular move," and "Israelis will never adopt this." Although some movement members did see potential for this innovation to spread beyond Habonim, they were realistic. Spencer, a *madrichol* at Tavor who crafted the resolution, realized that changing Hebrew would require a full restructuring of verbs, adjectives, and pronouns, not just nouns.[35] They (Spencer's preferred pronoun) told us, "I didn't really intend for it to be the solution to neutering all of Hebrew. I just wanted to start the conversation—start people thinking about how we can make this change further than just our community."

The suffix revolution was possible precisely because Habonim camps use Hebrew infusion, rather than immersion. When Hebrew nouns are inserted into English sentences, changes in the surrounding grammar are not necessary. Habonim camps do have routinized Hebrew sentences, such as *"Nitzanimot, kulam po?* [(Group name), is everyone here?]" and *"Acharei X, yesh lanu Y* [After X, we have Y]," which do not involve verbs agreeing with nouns. Some of the Habonim camps use nonroutinized Hebrew announcements, but these rarely include past, present, future, or command forms. They tend to use infinitives— which have no gender—instead of imperatives (*"Achshav kulam na lavo l'* . . . [Now everybody please to go to . . .]"). If a Habonim camp started an immersion program, much more elaborate changes would be necessary to accompany the innovative suffixes.

Staff members we spoke with at three Habonim camps pointed to several benefits of the change, beyond inclusivity. One woman said it led to more metalinguistic conversation about Hebrew plurals, which clarified for some non-Hebrew speakers how the masculine and feminine plurals work. Ironically, an innovation that made camp Hebrew even more different from Israeli Hebrew increased campers' understanding of Israeli Hebrew. Another staff member said the new suffixes were an "educational tool"—about language, inclusion, and change. She said, "Whenever we encounter resistance, whether it's from the kids, from the parents, or from whoever else in the community, our response as movement members was always, 'Hebrew was a language that people created, and that means that it's a language that we can change to meet our own needs, aims, and beliefs.'" This point about change being acceptable because (modern) Hebrew is an invented language did not come up at other camps. But we did hear participants at many camps tout the acceptability of innovation in Hebrew words. Although the suffix revolution is a radical change, any clippings, blends, innovative meanings, and syncretic morphology might also be seen as camps changing Hebrew or, more precisely, elements of it as used in CHE to meet their "needs, aims, and beliefs." Another conclusion we can draw from Habonim's suffix revolution is the role of language in creating specific communities. Camp leaders' language choices help socialize campers to be competent participants in American Jewish subgroups with specific religious or political orientations—in the case of Habonim, progressive Zionists.

As this chapter has shown, debates about language are not only about language. They are intertwined with broader questions regarding group identity—in our case what it means to be an American Jew, what the relationship between American and Israeli Jews should look like, and what role summer camps should play in socializing youth. Although this chapter focused on contemporary camps, it is clear from the historical section that camp leaders have long held such conflicting ideologies. At times the debates have been waged explicitly, sometimes in public spaces at camp, and other times they have loomed under the surface. At some camps and within some movements, evolving language ideologies have led to changes in language policies and practices, such as the transition from Ashkenazi to Israeli-influenced Hebrew pronunciation in Reform camps and the adoption of Hebrew infusion at Ramah camps. The establishment of Massad Poconos was premised on an ideology that American Jews should be proficient in Hebrew, and the success of the Zionist project was a factor in the camp's demise. All of these changes reflect the diversity and fluidity of American Jewish communities, as they regularly refine their educational offerings, influenced by Israel and Hebrew but presenting themselves as uniquely American.

# Epilogue

On October 23, 2018, Isaac Herzog, the newly elected chairman of the Jewish Agency for Israel, delivered remarks to the General Assembly of the Jewish Federations of North America. In speaking about Israeli and American Jews' lack of common ground, Herzog called for "new unity" that would recognize and honor the differences between these two Jewish populations. Hebrew was central to his vision:

> Our first act should be to find a common language. When I say common— I mean both literally and figuratively. We have a rare and sacred national treasure—the Hebrew language. The language of the Bible and of Israel. In order for us to be able to speak to one another and listen to one another and to debate, discuss, and delight one another—we must return to our national treasure. We must enable every young Jewish person in the world to learn Hebrew. Hence, I hereby call upon the state of Israel to honor its historic pledge to take care of the Jewish people in the Diaspora by allocating a substantial share of its annual budget to a national enterprise of spreading and teaching Hebrew all over the Jewish world. From here on, it will be every young Jew's birthright, wherever he or she may live, not only to visit this historic homeland but to learn the language of the Jewish people. Hebrew can be a common denominator of all Jews, from all streams of Judaism and of affiliated or nonaffiliated Jews. Our beautiful language can serve as a tool for unity.[1]

This mission statement was greeted with excitement by Hebrew educators in America, and it reignited the debate about the need for Diaspora Jews to learn Hebrew. It was also a form of linguistic manna for us as we began to write this epilogue. The speech drew on many of the tropes that have dominated conversations among Jewish educators and camp leaders about the place of Hebrew in the Diaspora over the last century. For Herzog and many others, Hebrew functions as a common denominator that enables people of different nationalities and levels of observance to feel part of the Jewish collectivity. Alluding to Taglit Birthright Israel, which sends Diaspora young adult Jews on free trips to Israel, Herzog identified Hebrew education as a birthright, a privilege that Jews are entitled to by dint of their ancestral connection to Judaism. Additionally, this speech demonstrates that promoting Hebrew learning in the United States remains an ideological project: many believe that language acquisition can facilitate the fulfillment of extralinguistic goals, such as building an attachment to Israel and sacred texts and creating a sense of collectivity among Jews of different nationalities and cultural and linguistic backgrounds.

The analysis we presented in *Hebrew Infusion* complicates these understandings. Leaders at the majority of American Jewish camps would probably agree with Herzog's figurative notion of Hebrew as a "common language" and "tool for unity," but not his literal interpretation. That is, they have approached Hebrew not as a "common denominator" for communicative purposes but as a shared "sacred national treasure" appropriate for liturgical performance and for symbolically expressing Diaspora Jews' bonds with Jews in Israel and around the world. Most leaders do not expect the majority of American Jews to become proficient enough in Hebrew to have Hebrew conversations or, outside of some elite institutions, to explicate Hebrew texts. Instead, they believe American Jews should love Hebrew, feel personally attached to it, and use fragments of it in their English-speaking communities. When American and Israeli Jews "debate, discuss, and delight one another," these conversations are expected to occur in English.

Although Hebrew can serve a unifying symbolic function, it can also divide. The language infusion practices highlighted in this book demonstrate how camps use Hebrew in flexible, creative ways unique to the English-speaking milieu and, in some cases, unique to an individual movement or camp. Users of CHE often have a genuine attachment to their local variety of the language and make no claims about knowing Hebrew or speaking like Israelis. This distinctiveness can be threatening to those who promote an ideology that full proficiency in Israeli Hebrew is needed for building an affective connection to Israel. As we argued, CHE actually reveals the vitality of American Jewry. Some lament that the Hebraists in the early to mid-twentieth century were unable to create a Hebrew-speaking culture in the United States. Yet what we see in CHE is a living and thriving Jewish language that serves identity- and community-building functions for those who speak, hear, and read it.

We can also look to discourses about Hebrew at camp to see how this register both affirms and challenges notions of diasporic Jewry. Positive and negative ideologies about CHE reveal the complex ways that American Jews evaluate their culture in relation to Israel. Quite different from Israeli Hebrew, Hebrew infusion and CHE are localized products that have evolved due to historical and social conditions to best serve the needs of camps. If the directors of some of the earliest Hebrew-rich camps did not succeed in realizing the immersive goals that their founders envisioned, many ended up with an approach to Hebrew that made sense, given their wider goals in the realms of education and enculturation. Thus, the vitality of CHE can be read as a political and cultural statement about the independence and distinctiveness of American Jewry in relation to Israeli Jewry.

Creating distinctive language practices and new registers is not a new phenomenon in Jewish communities, where bi- and trilingualism have historically been the rule rather than the exception. (Indeed, it is American Jewish monolingualism that is unusual, albeit reflective of broader American patterns.) That language mixing has taken hold in American summer camps is not surprising. CHE has thrived in the camp setting because residential summer camps are geographically, temporally, and culturally distinct from other Jewish educational and communal institutions and other American contexts. With ample opportunities for naming locations, activities, and roles, as well as interactive routines from wake-up to bedtime, camps use many Hebrew words not generally heard in American schools, synagogues, and homes. Without having to grapple with the Jewish/non-Jewish boundary-making conditions that permeate life during the rest of the year, camps are able to create their own language variety.

If we interpret through a symbolic lens Herzog's call for Hebrew as a common Jewish denominator, then American Jewish camps have been accomplishing his mission for decades. Through CHE, signs, prayers, songs, and other Hebrew-related activities and interactions, camps have socialized generations of Jews to feel part of a Hebrew-oriented metalinguistic community of worldwide Jewry. But they have not facilitated Hebrew learning in the literal meaning of Herzog's words. That would require immersive environments like that of Massad Poconos, which was a product of its time but did not endure. Quasi-immersive environments can be found today in a few North American overnight camps, including OSRUI, Massad Manitoba, and some Ramah camps. In addition, the Areivim Philanthropic Group,[2] which also funds Hebrew charter schools, has seeded immersion programs for younger children at several JCC and Ramah day camps. Underlying this initiative, called Kayitz Kef (Summer of Fun), is the belief that fluency in modern Hebrew enables American Jewish youth to connect with Israeli Jews and more broadly with Israel,[3] in line with Herzog's speech (but predating it by several years). Leaders also tout the ripple effect—the influence of the immersion program on the culture of Hebrew infusion within the broader camp.[4] Time will tell whether the social and cultural conditions are primed for the expansion of this new iteration of Hebrew-speaking camps.

The history of Hebrew at camp is the story of an American ethnoreligious community mobilizing language to serve its varying ideological and communal goals; it has never been a story of language just for language's sake. The debates about what it means to be Jewish in America have often been fought on the terrain of Hebrew, in its many varieties. The current push for Hebrew immersive camping and Herzog's call for Israeli-funded Diaspora Hebrew education demonstrate that the issues and dilemmas we raise in the book are still relevant today. Those who take on leadership roles in the education and socialization of American Jews continue to debate the best ways to approach their "sacred national treasure—the Hebrew language."

# Acknowledgments

Most importantly, thank you to the many camp leaders who engaged in the research process, whether by completing a survey, participating in interviews, connecting us with campers and parents for focus groups, or hosting us for several days of observations. And to the many campers who offered us interviews, directions, advice, and book title suggestions, thank you.

Dozens of support organization staff members spoke to us, and a few went above and beyond in their advice and assistance: Amy Skopp Cooper at the National Ramah Commission, Dan Lange at the URJ, Avi Orlow at FJC, and Aliza Goodman at the iCenter. The historical sections of this book would not have been possible without the cooperation of many archivists. In particular, Kevin Proffitt, Gary Zola, Dana Herman, Susan Malbin, Sean Martin, and Susan Woodland were generous with their time, suggestions, and encouragement. Lawrence Kobrin, co-chair of the Massad Archives Project, and filmmaker Elena Neuman Lefkowitz facilitated our access to invaluable interviews with former Massad Poconos campers and staff. Jacob Cytryn—and the pictured girls and their parents—granted us permission to use the cover photograph, and Leora Shudofsky allowed us access to a treasure-trove of Massad photographs collected by her late parents, Noam and Nechi Shudofsky, some of which appear in this volume.

This study was a project of the Jack, Joseph, and Morton Mandel Center for Studies in Jewish Education at Brandeis University. We are grateful to the Center's wonderful staff: Susanne Shavelson, Elizabeth DiNolfo, Rebecca Neville, Sarah Flatley, and Pam Endo. Thank you to director Jon Levisohn for inviting us to make this a Mandel Center project, arranging for funding, and being an all-around cheerleader and mensch.

The Consortium for Applied Studies in Jewish Education (CASJE) provided generous funding and support. Thanks also to the Wexner Foundation for a seed grant and to Hebrew Union College and CUNY for research funds and sabbaticals.

Thank you to Jessica Bonn for helping with translation, and thank you to our research assistants: Hannah Kober for compiling the database of Hebrew words, Talia Hurwich for editing interview transcripts, Stephen Brumbaugh for assisting with the survey analysis, Aluma Kepten for her excellent report on the *shlichim* training seminar, Madeline Scranton for help with the camp index, Kayla Flanagan for survey assistance, and Raphael Ellenson, Joey Barr, Ida Rose Levenson, and especially Caraid O'Brien for helping with qualitative coding. Thank you to Gail Chalew for her copyediting, and special thanks to Sue Fendrick for her in-depth editing of an earlier draft.

In the middle stages of the project, we convened sixteen scholars who are experts in summer camp, Jewish education, and/or Hebrew education: Barry Chazan, Judah Cohen, Steven M. Cohen, Sharon Feiman-Nemser, Talia Hurwich, Hannah Kober, Dan Lainer-Vos, Jon Levisohn, Leslie Paris, Alex Pomson, Riv-Ellen Prell, Vardit Ringvald, Jonathan Sarna, Shana Sippy, Jenna Weissman Joselit, and Dafna Zur. These scholars asked important questions and suggested new theoretical approaches.

Several other scholars—Isa Aron, Ayala Fader, Shaul Kelner, Angela Reyes, and Shuly Rubin Schwartz—served as respondents to our panels at the Network for Research in Jewish Education, Association for Jewish Studies, and New York Working Group on Jewish Orthodoxies. Thanks also to audience members at those sessions, particularly the late Alan Mintz, as well as at the FJC Leaders Assembly and various colloquium talks we gave.

We are grateful to Shaul Kelner for his careful reading of an earlier draft of the manuscript, which led to a much better book. Netta Avineri, Roberta and David Benor, Mark Benor, Christine Jacknick, Ari Kelman, Daniel and Ruth Krasner, Kate Menken, Joseph Reimer, Jonathan Sarna, and Elana Shohamy were helpful in reading chapter drafts. So many friends and colleagues—in person and via Facebook—expressed interest in the project at various stages, shared articles or tidbits, connected us to camps, or responded to requests for information. Many individuals answered questions, including Jerome Abrams, Ramie Arian, Raphael Arzt, David Behrman, Mary Baumgarten, Margie Berkowitz, Michael Berl, Burton Cohen, Mitchell Cohen, Julian Cook, Zvi Dershowitz, Loui Dobin, Sheldon Dorph, Gail Zaiman Dorph, Rachel Dulin, Avram Ettedgui, Dan Freelander, Fradle Freidenreich, Roey Gafter, Hillel Gamoran, Judy Gamoran, Einat Gonen, Yehudit Henshke, Joseph Honor, Naomi Goldberg Honor, Zvi Honor, Uri Horesh, Alvin Kaunfer, Stuart Kelman, Vicky Koltun Kelman, Ronald Klotz, Lawrence Kobrin, Anne Lapidus Lerner, Varda Lev, Harvey Leviton, Michael Lorge, Avi Orlow, Tamar Mayer, Mayer Moskowitz, Benjamin Ravid, Joseph Reimer, Vardit Ringvald, Herbert Rosenblum, Ora Schwarzwald, Judy Shulman, Lee Shulman, Debbie Sussman, David Tilman, Jerry Waldman, Sivan

Zakai, and Michael Zeldin. The information they provided us was invaluable, but we alone are responsible for any errors in this volume. Thanks to members of the Jewish Education Research Working Group at Brandeis University for their helpful ideas: Sharon Feiman-Nemser, Rabbi Elliot Goldberg, Ziva Hassenfeld, Danielle Igra, Jon Levisohn, Joseph Reimer, and Katka Reszke.

We are happy to be publishing this book with Rutgers University Press. Former editor Marlie Wasserman and current associate editor Elisabeth Maselli have been strong supporters of this project from its early stages, as have Jeffrey Shandler and Marcy Brink-Danan, editors of the (discontinued) Jewish Cultures of the World series. In particular, we thank Jeffrey for his careful readings and for pushing us to bring our analysis to the next level.

Our three husbands, Mark, Frank, and Yuval, and our seven children have been helpful and supportive throughout this project. *Toda raba.*

# Notes

INTRODUCTION

1. We use real names for public and historical figures, and for others we use pseudonyms.

2. See https://www.youtube.com/watch?v=zOj-U-FlmQQ.

3. Avni 2012c.

4. Anderson 1983; see also Avineri 2012.

5. Shandler 2006.

6. Avineri 2012: ii, Avineri 2014: 19. Emphasis added.

7. These theoretical treatments include linguistic survivance (Wyman 2012), emblematic language use (Canagarajah 2013a), and language as semiotic resource (Ahlers 2017). Related concepts include diglossia (Ferguson 1959; Fishman 1967), quasilect (Glinert 1993), and crossing (Rampton 1995). See also Dorian 1994; Kroskrity 1998; Ahlers 2006, 2014, 2017; Kroskrity and Field 2009; Wyman 2012; Sallabank 2013; Avineri and Kroskrity 2014; Meek 2014.

8. Benor 2018b, 2019.

9. Canagarajah 2013a.

10. Ahlers 2006, 2017.

11. Paris 2008: 86–95; Sarna 2006: 29–31.

12. Sales and Saxe 2002.

13. See http://jewishcamp.org/about/. On the "efficacy" of camp, see Cohen, Miller, Sheskin, and Torr 2011.

14. See https://www.acacamps.org/press-room/aca-facts-trends.

15. See https://jewishcamp.org/wp-content/uploads/2017/01/FJC-Census-2017_NIGHT _FINAL-1.pdf.

16. See https://jewishcamp.org/wp-content/uploads/2017/01/FJC-Census-2017_NIGHT _FINAL-1.pdf.

17. Goffman 1961.

18. Schwartz 1987; Joselit 1993; Sales and Saxe 2002, 2003; Lorge and Zola 2006; Prell 2007, 2009; Paris 2008; Krasner 2011; Reimer 2012; Lainer-Vos 2014; Rothenberg 2016.

19. On "transfer of learning" in education, see Perkins and Salomon 1988, 1992.

20. Although there has been much research on American Jewish summer camps and on Hebrew in America, very little research has addressed their intersection. On Hebrew in America see Glinert 1992; Mintz 1993. Two doctoral dissertations have analyzed the use of Hebrew at Ramah camps: Bekerman 1986 and Jakar 1995.

21. On music at Jewish camps, see Kent 2014; on Shabbat, see Reimer 2018.

22. Benor 2019.

23. Fishman 1981a; Steinmetz 1986.

24. Seidman 1997; Halperin 2014. On the term "revernacularization" rather than "revival," see Spolsky 2013.

25. Fishman 1980; Goldberg 1987; Shohamy 1999.

26. Fishman 1981b; Weinreich 2008 [1973].

27. On foreign influences on modern Hebrew, see Zuckermann 2003, 2006; Doron 2015.

28. For all of these methods, we obtained Institutional Review Board (IRB) approval from the University of Southern California's Office for the Protection of Research Subjects, Hebrew Union College's IRB of record (UP-14-00491).

29. Labov 1972.

30. For details on the survey methodology and results, see Benor, Krasner, and Avni 2016.

31. After this book manuscript was submitted, Sarah joined Gilboa's board.

32. For example, Sales and Saxe 2003; Sales, Samuels, and Boxer 2011.

33. García and Wei 2014.

34. For example, Shohamy and Gorter 2009; Blommaert 2010; Jaworski and Thurlow 2010.

35. Woolard 2016. See also Kroskrity et al. 1998; Blommaert 1999. On Hebrew ideologies in American Jewish educational contexts, see Avni 2011, 2012a, 2012b, 2014a, 2014b, 2016.

### CHAPTER 1 — HEBREW INFUSION IN AMERICAN JEWISH SUMMER CAMPS, 1900–1990

1. Samuel Dinsky, "End of Season Report" (1963) and "Cejwin Camp News" (Spring, 1958), Cejwin Camps Records, Special Collections, Jewish Theological Seminary of America, New York (JTSA); Steve Kushner, Staff Memorandum, n.d., c. 1970, box 2, Myron S. Goldman Union Camp Institute Records (GUCI), American Jewish Archives, Cincinnati, Ohio (AJA); Appel and Schoenfeld 1993: 1.

2. Steve Kushner, Staff Memorandum.

3. Paris 2008: 39–60, 86.

4. Paris 2002: 243.

5. Mykoff 2002: viii, 81–82; Bice 2001: 16.

6. The Yiddishist camps are beyond the scope of this volume. On their history, see Freidenreich 2010.

7. Cejwin was originally known as the Central Jewish Institute Camp, but became financially independent in 1929 and changed its name to the vaguely American Indian-sounding Cejwin, a play on the original name, CEntral JeWish INstitute.

8. On the history of Cejwin Camps and the Central Jewish Institute, see Krasner 2011: 268–322 and Stern 2007.

9. Jacob Wener, "Report of the Camp Committee," December 1926, box 18, folder 9, Schoolman Family Papers, American Jewish Historical Society (AJHS), New York, NY.

10. Albert Schoolman, "Memorandum on the Current Activities of the Central Jewish Institute," January 6, 1921, box 35, folder 12, Schoolman Family Papers, American Jewish Historical Society, AJHS.

11. Albert Schoolman, "The Central Institute Camp," n.d. (c. 1922), box 4, folder 7, Jerome Abrams Papers, JTSA; *Song Book of the Cejwin Camps*, n.d. (c. 1940), in the personal collection of Susan Addelston.

12. Albert Schoolman, "The Central Institute Camp."

13. Modin was relocated to Belgrade, Maine, in 1992.

14. Hurwitz 1994: 22–25, 31–33.

15. Grand 1958: 257–258.

16. "Habonim Prospectus (1935)," in Breslau 1961.

17. Interview, Allan Smith, March 27, 2017; interview, Herbert Rosenblum, May 6, 2016. All interviews were conducted by the authors, unless otherwise noted.

18. "The 1946 Season," in Breslau 1961; Breslau 1939; Altman 1934.

19. As we discuss later, Shulsinger expressed doubts about the long-term viability of Jewish life in the Diaspora, but he believed that it was pedagogically and practically problematic to advocate *shelilat hagolah* in an American Jewish camp context.

20. Sarna 2006: 35.

21. Potok 1993.

22. On the Americanization of Judaism, see Joselit 1995.

23. Our use of folk and elite culture corresponds to the distinctions made in Schoenfeld 1987.

24. Gerson Cohen, quoted in Schwartz 1987: 13; Jacob R. Marcus, quoted in Sarna 2006: 36.

25. Gans 1951.

26. May 1988, Hulbert 2003: 12.

27. See, for example, Robert Gordis's editorial in the inaugural issue of *Conservative Judaism* (January 1945, p. 33). Gordis characterized Kaplan's speech as "moving" and endorsed his call to "redeem" American Jewish youth by attending to their alleged ignorance and indifference.

28. Prell 2007: 81–86.

29. Potok 1993.

30. Goren 1999: 180–181. Young Judaea and its camps became more assertively proaliyah in the 1960s and '70s.

31. Schanin 2000: 71–97.

32. Correspondence, Zvi Dershowitz, January 21, 2018.

33. Correspondence, Zvi Dershowitz, January 24, 2018.

34. Kaufman 2012: 35.

35. Fermaglich 2006: 4, 9–11.

36. On the white ethnic revival, see Jacobson 2006.

37. Jacobson 2006: 7.

38. Kranson 2017.

39. Novak 1972: 62–63; Julian Cook, *A Manual for Hebrew Ulpan* (1972), GUCI, box 4, AJA. In the early 1970s, Cook introduced an ulpan-style Hebrew acquisition program while serving as director at Union Camp Institute, in Zionsville, Indiana.

40. Krasner 2016.

41. Bourdieu 1986; see also Kent's (2014) use of cultural capital in analyzing music at Jewish camps.

42. Brown 1989: 50–51.

43. Melzer 1993: 18; Melzer 1971: 4–10; Bice 2001: 90–91.

44. On the impact of the 1967 Six Day War on American Jewry, see Sklare 1968: 17–19.

45. Interview, Vicki Koltun Kelman, December 22, 2016; interview, Ray Arzt, March 28, 2017.

46. See Kent 2014.

47. "Union Institute, UAHC owned by the Chicago Federation of the Union of American Hebrew Congregations," n.d., c. 1952, box 2, Ernst Lorge Papers, AJA.

48. Sarna 2019: 202–203, 250–254.

49. Interview, Michael Lorge, September 24, 2016.

50. "Vocabulary Extracts," box 2, Olin-Sang-Ruby Union Institute Records (OSRUI), AJA.

51. J. Cohen 2006: 179–184.

52. Gamoran 2006: 135–136; Moore 1994, esp. 197–198. Solel was launched at Camp Saratoga because Kaelter's husband, Rabbi Wolfgang "Wolli" Kaelter, served as the camp's director.

53. Victor Weissberg to Philip Brin and Richard Hirsch, c. 1957, box 2, Ernst Mordecai Lorge Papers, AJA.

54. Stephen Passamaneck, "Report on Hebrew Program," Union Institute, 1959, box 4; "All Ready for Blast Off!!!" *Union Institute in Review*, Summer 1959, box 4, OSRUI, AJA.

55. "Intermediate Session I Daily Program," Union Institute, Summer 1962, box 5; "Intermediate Aleph Daily Program," Union Institute, 1966, box 7, OSRUI Records, AJA.

56. *Mogan David* (yearbook), 1962, box 5, OSRUI, AJA. On the Reform movement's transition to more Hebrew and from Ashkenazi to Israeli pronunciation, see Benor 2013.

57. "List of Hebrew Words Used at Union Institute," box 5, OSRUI; Union Institute Rabbinic Advisory Meeting, October 18, 1962, Ernst Mordecai Lorge Papers, AJA; interview, Donald Splansky, August 28, 2016.

58. Interview, Donald Splansky; interview, Fradle Freidenreich, March 28, 2017; interview, Hillel and Judith Gamoran, September 24, 2016.

59. Andy Miller, "Young Judaeans Complete Inspiring Year in Israel," *Jerusalem Post*, July 1, 1966, 16. Correspondence, Andrea Meiseles, August 8, 2017; interview, Mel Reisfield, January 8, 2015. Likewise, during this time, Tel Yehudah staff created a simulated kibbutz program with a strong Hebrew component, *Machaneh Avodah*, which was designed to hone leadership skills and excite campers about the prospect of future immigration to Israel.

60. An earlier Hebrew immersion program at Herzl Camp, "Ivriah," was established in 1960 but only lasted a few seasons. On the history of Herzl Camp, see the camp's website, http://herzlcamp.org/about/history/.

61. Interview, Mary Baumgarten, February 15, 2018; correspondence, Harvey Liviton, February 13, 2018; correspondence, Avram Ettedgui, February 17, 2018. At its height, MABA was attracting about seventy campers, mostly between the ages of 9 and 13, and was discontinued in 1995 because Herzl's core program was growing and a joint venture with the Talmud Torah no longer made sense financially.

62. On Chalutzim, see Gamoran 2006: 138–144.

63. Press Release, Union Institute Camp, October 26, 1962, box 2; Karl Weiner, Circular Letter, November 23, 1962, box 2; Brochure, 1965, Union Institute, Oconomowoc, box 2; Donald Splansky, Letter to Campers, "Information to Parents of Prospective Campers of the Pioneer Program," June 2, 1964, box 2, Ernst Mordecai Lorge Papers, AJA.

64. Splansky, Letter to Campers.

65. Interview, Michael Lorge, September 24, 2016.

66. Splansky, Letter to Campers; "General Information: Pioneer Program," 1964, box 2, Ernst Mordecai Lorge Papers, AJA.

67. Donald Splansky, "Pioneer Program—1964, Daily Log," July–August, 1964, box 6, OSRUI Records, AJA. Staff members that first summer also included Rabbis Sheldon Gordon and Hayim Goren Perelmuter.

68. Splansky, "Pioneer Program—1964, Daily Log."

69. Interview, Rachel Dulin, July 18, 2016; interview, Hillel Gamoran.

70. Interview, Rachel Dulin; interview, Michael Lorge; interview, Donald Splansky.

71. Interview, Rachel Dulin; interview, Hillel Gamoran.

72. *Halutzon, Shanah Bet*, 1966, box 7; *Eton Hahalutzim*, July 28, 1967, box 8, OSRUI, AJA.

73. Interview, Roy Splansky and Eric Schor, September 24, 2016; interview, Tamar Mayer, September 6, 2016.

74. "Program for Union Camp Institute, Summer—1962, Counselors' Handbook; "Junior Camp Session 2," July 16–August 1, 1965, box 1, GUCI, AJA.

75. Correspondence, Zvi Honor, April 7, 2017.

76. See Greenstein 1981.

77. See, for example, Zipperstein 1999; Diner, Shandler, and Wenger 2000; Diner 2002; Shandler 2014.

78. Shandler 2006.

79. Rosten 1968; see also Cohen 1969; Stavans 2006.

80. Quoted in Cohen 1969.

81. See https://www.youtube.com/watch?v=kF17M-m-Jvo.

82. Rosten 1968; on Rosten, see Stavans 2006.

83. UCI Junior Camp I Yearbook, July 1969, box 3, GUCI, AJA.

84. Hebrew Vocabulary List, c. 1970, box 8; "American in Israel," Program Description and Schedule, box 4, GUCI, AJA.

85. Steve Kushner, Staff Memorandum.

86. Interview, Julian Cook, March 23, 2017; interview, Ronald Klotz, March 14, 2017; Hebrew Memo and Vocabulary List, 1977, box 8, GUCI, AJA.

87. Posen 1957: 37.

88. Posen 1993: 30.

89. Posen 1957: 37–45.

90. Posen 1993: 28–36; see also Kent 2014.

91. Kent 2014: 15–24, 123–206.

92. Kligman 2001: 125.

93. Kelman 2011.

94. "Some Favorite Songs at Union Institute," November 16, 1956; "As Songs We Sing," box 2, OSRUI, AJA; J. Cohen 2006: 183–188; interview, Hillel Gamoran, September 24, 2016.

95. Schachet-Briskin 1996.

96. J. Cohen 2006, quote on p. 183.

97. Arian 2014.

98. J. Cohen 2006: 187–190; interview, Michael Lorge.

99. Klepper 2008.

100. Klepper 2008.

101. Schachet-Briskin 1996.

102. Interview, Karen Mindlin Kohn, March 17, 2017; interview, Michael Lorge, July 15, 2018; interview, Allan Smith; Schachet-Briskin 1996.

103. Schachet-Briskin 1996.

104. Judah Cohen (2015, 2017) has painstakingly documented Friedman's remarkable career and the crossover success of many of her best-known songs into Conservative, Reconstructionist, Renewal, and even Orthodox circles.

105. Cohen 2015: 20–22.

106. "Debbie Friedman: My Music . . . My Story," Jewish TV Network, n.d., https://www.youtube.com/watch?v=M_G9vFzrU6Q.

107. Interview, Dan Freelander, March 23, 2017.

108. Interview, Dan Freelander; interview, Ramie Arian, March 24, 2017; Meyer 1995: 374–375. In 2009, Rick Recht and Rabbi Brad Horowitz launched Songleader Boot Camp, which attracts scores of songleaders and educators from across the Jewish community to its annual conferences and workshops.

109. Interview, Dan Freelander.

CHAPTER 2 — CAMP MASSAD IN THE POCONOS AND THE RISE
AND FALL OF HEBREW IMMERSION CAMPING

1. In this chapter, Massad refers to the camps founded by Shlomo and Rivka Shulsinger Shear-Yashuv in Pennsylvania's Pocono Mountains region. The Canadian Massad camps near Montreal and Toronto, which were founded in 1947 and 1950, respectively, by the Keren Hatarbut Haivri under the leadership of Aron Horowitz, were inspired by but not officially connected to the Poconos camps; neither was Camp Massad in Manitoba, Canada, which was founded by a group of Winnipeg educators and Habonim members, including Soody Kleiman, in 1953.

2. Richard Starshefsky, interview with Chaim Feder, August 5, 1994. All subsequent quotations from Starshefsky were culled from this interview, Camp Massad Records (CM), box 8, AJHS.

3. Spiegel 1930.

4. Blumenfield, Samuel. 1937. "Why Hebrew?" *New Palestine*. Reprinted as a pamphlet by the Histadrut Hanoar Haivri. Moshe Davis Papers, box 2, folder 12, JTSA.

5. Frost 1994: 47.

6. Krasner 2011: 268–322; Prell 2007: 82–83.

7. Mintz 1991: 53

8. Shulsinger 1950: 8. See also Shulsinger 1946.

9. Shulsinger 1982.

10. Gordonia merged with another Labor Zionist youth movement, Habonim, in 1938, and Moshava became part of Habonim's camp network.

11. Shulsinger 1982; Frost 1994: 42–43.

12. Shulsinger 1982: 53–54; Sylvia Ettenberg, interview with Chaim Feder, July 24, 1994, CM, box 8, AJHS. All subsequent quotations from Ettenberg were culled from this interview.

13. Moshe Davis, interview with Mychal Springer, February 1, 1990. Moshe Davis Papers, JTSA.

14. Moshe Davis, interview with Mychal Springer, February 13, 1990.

15. Maslow 1964.

16. Moshe Davis, "Our Platform: Histadrut Ha'noar Haivri," n.d., Moshe Davis Papers, box 2, folder 12, JTSA.

17. On Kaplan's approach to Zionism, see Pianko 2010: 95–134.

18. Davis, "Our Platform."

19. Mintz 1993: 51–64; Pelli 1995. See also Pelli 1998.

20. Moshe Davis, interview, February 13, 1990.

21. Mintz 2012: 41–45, 51–58.

22. Leaf 1989; Katz 2015: 54; Moshe Davis, interview, February 1, 1990.

23. Frost 1994: 42.

24. Mintz 2002: 181.

25. This account of Camp Achvah is based on three essays in the Samson Benderly memorial issue of the journal *Jewish Education* (vol. 20, no. 3), which was published in Summer 1949: Rudavsky 2006, esp. 48–49; Menahem Barshad, "Some Memories of Abba," 59–60; Abraham Gannes and Levi Soshuk, "The Kvutzah and Camp Achvah," 61–69. A fourth essay in the volume, Samuel Citron, "Dr. Benderly's Love of Drama," 70–74, treats Camp Achvah between 1936 and 1944 after it was no longer a Hebrew-speaking camp. This section also draws on the treatment of Camp Achvah in Krasner 2011: 276–281.

26. Gannes and Soshuk 1949: 63–65.

27. Gannes and Soshuk 1949: 63.

28. Gannes and Soshuk 1949: 64.

29. Levi Soshuk became a Hebrew instructor in the New York public schools and, later, the director of Camp Ramah Poconos from 1953 to 1959. Abraham Gannes, who also made his career in Jewish education, directed Camp Keeyumah (1938–1951) and Cejwin Camps (1955–1968).

30. Gannes 2006: 64–65.

31. Thank you to Jeffrey Shandler for crystallizing this point.

32. Davis 1996.

33. Dushkin 1975.

34. The counselors were David Alster-Yardeni, Hayyim Kieval, Chana Wolman, and Rivka Wolman. There is some disagreement about the number of campers; Shulsinger said twenty-two and Frost twenty-three. Dushkin recalled that the camp opened with only seven campers. Dushkin 1975: 166; Shulsinger 1996; Frost 1994.

35. Shulsinger 1996: 10–11, Frost 1994: 42–43.

36. Shulsinger 1996: 11. The term "Kaytana Ivriah" (Hebrew Summer Camp) is used in early references to the camp, but it is unclear whether it was meant as a proper name or a placeholder.

37. Frost 1994: 43.

38. Shulsinger 1996: 10–11; Rivka Shulsinger, interview with Chaim Feder. March 20, 1997. CM, box 8, AJHS. (Hebrew) "Techezakna" had been similarly adopted a decade earlier by Gordonia and Habonim, and Shulsinger almost certainly recalled it from his summer employment at a Labor Zionist camp before moving to New York.

39. Shulsinger 1996: 17–18.

40. Frost 1994: 43, Ribalow 1946: 13.

41. Shulsinger, Shlomo. 1940. "Memorandum on Hebrew Camp Project." Moshe Davis Papers, Box 2, Folder 12, JTSA.

42. "Massad 1948 Season Camper List," Moshe Davis Papers, box 2, folder 25, JTSA.

43. Shulsinger, "Memorandum on Hebrew Camp Project."

44. Mark 2002.

45. Ribalow 1946: 13.

46. Frost 1994: 46.

47. Ribalow 1946: 13.

48. Philologos (Halkin) 2006.

49. Halkin 1989.

50. Israel Charny, interview with Elena Neuman Lefkowitz, c. 2013. Provided to the authors by Elena Neuman Lefkowitz.

51. Jack Bloom, interview with Elena Neuman Lefkowitz, c. 2013, provided to the authors by Elena Neuman Lefkowitz; Ray Arzt, interview with Chaim Feder, May 10, 1994. CM, box 8, AJHS. Subsequent quotes from Arzt are culled from this interview. See also Bloom 2012: 19–27.

52. Ileane Altman Colodner, interview with Chaim Feder, September 28, 1994. CM, box 8, AJHS. All subsequent quotes from Colodner were culled from this interview; interview, Jack Bloom; interview, Starshefsky.

53. Strigler 1963.

54. Mark 2002; Shlomo Shulsinger and Hillel Rudavsky, *Massad English-Hebrew Dictionary*, edited by Daniel Persky, n.d., CM, box 3, folder 1, AJHS.

55. Philologos (Halkin) 2006.

56. Philologos (Halkin) 2006; "Hebrew Doesn't Translate for Baseball," *National Public Radio's Morning Edition*, June 25, 2007.

57. Alster-Yardeni 1989.

58. Quoted in Leaf 1989: 352.

59. Alster-Yardeni 1989: 170.

60. *Nahal*, an acronym for *Noar Halutz Lohem*, is an Israeli paramilitary organization that combines military service and agricultural work in newly founded kibbutzim and villages on Israel's geographic periphery.

61. Alster-Yardeni 1989: 171.

62. For example, Deuteronomy 30:1–5 and Isaiah 11:11–12.

63. Alster-Yardeni 1989: 171–175.

64. Alster-Yardeni 1989: 171.

65. Tzippy Krieger Cedar, interview with Elena Neuman Lefkowitz, c. 2013, provided to the authors by Elena Neuman Lefkowitz.

66. Samama 2012: 89.

67. Alster-Yardeni 1989: 173.

68. Mark 2010.

69. Sharon Hyman Fogel, interview with Elena Neuman Lefkowitz, c. 2013, provided to the authors by Elena Neuman Lefkowitz; David Bernstein, interview with Chaim Feder, August 11, 1994, CM, box 8, AJHS.

70. Spiegel 2013: 6; Helman 2007: 99.

71. "Maccabiah Booklet," Massad Aleph, 1950. CM, Box 3, Folder 7, AJHS.

72. Shulsinger 1950: 14.

73. Bernstein 2008: 113–14.

74. "Maccabiah Booklet," Massad Aleph, 1950.

75. On performative language, see Austin 1975.

76. Gurock 2004: 159–166.

77. Frost 1984: 48; Peggy Frost, interview with Chaim Feder, July 15, 1994. CM, box 8, AJHS; Sylvia Ettenberg, interview with Chaim Feder; interview Hillel Gamoran.

78. Noam Shudofsky, interview with Chaim Feder, August 1, 1994, CM, box 8, AJHS; David Eliach, interview with Elena Neuman Lefkowitz, provided to the authors by Elana Neuman Lefkowitz; Ray Artz, interview with Chaim Feder; Sylvia Ettenberg, interview with Chaim Feder; David Bernstein, interview with Chaim Feder, August 11, 1994, CM, box 8, AJHS.

79. Stanley Sperber, interview with Chaim Feder, June 9, 1994, CM, box 8, AJHS.

80. David Bernstein, interview.

81. Charles Kleinhaus, interview with Chaim Feder, December 19, 1994, CM, box 8, AJHS.

82. Jack Bloom, interview; emphasis added.

83. Lainer-Vos 2014: 93.

84. Lainer-Vos 2014: 96.

85. Ileane Colodner, interview; Massad Dictionary.

86. Shulsinger 1946: 19–20; Shulsinger 1950: 10–11.

87. Interview, Bob Hyfler, August 31, 2016; Ben-Sorek 2015.

88. Shulsinger 1967: 8.

89. Frost 1994: 43.

90. Shulsinger 1967: 12.

91. Rivka Shulsinger, interview.

92. Quoted in Frost 1994: 48.

93. These programs, including Chalutzim (OSRUI), Ulpan (Tel Yehuda), and MABA (Herzl Camp), are discussed in chapter 1.

94. Frost 1994: 48–50; Bernstein 2008: 116–120. According to Lawrence Kobrin, an engineering survey commissioned by the schools revealed that Massad Aleph would require an investment of hundreds of thousands of dollars for deferred maintenance. Correspondence, Lawrence Kobrin, March 20, 2017.

95. Frost 1994: 48–50; Bernstein 2008: 116–120.

96. Frost 1994: 42.

97. Quoted in Frost 1994: 47.

98. Starshefsky, interview.

99. Interview, Michael Berl, September 8, 2016.

100. Starshefsky, interview; Noam Shudofsky, interview with Chaim Feder.

101. Mintz 1993: 17–18.

102. Cohen 1986.

103. Arleen Pilzer Eidelman, interview with Chaim Feder, March 13, 1997, CM, box 8, AJHS; Charles Kleinhaus, interview; interview Michael Berl.

104. Shulsinger 1978: 289–299; Shulsinger 1989: 244–247.

105. David Bernstein, interview with Chaim Feder.

106. Mayer Moskowitz, interview with Elena Neuman Lefkowitz, provided to the authors by Elana Neuman Lefkowitz.

CHAPTER 3 — CAMP RAMAH

1. In this chapter, the generic term "Ramah" is generally used to refer to the Ramah camping network as a whole. Unless the context is clear, individual Ramah camps are referred to by name, for example, Ramah Poconos, Ramah Wisconsin, and so on.

2. Interview, Raphael Arzt, March 28, 2017.

3. Freedman 1955.

4. Moshe Davis, interview with Shuly Rubin Schwartz, April, 1976. Abridged and published in Hebrew as "Camp Ramah: Outlook and Beginnings," Kovetz Massad.

5. Goldberg 1948.

6. Goldberg 1948.

7. Chaim Potok, "Camp Ramah: From Jerusalem to Tyre, a Temple to the Lord," Jerome Abrams Papers, box 2, JTSA.

8. Ackerman 2008: 229.

9. Potok, "Jerusalem to Tyre."

10. Stiebel 1952.

11. Freedman 1955.

12. Freedman 1955. These signage practices remained a telltale feature of the camp landscape at Ramah, as well as at other Hebrew-rich camps.

13. Wertheimer 2007.

14. Cohen 2012: 114–121.

15. Schwartz 1984: 150.

16. Elazar and Geffen 2000: 23.

17. Ackerman 1969: 22.

18. Fox and Novak 2000: 16–17.

19. Quoted in Freedman 1955.

20. Fox and Novak 2000: 17.

21. Examples include Moshe Greenberg, Louis Newman, Raphael Arzt, Hillel Silverman, Moshe Samber, Jerome Abrams, Leah Abrams, and David Mogilner.

22. Schwartz 1987: 18–19; interview, Arthur Elstein, September 27, 2016.

23. See https://www.ramahwisconsin.com/blog/2016/12/reflections-on-ramahs-first -summer; interview, Arthur Elstein.

24. Interview, Arthur Elstein; interview, Allan Smith, March 27, 2017.

25. Interview, Herbert Rosenblum, May 6, 2016. Former Yavneh head counselor Alvin Schiff, who arrived in 1949, was a product of Massad, and he stocked the staff with Massad buddies, many of whom also attended Yeshiva College.

26. Schwartz 1987: 19–20.

27. Potok, "Jerusalem to Tyre."

28. Freedman 1955.

29. Abramson 1989: 71–72, 79.

30. Paris 2008: 2–4.

31. Soshuk 1960: 25–26.

32. Henry Goldberg, "Report on Camp Ramah," Summer, 1947, Camp Ramah Records (CR), box 34, JTSA.

33. Interview, Burton Cohen, March 20, 2017.

34. See https://www.ramahwisconsin.com/blog/2016/12/reflections-on-ramahs-first -summer.

35. Camp Kinneret Brochure, 1947, Jerome Abrams Papers, box 2, JTSA; Ramah New England Brochure, 1948 and Ramah Poconos Brochure, n.d., CR, box 34, JTSA.

36. Camp Ramah Committee Minutes, September 25, 1951, CR, box 34, JTSA.

37. David Mogilner, "Hebrew at Ramah Camps," October 1962, CR, box 28, JTSA.

38. Mogilner, "Hebrew at Ramah Camps."

39. Lieberman 1931.

40. Cohen 1984: 25.

41. Schwartz 1984: 12; interview, Arthur Elstein.

42. Louis Newman, "Educational Program" c. 1953, Louis Newman Papers, box 8, AJA.

43. Interview, Allan and Margaret Auslander Silberman, September 25, 2016.

44. Interview, Arthur Elstein; the story was confirmed by Rabbi Dr. Joel Roth in an email dated July 18, 2017.

45. Newman, "Educational Program."

46. Louis Newman, "Progress Report—Camp Ramah Wisconsin," Summer 1953, Louis Newman Papers, box 8, AJA.

47. Interview, Jerome Abrams, March 27, 2017; interview, Arthur Elstein.

48. For an analysis of the pedagogical role of Hebrew dramatics at Ramah, see Reimer 2012.

49. Interview, Robert Mosenkis, April 28, 2016.

50. Melzer 1971: 4–10.

51. Interview, Jerome Abrams; interview, Sheldon Dorph, December 23, 2016; interview, Ray Arzt.

52. Simon Greenberg, "The Ramah Movement: Its History and Place in the Conservative Movement," p. 7, CR, box 34, JTSA.

53. Brown 1997: 833–835.

54. Interview, Neal Kaunfer, August 30, 2017.

55. Fox 1989: 35.

56. Fox and Novak 2000: 41.

57. Reimer 1989: 57. It is illuminating, in light of Ray Arzt's comment about Fox's seminars to compare this image to the one of Newman trying to balance Dewey with Torah.

58. Readings included John Dewey's *Experience in Education* (1938), Herbert Thelen's *Dynamics of Groups at Work* (1954), and Fritz Redl and David Wineman's *Children Who Hate* (1951).

59. Fox and Novak 2000: 20–22; Aviad 1988: 213; Brown 1997: 839–841. In theorizing the home haven, with its binary spheres, Schwab drew on the work of psychologist Bruno Bettelheim, who later would help Fox and his colleagues translate the home haven into a camp setting.

60. Interview, Raphael Arzt.

61. Elliot Dorff, "Home Havens," November 2003. https://www.aju.edu/ziegler-school-rabbinic-studies/our-torah/back-issues/home-havens.

62. Chaim Potok, "The 1963 Machon in Camp Ramah in New York: Report on the Schwabian Framework (Bunk Counselor)," c. August 1963, Jerome Abrams Papers, box 2, JTSA.

63. Lerner 1971: 14–16; Farago 1972: 197–202.

64. Interview, Joseph Wouk, September 2, 2017.

65. Interview, Joseph Reimer, August 29, 2017.

66. Robert Abramson, quoted in Farago 1972: 202.

67. Bekerman 1986: 119–120.

68. Interview, Jerome Abrams.

69. Novak 1972: 62.

70. Novak 1972: 62; emphasis added.

71. Shandler 2006.

72. Bekerman 1986: 160–194.

73. Abramson 1989: 71–72, 79.

74. Interview, Margie Berkowitz, October 22, 2014.

75. Interviews, Debbie Sussman, November 28, 2014; July 13, 2015.

76. Interview, Margie Berkowitz.

77. See, for example, Saul Wachs to David Mogilner, November 29, 1971, Jerome Abrams Papers, box 2; and, Burton Cohen, "Talk to Ramah Staff," 1969, CR, box 34, JTSA.

### CHAPTER 4　—　A FLEXIBLE SIGNIFIER

1. The phrase "flexible signifier" comes from Tavory (2016: 85); the concept is influenced by work on linguistic indexicality, including Ochs 1992; Silverstein 2003; Bucholtz and Hall 2005; Eckert 2008.

2. Shohamy 2008. See also Halperin 2014.

3. We heard this song in several camps, but more religiously oriented camps tended to end it differently: "and together we will walk in the path/way of *Hashem* [God]."

4. Technically Nigerian should be Ibo, the original language of the song. The song was written after the occupying British dropped a curfew (Silverman 2011: 62).

5. Goldberg and King 1993: 263–286 (Habonim at Camp).

6. Vanderbilt 1993, cited in Wilson 2005.

7. Raider 1998: 78–79. Whereas the invocation of the cowboy in the 1920s identified Zionism as a civilizing project, the contemporary Mr. Milon steers clear of this fraught discourse. Instead, it plays up another facet that resonated with earlier generations of American Zionists: Hollywood's image of the cowboy as a tough guy, a repudiation of the stereotypically weak, neurotic, bookish Jewish male.

8. Among camps that responded to our survey, only 20% report having more than a few non-Jewish staff members; most of these are part of the AIJC (which includes Beber), JCCA, or no network.

9. Steinmetz 1981, 1986; Gold 1985, 1986; Weiser 1995; Benor 2012.

10. See Fader 2009: 104.

11. See details in Benor, Krasner, and Avni 2016.

12. Ahlers 2006, 2017.

13. See the same finding in Bekerman 1986.

14. Avineri 2012.

15. See also Van Slyck 2006 and Paris 2008.

16. Paris 2008; Koffman 2018.

17. JDate, "Jewish Summer Camp," 2014, https://www.youtube.com/watch?v=wBv Q6S7NYwM.

18. Rabbi M. Cohen 2006.

19. Irvine and Gal 2000.

20. Zuckermann 2006; Benor 2018b.

21. Eckert 2008: 453.

22. On mediated indexicality, see Ochs 1992.

23. Benor 2011; Benor and Cohen 2011.

### CHAPTER 5 — THE BUILDING BLOCKS OF INFUSION

1. Postman 2006; Putnam 2001; cf. Silverstone 2003.

2. See Van Slyck 2006 on "the serious work of play" in early twentieth-century American summer camps and Chudacoff (2007: xii) on the "behavioral, social, intellectual, and physical rewards" of play more generally.

3. Wright, Betteridge, and Buckby 1983; Richard-Amato 1988; Engh 2013.

4. On the centrality of fun at camp, see Sales and Saxe 2004, 2008; Rothenberg 2016. See also Chazan 2003 and Kress 2014 on fun in "informal" or "experiential" Jewish education.

5. Ochs and Schieffelin 1984; Schieffelin and Ochs 1986; Garrett and Baquedano-López 2002; Duff and Hornberger 2008; Duranti et al. 2011.

6. Kulick 1992; Moore 2004, 2011; Makihara 2005; Garrett 2011; Duff 2007; Fader 2007, 2009; Baquedano-Lopez 2008; Friedman 2010.

7. See also Jakar 1995, which shows how the social and educational conditions at a Ramah camp give campers opportunities to comprehend and communicate newly acquired Hebrew items and concepts.

8. For example, Weinreich 1953; Thomason and Kaufman 1988; Myers-Scotton 1993, 2002; Romaine 1995; Muysken 2000; Thomason 2001; Winford 2003; Heller 2007; Matras 2009; Hickey 2010; Baker and Wright 2017.

9. Otheguy, García, and Reid 2015: 281. See also Lewis, Jones, and Baker 2012; Canagarajah 2013b; García and Wei 2014; Wei 2017.

10. Canagarajah 2013b.

11. Adapted from Matras 2009: 111–114, informed by Sankoff and Poplack 1984; Poplack, Sankoff, and Miller 1988; and Myers-Scotton 1993. In a bilingual context, there is a continuum between borrowing and code switching.

12. See Muysken 2000; Young 2009; Canagarajah 2011; Young and Martinez 2011; and Barrett 2013 regarding academic fields' diverse understandings of terms like "code switching," "code mixing," and "code meshing."

13. Weinreich 2008[1973]; Kahn and Rubin 2016; Hary and Benor 2018. See Weinreich's distinction between "Whole Hebrew" and "Merged Hebrew" in Yiddish and other Jewish languages.

14. Steinmetz 1981; Gold 1985; Glinert 1992; Benor 2009a, 2011, 2012.

15. Benor 2008, 2013, 2018a.

16. See Lebenswerd 2018 on Jewish Swedish and Dean-Olmsted and Skura 2018 on Jewish Latin American Spanish.

17. Leonard 2011.

18. A different performance of this song is found at https://www.youtube.com/watch?v=dH3KnftCPIY.

19. Woolard 1999. See also Muysken's (1990) "homophonous diamorphs."

20. See Richard-Amato 1995; Engh 2013 on "jazz chants" in language education.

21. See also Kent 2014.

22. See https://vimeo.com/120085721. See Schunk 1999 on singing paired with signing in language education.

23. For example, Shell 1993; Heller 1994; Piller 2001. Sometimes simultaneity is intentional, and speakers may compete playfully to produce the most creative blends. But sometimes it happens unintentionally because the speaker does not know enough of one of the languages to use it without influence from the other. Both intentional and unintentional instances of hybridity lead to multiple reactions: laughter, resignation that "mistakes" will happen, criticism, and attempts to stop the innovation.

24. On distinctive intonation in Yiddish and Jewish English and its relation to Talmud study, see Weinreich 1956; Heilman 1983; Benor 2012; Burdin 2017.

25. Several studies of child language socialization report caregivers using rituals to help children acquire specific words, politeness conventions, and other linguistic practices (but only in some cultures; others believe that children do not need explicit linguistic instruction). These include prompting children to repeat adults' utterances or attaching specific intonation to utterances. Like the Hebrew intonation patterns and jingles at camp, these caregiving rituals highlight the importance of certain linguistic practices over others; see Ochs and Schieffelin 1984; Demuth 1986; Watson-Gegeo and Gegeo 1986; Moore 2011.

26. See https://archive.org/details/KPNX_20161123_063700_Late_Night_With_Seth_Meyers/start/2580/end/2640.

27. Reimer (2012) analyzes a Hebrew play at Ramah Wisconsin as an "optimal experience" at camp, which can lead to educational growth.

28. On the role of song and embodied singing practices in fostering community at camp, see Kent 2014; Kramarz 2014.

29. Murphey 1992; Richard-Amato 1995; Schunk 1999; Engh 2013.

30. See Glinert 1993 on Hebrew as quasilect; Moore 2004, 2011 on rote language learning in Qur'anic schools; Ahlers 2006 on blessings in Elem Pomo ceremonies.

31. Haugen 1950; Muysken 1981; Berk-Seligson 1986; Winford 2010.

32. See Poplack et al. 1988 on "nonce borrowings."

33. On hybridity and simultaneity, see Bakhtin 1981; Muysken 1990; Woolard 1999.

34. Richard-Amato 1995.

35. Rabbi M. Cohen 2006.

36. See Lave and Wenger 1991 and Wenger 1998 on learning as "peripheral participation"; Wortham 2005 on the "trajectory of socialization"; Duff 2007 on the influence of "scaffolding" (Brunner 1977) and the "zone of proximal development" (Vygotsky 1978) on early language socialization research, as well as on critiques of the communities of practice approach; and Benor 2012 on newly Orthodox Jews' language socialization.

37. See https://machanehgilboa.blogspot.com/2017/07/shabbat-blogging-chotrimot-7th-graders.html.

38. Shandler 2006; Avineri 2012.

CHAPTER 6 — "SIGN" LANGUAGE: VISUAL DISPLAYS OF
HEBREW AND JEWISH SPACE

1. On summoning, see Tavory 2016.

2. Tuan 1977; Entrikin 1991; Lefebvre 1991; Low 2003; Johnstone 2004, 2006, 2010; Blommaert, Collins, and Slembrouck 2005; Shohamy and Gorter 2009; Blommaert 2010; Jaworski and Thurlow 2010; Cresswell 2014.

3. Leeman and Modan 2009.

4. See Davis 2018 on Chickasaw language revitalization efforts.

5. Davis 2018: 126.

6. Hill 2002; Davis 2018.

7. Jaworski and Thurlow 2010.

8. Coupland 2012.

9. For a historical and theoretical treatment of Jewish space, see Mann 2012.

10. Heilman 2006, chapter 7. On linguistic landscape in a Hasidic-Haredi community in England, see Reershemius, Gaiser, and Matras 2018. On visual culture more broadly in Chabad communities, see Katz 2010.

11. Wildstein 2016.

12. See https://www.bneiakiva.org/.

13. We did find a few other instances of written bivalency, such as a sign at Emunah, a Chabad camp, in which the cursive *mem* in *moshiach* (messiah) was also the *N* in Now: "We want משיחNow." A different type of written bivalency was the use of faux Hebrew lettering—English letters designed to resemble Hebrew letters (Shandler 2006: 156; Avni 2014b). This was also rare, but we found it in a Camp Shomria T-shirt.

14. Ramah Darom, https://www.pinterest.com/pin/104145810106200154/.

15. See Davis 2018 on community members' discourse about signage and their epistemic stances regarding correct and incorrect language use.

16. Spolsky and Shohamy 1999; Ben-Rafael, Shohamy, Amara, and Trumper-Hecht 2006; Yelenevskaya and Fialkova 2017.

17. See https://campcoleman.org/2016/06/13/camp-coleman-glossary-2016/.

18. See https://www.camptavor.org/camp-tavor-glossary.

19. For more on design feature analysis, see Kress and Van Leeuwen 1996; Van Leeuwen 2005; Scollon and Wong Scollon 2003.

20. Benor, Avineri, and Greninger forthcoming; personal communication, David Behrman, January 2018. Hebrew cursive was taught at more supplementary schools in the past. See example of a Hebrew school that stopped teaching cursive in Avni 2014a: 257.

21. The semiotic inflections of Hebrew typography have a long history. For example, Fishman (2001b: 38) showed that the rounded "Rashi" style of Hebrew script was associated with ultra-Orthodoxy, whereas block typography was associated with broader Jewish culture. See also Glinert 2017: 99.

22. On the social meanings of transliteration, see Coulmas 2003; Unseth 2005, 2008; Shandler 2006; Ahmad 2011; Androutsopoulos 2012.

23. Stolow 2010.

### CHAPTER 7 — BRINGING ISRAEL TO CAMP

1. "Golden Boy" was performed by Nadav Guedj and reached ninth place in the 2015 Eurovision contest.

2. "Golden Boy" was Israel's first Eurovision entry with entirely English lyrics.

3. On "Jewish peoplehood," see Pianko 2015.

4. See Kirshenblatt-Gimblett 1998.

5. Kelner 2012.

6. Bruner 2005; Avni 2014c.

7. Cohen 2011.

8. Interview, Tamar Mayer, September 6, 2016.

9. Rivka Shulsinger Shear-Yashuv, interview with Chaim Feder, March 20, 1997.

10. Interview, Burton Cohen, March 20, 2017; interview, Hillel Gamoran; interview, Herbert Rosenblum, May 6, 2016.

11. Woocher 1986.

12. Cummings 2012.

13. "Summer Camp Youngsters to Hear Shlichim," *Jewish Week*, July 22, 1979, 11.

14. Interview, Jerome Abrams, March 27, 2017; "Summer Camp Youngsters to Hear Shlichim," *New York Jewish Week*, July 22, 1979; Lauren Gelfond, "From the Holy Land with Love," *Jerusalem Post*, August 10, 2001, 18; Shulsinger 1978.

15. Correspondence, Hanoch Greenberg, AIJC Camps and Shlichim Coordinator, JAFI, March 18, 2018.

16. Interview, Tamar Mayer; Interview, Yitzhak B., February 28, 2015; Shulsinger 1978.

17. See https://jaficamps-community.herokuapp.com/.

18. In addition to this seminar, there are seminars for returning emissaries and for emissaries participating in other initiatives sponsored by the iCenter or Avi Chai.

19. Benor, Krasner, and Avni 2016.

20. *Chadar ochel* is grammatically "correct" according to the rules of *smichut* (the construct state), but several such forms are changing or have changed in Israeli Hebrew, reflecting variation (Ravid and Zilberbuch 2003: 389; Schwarzwald 2009: 197; Gonen 2013). Although there has not been systematic sociolinguistic research on this particular phrase, anecdotal evidence suggests that *cheder ochel* is used more by younger Israelis, whereas *chadar ochel* is used more by older Israelis, those who are concerned about standard grammar, and those who have lived on a kibbutz. According to the Academy of the Hebrew Language, both forms are normative (personal communication, Einat Gonen).

21. Katon 1978. For more about Israeli secular Jews embracing American Judaism, see Meiseles 2017.

22. The participating camps were B'nai B'rith Camp, B'nai B'rith Perlman Camp, BBYO CLTC, Camp B'nai B'rith Ottawa, Camp Daisy and Harry Stein, Camp Kinneret and Biluim, Camp Seneca Lake, Camp Tevya, Camp Young Judaea Texas, Habonim Dror Camp Tavor, Shwayder Camp, and Tamarack Camp.

23. On these performances in early camps, see Lainer-Vos 2014: 91.

24. Billig 1995.

25. On American tourists and campers participating in Israeli army experiences, see https://www.npr.org/sections/parallels/2013/06/02/180824990/U-S-Tourists-Become -Israeli-Commandos-For-A-Day; https://www.haaretz.com/israel-news/.premium-u-s -jewish-campers-turn-idf-recruits-in-controversial-video-1.5455928; and https://heller high.org/2015/03/04/gadna-too-easy/.

### CHAPTER 8 — CONFLICTING IDEOLOGIES OF HEBREW USE

1. Communities whose languages are endangered often work on prestige and image planning as an important step in enticing community members to learn and transmit the language (Ager 2005; Sallabank 2011).

2. Glinert 1991, 2017; Stein 2003; Avni 2014a; Halperin 2014; Efron 2016; Benor 2018b. Yiddish was called *zhargon* and Ladino *zhirgonza* (jargon), even in newspapers written in those languages.

3. Avni 2011, 2012b.

4. Lipstadt 1993; Benor 2018b.

5. Gal and Woolard 1995; Kroskrity et al. 1998; Heller 2007; Kroskrity and Field 2009; Woolard 2016.

6. Dorian 1994; Makihara 2005; Canagarajah 2013a.

7. Moore 2004, 2007; Omoniyi and Fishman 2006; Fader 2009.

8. Creese and Blackledge 2011. See also Blackledge and Creese 2010.

9. Shandler 2006.

10. Canagarajah 2013a.

11. Dorian 1994: 479.

12. Dorian 1994; Kroskrity and Field 2009; Sallabank 2013.

13. Figure 8.1 is from Benor, Krasner, and Avni 2016.

14. In contrast, some staff at Eden Village consider any modern Hebrew use to be inherently political because of its association with Israel. In addition, many Israel educators advocate for introducing complexity and multiple narratives, even to young children (Sinclair 2014; Chazan 2015; Zakai 2015).

15. Recently, enrollment in university Hebrew classes has declined (see Kushner 2019).

16. S. Cohen 2017.

17. As Fishman (1991) argued, schools should be supplemented by home-based efforts to encourage intergenerational language transmission.

18. Chazan 2003; Reimer 2007. See also Shohamy 1999 on the lack of explicit goals regarding the symbolic use of Hebrew.

19. Otheguy, García, and Reid 2015.

20. See how this tension plays out in Jewish day schools in Pomson and Wertheimer 2017. See also Shapiro-Rosenberg 2017.

21. A classic example is Novak 1972: 62–63.

22. The use of Hebrew as a secret language has a long history. Around the world, Jews have often used Hebrew words, sometimes in derogatory ways, to discuss non-Jews (e.g., *goyim* [nations], *arelim* [uncircumcised ones]) and non-Jewish figures and concepts (e.g., *meshuga* [crazy] for Muhammad, *tole* [hanging one] for Jesus), as well as to conceal business dealings from their non-Jewish neighbors (e.g., using Hebrew letters for numbers); see Weinreich [1973] 2008; Bunis 1993; Seidman 2006; Benor 2009b; Hary and Benor 2018. Minority groups, especially when oppressed, often use group-specific codes in secretive ways (Scott 1990; see an example from endangered Guernesiais in Sallabank 2013: 203).

23. Le Page and Tabouret-Keller 1985.

24. Research on language socialization has found that corrections and praise are not only about language use but also about broader ideologies and social categorizations in the community (Fader 2009; Friedman 2010).

25. Jefferson 1987.

26. Dorian 1994; Makihara 2005; Heller 2007; Garrett 2011.

27. Milroy and Milroy 1985; Lippi-Green 1997; Young, Barrett, and Lovejoy 2013.

28. Dorian 1994; Spolsky 2004; Canagarajah 2013a.

29. See Hobsbawm and Ranger 1983.

30. Rabbi M. Cohen 2006.

31. Rabbi M. Cohen 2006.

32. See Bekerman 1986 on the influence of context on whether Hebrew is interpreted as Jewish at camp.

33. Jacobs 2004; Levon 2010; Muchnik 2014.

34. Muchnik 2014: 225.

35. See Sales 2018 and https://www.nonbinaryhebrew.com/ regarding a nonbinary Hebrew system created by American Jews two years after the Habonim suffix revolution.

EPILOGUE

1. See http://www.jewishagency.org/news/isaac-herzog-ga.

2. The Areivim Philanthropic Group is a consortium of nine foundations with funding from the Steinhardt Foundation for Jewish Life and the AVI CHAI Foundation.

3. See https://jewishcamp.org/camp-professionals/immersive-learning/kayitz-kef/.

4. In Hawaiian-language immersion schools, parents also reported a ripple effect: increased pride in the language and culture among students' family members (Luning and Yamauchi 2010).

# References

Abramson, Robert. 1989. "The Indispensability of the Hebrew Language." In *The Ramah Experience: Community and Commitment*, edited by Sylvia Ettenberg and Geraldine Rosenfield, 71–84. New York: Jewish Theological Seminary of America.

Ackerman, Walter. 1969. "Jewish Education—For What?" *American Jewish Year Book* 70: 3–36.

———. 2008. "Becoming Ramah." In *"Jewish Education for What" and Other Essays*, edited by Ari Ackerman et al., 213–237. Jerusalem: Schechter Institute of Jewish Studies.

Ager, Dennis E. 2005. "Prestige and Image Planning." *Current Issues in Language Planning* 6: 1–43.

Ahlers, Jocelyn C. 2006. "Framing Discourse: Creating Community through Native Language Use." *Journal of Linguistic Anthropology* 16, no. 1: 58–75.

———. 2014. "Linguistic Variation and Time Travel: Barrier, or Border-Crossing?" *Language & Communication* 38: 33–43.

———. 2017. "Native California Languages as Semiotic Resources in the Performance of Identity." *Journal of Linguistic Anthropology* 27, no. 1: 40–53.

Ahmad, Rizwan. 2011. "Urdu in Devanagari: Shifting Orthographic Practices and Muslim Identity in Delhi." *Language in Society* 40, no. 3: 259–284.

Alster-Yardeni, David. 1989. "Music and Drama at Camp Massad," In *Kovetz Massad*. Vol. 2, *Hebrew Camping in America,* edited by Shlomo Shulsinger-Shear Yashuv and Rivka Shulsinger-Shear Yashuv, 170–176. Jerusalem: Alumni of Massad Camps. [Hebrew]

Altman, Shalom. 1934. *Judaean Songster.* New York: Young Judaea.

Anderson, Benedict. 1983. *Imagined Communities.* New York: Verso.

Androutsopoulos, Jannis. 2012. "'Greeklish': Transliteration Practice and Discourse in the Context of Computer-Mediated Digraphia." In *Orthography as Social Action: Scripts, Spelling, Identity and Power,* edited by Alexandra Jaffe, Jannis Androutsopoulos, Mark Sebba, and Sally Johnson, 359–392. Berlin: De Gruyter Mouton.

Appel, Mike, and Sharon Schoenfeld. 1993. *Choveret Ivrit.* New York: Young Judaea.

Arian, Merri Lovinger. 2014. "Spirited Singing of the Seventies." *eJewish Philanthropy.* http://ejewishphilanthropy.com/spirited-singing-of-the-seventies/.

Austin, J. L. 1975. *How to Do Things with Words*, 2nd ed. Cambridge, MA: Harvard University Press.

Aviad, Janet. 1988. "Subculture or Counterculture: Camp Ramah." *Studies in Jewish Education* 3: 197–225.

Avineri, Netta. 2012. "Heritage Language Socialization Practices in Secular Yiddish Educational Contexts: The Creation of a Metalinguistic Community." PhD diss., University of California, Los Angeles. https://www.bjpa.org/content/upload/bjpa/c__c /Avineri-%20Heritage%20Language%20Socialization.pdf.

———. 2014. "Yiddish Endangerment as Phenomenological Reality and Discursive Strategy: Crossing into the Past and Crossing out the Present." *Language & Communication* 38: 18–32.

Avineri, Netta, and Paul Kroskrity. 2014. "On the (Re-)production and Representation of Endangered Language Communities: Social Boundaries and Temporal Borders." *Language & Communication* 38: 1–7.

Avni, Sharon. 2011. "Toward an Understanding of Hebrew Language Education: Ideologies, Emotions, and Identity." *International Journal of the Sociology of Language* 208: 53–70.

———. 2012a. "Hebrew as Heritage: The Work of Language in Religious and Communal Continuity." *Linguistics and Education* 23: 323–333.

———. 2012b. "Translation as a Site of Language Policy Negotiation in Jewish Day School Education." *Current Issues in Language Planning* 13, no. 2: 76–104.

———. 2012c. "Hebrew-Only Language Policy in Religious Education." *Language Policy* 11: 169–188.

———. 2014a. "Hebrew Education in the United States: Historical Perspectives and Future Directions." *Journal of Jewish Education* 80, no. 3: 256–286.

———. 2014b. "Hebrew in the North American Linguistic Landscape." In *Challenges for Language Education and Policy: Making Space for People*, edited by B. Spolsky, M. Tannenbaum, and O. Inbar, 196–213. New York: Routledge.

———. 2014c. "Homeland Tour Guide Narratives and the Discursive Construction of the Diasporic." *Narrative Inquiry* 23, no. 2: 227–244.

———. 2016. "Hebrew Learning Ideologies and the Reconceptualization of American Judaism: Language Debates in American Jewish Schooling in the Early 20th Century." *International Journal of Sociology of Language* 237: 119–138.

Baker, Colin, and Wayne E. Wright. 2017. *Foundations of Bilingual Education and Bilingualism*, 6th ed. Bristol: Multilingual Matters.

Bakhtin, Mikhail M. 1981. *The Dialogic Imagination*, translated by Caryl Emerson and Michael Holquist and edited by Michael Holquist. Austin: University of Texas Press.

Baquedano-López, Patricia. 2008. "The Pragmatics of Reading Prayers: Learning the Act of Contrition in Spanish-Based Religious Education Classes (Doctrina)." *Text & Talk* 28, no. 5: 582–602.

Barrett, Rusty. 2013. "Be Yourself Somewhere Else: What's Wrong with Keeping Undervalued English out of the Classroom?" In *Other People's English: Code-Meshing, Code-Switching, and African American Literacy*, edited by Vershawn Ashanti Young et al., 33–54. New York: Teachers College Press.

Bekerman, Zvi. 1986. *The Social Construction of Jewishness: An Anthropological Interactional Study of a Camp System*. PhD diss., Jewish Theological Seminary of America, New York.

Benor, Sarah Bunin. 2008. "Towards a New Understanding of Jewish Language in the 21st Century." *Religion Compass* 2, no. 6: 1062–1080.

———. 2009a. "Do American Jews Speak a Jewish Language? A Model of Jewish Linguistic Distinctiveness." *Jewish Quarterly Review* 99, no. 2: 230–269.

———. 2009b. "Lexical Othering in Judezmo: How Ottoman Sephardim Refer to Non-Jews." In *Languages and Literatures of Sephardic and Oriental Jews: Proceedings of the Sixth International Congress*, edited by David M. Bunis, 65–85. Jerusalem: Bialik Institute and Misgav Yerushalayim.

———. 2011. "*Mensch, Bentsh*, and *Balagan*: Variation in the American Jewish Linguistic Repertoire." *Language and Communication* 31, no. 2: 141–154.

———. 2012. *Becoming Frum: How Newcomers Learn the Language and Culture of Orthodox Judaism*. New Brunswick, NJ: Rutgers University Press.

———. 2013. "From Sabbath to Shabbat: The Changing Language of Jewish Sisterhood Leaders, 1913–2012." In *Sisterhood: A Centennial History of Women of Reform Judaism*, edited by Carole Balin, Dana Herman, and Jonathan Sarna, 314–337. Cincinnati: HUC Press.

———. 2018a. "Jewish English in the United States." In *Languages in Jewish Communities, Past and Present*, edited by Benjamin Hary and Sarah Bunin Benor, 414–430. Berlin: De Gruyter Mouton.

———. 2018b. "Hebrew Infusion in American Jewish Life: Tensions and the Role of Israeli Hebrew." In *What We Talk about When We Talk about Hebrew (and Why It Matters to Americans)*, edited by Nancy Berg and Naomi Sokoloff, 124–138. Seattle: University of Washington Press.

———. 2019. "Ethnolinguistic Infusion at Sephardic Adventure Camp." In *The Routledge Companion to the Work of John Rickford*, edited by Renée Blake and Isabelle Buchstaller, 142–152. London: Routledge.

Benor, Sarah Bunin, Netta Avineri, and Nicki Greninger. Forthcoming. "Hebrew Education in Part-Time Jewish Schools: Rationales, boals, and Practices" (report). Washington, DC: Consortium for Applied Studies in Jewish Education.

Benor, Sarah Bunin, and Steven M. Cohen. 2011. "Talking Jewish: The 'Ethnic English' of American Jews." In *Ethnicity and Beyond: Theories and Dilemmas of Jewish Group Demarcation. Studies in Contemporary Jewry*, Vol. 25, edited by Eli Lederhendler, 62–78. Oxford: Oxford University Press.

Benor, Sarah Bunin, Jonathan Krasner, and Sharon Avni. 2016. *Connection, Not Proficiency: Survey of Hebrew at North American Jewish Summer Camps*. Waltham, MA: Brandeis University Mandel Center for Studies in Jewish Education. http://www.brandeis.edu/mandel/pdfs/2016-Hebrew-in-camp-survey-report.pdf.

Ben-Rafael, Eliezer, Elana Shohamy, Muhammad Hasan Amara, and Nira Trumper-Hecht. 2006. "Linguistic Landscape as Symbolic Construction of the Public Space: The Case of Israel." *International Journal of Multilingualism* 3, no. 1: 7–30.

Ben-Sorek, Eson. 2015. "Israel's Pagan Poet." *Times of Israel*, September 25. http://blogs.timesofisrael.com/israels-pagan-poet/.

Berk-Seligson, Susan. 1986. "Linguistic Constraints on Intrasentential Code-Switching: A Study of Spanish/Hebrew Bilingualism." *Language in Society* 15, no. 3: 313–348.

Bernstein, Louis. 2008. "The Jubilee that Was Not: Massad in Its Glory and Its Decline." In *Massad Reminiscences 3*, edited by Shlomo Shulsinger-Shear Yashuv, 108–120. Jerusalem: Camp Massad Alumni Project.

Bice, Wendy Rose. 2001. *A Timeless Treasure: 100 Years of Fresh Air Society Camp.* Bloomfield Hills, MI: Fresh Air Society.

Billig, Michael. 1995. *Banal Nationalism.* Thousand Oaks, CA: Sage.

Blackledge, Adrian, and Angela Creese. 2010. *Multilingualism, A Critical Perspective.* London: Continuum.

Blommaert, Jan, ed. 1999. *Language Ideological Debates.* Berlin: De Gruyter Mouton.

———. 2010. *The Sociolinguistics of Globalization.* Cambridge: Cambridge University Press.

Blommaert, Jan, James Collins, and Stef Slembrouck. 2005. "Spaces of Multilingualism." *Language & Communication* 25, no. 3, 197–216.

Bloom, Jack. 2012. *The Rabbi as Symbolic Exemplar: By the Power Vested in Me.* New York: Routledge.

Bourdieu, Pierre. 1986. "The Forms of Capital." In *Handbook of Theory and Research for the Sociology of Education,* translated by R. Nice and edited by John Richardson, 241–258. New York: Greenwood.

Breslau, David, ed., 1961. *Arise and Build: The Story of American Habonim.* New York: Ichud Habonim Labor Zionist Youth.

Breslau, R. 1939. "Palestine Comes to Boston." *Young Judaean* 28 (October 1939): 13–16.

Brown, Albert. 1989. *The Camp Wise Story, 1907–1988.* Cleveland: Jewish Community Federation of Cleveland.

Brown, Michael. 1997. "It's Off to Camp We Go: Ramah, LTF, and the Seminary in the Finkelstein Era." In *Tradition Renewed: A History of the Jewish Theological Seminary, Vol. 1,* edited by Jack Wertheimer, 823–854. New York: Jewish Theological Seminary of America.

Bruner, Edward M. 2005. *Culture on Tour: Ethnographies of Travel.* Chicago: University of Chicago Press.

Brunner, Jerome S. 1977. "Early Social Interaction and Language Acquisition." In *Studies in Mother–Infant Interaction,* edited by H. R. Schaffer, 52–78. London: Academic Press.

Bucholtz, Mary, and Kira Hall. 2005. "Identity and Interaction: A Sociocultural Linguistic Approach." *Discourse Studies* 7: 585–614.

Bunis, David M. 1993. *A Lexicon of the Hebrew and Aramaic Elements in Modern Judezmo.* Jerusalem: Magnes Press and Misgav Yerushalayim.

Burdin, Rachel Steindel. 2017. "New Notes on the Rise-Fall Contour." *Journal of Jewish Languages* 5, no. 2: 145–173.

Canagarajah, Suresh. 2011. "Translanguaging in the Classroom: Emerging Issues for Research and Pedagogy." *Applied Linguistics Review* 2: 1–28.

———. 2013a. "Reconstructing Heritage Language: Resolving Dilemmas in Language Maintenance for Sri Lankan Tamil Migrants." *International Journal of the Sociology of Language* 222: 131–155.

———. 2013b. *Translingual Practice: Global Englishes and Cosmopolitan Relations.* London: Routledge.

Chazan, Barry. 2003. "The Philosophy of Informal Jewish Education." In *Encyclopaedia of Informal Education.* http://www.infed.org/informaljewisheducation/informal-jewish-education.htm.

———. 2015. "Diverse Narratives." In *The Aleph Bet of Israel Education,* 89–96. Chicago: iCenter.

Chudacoff, Howard P. 2007. *Children at Play: An American History*. New York: New York University Press.

Cohen, Burton. 1984. "Louis Newman's Wisconsin Innovations and Their Effect upon the Ramah Camping Movement." In *Studies in Jewish Education and Judaica in Honor of Louis Newman*, edited by Alexander Shapiro and Burton Cohen, 23–38. New York: Ktav.

Cohen, Erik. 2011. *The Educational Shaliach 1939–2009: A Socio-History of a Unique Project in Formal and Informal Jewish Education. Dor Ledor*, 37. Ramat Aviv: Tel Aviv University.

Cohen, Judah. 2006. "Singing out for Judaism: A History of Song Leaders and Song Leading at Olin-Sang-Ruby Union Institute." In *A Place of Our Own: The Rise of Reform Jewish Camping*, edited by Michael Lorge and Gary Zola, 173–208. Tuscaloosa: University of Alabama Press.

———. 2015. "*Sing unto God*: Debbie Friedman and the Changing Sound of Liturgical Music." *Contemporary Jewry* 35, no. 1: 13–34.

———. 2017. "Higher Education: Debbie Friedman in Chicago." *Journal of Jewish Identities* 10: 7–26.

Cohen, Michael. 2012. *The Birth of Conservative Judaism: Solomon Schechter's Disciples and the Creation of an American Religious Movement*. New York: Columbia University Press.

Cohen, Mortimer. 1969. "*The Joys of Yiddish* by Leo Rosten." *Commentary*, March 1. https://www.commentarymagazine.com/articles/the-joys-of-yiddish-by-leo-rosten/.

Cohen, Rabbi Mitchell. 2006. *Report on the Shapiro Fellowship Seminar: המר הנחמב תירבע* [Hebrew at Camp Ramah]. New York: National Ramah Commission.

Cohen, Steven M. 1986. *Ties and Tensions: The 1986 Survey of American Jewish Attitudes toward Israel and Israelis*. New York: American Jewish Committee.

———. 2017. The Alumni of Ramah Camps: A Long-Term Portrait of Jewish Engagement. New York: National Ramah Commission.

Cohen, Steven M., Ron Miller, Ira Sheskin, and Berna Torr. 2011. *Camp Works: The Long-Term Impact of Jewish Overnight Camp*. New York: Foundation for Jewish Camp.

Coulmas, Florian. 2003. *The Blackwell Encyclopedia of Writing Systems*. New York: Wiley-Blackwell.

Coupland, Nikolas. 2012. "Bilingualism on Display: The Framing of Welsh and English in Welsh Public Spaces." *Language in Society* 41, no. 1: 1–27.

Creese, Angela, and Adrian Blackledge. 2011. "Separate and Flexible Bilingualism in Complementary Schools: Multiple Language Practices in Interrelationship." *Journal of Pragmatics* 43, no. 5: 1196–1208.

Cresswell, Tim. 2014. *Place: An Introduction*. Hoboken, NJ: John Wiley & Sons.

Cummings, Jonathan. 2012. "'Muddling through' Hasbara: Israeli Government Communications Policy, 1966–1975." PhD diss., London School of Economics and Political Science.

Davis, Jenny L. 2017. "Resisting Rhetorics of Language Endangerment: Reclamation through Indigenous Language Survivance." *Language Documentation and Description* 14: 37–58.

———. 2018. *Talking Indian: Identity and Language Revitalization in the Chickasaw Renaissance*. Tucson: University of Arizona Press.

Davis, Moshe. 1996. "Massad: Was, Is, Will Be." In *Massad Reminiscences*. Jerusalem: Abraham Harman Institute for Contemporary Jewry, Hebrew University.

Dean-Olmsted, Evelyn, and Susana Skura. 2018. "Jewish Spanish in Buenos Aires and Mexico City." In *Languages in Jewish Communities, Past and Present*, edited by Benjamin Hary and Sarah Bunin Benor, 383–413. Berlin: De Gruyter Mouton.

Demuth, Katherine. 1986. "Prompting Routines in the Language Socialization of Basotho Children." In *Language Socialization across Cultures*, edited by Bambi B. Schieffelin and Elinor Ochs, 51–79. Cambridge: Cambridge University Press.

Diner, Hasia. 2002. *Lower East Side Memories: A Jewish Place in America*. Princeton: Princeton University Press.

Diner, Hasia, Jeffrey Shandler, and Beth Wenger, eds. 2000. *Remembering the Lower East Side*. Bloomington: Indiana University Press.

Dorian, Nancy C. 1994. "Purism vs. Compromise in Language Revitalization and Language Revival." *Language in Society* 23, no. 4: 479–494.

———. 2014. *Small-Language Fates and Prospects: Lessons of Persistence and Change from Endangered Languages: Collected Essays*. Leiden: Brill.

Doron, Edit, ed. 2015. *Language Contact and the Development of Modern Hebrew* (thematic issue). *Journal of Jewish Languages* 3.

Duff, Patricia. 2007. "Second Language Socialization as Sociocultural Theory: Insights and Issues." *Language Teaching* 40: 309–319.

Duff, Patricia, and Nancy Hornberger, eds. 2008. *Encyclopedia of Language and Education*. Vol. 8, *Language Socialization*. New York: Springer.

Duranti, Alessandro, Elinor Ochs, and Bambi B. Schieffelin, eds. 2011. *The Handbook of Language Socialization*. Malden, MA: Wiley-Blackwell.

Dushkin, Alexander M. 1975. *Living Bridges: Memoirs of an Educator*. Jerusalem: Keter.

Eckert, Penelope. 2008. "Variation and the Indexical Field." *Journal of Sociolinguistics* 12, no. 4: 453–476.

Efron, John M. 2016. *German Jewry and the Allure of the Sephardic*. Princeton: Princeton University Press.

Elazar, Daniel, and Rela Mintz Geffen. 2000. *The Conservative Movement in Judaism: Dilemmas and Opportunities*. Albany: State University of New York Press.

Engh, Dwayne. 2013. "Why Use Music in English Language Learning? A Survey of the Literature." *English Language Teaching* 6, no. 2: 113–127.

Entrikin, J. Nicholas. 1991. *The Betweenness of Place: Towards a Geography of Modernity*. Baltimore: Johns Hopkins University Press.

Fader, Ayala. 2007. "Reclaiming Sacred Sparks: Linguistic Syncretism and Gendered Language Shift among Hasidic Jews in New York." *Journal of Linguistic Anthropology* 17, no. 1: 1–22.

———. 2009. *Mitzvah Girls: Bringing up the Next Generation of Hasidic Jews in Brooklyn*. Princeton: Princeton University Press.

Farago, Uri. 1972. *The Influence of a Jewish Summer Camp's Social Climate on Campers' Jewish Identity*. PhD diss., Brandeis University, Waltham, MA.

Ferguson, Charles. 1959. "Diglossia." *Word* 15, no. 2: 325–340.

Fermaglich, Kirsten. 2006. *American Dreams and Nazi Nightmares: Early Holocaust Consciousness and Liberal America, 1957–1965*. Hanover, NH: UPNE/Brandeis University Press.

Fishman, Joshua A. 1967. "Bilingualism with and without Diglossia; Diglossia with and without Bilingualism." *Journal of Social Issues* 23, no. 2: 29–38.

———. 1980. "Bilingualism and Biculturism as Individual and as Societal Phenomena." *Journal of Multilingual & Multicultural Development* 1, no. 1: 3–15.

———, ed. 1981a. *Never Say Die! A Thousand Years of Yiddish in Jewish Life and Letters.* Berlin: De Gruyter Mouton.

———. 1981b. "The Sociology of Jewish Languages from the Perspective of the General Sociology of Language: A Preliminary Formulation." *International Journal of the Sociology of Language* 30: 5–18.

———. 1991. *Reversing Language Shift: Theoretical and Empirical Foundations of Assistance to Threatened Languages.* Clevedon: Multilingual Matters.

———. 2001b. "Digraphia Maintenance and Loss among Eastern European Jews: Intertextual and Interlingual Print-Conventions in Ashkenazic Linguistic Culture since 1800." *International Journal of the Sociology of Language,* 150: 27–42.

Fox, Margalit. 2011. "Debbie Friedman, Singer of Jewish Music, Dies at 59." *New York Times,* January 11.

Fox, Seymour. 1989. "Ramah: A Setting for Jewish Education." In *The Ramah Experience: Community and Commitment,* edited by Sylvia Ettenberg and Geraldine Rosenfield, 19-37. New York: Jewish Theological Seminary.

Fox, Seymour, with William Novak. 2000. *Vision at the Heart: Lessons from Camp Ramah on the Power of Ideas in Shaping Educational Institutions.* New York: Council for Initiatives in Jewish Education.

Freedman, Morris. 1955. "Camp Ramah, Where Hebrew Is the Key: A Full Jewish Education for a Full Jewish Life." *Commentary,* May.

Freidenreich, Fradle Pomerantz. 2010. *Passionate Pioneers: The Story of Yiddish Secular Education in North America, 1910–1960.* New York: Holmes & Meier.

Friedman, Debra. 2006. *(Re)Imagining the Nation: Language Socialization in Ukrainian Classrooms.* PhD diss., University of California, Los Angeles.

———. 2010. "Speaking Correctly: Error Correction as a Language Socialization Practice in a Ukrainian Classroom." *Applied Linguistics* 31, no. 3: 346–367.

Frost, Shimon. 1994. "Camp Massad." *Avar ve 'Atid: A Journal of Jewish Education, Culture and Discourse* 1: 41–50.

Gal, Susan, and Kathryn A. Woolard. 1995. "Constructing Languages and Publics: Authority and Representation." *Pragmatics* 5: 129–138.

Gal, Susan, and Kathryn A. Woolard, eds. 2014. *Languages and Publics: The Making of Authority.* Oxon: Routledge.

Gamoran, Hillel. 2006. "The Road to Chalutzim: Reform Judaism's Hebrew-Speaking Program." In *A Place of Our Own: The Rise of Reform Jewish Camping,* edited by Michael Lorge and Gary Zola, 124–150. Tuscaloosa: University of Alabama Press.

Gannes, Abraham, and Levi Soshuk. 1949. "The Kvutzah and Camp Achvah." *Jewish Education* 20, no. 3: 61–69.

Gans, Herbert. 1951. "Park Forest: Birth of a Jewish Community: A Documentary." *Commentary* 11 (April 1): 333–334.

García, Ofelia, and Li Wei. 2014. "Translanguaging and Education." In *Translanguaging: Language, Bilingualism and Education,* 63–77. London: Palgrave Macmillan UK.

Garrett, Paul B. 2011. "Language Socialization and Language Shift." In *The Handbook of Language Socialization*, edited by Alessandro Duranti, Elinor Ochs, and Bambi B. Schieffelin, 515–535. Malden, MA: Wiley-Blackwell.

Garrett, Paul, and Patricia Baquedano-López. 2002. "Language Socialization: Reproduction and Continuity, Transformation and Change." *Annual Review of Anthropology* 31: 339–361.

Garvey, Catherine. 1990 [1977]. *Play*. Cambridge, MA: Harvard University Press.

Glinert, Lewis. 1991. "Language Choice and the Halakhic Speech Act." In *The Influence of Language on Culture and Thought: Essays in Honor of Joshua A. Fishman's Sixty-Fifth Birthday*, 157–182. Berlin: De Gruyter Mouton.

———. 1992. *The Joys of Hebrew*. New York: Oxford University Press.

———. 1993. "Language as Quasilect: Hebrew in Contemporary Anglo Jewry." In *Hebrew in Ashkenaz: A Language in Exile*, 249–264. New York: Oxford University Press.

———. 2017. *The Story of Hebrew*. Princeton: Princeton University Press.

Goffman, Erving. 1961. *Asylums: Essays on the Social Situation of Mental Patients and Other Inmates*. Garden City, NY: Anchor Books.

Gold, David. 1985. "Jewish English." In *Readings in the Sociology of Jewish Languages*, edited by Joshua A. Fishman, 280–298. Leiden: Brill.

———. 1986. "On Jewish English in the United States." *Jewish Language Review* 6: 121–135.

Goldberg, Harvey E. 1987. "Epilogue: Text in Jewish Society and the Challenge of Comparison." In *Judaism Viewed from Within and from Without*, 315–330. Albany: State University of New York Press.

Goldberg, Henry. 1948. "Camp Ramah—A Challenge." *Synagogue School* 6: 47–48.

Goldberg, J. J., and Elliot King, eds. 1993. *Builders and Dreamers: Habonim Labor Zionist Youth in North America*. New York: Herzl Press.

Gonen, Einat. 2013. "Reduction of Vowels: Modern Hebrew." *Encyclopedia of Hebrew Language and Linguistics*. Vol. 3. Leiden: Brill.

Goren, Arthur. 1999. *The Politics and Public Culture of American Jews*. Bloomington: Indiana University Press.

Grand, Samuel. 1958. "A History of Zionist Youth Organizations in the United States from their Inception to 1940." PhD diss., Columbia University, New York.

Greenstein, Howard. 1981. *Turning Point: Zionism and Reform Judaism*. Chico, CA: Scholars Press.

Gurock, Jeffrey. 2004. *Orthodox Jews in America*. Bloomington: Indiana University Press.

Halkin, Hillel. 1989. "My Massad Recollections." In *Kovetz Massad*. Vol. 2, *Hebrew Camping in America*, eds. Shlomo Shulsinger-Shear Yashuv and Rivka Shulsinger-Shear Yashuv, 278–279. Jerusalem: Alumni of Massad Camps. [Hebrew]

Halperin, Liora. 2014. *Babel in Zion: Jews, Nationalism, and Language Diversity in Palestine, 1920–1948*. New Haven: Yale University Press.

Hary, Benjamin, and Sarah Bunin Benor, eds. 2018. *Languages in Jewish Communities, Past and Present*. Berlin: De Gruyter Mouton.

Haugen, Einar. 1950. "The Analysis of Linguistic Borrowing." *Language* 26, no. 2: 210–231.

Heilman, Samuel. 1983. *The People of the Book: Drama, Fellowship, and Religion*. Chicago: University of Chicago Press.

———. 2006. *Sliding to the Right: The Contest for the Future of American Jewish Ortho-doxy.* Berkeley: University of California Press.

Heller, Monica, ed. 2007. *Bilingualism: A Social Approach.* New York: Palgrave Macmillan.

———. 1994. *Crosswords: Language, Education and Ethnicity in French Ontario.* Berlin: De Gruyter Mouton.

Helman, Anat. 2007. "Zionism, Politics, Hedonism: Sports in Interwar Tel Aviv." In *Jews, Sports, and the Rites of Citizenship,* edited by Jack Kugelmass, 95–113. Urbana: University of Illinois Press.

Hickey, Raymond. 2010. *The Handbook of Language Contact.* Hoboken, NJ: John Wiley & Sons.

Hill, Jane H. 2002. "'Expert Rhetorics' in Advocacy for Endangered Languages: Who Is Listening and What Do They Hear? *Journal of Linguistic Anthropology* 12, no. 2: 119–133.

Hobsbawm, Eric, and Terence Ranger. 1983. *The Invention of Tradition.* New York: Cambridge University Press.

Hulbert, Ann. 2003. *Raising America: Experts, Parents, and a Century of Advice about Children.* New York: Knopf.

Hurwitz, Ariel. 1994. *Against the Stream: Seven Decades of Hashomer Hatzair in North America.* Givat Haviva, Israel: Association North American Shomrim in Israel and Yad Yaari.

Irvine, Judith, and Susan Gal. 2000. "Language Ideology and Linguistic Differentia-tion." In *Regimes of Language: Ideologies, Polities, and Identities,* edited by Paul Kros-krity, 35–84. Santa Fe, NM: School of American Research Press.

Jacobs, Andrea Michele. 2004. "Language Reform as Language Ideology: An Examina-tion of Israeli Feminist Language Practice." PhD diss., University of Texas, Austin.

Jacobson, Matthew Frye. 2006. *Roots Too: White Ethnic Revival in Post-Civil Rights America.* Cambridge, MA: Harvard University Press.

Jakar, Valerie. 1995. "A Society Contained, a Cultured Maintained: An Ethnography of Second Language Acquisition in Informal Education." PhD diss., University of Penn-sylvania, Philadelphia.

Jaworski, Adam, and Crispin Thurlow, eds. 2010. *Semiotic Landscapes: Language, Image, Space.* London: A&C Black.

Jefferson, Gail. 1987. "On Exposed and Embedded Correction in Conversation." In *Talk and Social Organisation,* edited by Graham Button and J. R. E. Lee, 86–100. Clevedon: Multilingual Matters.

Johnstone, Barbara. 2004. "Place, Globalization, and Linguistic Variation." In *Sociolin-guistic Variation: Critical Reflections,* edited by Carmen Fought, 65–83. New York: Oxford University Press.

———. 2010. "Language and Geographical Space." In *Language and Space: An Interna-tional Handbook of Linguistic Variation.* Vol. 1, *Theories and Methods,* edited by P. Auer and Jacob Edward Schmidt, 1–18. Berlin: De Gruyter Mouton.

Johnstone, Barbara, Jennifer Andrus, and Andrew E. Danielson. 2006. "Mobility, Indexicality, and the Enregisterment of 'Pittsburghese.'" *Journal of English Linguistics* 34: 77–104.

Joselit, Jenna Weissman. 1993. *A Worthy Use of Summer: Jewish Summer Camping in America.* Philadelphia: National Museum of American Jewish History.

———. 1995. *The Wonders of America: Reinventing Jewish Culture, 1880–1950.* New York: Henry Holt.

Kahn, Lily, and Aaron D. Rubin, eds. 2016. *Handbook of Jewish Languages*. Leiden: Brill.

Katon, Ruth. 1978. "Some Activities of the Israeli Delegation to Massad." In *Kovetz Massad*, Vol. 1, edited by Meir Havatzelet and Shlomo Kornblum, 314–318. New York: Massad Camps. [Hebrew]

Katz, Emily Alice. 2015. *Bringing Zion Home: Israel in American Jewish Culture, 1948–1967*. Albany: State University Press of New York. [Hebrew]

Katz, Maya Balakirsky. 2010. *The Visual Culture of Chabad*. Cambridge: Cambridge University Press.

Kaufman, David. 2012. *Jewhooing the Sixties: American Celebrity & Jewish Identity*. Hanover, NH: UPNE/Brandeis University Press.

Kelman, Ari. 2011. "Hear Israel." *Tablet Magazine*, January 7.

Kelner, Shaul. 2012. *Tours that Bind: Diaspora, Pilgrimage, and Israeli Birthright Tourism*. New York: New York University Press.

Kirshenblatt-Gimblett, Barbara. 1998. *Destination Culture: Tourism, Museums and Heritage*. Berkeley: University of California Press.

Kent, Evan. 2014. "So Much More than Kumbaya: Music at Jewish Summer Camps and the Formation of Jewish Identity." PhD diss., Boston University.

Klepper, Jeff. 2008. "Songs of Israel, Part II." http://jeffklepper.blogspot.com/2008/05/songs-of-israel-part-2.html.

Kligman, Mark. 2001. "Contemporary Jewish Music in America." *American Jewish Yearbook 2001*: 88–141.

Koffman, David S. 2018. "Playing Indian at Jewish Summer Camp: Lessons on Tribalism, Assimilation, and Spirituality." *Journal of Jewish Education* 84, no. 4: 413–440.

Kramarz, Benjamin Max. 2014. "The Culture and Music of American-Jewish Summer Camp." Master's thesis, University of California, Berkeley.

Kranson, Rachel. 2017. *Ambivalent Embrace: Jewish Upward Mobility in Postwar America*. Chapel Hill: University of North Carolina Press.

Krasner, Jonathan B. 2011. *The Benderly Boys and American Jewish Education*. Hanover, NH: Brandeis University Press.

———. 2016. "On the Origins and Persistence of the Jewish Identity Industry in Jewish Education." *Journal of Jewish Education* 82: 132–158.

Kress, Gunther R., and Theo Van Leeuwen. 1996. *Reading Images: The Grammar of Visual Design*. New York: Psychology Press.

Kress, Jeffrey S. 2014. "Experiential Jewish Education Has Arrived! Now What?" *Journal of Jewish Education* 80, no. 3: 319–342.

Kroskrity, Paul V., and Margaret C. Field, eds. 2009. *Native American Language Ideologies: Beliefs, Practices, and Struggles in Indian Country*. Tucson: University of Arizona Press.

Kroskrity, Paul V., Bambi B. Schieffelin, and Kathryn Ann Woolard, eds. 1998. *Language Ideologies: Practice and Theory*. New York: Oxford University Press.

Kulick, Don. 1992. *Language Shift and Cultural Reproduction: Socialization, Self, and Syncretism in a Papua New Guinea Village*. Cambridge: Cambridge University Press.

Kushner, Aviya. 2019. "No One's Studying Hebrew Anymore—That's a Big Problem." *Forward*, July 11. https://forward.com/culture/427477/no-ones-studying-hebrew-anymore-thats-a-big-problem/.

Labov, William. 1972. *Sociolinguistic Patterns*. Philadelphia: University of Pennsylvania Press.

Lainer-Vos, Dan. 2014. "Israel in the Poconos: Simulating the Nation in a Zionist Summer Camp." *Theory and Society* 43: 91–116.

Lave, Jean, and Etienne Wenger. 1991. *Situated Learning: Legitimate Peripheral Participation*. Cambridge: Cambridge University Press.

Leaf, Haim. 1989. "The Hebrew Youth Movement in America: The First Five Years." In *Kovetz Massad*. Vol. 2, *Hebrew Camping in America*, edited by Shlomo Shulsinger-Shear Yashuv and Rivka Shulsinger-Shear Yashuv, 349–362. Jerusalem: Alumni of Massad Camps. [Hebrew]

Lebenswerd, Patric Joshua Klagsbrun. 2018. "Jewish Swedish in Sweden." In *Languages in Jewish Communities, Past and Present*, edited by Benjamin Hary and Sarah Bunin Benor, 431–452. Berlin: De Gruyter Mouton.

Leeman, Jennifer, and Gabriella Modan. 2009. "Commodified Language in Chinatown: A Contextualized Approach to Linguistic Landscape." *Journal of Sociolinguistics* 13, no. 3: 332–362.

Lefebvre, Henri. 1991. *The Production of Space*, vol. 142. Blackwell: Oxford.

Leonard, Wesley Y. 2011. "Challenging 'Extinction' through Modern Miami Language Practices." *American Indian Culture and Research Journal* 35, no. 2: 135–160.

Le Page, Robert B., and Andrée Tabouret-Keller. 1985. *Acts of Identity: Creole-Based Approaches to Ethnicity and Language*. Cambridge: Cambridge University Press.

Lerner, Stephen. 1971. "Ramah and its Critics," *Conservative Judaism* 24, no. 4: 1–28.

Levon, Erez. 2010. *Language and the Politics of Sexuality: Lesbians and Gays in Israel.* New York: Springer.

Lewis, Gwyn, Bryn Jones, and Colin Baker. 2012. "Translanguaging: Developing its Conceptualisation and Contextualisation." *Educational Research and Evaluation* 18, no. 7: 655–670.

Lieberman, Joshua. 1931. *Creative Camping: A Coeducational Experiment in Personality Development and Social Living.* New York: Association Press.

Lippi-Green, Rosina. 1997. *English with an Accent: Language, Ideology, and Discrimination in the United States.* New York: Psychology Press.

Lipstadt, Deborah. 1993. "Hebrew among Jewish Communal Leaders: Requirement, Elective, or Extra-Curricular Activity?" In *Hebrew in America: Perspectives and Prospects*, edited by Alan Mintz, 309–321. Detroit: Wayne State University Press.

Lorge, Michael M., and Gary P. Zola, eds. 2006. *A Place of Our Own: The Rise of Reform Jewish Camping.* Tuscaloosa: University of Alabama Press.

Low, Setha M. 2003. *The Anthropology of Space and Place.* New York: Wiley-Blackwell.

Luning, Rebecca J. I., and Lois A. Yamauchi. 2010. "The Influences of Indigenous Heritage Language Education on Students and Families in a Hawaiian Language Immersion Program." *Heritage Language Journal* 7, no. 2: 46–75.

Makihara, Miki. 2005. "Rapa Nui Ways of Speaking Spanish: Language Shift and Socialization on Easter Island." *Language in Society* 34: 727–762.

Mann, Barbara. 2012. *Space and Place in Jewish Studies.* New Brunswick, NJ: Rutgers University Press.

Mark, Jonathan. 2002. "Reliving the Zionist Dream." *New York Jewish Week*, April 19.

———. 2010. "Zamir's Long Road." *New York Jewish Week*, October 27.

Maslow, Abraham. 1964. *Religions, Values and Peak Experiences.* Columbus: Ohio State University Press.

Matras, Yaron. 2009. *Language Contact.* Cambridge: Cambridge University Press.

May, Elaine Tyler. 1988. *Homeward Bound: American Families in the Cold War Era.* New York: Basic Books.

Meek, Barbra A. 2014. "'She Can Do It in English Too': Acts of Intimacy and Boundary-Making in Language Revitalization." *Language & Communication* 38: 73–82.

Meiseles, Andrea. 2017. "'I Say Aggressive, You Say Assertive': The Intercultural Experiences of Israeli Shlichim at American Jewish Summer Camp." PhD diss., Jewish Theological Seminary of America. New York.

Melzer, Asher O. 1971. "The Utilization of Israelis as Counselors and Specialists in American Jewish Summer Camps." Jewish Community Center Program Aids. New York: JCCA.

———. 1993. "Reflections on Fifty Years of Work in Jewish Camping—A Labor of Love." *Jewish Education* 60.

Meyer, Michael. 1995. *Response to Modernity: A History of the Reform Movement in Judaism.* Detroit: Wayne State University Press.

Milroy, James, and Lesley Milroy. 1985. *Authority in Language: Investigating Language Prescription and Standardisation.* New York: Routledge.

Mintz, Alan. 1991. "The Erosion of the Tarbut Ivrit Ideology in America and the Consequences for the Teaching of Hebrew in the University." *Shofar* 9, no. 3: 50–54.

———, ed. 1993. *Hebrew in America: Perspectives and Prospects.* Detroit: Wayne State University Press.

———. 1993. "A Sanctuary in the Wilderness: The Beginnings of the Hebrew Movement in America in *Hatoren*." In *Hebrew in America: Perspectives and Prospects*, 29–67. Detroit: Wayne State University Press.

———. 2002. "Tarbut Ivrit in America: Act II." In *Essays on Hebrew Literature in Honor of Avraham Holtz*, edited by Zvia Ben Yosef Ginor, 177–183. New York: Jewish Theological Seminary. [Hebrew]

———. 2012. *Sanctuary in the Wilderness: A Critical Introduction to American Hebrew Poetry.* Stanford: Stanford University Press.

Mittelberg, David. 2011. "Jewish Peoplehood Education." In *International Handbook of Jewish Education*, edited by Helena Miller et al., 515–539. New York: Springer.

Moore, Deborah Dash. 1994. *To the Golden Cities: Pursuing the American Jewish Dream in Miami and L.A.* New York: Free Press.

Moore, Leslie C. 2004. "Learning Languages by Heart: Language Socialization in a Fulbe Community (Maroua, Cameroon)." PhD diss., University of California Los Angeles.

———. 2011. "Language Socialization and Repetition." In *The Handbook of Language Socialization*, edited by Alessandro Duranti, Elinor Ochs, and Bambi B. Schieffelin, 209–226. Malden, MA: Wiley-Blackwell.

Muchnik, Malka. 2014. *The Gender Challenge of Hebrew.* Leiden: Brill.

Murphey, Tim. 1992. "The Discourse of Pop Songs." *Tesol Quarterly* 26, no. 4: 770–774.

Muysken, Pieter. 1981. "Halfway between Quechua and Spanish: The Case for Relexification." In *Historicity and Variation in Creole Studies*, edited by Arnold Highfield and Albert Valdman, 52–78. Ann Arbor: Karoma.

———. 1990. "Concepts, Methodology and Data in Language Contact Research." *Papers for the Workshop on Concept, Methodology and Data. Network on Code-Switching and Language Contact, Basel, January 12–13.* Strasbourg: European Science Foundation.

———. 2000. *Bilingual Speech. A Typology of Code-Mixing*. Cambridge: Cambridge University Press.

Myers-Scotton, Carol. 1993. *Social Motivations for Codeswitching: Evidence from Africa*. Oxford: Clarendon Press.

———. 2002. *Contact Linguistics*. Oxford: Oxford University Press.

Mykoff, Nancy. 2002. "A Jewish Season: Ethnic-American Culture at Children's Summer Camp." PhD diss., New York University.

Novak, William. 1972. "Notes on Summer Camps: Some Reflections on the Ramah Dream." *Response: A Contemporary Jewish Review* 12 (Winter, 1971–1972): 58–63.

Ochs, Elinor. 1992. "Indexing Gender." In *Rethinking Context: Language as an Interactive Phenomenon*, edited by Alessandro Duranti and Charles Goodwin, 335–358. Cambridge: Cambridge University Press.

———. 2003. "Becoming a Speaker of Culture." In *Language Acquisition and Language Socialization*, edited by Claire Kramsch, 99–120. London: Continuum.

Ochs, Elinor, and Bambi B. Schieffelin. 1984. "Language Acquisition and Socialization: Three Developmental Stories and Their Implications." In *Culture Theory: Essays on Mind, Self, and Emotion*, edited by Richard A. Shweder and Robert A. LeVine, 276–320. Cambridge: Cambridge University Press.

———. 2011. "The Theory of Language Socialization." In *The Handbook of Language Socialization*, edited by Alessandro Duranti, Elinor Ochs, and Bambi B. Schieffelin, 1–21. Malden, MA: Wiley-Blackwell.

Omoniyi, Tope, and Joshua A. Fishman, eds. 2006. *Explorations in the Sociology of Language and Religion*. Amsterdam: John Benjamins.

Otheguy, Ricardo, Ofelia García, and Wallis Reid. 2015. "Clarifying Translanguaging and Deconstructing Named Languages: A Perspective from Linguistics." *Applied Linguistics Review* 6, no. 3: 281–307.

Paris, Leslie. 2002. "A Home though Away from Home: Brooklyn Jews and Interwar Children's Summer Camps." In *Jews of Brooklyn,* edited by Ilana Abramovitch and Sean Galvin, 236–263. Hanover, NH: Brandeis University Press.

———. 2008. *Children's Nature: The Rise of American Summer Camps*. New York: New York University Press.

Pelli, Moshe. 1995. "Ideology and Reality: The American Hebrew Movement in its Inception—In Search of Identity." *Hebrew Studies* 36: 73–85.

———. 1998. *Hebrew Culture in America: 80 Years of Hebrew Culture in the United States*. Tel Aviv: Reshafim. [Hebrew]

Perkins, David, and Gavriel Salomon. 1988. "Teaching Transfer." *Educational Leadership* 46, no. 1: 22–32.

———. 1992. "Transfer of Learning." In *International Encyclopedia of Education*, 2nd ed., 6452–6457. Oxford: Pergamon Press.

Philologos (Hillel Halkin). 2006. "Camp Massad." *The Forward*, September 8. https://forward.com/articles/2417/camp-massad/.

Pianko, Noam. 2010. *Zionism & the Roads Not Taken*. Bloomington: Indiana University Press.

———. 2015. *Jewish Peoplehood: An American Innovation*. New Brunswick: Rutgers University Press.

Piller, Ingrid. 2001. "Identity Constructions in Multilingual Advertising." *Language in Society* 30, no. 2: 153–186.

Pomson, Alex, and Jack Wertheimer. 2017. *Hebrew for What? Hebrew at the Heart of Jewish Day Schools*. March. New York: Avi Chai Foundation. http://avichai.org /knowledge_base/hebrew-for-what-hebrew-at-the-heart-of-jewish-day-schools/.

Poplack, Shana, and David Sankoff. 1984. "Borrowing: The Synchrony of Integration." *Linguistics* 22, no. 1: 99–136.

Poplack, Shana, David Sankoff, and Christopher Miller. 1988. "The Social Correlates and Linguistic Processes of Lexical Borrowing and Assimilation." *Linguistics* 26, no. 1: 47–104.

Posen, Ira Sheldon. 1957. "Song and Singing Traditions in Children's Summer Camps." PhD diss., Memorial University of Newfoundland, Canada.

———. 1993. "*Lomir Zingn, Hava Nashira* (Let Us Sing): An Introduction to Jewish Summer Camp Song." In *A Worthy Use of Summer: Jewish Summer Camping in America*, edited by Jenna Joselit and Karen Mittleman, 29–36. Philadelphia: National Museum of American Jewish History.

Postman, Neil. 2006. *Amusing Ourselves to Death: Public Discourse in the Age of Show Business*. New York: Penguin

Potok, Chaim. 1993. "Introduction." In *A Worthy Use of Summer: Jewish Summer Camping in America*, edited by Jenna Joselit and Karen Mittleman, 7–8. Philadelphia: National Museum of American Jewish History.

Prell, Riv-Ellen. 2007. "Summer Camp, Postwar American Jewish Youth and the Redemption of Judaism." *Jewish Role in American Life: An Annual Review* 5: 77–108.

———. 2009. "Jewish Summer Camping and Civil Rights: How Summer Camps Launched a Transformation in American Jewish Culture." Lecture, Frankel Center, University of Michigan. http://www.bjpa.org/Publications/details.cfm?PublicationID =6800.

Putnam, Robert D. 2001. *Bowling Alone: The Collapse and Revival of American Community*. New York: Simon & Schuster.

Raider, Mark. 1998. *The Emergence of American Zionism*. New York: New York University Press.

Rampton, Ben. 1995. *Crossing: Language and Ethnicity among Adolescents*. London: Longman.

Ravid, Dorit, and Shoshana Zilberbuch. 2003. "Morphosyntactic Constructs in the Development of Spoken and Written Hebrew Text Production." *Journal of Child Language* 30, no. 2: 395–418.

Reershemius, Gertrud K., Leonie Gaiser, and Yaron Matras. 2018. "Multilingual Repertoire Management and Illocutionary Functions in Yiddish Signage in Manchester." *Journal of Pragmatics* 135: 53–70.

Reimer, Joseph. 1989. "Changing Educational Strategies at Ramah." In *The Ramah Experience: Community and Commitment*, edited by Sylvia Ettenberg and Geraldine Rosenfield, 57–62. New York: Jewish Theological Seminary of America.

———. 2007. "Beyond More Jews Doing Jewish: Clarifying the Goals of Informal Jewish Education." *Journal of Jewish Education* 73, no. 1: 5–23.

———. 2012. "Providing Optimal Jewish Experiences: The Case of Camp Ramah in Wisconsin." *Journal of Jewish Education* 78, no. 2: 114–134.

———. 2018. "Shabbat-at-Camp at Three Jewish Camps: Jewish Learning through Ritual Participation." *Journal of Jewish Education* 84: 359–388.

Ribalow, Harold. 1946. "The Significance of Camp Massad." *Hebrew World* 3, no. 1: 13.

Richard-Amato, Patricia A. 1995. *Making It Happen: Interaction in the Second Language Classroom, From Theory to Practice*, 2nd ed. New York: Pearson.

Romaine, Suzanne. 1995. *Bilingualism*. New York: Wiley-Blackwell.

Rosten, Leo. 1968. *The Joys of Yiddish*. New York: McGraw-Hill.

Rothenberg, Celia E. 2016. *Serious Fun at a Jewish Community Summer Camp: Family, Judaism, and Israel*. London: Lexington Books.

Rudavsky, David. 2006. "The Bureau of Jewish Education after 1918." *Journal of Jewish Education* 20, no. 3: 38–52.

Sales, Amy L., Nicole Samuels, and Matthew Boxer. 2011. Limud by the Lake *Revisited: Growth and Change at Jewish Summer Camp*. New York: Avi Chai Foundation.

Sales, Amy L., and Leonard Saxe. 2002. *Limud by the Lake: Fulfilling the Educational Potential of Jewish Summer Camps*. New York: Avi Chai Foundation.

———. 2003. *How Goodly Are Thy Tents: Summer Camps as Jewish Socializing Experiences*. Waltham, MA: Brandeis University Press/UPNE.

———. 2008. "Summer Camps as Jewish Socializing Experiences." In *What We Now Know about Jewish Education: Perspectives on Research for Practice*, edited by Roberta Louis Goodman, Paul A. Flexner, and Linda Dale Bloomberg, 407–416. Los Angeles: Torah Aura Productions.

Sales, Ben. 2018. "This College Student Created a Way for Nonbinary People to Speak Hebrew." *Jewish Telegraphic Agency*, November 19. https://www.jta.org/2018/11/19 /united-states/college-student-created-way-transgender-people-speak-hebrew.

Sallabank, Julia. 2011. "Language Policy for Endangered Languages." In *Cambridge Handbook of Endangered Languages,* edited by Peter K. Austin and Julia Sallabank, 277–290. Cambridge: Cambridge University Press.

———. 2013. *Attitudes to Endangered Languages: Identities and Policies*. Cambridge: Cambridge University Press.

Samama, Leo. 2012. "Choral Music and Tradition in Europe and Israel." In *Cambridge Companion to Choral Music*, edited by Andres de Quadros, 79–103. Cambridge: Cambridge University Press.

Sarna, Jonathan. 2006. "The Crucial Decade in Jewish Camping." In *A Place of Our Own: The Rise of Reform Jewish Camping*, edited by Michael Lorge and Gary Zola, 27–51. Tuscaloosa: University of Alabama Press.

———. 2019. *American Judaism: A History*, 2nd ed. New Haven: Yale University Press.

Schachet-Briskin, Wally. 1996. "The Music of Reform Youth." Master's thesis, Hebrew Union College-Jewish Institute of Religion School of Sacred Music. http://cantorwally .weebly.com/masters-thesis.html.

Schanin, Norman. 2000. *In the Service of My People: Reflections of a Jewish Educator*. Jerusalem: Gefen.

Schieffelin, Bambi, and Elinor Ochs. 1986. *Language Socialization across Cultures*. Cambridge: Cambridge University Press.

Schoenfeld, Stuart. 1987. "Folk Judaism, Elite Judaism and the Role of Bar Mitzvah in the Development of the Synagogue and Jewish School in America." *Contemporary Jewry* 9, no. 1: 67–85.

Schunk, Heather A. 1999. "The Effect of Singing Paired with Signing on Receptive Vocabulary Skills of Elementary ESL Students." *Journal of Music Therapy* 36, no. 2: 110–124.

Schwartz, Shuly. 1984. "Ramah Philosophy and the Newman Revolution." In *Studies in Jewish Education and Judaica in Honor of Louis Newman,* edited by Alexander M. Shapiro and Burton M. Cohen, 7–21. New York: Ktav.

———. 1987. "Camp Ramah: The Early Years, 1947–1952." *Conservative Judaism* 40: 12–42.

Schwartz, Sidney. 1984. "Conservative Judaism's 'Ideology' Problem." *American Jewish History* 74: 143–157.

Schwarzwald, Ora (Rodrigue). 2009. "Hebrew Morphological Developments." In *Two Hundred Fifty Years of Modern Hebrew,* edited by Chaim E. Cohen, 177–209. Jerusalem: Hebrew Language Academy. [Hebrew]

Scollon, Ron, and Suzie Wong Scollon. 2003. *Discourses in Place: Language in the Material World.* New York: Routledge.

Scott, James C. 1990. *Domination and the Arts of Resistance: Hidden Transcripts.* New Haven: Yale University Press.

Seidman, Naomi. 1997. *A Marriage Made in Heaven: The Sexual Politics of Hebrew and Yiddish.* Berkeley: University of California Press.

———. 2006. *Faithful Renderings: Jewish-Christian Difference and the Politics of Translation.* Chicago: University of Chicago Press.

Shandler, Jeffrey. 2006. *Adventures in Yiddishland: Postvernacular Language and Culture.* Berkeley: University of California Press.

———. 2014. *Shtetl: A Vernacular Intellectual History.* New Brunswick, NJ: Rutgers University Press.

Shapiro-Rosenberg, Alisa. 2017. "What the Avi Chai Hebrew Report Tells Us (and What It Doesn't)." *Cmovan blog.* http://cmovan.edublogs.org/2017/04/14/what-the-avi-chai -hebrew-report-tells-us-and-what-it-doesnt/.

Shell, Marc. 1993. *Children of the Earth: Literature, Politics and Nationhood.* New York: Oxford University Press.

Shohamy, Elana. 1999. "Contextual and Pedagogical Factors for Learning and Maintaining Jewish Languages in the United States." *Journal of Jewish Education* 65, no. 3: 21–29.

———. 2008. "At What Cost? Methods of Language Revival and Protection: Examples from Hebrew." In *Sustaining Linguistic Diversity: Endangered and Minority Languages and Language Varieties,* edited by Kendall A. King, 205–218. Washington, DC: Georgetown University Press.

Shohamy, Elana, and Durk Gorter, eds. 2009. *Linguistic Landscape: Expanding the Scenery.* New York: Routledge.

Shoshuk, Levi. 1960. "The Ramah Camps." *The Synagogue School* 18, no. 3.

Shulsinger, Rivka. 1978. "The Israeli Delegation to Jewish Camps in the United States." In *Kovetz Massad,* Vol. 1, edited by Meir Havatzelet and Shlomo Kornblum, 289–299. New York: Massad Camps. [Hebrew]

Shulsinger, Shlomo. 1946. "Hebrew Camping: Five Years of Massad." *Journal of Jewish Education* 17, no. 3: 16–23.

———. 1950. *Hebrew Camping in the United States: Ten Years of the Massad Camps.* New York: Histadruth Ivrith of America.

———. 1967. "Hebrew Camping: The Creator of a Hebrew World." *Journal of Jewish Education* 37: 6–17.

———. 1982. "Memoirs of a Hebrew Educator." *Journal of Jewish Education* 50: 50–54.

————. 1989. "The Israeli Delegation to Massad." In *Kovetz Massad*. Vol. 2, *Hebrew Camping in America*, edited by Shlomo Shulsinger and Rivka Shulsinger, 244–245. Jerusalem: Alumni of Massad Camps. [Hebrew]

————. 1996. "Massad Memoirs: How It All Began." *Massad Reminiscences*, 10. Jerusalem: Abraham Harman Institute for Contemporary Jewry at Hebrew University.

Silverman, Jerry. 2011. *Songs that Made History around the World*. St. Louis: Mel Bay Productions.

Silverstein, Michael. 2003. "Indexical Order and the Dialectics of Sociolinguistic Life." *Language and Communication* 23: 193–229.

Silverstone, Roger. 2003. *Television and Everyday Life*. London: Routledge.

Sinclair, Alex. 2014. "The Complexity of 'Complexity' in Jewish Education." *eJewish Philanthropy*, May 11.

Sklare, Marshall. 1968. "Lakeville and Israel: The Six Day War and Its Aftermath." *Midstream* (October 1968): 2–19.

Spiegel, Nina. 2013. *Embodying Hebrew Culture: Aesthetics, Athletics, and Dance in the Jewish Community of Mandate Palestine*. Detroit: Wayne State University Press.

Spiegel, Shalom. 1930. *Hebrew Reborn*. New York: MacMillan.

Spolsky, Bernard. 2004. *Language Policy*. Cambridge: Cambridge University Press.

————. 2013. "Revernacularization and Revitalization of the Hebrew Language." *The Encyclopedia of Applied Linguistics*. New York: John Wiley.

Spolsky, Bernard, and Elana Shohamy. 1999. *The Languages of Israel: Policy, Ideology and Practice*. Clevedon: Multilingual Matters.

Stavans, Ilan. 2006. "O Rosten! My Rosten!" *Der Pakn Treger* 52: 16–23.

Stein, Sarah Abrevaya. 2003. *Making Jews Modern: The Yiddish and Ladino Press in the Russian and Ottoman Empires*. Bloomington: Indiana University Press.

Steinmetz, Sol. 1981. "Jewish English in the United States." *American Speech* 56, no. 1: 3–16.

————. 1986. *Yiddish and English: A Century of Yiddish in America*. Tuscaloosa: University of Alabama Press.

Stern, Miriam Heller. 2007. "'Your Children—Will They Be Yours?' Educational Strategies for Jewish Survival, the Central Jewish Institute, 1916–1944," PhD diss., Stanford University.

Stiebel, Mayer. 1952. "Camp Ramah Uses Hebrew in Every Activity on the Camp Schedule." *Chicago Jewish Sentinel*, July 3.

Stolow, Jeremy. 2010. *Orthodox by Design: Judaism, Print Politics, and the ArtScroll Revolution*. Berkeley: University of California Press.

Strigler, Mordechai. 1963. "Points of Light: A Visit to the Massad Camps in the United States." *HaDoar, Massad Supplement* (Tishrei). Reprinted in *Kovetz Massad*. Vol. 2, *Hebrew Camping in America*, edited by Shlomo Shulsinger and Rivka Shulsinger, 97–101. Jerusalem: Alumni of Massad Camps. [Hebrew]

Tavory, Iddo. 2016. *Summoned: Identification and Religious Life in a Jewish Neighborhood*. Chicago: University of Chicago Press.

Thomason, Sarah G. 2001. *Language Contact. An Introduction*. Edinburgh: Edinburgh University Press.

Thomason, Sarah G., and Terrence Kaufman. 1988. *Language Contact, Creolization, and Genetic Linguistics*. Berkeley: University of California Press.

Tuan, Yi-Fu. 1977. *Space and Place: The Perspective of Experience.* Minneapolis: University of Minnesota Press.

Unseth, Peter. 2005. "Sociolinguistic Parallels between Choosing Scripts and Languages." *Written Language & Literacy* 8, no. 1: 19–42.

———. 2008. "The Sociolinguistics of Script Choice: An Introduction." *International Journal of the Sociology of Language* 192: 1–4.

Vanderbilt, Tom. 1993. "The Nostalgia Gap." *The Baffler* 5. https://thebaffler.com/salvos/the-nostalgia-gap.

Van Leeuwen, Theo. 2005. *Introducing Social Semiotics.* New York: Psychology Press.

Van Slyck, Abigail A. 2006. *A Manufactured Wilderness: Summer Camps and the Shaping of American Youth, 1890–1960.* Minneapolis: University of Minnesota Press.

Vygotsky, Lev Semyonovich. 1978. *Mind in Society.* Cambridge, MA: Harvard University Press.

Watson-Gegeo, Karen A., and Gegeo, David W. 1986. "Calling-Out and Repeating Routines in Kwara'ae Children's Language Socialization." In *Language Socialization across Cultures*, edited by Bambi B. Schieffelin and Elinor Ochs, 17–50. Cambridge: Cambridge University Press.

Wei, Li. 2017. "Translanguaging as a Practical Theory of Language." *Applied Linguistics* 39, no. 1: 9–30.

Weinreich, Max. 2008 [1973]. *History of the Yiddish Language.* New Haven: Yale University Press.

Weinreich, Uriel. 1953. *Languages in Contact.* The Hague: Mouton.

———. 1956. "Notes on the Yiddish Rise-Fall Intonation Contour." In *For Roman Jakobson*, edited by Morris Halle, 633–643. The Hague: Mouton.

Weiser, Chaim. 1995. *Frumspeak: The First Dictionary of Yeshivish.* Northvale, NJ: Jason Aronson.

Wenger, Etienne. 1998. *Communities of Practice: Learning, Meaning, and Identity.* Cambridge: Cambridge University Press.

Wertheimer, Jack. 2007. "The Perplexities of Conservative Judaism." *Commentary*, September 1. https://www.commentarymagazine.com/articles/the-perplexities-of-conservative-judaism/.

Wildstein, Tristin J. 2016. "Missions, Methods, and Assessment in Hebrew Language Education: Case Studies of American Jewish Day Schools." PhD diss., New York University.

Wilson, Janelle L. 2005. *Nostalgia: Sanctuary of Meaning.* Lewisburg, PA: Bucknell University Press.

Winford, Donald. 2003. *An Introduction to Contact Linguistics.* Oxford: Blackwell.

———. 2010. "Contact and Borrowing." In *The Handbook of Language Contact*, edited by Raymond Hickey, 170–187. Hoboken, NJ: John Wiley & Sons.

Woocher, Jonathan. 1986. *Sacred Survival: The Civil Religion of American Jews.* Bloomington: Indiana University Press.

Woolard, Kathryn A. 1999. "Simultaneity and Bivalency as Strategies in Bilingualism." *Journal of Linguistic Anthropology* 8, no. 1: 3–29.

———. 2016. *Singular and Plural: Ideologies of Linguistic Authority in 21st Century Catalonia.* New York: Oxford University Press.

Wortham, Stanton E. F. 2005. "Socialization beyond the Speech Event." *Journal of Linguistic Anthropology* 15: 95–112.

Wright, Andrew, David Betteridge, and Michael Buckby. 1983. *Games for Language Learning*. Cambridge: Cambridge University Press.

Wyman, Leisy T. 2012. *Youth Culture, Language Endangerment and Linguistic Survivance*. Bristol: Multilingual Matters.

Yelenevskaya, Maria, and Larisa Fialkova. 2017. "Linguistic Landscape and What It Tells Us about the Integration of the Russian Language into the Israeli Economy." *Вестник Российского университета дружбы народов. Серия: Лингвистика* 21, no. 3: 557–586.

Young, Vershawn Ashanti. 2009. "'Nah, We Straight': An Argument against Code Switching." *JAC: A Journal of Rhetoric, Culture, and Politics* 29, no. 1–2: 49–76.

Young, Vershawn Ashanti, Rusty Barrett, and Kim Brian Lovejoy. 2013. *Other People's English: Code-Meshing, Code-Switching, and African American Literacy*. New York: Teachers College Press.

Young, Vershawn Ashanti, and Aja Y. Martinez, eds. 2011. *Code-Meshing as World English: Pedagogy, Policy, Performance*. Urbana, IL: National Council of Teachers of English.

Zakai, Sivan. 2015. "'Israel Is Meant for Me': Kindergarteners' Conceptions of Israel." *Journal of Jewish Education* 81: 4–34.

Zipperstein, Steven. 1999. *Imagining Russian Jewry: Memory, History, Identity*. Seattle: University of Washington Press.

Zuckermann, Ghil'ad. 2003. *Language Contact and Lexical Enrichment in Israeli Hebrew*. London: Palgrave Macmillan.

———. 2006. "A New Vision for 'Israeli Hebrew': Theoretical and Practical Implications of Analyzing Israel's Main Language as a Semi-Engineered Semito-European Hybrid Language." *Journal of Modern Jewish Studies* 5: 57–71.

# Index

Page references in italics refer to illustrative matter.

Abrams, Jerome, 106–107, 266n21
Abrams, Leah, 98–99, 266n21
Abramson, Robert, 93, 106, 108
Ackerman, Walter, 88
acronyms, 243–244
AIJC. *See* Association of Independent
　Jewish Camps (AIJC)
alienation, 230–232
*aliyah,* 40, 76–77, 113, 115, 259n30
Alpert, Sam "Shmulik," 36
Alster-Yardeni, David, 66, 67, 68
Altman, Shalom, 24
Americamp, 122
American Association for Jewish
　Education, 29
American Camping Association, 6
American Jewish summer camps. *See*
　Jewish summer camping
*American Jewish Year Book,* 88
Amharic language, 207
announcements: in English, 27, 107, 115; in
　Hebrew and CHE, 50, 108–110, 116–119,
　128–130, 157–159, 161, 168–169, 227–229.
　*See also* Hebrew language
Arabic language, 73, 115, 117, 118, 184, 207,
　212, 216
Arabs, 66, 73, 105, 199, 210
Aramaic language, 9, 146, 216
Areivim Philanthropic Group, 250, 274n2
Arian, Merri Lovinger, 44, 46
Arian, Philip "Shraga," 102
Arzt, Raphael "Ray," 82–83, 104, 105, 106,
　254, 267n57

Ashkenazi Hebrew, 32, 43, 45, 123–125, 206,
　235–237, 247. *See also* Hebrew language
Association of Independent Jewish Camps
　(AIJC), 10, 119, 127, 268n8, 272n22
authenticity, 15, 73–74, 199, 202–214,
　238–244
Avineri, Netta, 4
Avni, Sharon, 12

banal nationalism, 208
baseball, 61, 63–64, 76, 91, 92, 93, 96,
　106, 202
Beber Camp, 113, 119–123, 126, 134, 136, 148,
　165, 186
Bekerman, Zvi, 106, 108
Ben-Ari, Moshe, 43
Benderly, Samson, 21, 56
Bengali language, 217–218
Benor, Sarah Bunin, 11–12
Ben-Yehuda, Eliezer, 37, 138
Berkowitz, Margie, 109
Berkson, Isaac and Libbie, 22
Bernstein, David, 68
Bernstein, Louis, 71, 82–83
Betar camp, 23, 24, 54
Bettelheim, Bruno, 267n59
Bialik, Chaim Nachman, 58, 66, 68, 75;
　"Techezakna," 58, *59,* 75, 263n38
biblical Hebrew, 137, 235, 238. *See also*
　Hebrew language
bilingual signage, 86–87, 114, 115, 177–183,
　189–190. *See also* linguistic hybridity;
　signage

bilingual wordplay, 150–152, 239. *See also* camp Hebraized English (CHE)

Birthright Israel, 249

bivalency, 178, 194, 271n13

Bloom, Jack, 62–63, 73

Blue Star camp, 22, 44

Blumenfield, Samuel, 51

B'nai B'rith / BBYO (B'nai B'rith Youth Organization), 10, 119, 272n22

Bnei Akiva camp network, 74, 231; Hebrew practices of, 113, 127, 128–130, 138, 152, 160, 237; on Israel connection, 138; Mizrachi, 23; Moshava Indian Orchard (IO), 74, 137, 156, 177–178, 186–187, 191, 207, 221, 227, 232, 243–244; Moshava Malibu (Alevy), 11, 53, 113, 134, 230, 232, 243; origin of, 23; rituals at, 74, 152; signage at, 173, 177–178; Stone, 130. *See also* Zionist camp network

Bogot, Howard, 33

Brandeis Camp Institute, 26. *See also* Camp Alonim

Bringing Israel to Camp Workshop, 207–214

Bureau of Jewish Education, Los Angeles, CA, 32

Bureau of Jewish Education, New York, NY, 21, 56. *See also* Jewish Education Committee, New York, NY

Camp Achvah, 56–57, 263n25

Camp Alonim, 133, 147, 150, *193*, 206–207, 240

Camp Avodah, 32, 34

Camp Bechol Lashon, 137, 152, 229

Camp Boiberik, 79

Camp Che-Na-Wah, 20

Camp Coleman. *See* URJ camp network

Camp Daisy and Harry Stein, 183, 184, 272n22

Camp Emunah, 8, 271n13

Camp Galil. *See* Habonim Dror camp network

Camp Gesher (Russian-American), 8, 137

Camp Gilboa. *See* Habonim Dror camp network

Camp Harlam. *See* URJ camp network

Camp Havaya. *See* Camp JRF

camp Hebraized English (CHE), 1–2, 249–251; acronyms and, 243–244; bilingual wordplay, 150–152; camp announcements in, 50, 108–110, 116–119, 128–130, 157–159, 161, 168–169, 227–229; camp music in, 33–34, 46–49, 116–117;

154–157; camp rationale for using, 131–140, 219–224; dictionaries of, 23, 63, 64, *65*, 91–92, 187, 202; ethnic revival through, 28–30; gendered language and, 244–246; informal teaching of, 165–167; inter-camp diversity of, 126–128; intra-camp diversity of, 128–131; Israeli emissaries and, 198–214, 242–243; Jewish cultural programming at, 38–41; language contact and, 144–147; loanwords in, 24, 39, 48, 74, 133, 136, 145–146, 159–162; Lovitt on learning, 1; Novak on, 107; at Ramah, 85–94; translanguaging and, 15, 86, 144–146, 218, 226; translation and language exposure through, 167–170, 234–235; type of Hebrew for, 235–238; Union Institute's use of, 30–34; word lists of, *64, 65*, 185, *186*, 192, 215, 221, 226; word-of-the-day skits, 115, 120–121, 147–150, 168, 204; as wordplay, 150–152, 239, 270n23. *See also* Hebrew language; signage

Camp Hess Kramer. *See* Wilshire Boulevard Camps

Camp Institutes for Living Judaism. *See* URJ camp network

Camp Jacobs. *See* URJ camp network

Camp JCA Shalom, 180

Camp JRF (Havaya), 11, 127, 184

Camp Kalsman. *See* URJ camp network

Camp Kawanga, 20

Camp Keeyumah, 263n29

Camp Kennebec, 20

Camp Kinder Ring, 8

Camp Kinderwelt, 79

Camp Kinneret and Biluim, 272n22

Camp Lavi, 132, 178, *179*, 209

Camp Massad. *See* Massad Poconos camp network

Camp Modin, 21, 22, 186, 259n13

Camp Morasha, 77

Camp Newman. *See* URJ camp network

Camp Perlman, 165, 272n22

Camp Raleigh, 12, 80

Camp Ramah. *See* Ramah camp network

Camp Saratoga, 30, 43. *See also* URJ camp network

Camp Seneca Lake, 272n22

Camp Sharon, 21, 24, 34

Camp Shomria. *See* Hashomer Hatzair camp network

Camp Solomon Schechter, 11, 153–154, 166, 171, 195, 212, 219, 240, 241–242

Camp Sprout Lake. *See* Young Judaea camp network
Camp Sternberg, 10, 113, 123–126
Camp Stone. *See* Bnei Akiva camp network
Camp Tavor. *See* Habonim Dror camp network
Camp Tevya, 272n22
Camp Wise, 20
Camp Yavneh, 21, 23, 24, 35, 45, 63, 68, 81, 92, 96, 109–110, 127, 137, 158, 160, 186–187, 201, 202, 206, 221, 226, 230, 266n25
Camp Young Judaea. *See* Young Judaea camp network
Canada, 5, 13, 27, 77, 102, 218, 262n1
Canadian Young Judaea camp network, *129*
Capital Camps, 207
Cedar, Tzippy Krieger, 67
Cejwin Camps, 19, 21–22, 57, 59, 70, 258n7
Central Jewish Institute Camp. *See* Cejwin Camps
Chabad, 10, 138, 271n10, 271n13. *See also* Camp Emunah; Lubavitch
*chadar ochel*, as term, 16, 23, 27, 38, 113, 114, *181*, 202, 225, 272n20. *See also* camp Hebraized English (CHE)
Chalutzim Hebrew immersion program, 34–38, 137, 260n62, 265n93; competitions at, 163–164; Hebrew language at, 130, 132, 148, 158, 162–163, 225, 226, 231, 234, 239; Israeli emissaries at, 200–201; writing at, 190. *See also* Olin-Sang-Ruby Union Institute
*chalutziut*, 26–27, 30
Chassidic Song Festival, 45, 78
CHE. *See* camp Hebraized English (CHE)
Chicago College of Jewish Studies, 21
*Chicago Jewish Sentinel*, 85
Chickasaw Indians, 270n4
Chinese language, 117, 174, 217–218
choral groups, 68, *69*. *See also* music
code switching, 48, 95, 145, 160, 217, 269nn11–12. *See also* camp Hebraized English (CHE); loanwords, Hebrew; translanguaging
Cohen, Burton, 94
Cohen, Judah, 45, 262n104
Colodner, Ileane "Chaya" Altman, 63
color war. *See maccabiah*
*Commentary Magazine*, 86
Committee on Jewish Law and Standards, 85
communal singing. *See* music

connection, 3, 7–9, 213, 224, 231–232, 248–251
Conservative movement. *See* Ramah camp network
Cook, Julian, 259n39
cowboy, as character, 122, 268n7
culture camp model, 21–22, 38–41, 134

Daber program, 164, 225, 232
Davis, Moshe, 24, 53–55, 57–58, 70, 71, 77, 82, 84, 89, 91, 92. *See also* Ramah camp network
day camps, 6, 11, 13, 58, 250
Debbie Friedman School of Sacred Music, Hebrew Union College-Jewish Institute of Religion, New York, NY, 44
decorative plaques, 179–180. *See also* signage
denominations, 52, 72, 77, 194
Dershowitz, Zvi, 27
Dewey, John, 97, 267n57
dictionaries, 23, 63, 64, *65*, 91–92, 187, 202
directional signposts, 120, 182–183. *See also* linguistic landscape
displaced nostalgia. *See* nostalgia
Dolgin, Etty, 38
Dorff, Elliot, 104
dramatic arts, 66–70. *See also* theatrical productions
Dulin, Rachel Zohar, 36–37
Dushkin, Alexander, 22, 58, 263n34
Dushkin, Julia, 22
Dworkin, Moshe, 27

Eden Village Camp, 12, 137, 150, 165, 235–236, 273n14
Eidelman, Arleen Pilzer, 79–80
Einstein, Arik, 43
Eisentein, Ike, 40
Eisner Camp. *See* URJ camp network
Elazar, Daniel, 88
Elem Pomo Indian communities, 5, 270n30
Elstein, Arthur, 91–92
emissaries, Israeli, 10, 15, 30, 44, 45, 80, 101, 105, 120–122, 127, 131, 139, 147, 163, 166, 169, 170, 184, 191, 198–214, 237, 242–243
endangered languages, 5, 174–175, 218, 272n1, 273n22
English language, 5, 27, 107, 115, 167, 198. *See also* camp Hebraized English (CHE); Orthodox Jewish English
Erikson, Erik, 29

Ettenberg, Sylvia Cutler, 24, 57, 70–72, 82, 83, 89, 91, 92. *See also* Ramah camp network
Eurovision Song Contest, 78, 198, 271nn1–2
exchange programs, 39

Farband, 20
Fermaglich, Kirsten, 28
Finkelstein, Louis, 82, 89
FJC. *See* Foundation for Jewish Camp
flags, 82, 89, 115, 148
flexible bilingualism, 217–218
flexible signifier, Hebrew as a, 113 (defined), 126, *140*, 141, 159, 244, 268n1
folk music. *See* music
Foundation for Jewish Camp (FJC), 6, 10, 147, 170, 188
Fox, Seymour, 89, 101, 103–104, 267n57, 267n59
Freedman, Morris, 86–87
Freelander, Daniel, 46, 48
Freidenreich, Fradle Pomp, 34
Friedman, Debbie, 46–49, 262n104
Frost, Shimon, 52, 58, 78

games, 39, 123, 163–165
Gamoran, Hillel, 37, 44, 201
Gannes, Abraham, 263n29
Gaza conflict (2014), 211–213
Geffen, Rela Mintz, 88
gender and Hebrew language, 119, 125, 244–247; grammatical gender, 101
glossaries. *See* dictionaries
Goldberg, Henry, 84, 91, 94
Goldin, Judah, 89, 93
Goldman Union Camp Institute (GUCI). *See* URJ camp network
Goodman Camping Initiative, 10, 184, 207–208
Gordon, A. D., 54
Gordonia movement, 23, 53, 262n10, 263n38. *See also* Zionist camp network
Goren, Arthur, 26
Greek language, 216
Green, Arthur, 105
Greenberg, Moshe, 266n21
Greenberg, Simon, 102

Habonim Dror camp network: Camp Galil, 113, 114–119, 123, 128, 130, 186, 206, 219, 232, 234, 244, 245; Camp Gilboa, 11, 131, 134, 150, 153, 154, 169, 185, *193*, 212, 226, 234, 245, 258n31; Camp Miriam, 162;

Camp Moshava, 53, 262n10; Camp Tavor, 187, 246, 271n18, 272n22; Hebrew practices of, 222; as *kvutzot,* 22; origin of, 23; resolution on gendered language, 245–247. *See also* Gordonia movement; Labor Zionist organizations; Zionist camp network
*hachshara,* 24, 53
Halkin, Hillel, 61, 63–64
Hanoar Haivri. *See Histadrut Hanoar Haivri* (Hebrew Youth Cultural Federation)
Haredi communities, 113, 176, 236
Hashomer Hatzair camp network, 11, 22–24, 54, 128–129; Shomria, 137, 185–186, 271n13
Hasidic communities, 8, 176
*havdalah,* 38, 75, 116–117, 119, 120, 122, 150, 186, 235, 240
*havurah* movement, 28, 104–105
Havurat Shalom, 105
Hawaiian language, 274n4
Hebrew language: alienation and, 230–231; Ashkenazi Hebrew, 32, 43, 45, 123–125, 206, 235–237, 247; authenticity critiques of, 15, 73–74, 199, 202–214, 238–244; biblical Hebrew, 137, 235, 238; bivalency and, 178, 194, 271n13; camp announcements in, 50, 108–110, 116–119, 128–130, 157–159, 161, 168–169, 227–229; camp music in, 32–34, 41–49, 116–117, 154–157, 198, 209–210; concept of connection through, 3, 8–9, 213, 224, 231–232, 248–251; conflicting ideologies on, 215–219; considerations on types of, 235–238; dictionaries/glossaries of, 23, 63, 64, *65*, 91–92, 116, 187, 202; education through the arts, 66–71, 93–94, 97–99; ethnic revival and, 28–30; gender and, 244–247; goals of camp use, 131–140, 219–224; immersion programs, 3, 19, 34–38, 56–57, 83, 148, 200, 225–228, 250, 259n39; infusion, 2–5 (overview), 113–114, 142–144, 225–234; Israeli Hebrew, 15, 199, 202–213, 228; as lens into Jewish life, 7–9; mishnaic Hebrew, 216, 235; origin of use in American Jewish camps, 20–22; secrecy and, 39, 136, 146, 231, 273n22; Sephardi Hebrew, 10, 45, 56, 161, 194, 235–237; textual *vs.* modern, 9, 133, 137–138, 190–197, 205; theatrical productions and, 97–99, 105–106, 126, 127, 143, 154–157, 196; tipping point of, 6–7, 144, 188, 228–232;

translanguaging and, 15, 86, 144–146, 218, 226; translation considerations and, 167–170, 234–235; transliteration of, 13, 194–197; typography of, 191–194, 271n21; in Zionist youth movement camps, 22–24. *See also* camp Hebraized English (CHE); signage

*Hebrew Reborn* (Spiegel), 51

Hebrew Teachers College, 21

Hebrew Union College, 39, 44

Hebrew Youth Cultural Federation. *See* *Histadrut Hanoar Haivri* (Hebrew Youth Cultural Federation)

Henry S. Jacobs Camp. *See* URJ camp network

Herzl, Theodor, 66, 156

Herzl Camp, 27, 35, 260nn60–61

Herzliya Hebrew Teachers College, 67, 72

Herzog, Isaac, 248

Hilltop (Gindling Hilltop Camp). *See* Wilshire Boulevard Camps

*Histadrut Hanoar Haivri* (Hebrew Youth Cultural Federation), 14, 24, 51–56, 91

"home haven" model, 103, 104, 267n59

Honor, Herzl, 38, 40

Horowitz, Bernard "Bernie," 50

Hyfler, Robert "Bob," 75

iCenter, 10, 184, 207–208, 272n18

Ichud Habonim, 23. *See also* Habonim Dror camp network

identity, as term, 29

IDF. *See* Israel Defense Forces

imagined communities, 3, 126, 134, 135, 141, 218, 221

immigrant groups, 4–5, 174–175, 217–218

incentives for language use, 37, 91, 101, 163–164, 221

indexicality, 39, 208, 268n1, 269n22; indexical field, 139

indigenous groups, 4–5, 130, 174–175, 218

Isaacson, Michael, 46

Israel: as camps' rationale for using Hebrew, 15, 131–133, 138–139; emissaries at camps, 30, 44, 101, 198–214, 242–243; IDF, 209–211; Palestine conflict, 115, 118; signage of, 184; statehood of, 9, 14, 16, 26, 29, 66, 211. *See also* Labor Zionist organizations; military experience and camp; Six Day War (1967); Zionism; Zionist camp network

Israel Day celebrations, 186, 207, 208–209

Israel Defense Forces (IDF), 204, 209–211, 212, 272n25

Israeli American Council, 127

Israeli Hebrew, 15, 199, 202–213, 228. *See also* Hebrew language

*Israel Today* (Essrig and Segal), 39

Ivriah program, 260n60

*Ivrit. See* Hebrew language

Jacobson, Matthew Frye, 28

JCC Association (JCCA), 127–133, 187, 189, 226, 239, 268n8

Jewish Agency for Israel (JAFI), 10, 27, 200, 201, 202, 204, 248

*The Jewish Catalog* (publication), 29

Jewish Community Center Association. *See* JCC Association

Jewish Education Committee, New York, NY, 58. *See also* Bureau of Jewish Education, New York, NY

Jewish English, 11, 123–125, 140, 146, 204, 225–226, 236–237

Jewish Federations of North America, 20, 248; federation camps, 22, 29, 30, 200, 201

Jewish Spanish language, 146

Jewish summer camping: creating a bubble, 177; history of, 5–7; inter-camp diversity in, 126–128; intra-camp diversity in, 128–131; Israeli emissary programs at, 30, 44, 101, 198–213; origin of Hebrew in, 20–22; rationale for using Hebrew in, 131–140; traditions of, 136. *See also names of specific camps and camp networks*

Jewish Swedish language, 146

Jewish Telegraphic Agency, 40

Jewish Theological Seminary (JTS), 21, 45, 54, 82, 84, 85, 88, 89, 93, 97, 98, 103, 106

*Joys of Yiddish, The* (Rosten), 40

*Judaean Songster* (Altman), 24

Judaism: as rationale for camp Hebrew use, 133; services and rituals in, 29, 39, 42, 72, 93, 108–109, 124, 133, 169

Judeo-Arabic, 146

Kaelter, Sarah, 32

Kaminker, Samuel, 32

Kamp Kohut, 20

Kaplan, Irv, 33–34

Kaplan, Louis, 53

Kaplan, Mordecai, 25, 27, 54, 88, 259n27

Katon, Ruth, 204

Kaunfer, Neal, 102

Kayitz Kef program, 250

Kelman, Ari, 43

Kelner, Shaul, 199
kibbutz life and movement, 23, 24, 35, 38,
    43, 47, 53, 61, 66, 80, 114–119, 202, 237,
    260n59, 264n60, 272n20
Kibbutz Max Straus (camp), 222
Kimmel, Jimmy, 39
Kleinhaus, Charles, 79–80
Klepper, Jeffrey, 45, 46, 47, 48
Kligman, Mark, 43
Krasner, Jonathan, 12
Kraushar, Abraham "Abie," 82–83
Kutz Camp. See URJ camp network
Kvutzah initiative at Camp Achvah, 56–57

Labor Zionist organizations, 20, 23, 114,
    262n10, 264n38. See also Habonim Dror
    camp network; Zionism
Ladino (Judeo-Spanish) language, 8, 42,
    146, 236–237, 272n2
Lainer-Vos, Dan, 73–74
Lang, Leon, 95
language. See names of specific
    languages
language endangerment, 5, 174–175, 218,
    272n1, 273n22
language ideology, 2–3, 4–5, 8, 9, 14, 45,
    88–89, 131–141, 170, 173, 175–176, 188–189,
    195, 206–208, 215–247
language policing, 61–63, 73, 215–216, 226,
    232–234, 241–243
language policy, 3, 61, 73, 79, 108, 175–176,
    225–247
language revitalization, 218, 224, 270n4
Levi, S. Gershon, 95
LGBTQ individuals and Hebrew
    language, 244–245. See also gender and
    Hebrew language
Lieberman, Joshua and Leah, 97
linguistic hybridity, 4, 15, 73, 114, 122,
    144–147, 161–162, 175, 178, 214, 217, 226,
    238–241, 270n23. See also camp
    Hebraized English (CHE);
    translanguaging
linguistic landscape, 114, 174 (defined),
    172–197. See also camp Hebraized
    English (CHE); Hebrew language
linguistic purism, 217, 238. See also
    authenticity
liturgy. See music
loanwords, Hebrew, 24, 39, 48, 74, 133, 136,
    145–146, 159–162. See also camp
    Hebraized English (CHE)
location signage, 180–182. See also signage;
    linguistic landscape

Lorge, Ernst, 31
Lorge, Michael, 31
Lovitt, Benji, 1
Lubavitch, 105. See also Camp Emunah

MABA program at Herzl camp, 35,
    260n61, 265n93
maccabiah, 68–71, 76, 81, 91, 120, 131, 156,
    165, 172
machanayim, 39, 123
Machaneh Kachol-Lavan, 127
Machon L'Madrichei Chutz La'Aretz
    (Institute for Youth Leaders from
    Abroad), 27
Mandarin language. See Chinese
    language
Maslow, Abraham, 54
Massad Dictionary (Milon Massad), 23,
    63, 64, 65, 91–92, 202
Massad Manitoba, 13, 81, 127, 135, 149, 154,
    158, 196, 234, 250, 262n1
Massad Poconos camp network, 9, 14;
    airborne leafleting by Massad Poconos
    staff members, 82–83; decline of, 77–81,
    84; denominationalism of, 72; dramatics
    at, 66–68, 69, 78, 96; emissaries
    program at, 200–201; as an ersatz Israel,
    72–77; establishment of, 23, 24, 52–62,
    71, 262n1, 263n34; Hebrew immersion at,
    23, 50–52, 62–66; images of, 53, 59, 62,
    64, 65, 67, 69, 70, 75, 87; learning Hebrew
    through the arts at, 66–71, 155; macca-
    biah (color war) at, 68–71, 76, 81; Massad
    Aleph, 59, 69, 265n94; Massad Bet, 12,
    59, 61, 68, 69, 71, 72, 78, 81; Massad
    Gimel, 81; music at, 66, 68, 78, 79;
    relationship with Ramah, 82–83, 91–92;
    signage of, 64, 65, 87; zimriya (song
    festival) at, 68, 76
Massad Quebec, 81, 262n1
Mayer, Tamar "Timi," 38, 200
Meah Milim program, 164, 185, 215, 221,
    223, 226, 233. See also word lists
Meiseles, Andrea, 260n59
Melzer, Asher, 29
metalinguistic community, 4, 15, 134, 170,
    221, 250
metalinguistic conversation, 8, 15, 126, 136,
    143, 165–168, 206–207, 215, 231–238,
    242–243, 246
Miami Indians, 147
military experience and camp, 209–213.
    See also Israel
Miller, Oscar, 33, 34

*Milon Massad (Massad Dictionary)*, 23, 63, 64
Mintz, Alan, 52, 79
Mishkin, Doug, 46
mishnaic Hebrew, 216, 235. *See also* Hebrew language
Mizrachi. *See* Bnei Akiva camp network
modern Hebrew, 9, 133, 137–138, 190–197, 205, 235. *See also* Hebrew language; signage
Mogilner, David, 95–96, 266n21
Mosenkis, Matthew, 101
Mosenkis, Robert, 101
Moshava camps. *See* Bnei Akiva camp network
*moshavot,* 22
Moskowitz, Mayer, 61, 81
murals, 179–180. *See also* signage
music, 32–34, 41–49, 116–117, 154–157, 198, 209–210; Ethnix, 210; Hadag Nahash, 209–210. *See also* choral groups; theatrical productions
myaamia language. *See* Miami Indians

Nahal, 66, 264n60
Nathanson, Moshe, 46
nationalism, 15, 27, 134, 135, 198, 199, 203, 207–209, 213. *See also* Zionism
National Jewish Population Survey (1990), 6
National Jewish Welfare Board (JWB), 29–30
National Ramah Commission, 223
neo-Hasidic music, 45, 46, 78
Newman, Louis, 71, 91, 96–99, 101, 103, 266n21, 267n57
Newman, Shirley, 98
NFTY, 39, 46, 48
*NFTY Sings,* 46, 48
*nikud,* 172, 192–194, 197
*Niv* (publication), 55–56
nonbinary gender and Hebrew language, 244–247
nostalgia, 39, 207; displaced nostalgia, 118–119, 213; for past Hebrew use at camp, 108, 109, 227, 229
Novak, William, 28, 107

Olin-Sang-Ruby Union Institute. *See* URJ camp network
online camp presence. *See* websites
Orthodox Jewish English, 124–126, 236. *See also* Jewish English
overnight camps. *See* Jewish summer camping

Palestine: agricultural settlements in, 23, 56–57; camp celebration of, 22, 60, 69, 73, 74, 76; emigration to, 24, 27, 36, 53; Hebrew culture of, 20, 45, 54, 88, 91, 202; Israel conflict, 115, 118. *See also* military experience and camp
Passamaneck, Stephen, 33
pedagogical labels, 185, 192–194
Persky, Daniel, 63, 81
Pioneer Program at Union Institute, 34, 36–38. *See also* Chalutzim Hebrew immersion program
Pioneer Youth Camp, 97
Platt, Ben, 155
plays. *See* theatrical productions
Posen, I. Sheldon, 41, 42
postvernacularity, 4, 39, 107, 170
postwar survival and Jewish summer camps, 25–27
Potok, Chaim, 25, 26, 84–85, 92–93, 104
prayer rituals, 151–152, 204–205, 211–212, 215–216, 236. *See also* religious services and rituals
Prell, Riv-Ellen, 25, 26
progressive educational pedagogy, 97

queer individuals and Hebrew language, 244–247. *See also* gender and Hebrew language

rabbinic Hebrew. *See* textual Hebrew
Ramah camp network, 3, 6, 14, 21, 266n1; airborne leafleting of Ramah Poconos, 82–83; core objectives of, 84, 215; Daber program of, 164, 225, 232; dramatics at, 98–99, 105–106, 155–156; emissary program at, 200, 201; establishment of, 24, 72, 82–84; Hebrew language objectives and infusion at, 85–94, 132, 158, 222; images of, *86, 90, 99, 100*; maccabiah at, 91; *Meah Milim* program at, 164, 185, 215, 221, 223, 226, 233; music at, 43; Potok on, 84–85; as pseudo-Hebraic environment, 94–101; Ramah Berkshires, 102, 154; Ramah California, 10, 11, 101, 128, 135, 145, 149, 155–158, 167, 169, 170, 192, 210, 222, 223, 230, 232–233, 234, 236, 243; Ramah Canada, 102; Ramah Connecticut, 84, 86–87, 101; Ramah Darom, 163, 221, 222, 271n14; Ramah Glen Spey, 102; Ramah in the Rockies, 11, 158, 224, 229, 230, 231, 234; Ramah Maine, 95; Ramah New England, 93, 102, 104–108, 137, 223; Ramah Nyack, 12, 102, 104; Ramah

Ramah camp network (cont.)
  Poconos, 26, 82–83, 89, 95, *100*, 101, 155,
    156, 164, 166, 168, 186, 207, 215–216, 222,
    224, 226, 227, 233, 263n29; Ramah
    Wisconsin, 63, 82, 84, 85, 89, *90*, 91–92,
    94, 96–101, 103, 156, 231, 238; relationship
    with Massad, 82–83, 91–92; shifting
    priorities of Hebrew infusion at, 101–110;
    signage at, *86*, 266n12; statistics on, 6;
    on textual literacy, 26; *Yom Yisrael*
    celebrations at, 186, 207, 208–209;
    zimriya at, 109. *See also* emissaries,
    Israeli
Ramaz School, 60, 61, 79
Reimer, Joseph, 103, 105–106, 270n27
Reisfield, Mel, 35, 243
religious services and rituals, 29, 39, 42,
    72, 93, 108–109, 124, 133, 169. *See also*
    Judaism; prayer rituals; rituals and
    language acquisition
research methods, 9–13
*Response* (publication), 107
revernacularization of Hebrew, 8–9, 175,
    258n24
reward systems. *See* incentives for
    language use
rituals and language acquisition, 74, 85,
    93, 108–109, 117, 152–154, 270n25. *See also*
    prayer rituals; religious services and
    rituals
*Rocket to Mars* (textbook), 33
Rosenblum, Herbert, 92
Rosten, Leo, 39, 40
Roth, Joel, 98
Rudavsky, Hillel, 63
Russian Jewish summer camps, 6,
    8, 137
Russian language, 6, 8, 184, 207

Samber, Moshe, 266n21
Schaalman, Herman, 31
Schachter-Shalomi, Zalman, 105
Schanin, Norman, 27
Schiff, Alvin, 266n25
Schoolman, Albert P., 21–22, 57, 60, 70
Schroon Lake camp, 20
Schwab, Joseph, 103, 104, 105, 267n59
Schwartz, Shuly Rubin, 97
secrecy and Hebrew language, 39, 136, 146,
    231, 273n22
semiotic landscape, 174. *See also* linguistic
    landscape
Sephardic Adventure Camp, 8, 137, 235,
    236–237

Sephardi Hebrew, 10, 45, 56, 161, 194,
    235–237. *See also* Hebrew language
Shabbat, 1, 3, 10, 23, 68, 116–118, 122, 123,
    133, 150, 151, 153, 177, 258n21; *Ivrit shel*, 237
Shandler, Jeffrey, 4, 107
Sharlin, William, 43, 44
*shelilat hagolah*, 24, 259n19
*Shirei Eretz Yisrael*, 43
*shlichim*. *See* emissaries, Israeli
Sholem Aleichem Folk Institute, 20
Shulsinger, Rivka Wolman, 58, 59, 77, 79,
    80, 202, 263n34
Shulsinger, Shlomo, 53; background of,
    52–53; camp dictionary by, 63; as
    counselor at Gordonia camp, 23; on
    denominationalism, 72; on enforcement
    of Hebrew speaking at Massad, 60–64;
    founding of Camp Massad Poconos by,
    24, 57–62, 71; and Histadrut Hanoar
    Haivri, 55–56; influence of Zionist
    movement on, 23, 91; on Massad as an
    ersatz Israel, 72–73, 76–77; on Massad's
    mission, 52; and the religious obser-
    vance level of Massad, 72; *shelilat
    hagolah* and, 24, 259n19; on using the
    arts for Hebrew education, 66–68.
    *See also* Massad Poconos camp network
Shwayder Camp, 272n22
Siegel, Morton, 84
signage, 172–174; bilingual, 86–87, 114, 115,
    177–183, 189–190; at Camp Massad, *64,
    65, 87*; at Camp Ramah, *86*, 266n12;
    decorative plaques and murals, 179–180;
    directional signposts, 120, 182–183;
    impacts of, 187–189; of Israel, 184;
    linguistic decisions on, 190–197;
    location signs, 180–182; pedagogical
    labels and word lists, 185, *186*, 192;
    welcome signs, 177–179. *See also* camp
    Hebraized English (CHE); Hebrew
    language; textual Hebrew
Silberman, Alan, 97
Silverman, Hillel, 91, 266n21
Simon, Ralph, 91
Six Day War (1967), 28, 30, 44, 46, 60, 105,
    109, 201, 209, 260n44
Sleeper, Jim, 105
Smith, Allan, 46, 92
sociolinguistic projection, 16, 217,
    238, 243
Solel program, 32, 35, 260n52
Songleader Boot Camp, 262n108
song leaders, 42–48, 157. *See also* music;
    songs

songs: *"Ani v'Ata"* (Einstein), 43; *"Bashana Habaa"* (Hirsh), 45–46; "Golden Boy," 198, 271nn1–2; *"Mi Shebeirach"* (Friedman, Setel), 48; "Oseh Shalom" (Hirsh), 45–46; *"Salaam/Od Yavo Shalom Aleinu"* (Ari), 43; *"Shirat Hasticker,"* 209–210; *"Shir Shomer"* (Livni), 66; *Sing unto God* (Friedman), 47–48; *"Tootim,"* 210; *"Tzena, Tzena"* (Miron and Haggiz), 43; *"V'Haer Einenu"* (Carlebach), 45; *"Zog Nit Keyn Mol"* (Glik), 73. *See also* music; theatrical productions
*Songs NFTY Sings* series, 48
Soref, Irwin, 32
Soshuk, Levi, 263n29
Spanish language, 146, 174
Sperber, Stanley, 68
Spiegel, Shalom, 51
Splansky, Donald, 34, 36, 37
sports competitions. *See maccabiah*
Sri Lankan immigrant communities, 5, 218
Starshefsky, Richard "Rafi," 50–51, 69–71
Stewart, Jon, 39
Strigler, Mordechai, 63
Summer Shlichim (Emissaries) Program, 30, 44, 101, 202. *See also* Ramah camp network
Surprise Lake Camp, 20, 29, 212, 222
survey of camp directors, 11, 118, 126–128, 131, 138, 147, 155, 156, 200, 219–220, 258n30, 268n8
Swig Camp Institute. *See* URJ camp network
Switkin, Shelly, 91, 94

Taglit. *See* Birthright Israel
Talmud Torah, 21, 35, 53, 88, 260n61
Tamarack Camp, 20, 29, 208, 272n22
Tamil language, 5, 218
Tarbut Ivrit movement, 51, 52, 54–55, 77–79
Tchernichovsky, Shaul, 66, 75; "I Believe"/*"Tzachki, Tzachki,"* 75
Tel Yehudah. *See* Young Judaea camp network
textual Hebrew, 9, 133, 137–138, 190–197, 205. *See also* Hebrew language; signage
theatrical productions, 97–99, 105–106, 126, 127, 143, 154–157, 196; *Annie Get Your Gun*, 99, 155, 156; *The Book of Mormon*, 196; *Bye Bye Bernstein*, 155; *Chalom v'Hagshama* (Alster-Yardeni), 66; *A Chorus Line*, 155; *Frozen*, 155; *Guys and Dolls*, 155; *Hair*, 105, 106; *Hairspray*, 155; *Hakosem m'eretz oz*, 155–156; *Hoi Ad Matai?* (Alster-Yardeni), 66; *Joseph and the Amazing Technicolor Dreamcoat*, 156; *The Lion King*, 155; *Oklahoma!*, 99; *The Pirates of Penzance*, 155; *South Pacific*, 155. *See also* music
"tipping point" argument on Hebrew infusion, 6–7, 144, 188, 228–232
Tisha B'Av, 10, 108–109, 133, 196, 204
Torah Corps, 35
tourism, 47, 79, 132, 174, 208, 210, 272n25
traditions of camp, 136, 241–242
translanguaging, 15, 86, 144–146, 160–161, 166, 217–218, 226. *See also* camp Hebraized English (CHE); Hebrew language; loanwords, Hebrew
translation considerations, 167–170, 234–235
transliteration, 13, 194–197. *See also* camp Hebraized English (CHE); Hebrew language; signage; textual Hebrew
Turkish language, 217–218
typography, 191, 194, 271n21

Ulpan immersion program at Tel Yehudah, 35, 200, 259n39
Union for Reform Judaism. *See* URJ camp network
Union Institute. *See* URJ camp network
Union of American Hebrew Congregations (UAHC), 30, 32, 38–39. *See also* URJ camp network
*Union Prayer Book*, 32, 33, 48
United Kingdom, 217, 218
United Synagogue Youth, 84, 94
URJ (Union for Reform Judaism) camp network, 10, 13, 30–34, 38–41, 127–130, 132, 133, 157, 195, 209, 212, 222, 223, 242, 244; Coleman, 38, 187; Eisner, 44, 212; Goldman Union Camp Institute (GUCI, Zionsville), 19, 38–41, 259n39; Harlam, 212; Jacobs, 131, 181, *181*, 209; Kalsman, 151–152, 157, 221, 241; Kutz, 35, 38, 46, 127; Newman, 131, 134, 150, 160–161, 185, 230, 239; Olin-Sang-Ruby Union Institute (OSRUI, Union Institute, Oconomowoc), 3, 10, 30–38, 127, 130, 132, 137, 142–143, 149, 158, 160, 162–163, 165, 168, 170, 187–192, 200–201, 210, 211, 221, 223, 225, 230, 232, 243, 244, 250; Swig, 30, 35–36, 44, 244. *See also* Chalutzim Hebrew immersion program; Solel program

Vardi, Dov, 22–23
*Vision at the Heart* (Fox), 89
vowel markings, 172, 192–194, 197

Wales, 176
war. *See* Gaza conflict (2014); military
    experience and camp; Six Day War
    (1967)
websites, 16, 185–187, 189. *See also* signage
Weiner, Karl, 31
Weissberg, Victor, 32
welcome signs, 177–179. *See also* signage
Welsh language, 176
Wertheimer, Jack, 88
Wilshire Boulevard Camps: Gindling
    Hilltop, 151, 165, 166–167, *193*, 238; Hess
    Kramer, 46
Wolman, Rivka. *See* Shulsinger, Rivka
    Wolman
word lists, *64, 65,* 185, *186,* 192, 215, 221,
    226. *See also Meah Milim* program
word-of-the-day skits, 115, 120–121,
    147–150, 168, 204
wordplay, 148–152, 161, 210, 239–240,
    270n23
World Habonim, 23
Wouk, Joseph, 105

Ya'ari, Yudke, 22
Year Course program of Young Judaea, 35
Yeats, W. B., 223
Yeshivah of Flatbush, 53, 60, 79
Yiddish language: Camp Massad and, 73;
    camp music in, 42; ideologies about,
    272n2; influence on Jewish English, 11,
    123–125, 140, 146, 204, 225–226, 236–237;
    influence on modern Hebrew, 9; as
    insider language, 39, 231; in Israel, 207;

linguistic landscape, 176; metalinguistic
    communities, 170; postvernacularity
    of, 4, 170; use at Jewish summer camps,
    5, 8, 20, 22–23, 38–44, 176, 225–226;
    value of, 4, 146; Yiddish summer camps,
    57, 79
*Yom Yisrael* celebrations, 186, 207,
    208–209
Young Judaea camp network: on *aliyah,*
    259n30; Camp Judaea, 12, 135, 209;
    Hebrew practices of, 127–130, 222; Lovitt
    on, 1; origin of, 23; Sprout Lake, 12, 137,
    166, 182, 223, 240; Tel Yehudah, 10, 12, 19,
    26, 35, 132, 148, 155, 157, 172–173, 196, 210,
    225, 230, 240, 243; in Texas, 272n22;
    Ulpan program, 35, 200, 265n93; in
    Winnipeg, 27
Young Men's Zionist Organization of
    America, 27

Zak, Jonathan, 68
Zaks, Michael, 29
Zamir Chorale, 68
Zieger, Abraham, 22
*zimriya,* 33–34, 41, 46, 68, 76
Zionism: music of, 44; political expression
    of, 31, 82; Ramah camp and, 82–83, 89,
    *90,* 101, 109; *shelilat hagolah,* 24, 259n19.
    *See also* Labor Zionist organizations;
    nationalism
Zionist camp network, 1; culture model
    in, 22, 27, 82–83; Hebrew in, 22–24,
    114–119, 132; as *moshavot,* 22; origin of,
    20–21. *See also* Gordonia movement;
    Habonim Dror camp network; Massad
    Poconos camp network; Young Judaea
    camp network
*zman Ivrit,* 162–163

# About the Authors

Sarah Bunin Benor is a professor of contemporary Jewish studies at Hebrew Union College—Jewish Institute of Religion and a professor of linguistics at the University of Southern California. Her books include *Becoming Frum: How Newcomers Learn the Language and Culture of Orthodox Judaism* (2012) and *We the Resilient: Wisdom for America from Women Born before Suffrage* (2017).

Jonathan Krasner is the Jack, Joseph, and Morton Mandel Associate Professor of Jewish Education Research at Brandeis University. He is the author of *The Benderly Boys and American Jewish Education*, which won the 2011 National Jewish Book Award in American Jewish Studies, and was a 2012 finalist for the Sami Rohr Prize in Jewish Literature.

Sharon Avni is a professor of literacy and linguistics at BMCC–CUNY (City University of New York) and a research associate at the Research Institute for the Study of Language in Urban Society (RISLUS) at the CUNY Graduate Center.